THE
MIDDLE
EAST

History of Civilisation

For more than thirty years Weidenfeld & Nicolson have produced, within the *History of Civilisation* series, wide-ranging scholarly studies of the world's civilisations for the general reader. Previous authors in the series include Maurice Bowra, J.H. Parry, Frederick Heer, Richard Frye, George Rudé, Michael Grant and E.J. Hobsbawm.

THE
MIDDLE
EAST

2000 years of History
from the Rise of Christianity
to the Present Day

Bernard Lewis

Weidenfeld & Nicolson
LONDON

Weidenfeld & Nicolson
The Orion Publishing Group Ltd
Orion House
5 Upper Saint Martin's Lane
London WC2H 9EA

A catalogue record for this book is available
from the British Library.

ISBN 0 297 81345 5

Filmset by Selwood Systems, Midsomer Norton
Printed by Butler & Tanner, Frome and London

CONTENTS

MAPS

ILLUSTRATIONS

Between pages 82 and 83

The Roman emperor Constantine (Weidenfeld Archives)

The land walls of Constantinople (Weidenfeld Archives)

Rock carving of the triumph of the Persian emperor Shapur (Weidenfeld Archives)

Early Christian mosaic at Ma'daba (Weidenfeld Archives)

Justinian medallion (Ancient Art & Architecture Collection, London)

Synagogue at Dura Europoss (National Museum, Damascus/ Weidenfeld Archives)

Abraham prepares to sacrifice Ishmael (Turkish postcard)

Muḥammad receives revelation from Archangel Gabriel (Edinburgh University Library/Weidenfeld Archives)

The Dome of the Rock, Jerusalem (Weidenfeld Archives)

Inside the Dome of the Rock (Weidenfeld Archives)

The Church of the Holy Sepulchre, Jerusalem (Ancient Art & Architecture Collection, London)

Quṣayr 'Amra (Bridgeman Art Library)

Byzantine, Umayyad and 'Abbasid coins (Weidenfeld Archives)

The 'Tower of Victory' in Ghazna (author's collection)

The assassination of Niẓām al-Mulk (Topkapi Museum, Istanbul/ Weidenfeld Archives)

Between pages 146 and 147

Crac des Chevaliers (Weidenfeld Archives)

Saladin's *minbar* from Aleppo (Weidenfeld Archives)

Mongol horseman (Victoria & Albert Museum, London/ Weidenfeld Archives)

Jenghiz Khan in Bokhara (British Library/Weidenfeld Archives)

The Mongols storm Baghdad in 1258 (Bibliothèque Nationale, Paris/Bridgeman Art Library)

The tomb of Timur Lang in Samarqand (Weidenfeld Archives)

Sultan Bayezid I (Topkapı Museum, Istanbul/Weidenfeld Archives)

Sultan Murad II (Topkapı Museum, Istanbul/Weidenfeld Archives)

The castle of Rumeli Hisar (Weidenfeld Archives)

Mehmed the Conqueror (National Gallery, London)

The mosque of Aya Sofya, Istanbul (Weidenfeld Archives)

The mosque of Sultan Ahmed, Istanbul (Turkish Ministry of Tourism and Press/Weidenfeld Archives)

The helmet of Shah 'Abbās (British Museum/Weidenfeld Archives)

Crossing the Drava (Chester Beatty Library & Gallery of Oriental Art, Dublin/Weidenfeld Archives)

Ottoman galleys (British Library/Weidenfeld Archives)

Spanish galleon (Mary Evans Picture Library)

Ottoman military parade (Gennadios Library, Athens/Weidenfeld Archives)

Janissary musketeers (Gennadios Library, Athens/Weidenfeld Archives)

Between pages 210 and 211

Ottoman palace festivities (Topkapı Museum, Istanbul)

Early Islamic woodcarving (Ancient Art & Architecture Collection, London)

The Baptistery of St Louis (Louvre, Paris. Lauros-Giraudon/ Bridgeman Art Library)

Detail from the Baptistery of St Louis (Louvre, Paris/Weidenfeld Archives)

Prayer rug (Bridgeman Art Library)

The astronomer Taqī al Dīn in his observatory (Weidenfeld Archives)

Thirteenth-century astrolabe (British Museum/Weidenfeld Archives)

Illustration from Persian medical text (Bodleian Library, Oxford)

The Shah mosque, Isfahān (Weidenfeld Archives)

The madrasa Chehār Bāgh, Isfahān (Ancient Art & Architecture Collection, London)

Shah 'Abbās receiving an ambassador (Ancient Art & Architecture Collection, London)

Turkish banquet scene (Chester Beatty Library & Gallery of Oriental Art, Dublin/Bridgeman Art Library)

Turkish merchants (Weidenfeld Archives)

An Englishman in Ottoman service (Bodleian Library, Oxford)

Jewish doctor and merchant in Istanbul (Gennadios Library, Athens)

Dervishes (Weidenfeld Archives)

Dragoman (from O. Dalvimart, *The Costume of Turkey*, 1802)

Persian hunting scene (British Library/Weidenfeld Archives)

Turkish coffee-house (Mary Evans Picture Library)

Between pages 274 and 275

Thirteenth-century slave market (Bibliothèque Nationale, Paris/Bridgeman Art Library)

Nineteenth-century slave caravan (Syndication International)

Two eunuchs on horseback (Gennadios Library, Athens)

The Aga of the Girls (Gennadios Library, Athens)

The sultan's mother (Harlingue-Viollet, Paris)

Turkish lady and servant (from miniature reproduced in F. Taeschner, *Alt-Stambuler Hof- und Volksleben*, 1925)

Ladies at a wedding reception (Nationalbibliothek, Vienna/ Weidenfeld Archives)

Ladies sitting in a drawing room (Nationalbibliothek, Vienna/ Weidenfeld Archives)

The grand vizier grants an audience to a European ambassador (Bridgeman Art Library)

The Nuruosmaniye mosque, Istanbul (Weidenfeld Archives)

The aga of the girls, a jester and a eunuch (Turkish postcard collection)

Ottoman military uniforms (Turkish postcard collection)

Ottoman officials with ambassadors (Turkish postcard collection)

Bonaparte and his troops in Egypt (Weidenfeld Archives)

Selim III (Topkapı Museum, Istanbul)

Murad II before and after the destruction of the Janissaries (Topkapı Museum, Istanbul)

Muḥammad ʿAlī Pasha (Victoria & Albert Museum, London/ Weidenfeld Archives)

Persians resist Russian advance (Victoria & Albert Museum, London)

Russians destroy the Ottoman fleet, 1853 (Mansell Collection)

Between pages 338 and 339

The opening of the Suez Canal (Mary Evans Picture Library)

French comment on the British in Egypt (Mary Evans Picture Library)

The Dolmabahçe Palace (Weidenfeld Archives)

Silk mercers' bazaar, Cairo (Mary Evans Picture Library)

European and Turkish ladies in Istanbul, 1907 (from the French magazine, *L'Illustration*)

Atatürk in uniform (Weidenfeld Archives)

Atatürk: the leader as teacher (Weidenfeld Archives)

The Arabian revolt, 1917 (Imperial War Museum, London)

Outside Jerusalem, 1917 (Weidenfeld Archives)

Jerusalem in 1947 (Weidenfeld Archives)

Bedouin tribesmen (Aramco)

Oil pipelines (Aramco)

Demonstration in support of Ayatollah Khomeini (photo by A. Mingam/Frank Spooner Pictures)

Iranian women voting, 1979 (photo by A. de Wildenberg/Frank Spooner Pictures)

The Great Mosque and the Kaʿba in Mecca (photo by M. Lounes/ Frank Spooner Pictures)

The faithful at prayer, Cairo (Camera Press)

Istanbul, 1988 (photo by A. Abbas/Magnum)

PREFACE

There are by now many one-volume histories of the Middle East. Most of them either end with the advent of Christianity or start with the advent of Islam. In commencing my history at the beginning of the Christian era, I seek to accomplish two purposes. The first is to rescue the two great empires of Persia and Byzantium from the modest place usually assigned to them, along with pre-Islamic Arabia, as part of the backdrop to the career of the Prophet and the founding of the Islamic state. These rival powers, which between them shared or divided the Middle East for many centuries, deserve more than cursory mention.

My second purpose is to establish some link between the Middle East that we know today and the ancient civilizations of the region that we know from ancient texts and monuments. During the early centuries of the Christian era, that is to say, in the period between Jesus and Muḥammad, the regions west of the Persian Empire were transformed by the consecutive processes of Hellenization, Romanization and Christianization, and the memory (though not all the traces) of these ancient civilizations was obliterated. That memory was not restored until comparatively modern times, through the work of archaeologists and orientalists. But the direct continuing connection from the ancient to the modern Middle East, through Late Antiquity and the Middle Ages, deserves attention.

The earliest modern attempts to write the history of the region have necessarily concentrated on the sequence of political and military events, without which the deeper levels of history are difficult, if not impossible, to fathom. Thanks to the work of my predecessors, I have felt freer than they to reduce the political narrative to a minimum and to devote more attention to social, economic and, above all, cultural change. With this in view, I have made frequent use of direct quotations from contemporary sources – chronicles and travels, documents and inscriptions, and sometimes even poetry and anecdote. Where suitable English translations are available, I have used and cited them. Where they are not, I have made my own. The illustrations may also serve a similar purpose. From these, one may hope to obtain insights which neither narrative nor even analysis can readily yield.

Any attempt to present two thousand years of the history of a rich, varied and vibrant region within the compass of a single volume must necessarily omit much that is of importance. Every student of the region will make his or her own choice. I have made mine, and it is inevitably personal. I have tried to give due prominence to what seemed to me the most characteristic and most instructive careers, events, trends and achievements. The reader will judge how far I have succeeded.

Finally, it is my pleasant duty to record my thanks and appreciation to four young scholars at Princeton University, David Marmer, Michael Doran, Kate Elliott and Jane Baun. All of them have helped in various ways in the preparation and production of this book. I am particularly indebted to Jane Baun, whose meticulous scholarship and critical acuity were at all times of the greatest value. I should also like to express my gratitude to my assistant Annamarie Cerminaro, for her careful and patient handling of the many versions of this book, from first draft to final copy. In the editing, illustration and publication of this book I benefited enormously from the skill and patience of Benjamin Buchan, Tom Graves, and the indexer Douglas Matthews. They did much both to speed the process of production and to improve the quality of the product.

To all of them I offer my thanks for those of their many suggestions which I accepted, and my apologies for those that I resisted. From this it will be clear that whatever faults remain are entirely my own.

BERNARD LEWIS
PRINCETON, APRIL 1995

Transcription
Arabic and Persian names and terms have been transcribed in accordance with the system generally used in English-speaking countries; Turkish in a slightly modified form of the standard Turkish orthography. A few familiar names (e.g. Saud, Nasser) are cited in the form commonly used in the press.

PART I

Introduction

INTRODUCTION

A common sight in most Middle Eastern cities is the coffee-house, or sometimes the tea-house, where at almost any hour of the day you may find men – usually only men – sitting at a table, drinking a cup of coffee or tea, perhaps smoking a cigarette, reading a newspaper, playing a board game, and listening with half an ear to whatever is coming out of the radio or the television installed in the corner.

In outward appearance this Middle Eastern café patron does not look very different from a similar figure sitting in a café in Europe, particularly in Mediterranean Europe. He will look very different from his predecessors in the same place fifty years ago, still more a hundred years ago. That of course is also true of the European sitting in his café, but the two cases are far from being the same. The changes that have taken place in the appearance, the demeanour, the garb, the behaviour of the European during that period of time are almost entirely of European origin. They are changes which, with few exceptions, arose from within the society, and even these recent exceptions came from the closely related society of America.

In the Middle East, on the other hand, the changes, for the most part, originated from outside, from societies and cultures profoundly alien to the indigenous traditions of the Middle Easterner. The man in a coffee-house, sitting in a chair, by a table, reading a newspaper, encapsulates the changes that have transformed his life and that of his parents – how he looks, what he does, how he dresses, even what he is, symbolizing the immense and devastating changes which, coming out of the West, have affected the Middle East in modern times.

The first, most obvious and visible change is in the clothes that he wears. It is still possible that he may be wearing traditional dress, but this is becoming less and less frequent in the cities. Most probably he will be dressed Western-style, with shirt and slacks or, nowadays, a T-shirt and jeans. Clothes, of course, have a tremendous importance, not merely as a way of keeping out the cold and damp and preserving decency, but also – and particularly in this part of the world – as a way of indicating one's identity, as an affirmation of one's origins and a recognition signal to others who share them. Already in the seventh century BCE in the book of the prophet Zephaniah (1:8), it is stated that 'In the day of the Lord's sacrifice' God will punish 'all such as are clothed with strange apparel.' In Jewish and later in Muslim writings, the believers are urged not to dress like the unbelievers but to maintain their own distinctive garb. 'Do not dress like the infidels lest you become like them', is a common injunction. 'The turban', according to a tradition ascribed to the Prophet, 'is the barrier between unbelief and the Faith'. According to another tradition, 'He who tries to resemble people becomes one of them.' Until very recently, in some areas even today, each ethnic group, each religious denomination, each tribe, each region, sometimes even each occupation had its own distinctive way of dressing.

It is very likely that the man sitting in the coffee-house is still wearing some form of headgear, perhaps a cloth cap, probably – except in Turkey – something more traditional. Anyone who has ever visited a cemetery of the Ottoman period will recall that many of the head-stones over the graves include a carved representation of the form of headgear worn by the deceased during his lifetime. If he was a *kadi*, there is a *kadi*'s cap; if he was a janissary, the headstone is topped by the distinctive headcover, like a folded sleeve, that the janissaries wore on their heads. Whatever other walk of life he followed during his lifetime, the appropriate headgear, as a symbol indicative of his pro-fession, appears on his grave. A distinction so important that it followed a man into his tomb was clearly of great importance during his lifetime. In Turkish until not so long ago, the phrase '*şapka giymek*', to put on a hat, had much the same significance as the earlier English phrase, 'to turn one's coat'. It meant to become a renegade, an apostate, to go over to the other side. Nowadays, of course, most Turks who wear any kind of headgear wear a hat, cap, or – for the pious – a beret, and the phrase, having lost its meaning, is no longer current. Western-style headgear is however still rare in the Arab lands, and even rarer in Iran. We can, in a sense, document the stages of modernization in the Middle East through the Westernization of clothing and, more particularly, of headgear.

Change in dress began, as did most aspects of modernization, with the military. For the reformers, Western military uniforms had a certain magic. As Muslim armies were defeated again and again on the battlefield by their infidel enemies, Muslim rulers reluctantly adopted not only the weaponry but also the organization and equipment of their opponents, including Western-style uniforms. When the first Ottoman reform troops were organized at the end of the eighteenth century, it was necessary for them to adopt Western drill and weapons; it was not necessary for them to adopt Western uniforms. This was a social, not a military choice, and it has been followed in virtually all modern armies in Muslim lands, including even Libya and the Islamic Republic of Iran. They have to use Western weapons and tactics because these are the most effective; they do not have to wear fitted tunics and peaked caps, but they still do. This change of style remains as a continuing testimony to the authority and attraction of Western culture, even among those who explicitly and vehemently reject it.

Even in military uniforms, headgear was the last to be changed, and still today it is probable that in most Arab countries the man in the coffee-house will be wearing some traditional form of head covering – perhaps a *kefiya*, the design and colour of which may also indicate his tribal or regional affiliation. The symbolic centrality of the head and its covering is obvious. For Muslims, there was the additional point that most European forms of headgear with peaks or brims were an obstruction to Muslim worship. Muslim men, like Jewish men and unlike Christian men, pray with covered, not bared heads, as a sign of respect. In the prostrations required by Muslim prayer rituals, with the worshipper's brow touching the ground, the brim or peak gets in the way. For a long time, even when Middle Eastern Muslim armies were wearing uniforms of more or less Western type, they did not wear Western headgear, and retained coverings of a more traditional kind. Sultan Mahmud II (r. 1808–1839), one of the first major reformers of the nineteenth century, introduced a new headgear, the fez, also known in Arabic as the *tarbush*. At first resented and hated as an infidel innovation, it was finally accepted and even became a Muslim symbol. Its abolition in 1925, by the first president of the Turkish Republic, Kemal Atatürk, was opposed as fiercely as its introduction and for precisely the same reasons. Atatürk, the master of social symbolism, was not pursuing the idle caprice of a despot when he decreed that the fez and all other forms of traditional male headgear must be abandoned and European hats and caps adopted in their place. This was a major social decision, and he and those around him knew perfectly well what he was doing. So too, of course, did those who resisted him.

It was not the first time that such a change had taken place. In the thirteenth century, when the great Mongol conquests subjected the Muslim heartlands of the Middle East, for the first time since the days of the Prophet Muḥammad, to the rule of a non-Muslim conqueror, the Muslims themselves began to adopt Mongol ways, at least in military matters. The great Muslim amirs, even in Egypt, which was never conquered by the Mongols, began to wear Mongol-style dress, to ride their horses with Mongol harness, and to let their hair grow long in the Mongol fashion instead of cutting it short according to Muslim usage. Muslim armies used Mongol dress, accoutrements and harness for the same reason that they wear fitted tunics and peaked caps today; this was the dress of victory, representing the appearance and manner of the greatest military force in the world of their day. They continued with Mongol hairstyles and accoutrements until, we are told, the year 1315 CE, when, after the conversion and assimilation of the Mongol rulers of the Middle East, the Sultan of Egypt gave orders to his officers to shear their flowing locks, abandon the Mongol style for themselves and their horses, and return to traditional Muslim dress and caparisons. No such restoration has yet taken place in the armies of modern Islam.

After the military came the palace. The sultan himself appeared in a form of Western dress, modified to look somewhat different from that of Westerners, but not too different. There are two charming portraits of Sultan Mahmud II in the Topkapı Palace in Istanbul before and after the military vestimentary reform. The two portraits, obviously by the same artist, depict the same sultan on the same horse, prancing at exactly the same angle. But in one of them he is wearing traditional Ottoman costume, in the other a frogged coat and trousers. The horse has undergone a similar change of attire. Atatürk, as usual, went straight to the root of the matter. 'We want to wear civilized clothes', he said. But what does that mean? And why should the clothes of much more ancient civilizations be considered uncivilized? For him, civilization meant modern, that is Western, civilization.

After the sultan, the palace, too, began to adopt a Western style of dress. This was the first place in which it was feasible for the rulers to issue orders to civilians and enforce obedience concerning dress. Ottoman court officials began to wear frock-coats and trousers. From the palace, the new style spread to officialdom in general, and by the end of the nineteenth century, civil servants all over the Ottoman lands were wearing coats and trousers of various cuts, symbolizing a significant change in social values. From the civil servant, an important element in society, the new style of dress spread gradually among the rest of the population, eventually reaching the common people, at least in cities. Iran came somewhat later, and in both the Ottoman and Iranian worlds the sartorial Westernization of the working class and rural population took much longer, and is incomplete. After the Islamic revolution of 1979, even the representatives of the Republic of Iran still wore Western coats and trousers; only the missing necktie symbolized their refusal to submit to Western conventions and constraints.

There was greater resistance to Westernizing or modernizing the dress of the female half of the population. This did not come until much later, and was never as extensive, even to the present day, as among males. Muslim rules regarding female modesty make this a sensitive point, and a recurring matter of contention. Even Atatürk, though he prohibited the fez and other forms of non-Western headgear for males, never prohibited the veil. There were some local regulations here and there in the Turkish Republic at the municipal level, and even that in very few places. The abolition of the veil was accomplished by a kind of social pressure and osmosis, without the apparatus of legal enforcement which procured the abolition of traditional headgear for men. In this, as in other respects, change of dress reflects the different feminine realities. There will be few, if any, women, in the coffee-house or tea-house, and if any appear at all, they are likely to be thoroughly covered in traditional style. Elegant ladies in fashionable, i.e. Western dress may, however, be found, in some countries, in the more expensive hotels and cafés frequented by the wealthier classes.

The change in dress also symbolizes a larger change, even in the radical, anti-Western states. Just as the individual still wears at least partial Western dress, so the state still wears a Western coat and hat in the form of a written constitution, a legislative assembly, and some form of elections. All of these were maintained in the Islamic Republic of Iran, though there is of course no precedent for them either in the ancient Iranian or the sacred Islamic past.

Our patron in the café is sitting on a chair next to a table, and these two items of furniture are also innovations due to Western influence. There were tables and chairs in the Middle East in antiquity and still in Roman times, but they disappeared after the Arab conquest. The Arabs came from a land where trees are few, and wood is rare and precious. They had plenty of wool and leather, and they used them for furnishing their homes and public places, as well as for making clothes. One reclined or sat on cushions or hassocks of many different kinds, on divans and ottomans – both names are Middle Eastern – covered with carpets or tapestries, and one took food and drink from elegantly adorned metal trays. Ottoman miniatures of the early eighteenth century depict European visitors at Ottoman court celebrations. They are clearly distinguished by their fitted jackets and

7

breeches, and their hats, and also because they alone are sitting on chairs. The Ottomans were gracious hosts and provided chairs for their European guests. They did not use them themselves.

The man in the café is probably smoking a cigarette – an import of Western, indeed of American origin. As far as we know, tobacco was first introduced to the Middle East by English merchants at the beginning of the seventeenth century, and it soon became very popular. Coffee came a little earlier, in the sixteenth century. Originating in Ethiopia, it was introduced first to southern Arabia and thence to Egypt, Syria, and Turkey. According to Turkish chronicles, it was brought to Istanbul during the reign of Sultan Süleyman the Magnificent (1520–1566) by two Syrians, one from Aleppo and the other from Damascus, who opened the first coffee-houses in the Turkish capital. The new drink proved enormously fashionable, and the café owner from Aleppo is said to have returned to his native city after only three years with a profit of five thousand gold pieces. The development of a café society caused some alarm to both the political authorities, who feared the plotting of sedition, and the religious authorities, concerned about the lawfulness of such stimulants under Islamic law. In 1633, Sultan Murad IV prohibited both coffee and tobacco, and ordered the execution of a number of smokers and coffee-drinkers. Finally, after long arguments between its opponents and defenders, tobacco was declared lawful in a *fatwā* by the chief *mufti* Mehmed Bahai Efendi, a heavy smoker who in 1634 had been dismissed from his position and sent into exile for smoking. His contemporary, the Ottoman author known as Kâtib Chelebi, says that his ruling in favour of the lawfulness of tobacco was due not to his own addiction but to a belief in the legal principle that all that is not forbidden is permitted, and to a concern for 'what was best suited to the condition of the people'.[1]

Quite likely, the man in the café will be reading a newspaper, or perhaps will form one of a group to whom a newspaper is being read. This represents what must surely have been one of the most explosive and far-reaching changes affecting both the individual and the society. In most of the region, the newspaper will be printed in Arabic, the language which prevails over the greater part of the Middle East. In the Fertile Crescent, in Egypt, and in North Africa, the languages spoken in antiquity have disappeared, surviving if at all only in religious rituals or among small minorities. The one exception is Hebrew, which was preserved as a religious and literary language by the Jews and revived as a political and everyday language in the modern state of Israel. In Persia, the old language was not replaced by Arabic, but it was transformed. After the advent of Islam, it was written in the Arabic script, with a very large admixture of Arabic vocabulary. What happened to Persian also happened to Turkish, but in Turkey the reforming president Kemal Atatürk inaugurated a major cultural change by abolishing the Arabic alphabet in which Turkish had hitherto been written, and replacing it with a new Latin script. The Turkish example is being followed in some of the former republics of the Soviet Union where languages of the Turkic family are used.

The art of writing has been practised in the Middle East since remote antiquity. The alphabet was a Middle Eastern invention, a vast improvement on the various systems of signs and pictures which preceded it, and which still prevail in some parts of the world. The Latin, Greek, Hebrew, and Arabic alphabets are all derived from the first alphabet devised by the mercantile people of the Levant coast. While the alphabet enormously simplified the preparation and decipherment of written texts, the introduction of paper from China in the eighth century CE greatly helped in their production and dissemination. But another Far Eastern invention, printing, seems for some reason to have bypassed the Middle East on its way to the West. Printing was not entirely unknown, and there are some traces of a form of woodblock printing in the Middle Ages. There was even one ill-fated attempt by the Mongol rulers of Persia in the late thirteenth century to print bank notes, but as they paid their employees in paper and insisted on receiving taxes in gold, there was a certain loss of confidence in the currency. The experiment was unsuccessful and was not repeated. When printing eventually reached the Middle East, it came not from China but from the West, where its introduction, remarkably, was known and reported in Turkey. The Ottoman chroniclers, who did not normally have much to say about what was going on in the lands of the infidels, reported the invention of printing and even devoted a few lines to Gutenberg and his first printing press. Printing seems to have been introduced to the Middle East by Spanish Jewish refugees following the expulsion of the Jews from Spain in 1492. Among other Western artefacts, skills, and ideas, they brought printed books and the knowledge of how to produce them. The example of the Jews was followed by the other non-Muslim communities. These activities, though they had no direct impact on the majority culture, nevertheless helped to prepare the way. Books in the

9

Arabic script, printed in Europe, were imported and purchased by Muslims, as is attested by the inventories of the estates of deceased persons preserved in the Ottoman archives. And when eventually, in the early eighteenth century, the first Muslim printing press was established in Istanbul, there were Jewish and Christian typesetters to provide the necessary skilled labour.

Newspapers did not appear until much later, though there are early signs of an awareness among Muslim intellectuals of the possibilities – and dangers – of the newspaper press. As early as 1690, a certain Muḥammad ibn ʿAbd al-Wahhāb, known as al-Wazīr al-Ghassānī, a Moroccan ambassador to Spain, speaks in his report of 'the writing mills which publish reports, purporting to contain the news, but full of sensational lies'.[2] In the course of the eighteenth century, there are indications that the Ottomans were aware of the European press. There are even occasional expressions of interest in what was being said about them in the newspapers, but that interest was limited and had little effect. The introduction of the press in the Middle East was a direct and immediate consequence of the French Revolution, when the French established what seems to be the first newspaper ever printed in that part of the world, the *Gazette Française de Constantinople*, published from the French Embassy in 1795. It was intended principally for French citizens, but was also read – one gathers – by other people. This was followed, after the arrival of the French Revolution in Egypt in the person of General Bonaparte, by French newspapers and official gazettes published in Cairo. There are reports of a French plan to publish an Arabic newspaper in Cairo, but no copy of this has yet come to light, and it seems likely that this project was never put into effect.

In traditional Muslim societies, there were several ways in which the ruler could bring news of important changes to the public. Two of them, conventionally listed among the prerogatives of sovereignty, are the inscription on the coinage and the Friday sermon in the mosques. Both name the ruler and his suzerain if any. The removal or addition of a name in the bidding prayer could signal a change of ruler, by succession or rebellion, or a transfer of allegiance. The rest of the Friday oration could serve to announce new measures and policies. The removal of taxes – though not the imposition of taxes – was also made known through inscriptions in public places. The praises of the ruler were sung by court poets, whose songs, easily memorized and widely disseminated, provided a kind of public relations. Written documents, issued by official chroniclers, were also distributed to bring news of important events. Such, for example, were the *fathname,* victory letters, with which the Ottoman sultans made known their military successes. Muslim rulers were long familiar with the use of the written and spoken word as an adjunct to government, and knew how to use this new, imported device – the newspaper.

The founding of the local vernacular press in the Middle East was the work of the two great reforming rulers, contemporaries and rivals, Muḥammad ʿAlī Pasha of Egypt and Sultan Mahmud II of Turkey. In this as in so many other matters, Muḥammad ʿAlī Pasha got in first and Sultan Mahmud followed, acting on the principle that anything that a pasha can do a sultan can do better. The Egyptian ruler began with an official gazette, first in French, then also in Arabic; the Turkish sultan began with one in French and Turkish. For quite a long time, the only newspapers published in the Middle East were official government newspapers, the purpose of which is well expressed in a Turkish editorial of the time: 'The aim of the newspaper is to make known to the subjects the intentions and orders of the government.'³ This perception of the nature and function of the press has not yet entirely disappeared in the region.

The history of the newspaper press in the Middle East is not easy to write. Many newspapers were ephemeral, appearing and dis-appearing after only a few issues. There are no full standard collections, only a number of fragmentary assemblages in various places. As far as can be ascertained, the earliest non-official newspaper was one started in Istanbul in Turkish in 1840, called *Jeride-i Havadis,* 'The Journal of Events'. Its owner and editor was an Englishman called William Churchill, who managed to get a *ferman* authorizing this enterprise. It was published at infrequent and irregular intervals, but survived.

The decisive turning-point, not only in the history of this paper but in the history of the whole newspaper press in the Middle East, came with the Crimean War, when for the first time the telegraph was brought to the region, providing a means of communication without precedent. The Crimean War brought many British and French war correspondents, and Mr Churchill was able to make a deal with one of them in the Crimea to provide him with copies of his dispatches to his paper in London. Churchill's *Jeride-i Havadis* – and this was something completely new – now appeared five times a week, and in this way first the Turks and then the rest of the Middle East became hooked on something far more addictive, and some would say far more pernicious, than either coffee or tobacco, namely a daily fix of news. A little later, a Crimean-War-vintage newspaper was produced in Arabic for those parts of the Ottoman Empire where Arabic, not Turkish, was the dominant language. The Arabic newspaper ceased publication after the end of the war; the Turkish paper continued and was followed by many others.

In 1860 the Ottoman government sponsored an Arabic daily news-paper in Istanbul – not just a medium for official decrees and the like, but a genuine newspaper containing news from inside and outside the Empire, editorials, and features. At about the same time, the Jesuit fathers in Beirut produced what was almost certainly the first daily newspaper in the Arab lands. When Muslims complain about the two great dangers of imperialists and missionaries, they are right at least in this respect; it was the imperialists and the missionaries who gave them the daily newspaper. And with the growth of the press, editors, journalists, and readers confronted two major problems, propaganda and censorship.

In the late nineteenth and early twentieth century, there was a very rapid and extensive development of the press – daily, weekly, and monthly – especially in Egypt, where the British occupation created favourable conditions. Egyptian publications circulated widely in other Arabic-speaking countries, all of which, in due course, developed their own newspapers and magazines. The effect of the growth of the press was enormous. The provision of regular news from both home and abroad gave the ordinary person who could read, or listen to someone else reading, an awareness of the world in which he lived, the city, the state, the country, the continent, that was totally impossible in earlier times. The press involved a new kind of socialization and politicization. The Crimean War had brought other things besides the press, and these too were reported in the press – the creation of municipalities in the Western style, and the introduction of Western-style state finances and notably of the public loan.

Another change of fundamental importance was in language. In Turkish and Arabic, and later in Persian, there was a rapid development from the ponderous style of the early newspapers, which read like court chronicles or official decrees, to the more athletic journalistic style that emerged in the course of decades and continues to the present time. Middle Eastern journalists had to forge a new medium of communication to discuss the problems of the modern world. Nineteenth-century newspapers report and discuss such matters as the Polish insurrection against Russia, the American Civil War, the speeches of Queen Victoria at the opening of Parliament in London, and other similarly incomprehensible topics. The need to report and explain these matters was in large measure responsible for the creation of the modern journalistic and political languages of the Middle East.

Another development, perhaps even more portentous than the language of journalism, was the journalist himself, an entirely new figure in Middle Eastern society, following a profession which had no precedent, but which acquired enormous importance.

Nowadays newspapers will not be the only mass media represented in the coffee-house. There will certainly be a radio, possibly also a television set. Radio broadcasting in the Middle East was inaugurated in Turkey in 1925, only three years after London. In most countries, however, where the control of communications was in the hands of foreign rulers, the introduction of broadcasting was delayed for some time. In Egypt, broadcasting did not begin until 1934, and was not really developed on a large scale until after the revolution of 1952. Turkey again was the pioneer in setting up an independent broadcasting authority, in 1964, not under direct government control. More generally, the degree of independence enjoyed by broadcasters is determined by the nature of the regime in any given country. Direct propagandist broadcasting from abroad appears to have been initiated by the Italian fascist government, which inaugurated a regular Arabic service from Bari in 1935. This was the beginning of a propaganda war in which first Britain and Germany, then France and later the USA and the USSR participated. Middle Eastern countries also began to broadcast extensively to one another, for information, guidance, and, on occasion, subversion. The introduction of television was, because of the greater costs, somewhat more difficult, but by the present time television services are widely available all over the Middle East.

In a region where illiteracy remains a major problem, the introduction of direct communication in the spoken word had a revolutionary impact. Indeed, the Iranian Revolution of 1979, in which the Ayatollah Khomeini's orations were distributed on cassettes and his instructions transmitted by telephone, must surely be the first electronically operated revolution in world history. This gave oratory a new dimension, a way of delivering speeches to reach audiences not conceivable in earlier times.

What comes out of the radio and television set will be very largely determined by the form of government that prevails in the country, and by the head of state or head of government who operates it. Probably, his picture will hang on the coffee-house wall. In a very few countries, which have successfully introduced and still operate Western-style democracy, he, or now she, may be a democratically elected leader, and the media will reflect a wide range of opposition as well as governmental views. In most countries of the region, the ruler will head a more or less autocratic form of government. In some, a traditional and moderate form of authoritarianism prevails, in which the classical decencies are observed and some variety of difference of opinion is permitted. In others, military or party dictators have established totalitarian regimes, and their media – press, radio, and television alike – express a totalitarian unanimity.

Irrespective of the form of government and the kind of authority that the ruler exercises, his picture on the wall, by its mere presence, marks an innovation and a radical departure from tradition. A Turkish ambassador in France in 1721 explains in his report that the French custom was for the king to give foreign ambassadors his portrait. However, 'since pictures are not permitted among Muslims', he requested and was given other presents.[4] Portraiture was, however, by no means unknown. Sultan Mehmed II, the Conqueror, allowed his portrait to be painted by the Italian artist Bellini, and even collected pictures by European artists. His son and successor, more pious than he, disposed of the collection, but later sultans were less fastidious, and the Topkapı Palace in Istanbul contains a rich collection of portraits of the sultans and others. In modern times a kind of Islamic iconography developed, with portraits, obviously mythical, of ʿAlī and Ḥusayn in Shīʿa countries, and of others, to a much lesser extent, in Sunni countries. There are few precedents of portraiture on the coinage, of the type customary in Europe since ancient Greece and Rome. A coin of one ʿAbbasid caliph, showing what is presumed to be the caliph's portrait, is intentionally provocative, in that it not only portrays the ruler, but portrays him drinking from a cup. There are a few Seljuk coins from Anatolia, from minor principalities, showing portraits of the amirs, but this is entirely local, and was in imitation of the local custom of Byzantine rulers.

There are unlikely to be any other pictures on the wall, but there will almost certainly be a framed calligraphic text, probably a verse from the Qurʾān or a saying of the Prophet. For some fourteen centuries, Islam has been the predominant and for most of the time the dominant religion of the region. The worship of the mosque is simple and austere, consisting of a few verses from the Qur'ān. Public prayer is a disciplined, communal act of submission to the Creator, to the one remote and immaterial God. It admits of no drama and no mystery. It has no place for liturgical music or poetry, still less for representational painting or sculpture, which Muslim tradition rejects as idolatrous. In their place, Muslim artists use abstract and geometrical design, and base their decorative schemes on the extensive and systematic use of inscriptions. Verses or even whole chapters of the Qur'ān are used to decorate the walls and ceilings of the mosque and also of homes and public places.

It is perhaps in the arts that one can see the earliest signs of the penetration of Western cultural methods and values. Even in Iran, much remoter from the West and less open to Western influences, Western influence can be seen in painting as early as the sixteenth century – in the use of shadow and perspective and the transformation of the way that human figures are depicted. In defiance of Islamic aniconism, there had for long been human figures in both Persian and Ottoman art, but they now became more individual, more personal, less stereotyped. There was even some portraiture, though the public display of the ruler's countenance, whether on the coinage, the postage stamp, or the wall, is very recent, and in the more conservative countries is still regarded as a blasphemy verging on idolatry.

The theatre as an art form has had limited impact in Middle Eastern countries, but the cinema has been overwhelmingly successful. There is evidence that silent films were imported into Egypt from Italy as far back as 1897. During the First World War, film shows arranged for Allied troops gave many Middle Easterners the opportunity to become acquainted with this new medium. Local films were already in production in Egypt in 1917, and the first full-length features films were produced and presented in 1927. Since then, the cinema has developed into a major enterprise, principally in Egypt but also in many other countries of the region. The Egyptian film industry is now the third largest in the world, after the USA and India.

Other innovations of Western provenance are by now so old and well established that their alien origin is no longer remembered. If the man in the coffee-house belongs to the educated classes and has ruined his eyesight by reading, he may be wearing eyeglasses, a European invention attested in the Middle East as far back as the fifteenth century. The coffee-house may offer a clock, the customer may carry a watch, both European inventions and probably even today still of foreign – European or Far Eastern – manufacture. The precise measurement of passing time marks a major change in social habits – a change still in progress.

It is likely that if the coffee drinker is with friends, they will be passing time in a way for which no measurement is needed – in playing board games, which have a very long history in the region. The two most popular are a form of backgammon and – among the better educated – chess. Both came to the West from the Middle East, and chess may originally have come from India. Both are already attested in pre-Islamic Persia. In the great debate among medieval Muslim theologians on the question of predestination or free will, these two games sometimes served as symbols and prototypes. Is life a game of chess, where the player has a choice at every move, where skill and foresight can bring him success? Or is it rather backgammon, where a modicum of skill may speed or delay the result, but where the final outcome is determined by the repeated throw of the dice, which some might call blind chance and others the predetermined decision of God? The two games provide arresting metaphors of one of the major debates in Muslim theology, one in which predestination – backgammon rather than chess – was victorious.

Between intervals of news and speeches, there will be music. In most coffee-houses the clients will be offered either traditional or popular Middle Eastern music which may, however, include semi-orientalized Western pop music. It is very unlikely that there will be any kind of Western art music. Even among the most Westernized elements, socially and culturally, the appreciation of Western art music is still very limited – in marked contrast with Japan or even China, other non-Western societies where Western-style art music is widely appreciated, performed and even composed. Among Westernized populations, such as Lebanese Christians and Israeli Jews, there is a public for Western art music. In Turkey, too, Westernization has reached the musical world, and there are now Turkish orchestras, operas, and composers. Music, at least instrumental music, is, like art, independent of language, and might therefore seem more accessible to those of other cultures. But in most of the Middle East, perhaps in part because of the centrality of song, it has not been so, and audiences for Western art music remain relatively small. This is in striking contrast with the other arts – with painting and architecture, where the change began and was completed at an early stage of the impact of the West, and literature, where traditional forms of artistic expression are virtually dead, and where fiction, drama, and even poetry conform to the general patterns of the modern world. Just as art was the first and most extensive, so music is the last and least effective in the artistic processes of Westernization. And that may perhaps tell us something, since music, among the arts of a civilization, is the very last which a newcomer entering from outside can understand, accept, and perform.

For the Western visitor, one of the most striking features of the coffee-house in almost any part of the Middle East is that there are few, if any, women in sight, and such as appear are likely to be foreigners. The tables are occupied by men, singly or in groups, and in the evening groups of young men will wander through the streets in search of entertainment. The emancipation of women lags far behind changes in the status of men, and in many parts of the region is now in reverse.

The picture which emerges is of a region of ancient and deep-rooted culture and tradition. It has been a centre from which ideas, commodities, and sometimes armies have radiated in all directions. At other times it has been a magnet which attracted many outsiders, sometimes as disciples and pilgrims, sometimes as captives and slaves, sometimes as conquerors and masters. It has been a crossroads and a marketplace where knowledge and merchandise were brought from ancient and distant lands, and then sent, sometimes much improved, to continue their journey.

In modern times, the dominating factor in the consciousness of most Middle Easterners has been the impact of Europe, later of the West more generally, and the transformation – some would say dislocation – which it has brought. The modern history of the region is one of rapid and enforced change – of challenge from an alien world and of different phases and aspects of reaction, rejection, and response. In some respects, the change has been overwhelming and is probably irreversible, and there are many who would wish to carry these changes further. In other respects, changes have been limited and superficial, and in parts of the region are now being reversed. There are many, both conservative and radical, who wish to continue and extend this reversal, and who see the impact of Western civilization as the greatest disaster ever to befall their region, greater even than the devastating Mongol invasions of the thirteenth century. At one time, the word 'imperialism' was commonly used to describe the Western impact, but this becomes increasingly implausible as the brief period of direct European rule recedes into the past, and the United States remains remote and uninvolved. A more accurate expression of how the Western impact is perceived by those who oppose it was given by Khomeini, when he spoke of the United States as 'the Great Satan'. Satan is not an imperialist; he is a tempter. He does not conquer; he seduces. The battle is still going between those who hate and fear the seductive and, in their view destructive, power of the Western way of life, and those who see it as a new advance and a new opportunity in a continuing and fruitful interchange of cultures and civilizations.

The outcome of the struggle in the Middle East is still far from clear. The sources, processes, and issues that determine its course may perhaps be better understood against the background of Middle Eastern history and civilization.

PART II

Antecedents

CHAPTER I

BEFORE CHRISTIANITY

At the beginning of the Christian era, the region which we now call the Middle East was disputed, for neither the first nor the last time in the thousands of years of its recorded history, between two mighty imperial powers. The western half of the region, consisting of the countries round the eastern Mediterranean from the Bosphorus to the Nile delta, had all become part of the Roman Empire. Its ancient civilizations had fallen into decline, and its ancient cities were ruled by Roman governors or native puppet princes. The eastern half of the region belonged to another vast empire, which the Greeks, and after them the Romans, called 'Persia', and which its inhabitants call 'Iran'.

The political map of the region, both in its outward form and in the realities which it represents, was very different from the present day. The names of the countries were not the same, nor were the territorial entities which they designated. Most of the peoples who lived in them at that time spoke different languages and professed different religions from those of today. Some even of the few exceptions are more apparent than real, representing a conscious evocation of a rediscovered antiquity rather than an uninterrupted survival of ancient traditions.

The map of southwest Asia and northeast Africa, in the era of Perso-Roman domination and rivalry, was also very different from that of the more ancient Middle Eastern empires and cultures, most of which had been conquered and assimilated by stronger neighbours long before the Macedonian phalanx, the Roman legion, or the Persian cataphract established their domination. Of the older cultures that had survived until the beginning of the Christian era, retaining something of their old identity and their old language, the most ancient was surely that of Egypt. Sharply defined by both geography and history, Egypt consists of the lower valley and the delta of the Nile, bounded by the eastern and western deserts and the sea in the north. Its civilization was already thousands of years old when the conquerors came, and yet, despite successive conquests by the Persians, the Greeks, and the

Romans, Egyptian civilization had preserved much of its distinctive quality.

The ancient Egyptian language and writing had, in the course of the millennia, undergone several changes, but show a remarkable continuity. Both the ancient hieroglyphic script and the so-called demotic, a more cursive style of writing which succeeded it, survived into the early Christian centuries, when they were finally supplanted by Coptic – the last form of the ancient Egyptian language, transcribed in an alphabet adapted from the Greek, with additional letters derived from demotic. The Coptic script first appears in the second century BCE and was stabilized in the first century CE. With the conversion of the Egyptians to Christianity, it became the national cultural language of Christian Egypt under Roman and then under Byzantine rule. After the Islamic Arab conquest and the subsequent Islamization and Arabization of Egypt, even those Egyptians who remained Christian adopted the Arabic language. They are still called Copts, but the Coptic language gradually died out and survives at the present day only in the liturgy of the Coptic Church. Egypt had acquired a new identity.

The country has had many names. The name used by the Greeks, the Romans, and the modern world, though not by the Egyptians, is 'Egypt', a Greek adaptation from an ancient Egyptian original. The second syllable is probably from the same root as the name 'Copt'. The Arabic name is Miṣr, brought by the Arab conquerors and still in use at the present day. It is related to the Semitic names for Egypt found in the Hebrew Bible and other ancient texts.

The other early river valley civilization of the Middle East, that of the Tigris and the Euphrates, may be even older than that of Egypt, but it shows neither the unity nor the continuity of Egyptian state and society. The south, the centre, and the north were often the seats of different peoples speaking different languages, and known by a number of names – Sumer and Akkad, Assyria and Babylonia. In the Hebrew Bible, it is called Aram Naharayim, Aram of the Two Rivers. In the Graeco-Roman world, it was called Mesopotamia, which conveys much the same meaning. In the early Christian centuries, the centre and the south were firmly in the hands of the Persians, who indeed had their imperial capital at Ctesiphon, not far from the present site of Baghdad. The name Baghdad itself is Persian, and means 'God gave'. It was the name of a village at the place where, centuries later, the Arabs established a new imperial capital. The name Iraq in medieval

Arab usage was that of a province, consisting of the southern half of the present country of that name from Takrit southwards to the sea. It was sometimes also called 'Irāq 'Arabī to distinguish it from 'Irāq 'Ajamī, the adjoining area of southwestern Iran.

Northern Mesopotamia was disputed territory, sometimes ruled by Rome, sometimes by Persia, sometimes by local dynasties. Sometimes it was even considered to be part of Syria, a term more commonly used, rather loosely, to designate the area bounded by the Taurus Mountains in the north, the Sinai desert in the south, the Arabian desert in the east, and the Mediterranean Sea in the west. The name Syria is of uncertain origin. Herodotus explains it as a shortened form of Assyria. Modern scholars have traced it to various local place names. It first appears in Greek and has no recognizable antecedents, either in its form or in its usage, in pre-Hellenistic texts. Well established in Roman and in Byzantine official usage, this Greek term virtually disappeared after the Arab conquest in the seventh century. It remained in occasional use in Europe, especially after the revival of classical learning, and with it of Graeco-Roman terminology, that followed the Renaissance. In the Arab, and more generally, the Muslim world, the region formerly called Syria was known as Shām, a name also given to its major city, Damascus. The name Syria – in Arabic Sūriya – makes an occasional rare appearance in geographical writings, but was otherwise unknown until the latter part of the nineteenth century, when it reappeared under European influence. It was officially adopted as the name of a province – the vilayet of Damascus – by the Ottoman administration in 1865, and first became the official designation of a country with the establishment of the French Mandate after the First World War. Of the older, local names of the country that have come down to us, the most widely used was 'Aram', after the name of the Aramaean peoples who had settled both Syria and Mesopotamia. As Mesopotamia was known as 'Aram of the Two Rivers', so were southern and northern Syria known as 'Aram of Damascus' and 'Aram of Zoba' (i.e. Aleppo) (see, for example, 2 Samuel 8:6 and 10:8).

More commonly, however, the countries forming the western arm of the Fertile Crescent were called by the names of the various kingdoms and peoples that ruled and inhabited them. Of these, the most familiar, or at least the best documented, are the southern lands, known in the earlier books of the Hebrew Bible and some other ancient writings as Canaan. After the Israelite conquest and settlement, the area inhabited by them came to be described as 'land of the children of Israel' (Joshua 11:22) or simply 'land of Israel' (1 Samuel 13:19). After the break-up of the kingdom of David and Solomon in the tenth century BCE, the southern part, with Jerusalem as its capital, was called Judah, while the north was called Israel, or, later, Samaria. The northern and southern coastal areas were known, after the peoples who inhabited them, as Phoenicia and Philistia. The Philistines disappeared at the time of the Babylonian conquests and were not heard of again. The Phoenicians remained until Roman and early Christian times on the coastal plain of what is now northern Israel and southern Lebanon. After the Persian conquest in the sixth century BCE, the area resettled by the returning exiles was known as Yehud (cf. the Aramaic texts in Daniel 2:25, 5:13; Ezra 5:1, 5:8). In Roman usage, also reflected in the New Testament, the south, centre, and north of the country are called respectively, Judaea, Samaria and Galilee. To these one may add the southern desert, which the Romans called Idumea, from the Biblical Edom, and which today is known as the Negev, and Peraea, in the lands east of the Jordan river.

The dominant languages in both Mesopotamia and Syria were Semitic, but subdivided into several different families. The oldest of these was the Akkadian family, to which both Assyrian and Babylonian belong, and which was generally used in Mesopotamia. Another was the Canaanite family, including biblical Hebrew, Phoenician, with its North African offshoot, Carthaginian, as well as a number of other closely related languages known from inscriptions in both northern and southern Syria. By the beginning of the Christian era, most of these languages had virtually disappeared, and had been replaced by a group of closely related languages belonging to another Semitic family, called Aramaic. Of the Canaanitic languages, Phoenician was still spoken in the Levant seaports and the North African colonies; Hebrew, though no longer the common spoken language of the Jews, survived as a language of religion, literature, and scholarship. Assyrian and Babylonian appear to have died out completely. Aramaic became an international medium of communication for commerce and diplomacy, and was widely used, not only in the Fertile Crescent, but also in Persia, Egypt and what is now southern Turkey.

At the beginning of the Christian era, Arabic, historically the last of the Semitic languages to enter the region, was in the main confined to the central and northern parts of the Arabian peninsula. The more advanced city cultures of the southwest, in the present-day Yemen, spoke yet another Semitic language, known as South Arabian, and closely related to Ethiopic, which had been carried by south Arabian colonists to the Horn of Africa. In the north, there is evidence that Arabic speakers had entered and settled the Syrian and Iraqi borderlands even before the great Arab conquests of the seventh century, which led to the triumph of Arabic all over the region. In the Fertile Crescent, Aramaic was replaced by Arabic. At the present day it survives in the rituals of some of the Eastern Churches and is still spoken in a few remote villages.

The country now called Turkey did not acquire that name – and then only in Europe – until the Middle Ages, when the people known as Turks arrived from further east. The commonest names used in the early Christian centuries were Asia or Asia Minor, and Anatolia. Both originally designated the eastern shores of the Aegean Sea, and were gradually extended eastwards in a somewhat vague and variable manner. The country was more usually referred to by the names of the different provinces, cities, and kingdoms that divided it. Greek was the dominant language and the principal medium of communication.

'Anatolia' comes from a Greek word meaning 'sunrise', as do 'Orient', from Latin, and 'Levant', from Italian. Such names reflect the outlook of peoples for whom the eastern Mediterranean lands were the limits of the known world. It was only gradually that the Mediterranean peoples, becoming aware of a remoter and vaster Asia to the East, renamed the familiar one 'Asia Minor'. In the same way, many centuries later, the ancient and immemorial 'East' became the 'Near' and then the 'Middle' East, when a more distant East dawned on the Western horizon. Of these more distant eastern lands, by far the most important, the most portentous for the Middle East was Iran, better known in the West as Persia.

Strictly speaking, Persia, or Persis, is the name not of a country nor of a nation, but of a province – the southwestern province of Pars or Fars, on the eastern shore of the gulf which takes its name from it. The Persians have never applied that name to the whole country. They have, however, used it of their language, since the regional dialect of Pars became the dominant cultural and political language of the country in the same way that Tuscan became Italian, Castilian became Spanish, and the dialect of the Home Counties became English. The name always used by the Persians, and imposed by them on the rest of the world in 1935, was Iran. This was derived from the ancient Persian *aryānam*, a genitive plural form meaning '[the land] of the Aryans', and dating back to the early migrations of the Indo-Aryan peoples.

The religious map of the Middle East was even more complex – and confused – than the ethnic and linguistic map. Some of the old gods had died and been forgotten, but many still survived, albeit in strange and altered forms. The long record of conquest and migration among Middle Eastern peoples, followed by the immensely powerful impact of Hellenistic culture and Roman rule, gave rise to new and syncretistic forms of belief and worship. Some of the eastern cults even found followers among the Romans – some of them even in Rome itself. Isis from Egypt, Adonis from Syria, Cybele from Phrygia in Asia Minor, all gained adherents among the new masters of the Middle East.

Within a comparatively short time, a period measured in centuries not millennia, all these ancient gods and cults had been abandoned or superseded, and had been replaced by two new and competing monotheistic world religions which arose successively in the region: Christianity and Islam. The advent and triumph of Islam in the seventh century was preceded and in a sense made possible by the rise and spread of Christianity, which itself was deeply indebted to its religious and philosophic predecessors. Both Christian and Islamic civilization have common roots in the encounter and interaction in the ancient Middle East of three universalist traditions – those of the Jews, the Persians, and the Greeks.

The idea of monotheism was not entirely new. It appears, for example, in the hymns of Akhenaton, pharaoh of Egypt in the fourteenth century BCE. But such ideas were sporadic and isolated, and their impact was temporary and local. The first to make ethical monotheism an essential part of their religion were the Jews, and the evolution of their beliefs from a primitive tribal cult to a universal ethical monotheism is reflected in the successive books of the Hebrew Bible. The same books reflect the growing Jewish awareness of how this belief isolated them among their idol-worshipping and polytheistic neighbours. In modern times, those who believe themselves to be in unique possession of the truth are easily convinced that the discovery of this truth was their achievement. For a devout people in ancient times, such a conviction would have been impossibly presumptuous. Confronted with the extraordinary fact of their uniqueness in knowing the truth about one God, the ancient Jews, unable even to consider the idea that they had chosen God, adopted the more humble belief that God had chosen them. This was a choice that imposed duties, as well as, indeed more than, privileges, and could sometimes be a difficult burden to bear. 'You only have I known of all the families of the earth: therefore I will punish you for all your iniquities' (Amos 3:2).

The Jews were, however, not alone in recognizing and worshipping one universal ethical God. Far away to the east, on the high plateau of Iran, two kindred peoples, known to history as the Medes and the Persians, had evolved out of their ancient paganism a belief in a single, supreme deity, the ultimate power of good, engaged in constant struggle with the forces of evil. The emergence of this religion is associated with the name of the prophet Zoroaster, whose teachings are preserved in the ancient Zoroastrian scriptures, written in a very early form of the Persian language. The date when the Persian prophet lived and taught is not known, and scholarly estimates vary by a thousand years or more. It seems clear, however, that the sixth and fifth centuries BCE were a time of major Zoroastrian religious activity. For centuries, these two God-seeking peoples went their separate ways, unknown, it would seem, to one another. The cataclysmic events of the sixth century BCE brought them into contact, with consequences that were to reverberate around the world and through the ages.

In 586 BCE Nebuchadnezzar, King of Babylon, in the course of a series of wars of conquest, captured Jerusalem, destroyed the kingdom of Judah and the Jewish Temple, and, in accordance with the custom of the time, sent the conquered people into captivity in Babylonia. Some decades later, the Babylonians themselves were overthrown by another conqueror, Cyrus the Mede, the founder of a new, Persian, empire, which in time extended to the Syrian lands and far beyond. It seems that both sides, the conquerors, and one small group among the many conquered peoples in their vast and polyglot domains, recognized a certain basic affinity of outlook and belief. Cyrus authorized the return of the Jews from the Babylonian captivity to the land of Israel, and gave orders for the rebuilding of the Temple in Jerusalem at government expense. In the Hebrew Bible, Cyrus is accorded a degree of respect given to no other non-Jewish ruler, and indeed to few Jewish rulers. The last chapters of the book of Isaiah, written after the Babylonian captivity, are dramatic: 'He [Cyrus] is my shepherd, and shall perform all my pleasure: even saying to Jerusalem, Thou shalt be built; and to the temple, Thy foundation shall be laid' (Isaiah 44:28). The immediately following chapter goes even further: 'Thus saith the Lord to his anointed, to Cyrus, whose right hand I have holden, to subdue nations before him ...' (Isaiah 45:1).

Between the earlier and later books of the Hebrew Bible, those written before the Babylonian captivity, and those written after the return, there are notable differences in belief and outlook, some of which at least may plausibly be attributed to influences from the religious thought-world of Iran. Notable among these are the idea of a cosmic struggle between the forces of good and the forces of evil, between God and the Devil, in which mankind has a role to play; the more explicit development of the notion of judgement after death, and reward or retribution in heaven or hell; the notion of an anointed saviour, born of a holy seed, who will come at the end of time and ensure the final triumph of good over evil. The importance of such ideas in late Judaism and early Christianity will be obvious.

The Jewish–Persian connection also had political implications. Cyrus had shown favour to the Jews, who in turn had served him loyally. For centuries after, Jews, both in their homeland and in other countries under Roman rule, were suspected, sometimes with good reason, of sympathy or even collaboration with the Persian enemies of Rome.

The German philosopher and historian Karl Jaspers has spoken of the period between 600 and 300 BCE as an 'axial age' in human history, when people in remote and apparently unrelated lands achieved major spiritual and intellectual breakthroughs. This was the time of Confucius and Lao-Tse in China, of Buddha in India, of Zoroaster or his major disciples in Iran, of the prophets in Israel, and the philosophers in Greece. These were to a very large extent unknown to one another. There seems to have been some activity in the Middle East by Buddhist missionaries from India, but it is little known, and appears to have had little effect. The fructifying mutual relations between Jews and Persians date from the time of Cyrus and of his successors. These same successors, extending their domain westwards across Asia Minor to the Aegean, came into contact and conflict with the Greeks, and thus established lines of communication between the rising Greek civilization and the many peoples of the Persian Empire. The Greek genius was philosophical and scientific rather than religious, but the insights achieved by Greek philosophers and scientists were to have a profound impact on the subsequent religious civilizations of the Middle East, and indeed, of the world.

Greek traders and mercenaries explored the various regions of the Middle East from an early date, and brought back information about these strange lands to whet the growing intellectual curiosity of Greek philosophers and scientists. The expansion of the Persian Empire offered new opportunities – easier travel and communication, knowledge of languages, and employment for Greek skills at many levels of the Persian imperial government. A new age began with the eastern conquests of Alexander the Great (356–323 BCE) of Macedon, which extended Macedonian rule and Greek cultural influence across Iran to Central Asia and the borders of India and southwards through Syria into Egypt. After his death, his conquests were divided among his successors into three kingdoms, based on Iran, Syria, and Egypt.

The Greeks had already known something of Persia before the conquests of Alexander; they now became familiar with the mysterious lands of Mesopotamia, Syria, and Egypt, where they established a political supremacy that eventually gave way to that of the Romans, and a cultural supremacy that continued even under Roman rule. In 64 BCE, the Roman general Pompey conquered Syria, and soon after took over Judaea. In 31 BCE, after the defeat of Antony and Cleopatra at the battle of Actium, the Graeco-Macedonian rulers of Egypt too were obliged to submit to Roman domination. In the universal triumph of Hellenistic culture and Roman domination, only two peoples dared to resist: the Persians and the Jews, with very different results.

In about 247 BCE, a certain Arshak led a successful revolt against Greek rule, and established an independent dynasty known to history as the Parthians, after their tribe and region of origin. Despite several attempts to restore Macedonian supremacy, the Parthians managed to preserve, and even to extend, their political independence, becoming in time a major power and a dangerous rival to Rome. They remained, however, open to Greek cultural influence, which appears to have been considerable. This too was changed, after the overthrow of the Parthian dynasty by Ardashīr (226–240 CE), the founder of the Sasanid dynasty and the restorer of the Zoroastrian faith. Zoroastrianism now became the state religion in Iran, part of the apparatus of sovereignty, of society, and of government. This may well be the first example in history of a state religion with a state-imposed orthodoxy and a hierarchic priesthood, much concerned with the detection and repression of heresy. Sasanid practice in this respect was in marked contrast with the broad tolerance and eclecticism both of their Parthian predecessors and of imperial Rome.

The Zoroastrian faith and priesthood gained great power from this link with the state, but they suffered the consequences of this relationship when that state was itself overthrown. The Zoroastrian priestly establishment perished with the Persian Empire. After the destruction of that empire by the Arab conquest, Zoroastrianism entered into a long decline, unbroken by any kind of revival, even by any share in later revivals of Iranian political and cultural life in Islamic times. Such religious resistance as was offered to the advance of Islam in Iran came not from the orthodox Zoroastrian priesthood, but rather from Zoroastrian heresies, that is, from those who were accustomed to opposition and repression, not from those accustomed to the exercise of authority.

Some of these Zoroastrian heresies came to be of considerable importance in Middle Eastern and indeed in general history. One of the best known is Mithraism, which won many followers in the Roman Empire, especially among the military, and was practised even in England, where traces of a Mithraistic temple have been found. Another, better known, was Manicheism, the creed of Mani, who lived from 216 to 277 CE, and founded a religion based on a blend of Christian and Zoroastrian ideas. He suffered martyrdom in the year 277, but his religion proved remarkably vigorous, and survived severe persecution at the hands of both Muslims and Christians in both the Middle East and Europe. A third, more local in character but of great importance, was the heresy of Mazdak, who flourished during the early sixth century in Iran, and established a kind of religious communism. It inspired a number of later, dissident Shi'ite movements in Islam.

Zoroastrianism was the first imperial and exclusive orthodoxy. It was however a religion of Iran, and does not seem to have been seriously offered to any other people outside the Iranian imperial and cultural world. It was not exceptional in this, since virtually all civilized ancient religions were initially ethnic, became civic and political, and in due course perished along with the polity which had maintained their cult. There was one exception to this rule, one only of the religions of antiquity, which survived the destruction of its political and territorial base, and managed to live on without either, by a process of radical self-transformation. This was the process by which the children of Israel, later the people of Judaea, became the Jews.

In their political resistance to Greece and Rome, the Jews failed. Initially, under the Maccabees, they were successful in asserting their independence against the Macedonian ruler of Syria, who claimed lordship over them, and for a while restored the independence of the kingdom of Judaea. But against the might of Rome they could not prevail, and in revolt after revolt, some of them perhaps with Persian instigation or help, they were crushed and reduced to slavery. Their kings and high priests became Roman puppets, and a Roman procurator ruled in Judaea. The most important of these revolts began in 66 CE. Despite a long and bitter struggle, the rebels were overwhelmed, and in 70 CE, the Romans captured Jerusalem and destroyed the second Temple, which had been built by the exiles returning from Babylon. Even this did not end Jewish resistance. After the revolt of Bar-Kokhba in 135 CE, the Romans decided once and for all to rid themselves of this troublesome people. Like the Babylonians before them, they sent a large part of the Jewish population into captivity and exile, and this time there was no Cyrus to restore them. Even the historic nomenclature of the Jews was to be obliterated. Jerusalem was renamed Aelia Capitolina, and a temple to Jupiter built on the site of the destroyed Jewish Temple. The names Judaea and Samaria were abolished, and the country renamed Palestine, after the long-forgotten Philistines.

A passage in an ancient Jewish text vividly illustrates how the benefits and penalties of Roman imperial rule were seen by their Jewish and no doubt other Middle Eastern subjects. The passage describes a conversation between three rabbis sometime in the second century CE:[1]

> Rabbi Judah began by saying: 'How fine are the works of these people [the Romans]. They have built markets, they have built bridges, they have built bathhouses.' Rabbi Jose was silent, and Rabbi Simeon Bar-Yohai answered: 'All that they built, they built only for their own needs. They built markets to set whores in them; bathhouses, to beautify themselves; bridges, to collect tolls.' Judah, the son of proselytes, went in and reported their words to the authorities, and they said: 'Let Judah, who exalted us, be exalted. Let Jose, who was silent, be exiled to Sepphoris, and let Simeon, who denounced us, be executed.'

In one important respect, Jews, Greeks and Romans resembled each other and differed from the other peoples of antiquity – a resemblance and a difference that gave all three of them a crucial role in shaping the civilizations that were to follow. In the Middle East as elsewhere in the world, it was the universal custom of human groups to draw a sharp line between themselves and others – to define the group and reject the outsider. This basic primal need goes back to the beginnings of humanity and beyond them to most forms of animal life. Invariably, the distinction between insiders and outsiders was determined by blood; that is, by kinship or by what we would nowadays call ethnicity. The Greeks and the Jews, the two most articulate peoples of Mediterranean antiquity, have bequeathed two classical definitions of the Other – the barbarian who is not Greek and the gentile who is not Jewish. The barriers expressed by these terms were formidable but – and herein lay an immensely important innovation – they were not insuperable, and in this they differed from the more primitive and more universal definitions of difference based on birth and blood. These barriers could be crossed or even removed, in the one case by adopting the language and culture of the Greeks, in the other by adopting the religion and laws of the Jews. Neither group sought new members, but both were willing to accept them, and by the beginning of the Christian era, Hellenized barbarians and Judaized gentiles were a common feature in many Middle Eastern cities.

There is another respect in which Greeks and Jews were unique in the ancient world – in their compassion for an enemy. There is nothing elsewhere to compare with the sympathetic portrayal by the Greek dramatist Aeschylus – himself a veteran of the Persian wars – of the sufferings of the vanquished Persians, or the concern for the people of Assyrian Nineveh expressed in the Biblical book of Jonah.

The Romans carried the principle of inclusiveness an important step further, by the gradual development of a common imperial citizenship. The Greeks had developed the idea of citizenship – the citizen, that is, as a member of a polity with the right to participate in the formation and conduct of its government. But membership of a Greek city was limited to its original citizens and their descendants, and the most that a foreigner could aspire to was the status of resident alien. Roman citizenship was originally of the same kind, but in gradual stages the rights and duties of a Roman citizen were extended to all the provinces of the Empire.

This accessibility of Hellenistic culture, Jewish religion and Roman polity all helped to prepare the way for the rise and spread of Christianity, a missionary religion whose followers believed that they were the possessors of God's final revelation, which it was their sacred duty to bring to all mankind. A few centuries later, a second universal religion arose, Islam, and inspired its adherents with a similar sense of certitude and mission, albeit with a different content and method. With two world religions, sustained by the same convictions, driven by the same ambitions, living side by side in the same region, it was inevitable that, sooner or later, they would clash.

CHAPTER 2

BEFORE ISLAM

The period from the advent of Christianity to the advent of Islam, that is, roughly the first six centuries of the Christian era, was shaped by a series of major developments both in the course of events and in the movement of civilizations.

The first of these developments, and in many ways by far the most important of them, was the rise of Christianity itself – the gradual spread and adoption of the Christian religion, and the consequent disappearance, or at least submersion, of all the pre-Christian religions except for those of the Jews and the Persians. For a while, classical Graeco-Roman paganism lingered on, and even had a last flicker of revival during the reign of the emperor Julian (361–363), known to Christian historians as Julian the Apostate. For the first half of this period, until the early fourth century, Christianity grew and spread as a protest against the Roman order. Sometimes tolerated, more often persecuted, it was perforce separated from the State, and developed its own institution – the Church, with its own structure and organization, its own leadership and hierarchy, its own laws and tribunals, which gradually embraced the whole of the Roman world.

With the conversion of the emperor Constantine (311–337), Christianity captured the Roman Empire, and was, in a sense, captured by it. The conversion of the emperor was followed in gradual stages by the Christianization of the Roman state. Authority was now added to persuasion in the promotion of the new faith, and by the time of the great Christian emperor Justinian (527–569), the full panoply of Roman power was used, not only to establish the supremacy of Christianity over other religions, but also to enforce the supremacy of one state-approved doctrine among the many schools of thought into which Christians were now divided. By this time there was not one, but several Churches, disagreeing primarily on questions of theological doctrine, but often divided also by personal, jurisdictional, regional, or even national loyalties.

The second major change was the shift of the centre of gravity of the Roman Empire from west to east, from Rome to Constantinople, the city founded by Constantine to be his eastern capital. After the death of the emperor Theodosius in 395 CE, the Empire was split into two, a western empire ruled from Rome, and an eastern empire ruled from Constantinople. Within a comparatively short time, the western empire was submerged in a series of barbarian invasions, and in effect ceased to exist. The eastern empire survived these difficulties, and was able to maintain itself for another thousand years.

The name Byzantine, which is nowadays generally applied to the eastern empire, is a term of modern scholarship, and is derived from the name of the settlement which previously existed on the site of the city of Constantinople. The Byzantines never called themselves Byzantines. They called themselves Romans, and were ruled by a Roman emperor, purporting to enforce the Roman law. True, there were differences. The emperors and their subjects were Christian, not pagan, and although the citizens of Byzantium called themselves Romans, they did so not in Latin, but in Greek – not *romani*, but *rhomaioi*. Even the provincials were affected. Greek inscriptions, in various places, pray for the 'domination of the Romans' – *hēgēmonia tōn Rhomaiōn* – and a client prince in the border principality of Edessa, ousted by the Persians and restored by the Romans, proudly adopts the title *philorhomaios*, 'friend of the Romans' – in Greek. Even at the height of Roman power, Greek in effect had the status of the second language of the Roman Empire. In the eastern Roman Empire, it became the first language. Latin lingered for a while, and Latin terms can be traced in the Greek of Byzantium, and even, centuries later, in the Arabic of the caliphate. But Greek had become, and for long remained, the language of government as well as of culture. Even the surviving non-Greek languages and literatures of the eastern provinces, Coptic, Aramaic, and later, Arabic, were profoundly influenced by the Hellenistic philosophic and scientific tradition.

The third major development, the Hellenization of the Middle East, had begun centuries earlier, in the empires of Alexander the Great and of his successors in Syria and Egypt. Both the Roman state and the Christian Churches were profoundly affected by Greek culture. Both of them contributed to its wider dissemination. The governmental institutions of the east Roman state were influenced by the traditions of the late Greek monarchies of Alexander and his successors, a conception of monarchy in many ways significantly different from that of the Roman caesars. In their religion, too, the early Christians were concerned with philosophical subtleties of a kind that had long preoccupied the Greeks, but had never much troubled either the Romans or the Jews. The Christian scripture, the New Testament, was written in a language which, though no longer that of the Athenian dramatists and philosophers, was unmistakably Greek. Even the Old Testament was available in a Greek translation, made centuries earlier in the Greek-speaking Jewish community of Alexandria.

Another major change, perhaps also to be attributed in part to earlier influences, was the steady growth of what would nowadays be called a command economy – the attempt to plan or direct the economy through the use of state authority. It was natural enough to develop such policies in the river valley societies, especially in Egypt, where the directed economy reached an advanced stage under the Ptolemaic Dynasty, founded by one of Alexander's generals. In the early Christian centuries, and especially from the third century onwards, the state became increasingly involved in industry, in trade and manufacture, and even in agriculture. More and more, state authorities exercised control over the economic activities of such private entrepreneurs as remained, and attempted to formulate and impose state economic policies. In many fields, the state simply bypassed the private traders and organized its own affairs. The army, for example, relied very largely on state enterprises for the manufacture of armaments, equipment and, in some periods, even uniforms. Provisions for the army were usually collected in the form of taxes in kind, and issued to the troops in the form of rations. The growing economic activities of the state left less and less room for the entrepreneur, the purveyor, the supplier, and their colleagues.

There was also growing state intervention in agriculture. There is some evidence of a continuous shrinkage in the area of cultivated land. Imperial legislation, of which a fair amount survives, reveals again and again the concern of the state at the increase in abandoned and deserted lands, and its desire to induce peasants and landowners, by various fiscal and other incentives, to resettle these lands. This appears to have been a major problem, especially from the third to the sixth centuries, that is to say, from the time of Diocletian (284–305), a leading exponent of economic interventionism, until the Islamic conquests and the resulting restructuring of economic function and power.

Both the Byzantine and the Persian empires were overwhelmed by the advancing tide of Islam in the early decades of the seventh century, but there is an important difference between their fates. The Byzantine

35

armies suffered crushing defeats, and lost many provinces to the Arabs, but the core province of Asia Minor was still Greek and Christian, and the imperial capital, Constantinople, despite many assaults, remained inviolate behind its land and sea walls. The Byzantine Empire was weakened and diminished, but it survived for another seven hundred years, and its language, its culture and its institutions continued to develop at their own natural rhythm. When finally the last remnant of the Greek Christian empire was overwhelmed in 1453, there was a Christian world to which the Byzantines could bequeath their memory and their record of earlier times.

The fate of Persia was very different. Not only its outlying provinces, but its capital and the entirety of its territories were conquered and incorporated in the new Arab Islamic empire. The Byzantine magnates of Syria and Egypt could flee to Byzantium; the Zoroastrians of Persia had no choice but to remain under Muslim rule, or to seek refuge in the only place that was open to them, India. During the early centuries of Muslim domination in Iran, the old language, and with it the old script, were gradually forgotten, except among a small and dwindling minority. Even the language was transformed by conquest, in much the same way that Anglo-Saxon became English. It is only in comparatively modern times that scholarship has undertaken the recovery and decipherment of old Persian writings and inscriptions, and thus begun the exploration of the pre-Islamic history of Iran.

During the first six centuries of the Christian era, there are two major phases in the history of the Iranian Empire: the first that of the Parthians; the second, that of the Sasanids. The first Sasanid ruler, Ardashir (226–240 CE), launched a new series of wars against Rome. His successor, Shapur I (240–271 CE), even succeeded in capturing the Roman emperor Valerian in battle, an achievement which so delighted him that he had representations of it carved in stone on several mountains in Iran, where they can still be seen. They depict the Persian shah on horseback with the Roman emperor at his feet; the shah's foot is on the emperor's neck. Valerian died in captivity.

This Perso-Roman, later Perso-Byzantine rivalry was the dominating political fact in the history of the area until the rise of the Islamic caliphate, which destroyed one of the rivals and greatly weakened the other. The long and apparently endless sequence of wars, with one exception interrupted only by brief intervals of peace, must surely have contributed significantly to this final result.

The one exception, the Long Peace, endured for more than a

century. In 384 Shapur III (383–388 CE) made peace with Rome. Apart from a brief frontier clash in 421–2, war did not resume until the beginning of the sixth century, when it continued, with only minor pauses, until 628. By that time, a new power was rising that would soon overshadow both belligerents.

For contemporary and medieval historians, the principal issues at stake in these wars were, as one would expect, territorial. The Romans laid claim to Armenia and Mesopotamia, which during most of this period were ruled by the Persians. The Romans had claimed these lands because the emperor Trajan had conquered them, thus establishing, according to a doctrine shared by Romans, Persians, and later, Muslims, a permanent entitlement. The Byzantines had a further argument, that the inhabitants of Armenia and Mesopotamia were largely Christian, and therefore owed allegiance to the Christian emperor. The Persians claimed Syria, Palestine, and even Egypt, which had been conquered by Cambyses, the son of Cyrus, in 525 BCE. In the course of the wars, they were from time to time able to invade and devastate these lands, and even, for brief periods, to hold them. There were no Persians or Zoroastrians in these countries, but there were other groups of non-Christians among whom the Persians found sympathizers.

Modern historians have been able to detect and document other issues besides territorial claims. Among the most important is the control of the trade routes between East and West. Two eastern imports were of particular importance to the Mediterranean world: silk from China and spices from India and Southeast Asia. The traffic in these commodities became very extensive; and Roman legislative enactments reveal a continuing concern to protect it from interference. Because of this trade, the Roman and Byzantine world was in touch with the civilizations of further Asia, with China and with India. There were no regular relations, and very few recorded exchanges of visitors. There were however imports from both, for which the Romans, and after them the Byzantines, seem to have paid principally in gold coin. There was little if anything that the Mediterranean world could offer in exchange for Chinese silk or Indian spices. Gold, however, was always acceptable, and great quantities of Roman gold coins were sent to eastern Asia to pay for the imports that came to the Mediterranean basin – and not only to eastern Asia, since the Persians made substantial profits as middlemen in the silk trade for China, especially when, as at certain periods, they were able to extend their rule eastwards into Central Asia and thus dominate the silk trade at its point of departure. There are occasional complaints of the drain of bullion to the East, but on the whole the Roman world seems to have survived this drain surprisingly well.

The most direct route from the Mediterranean lands to the further east lay through the territories ruled or dominated by Persia, but there were obvious advantages, both economic and strategic, in developing routes beyond the reach of Persian arms. The choices were the northern overland route from China through the Turkish lands in the Eurasian steppe towards the Black Sea and Byzantine territory, or the southern sea routes through the Indian Ocean. These led either to the Persian Gulf and Arabia or to the Red Sea, with overland connections, through Egypt and the isthmus of Suez, or through the caravan routes of western Arabia from Yemen to the borders of Syria. The Roman, and then Byzantine interest, was to establish and preserve these external commercial links with China and with India, thus bypassing the Persian-dominated centre. The Persian Empire tried to use its position athwart the transit routes to control Byzantine trade, so as to exploit it in times of peace, or stop it in times of war. This meant a recurring struggle for influence between the two imperial powers in the countries beyond the imperial borders of both of them. The effect of these interventions – commercial, diplomatic, and on rare occasions, military – was considerable in both areas. Those primarily affected were the Turkish tribes and principalities in the north, and the Arab tribes and principalities in the south. Neither Turks nor Arabs are recorded as playing much role in the ancient civilizations of the region. Both of them, in consecutive waves of invasion, later played a dominant role in the Islamic heartlands in the Middle Ages.

For the first six centuries of the Christian era, Turks and Arabs alike were still beyond the imperial frontiers, in the barbarous or semi-barbarous steppe and desert lands. Neither Persians nor Romans, even in their periods of imperial expansion, showed much interest in conquering the steppe or desert peoples, and took care not to get too closely involved with them. The fourth-century Roman historian Ammianus Marcellinus, himself a native of Syria, has something to say of both. Of the steppe peoples, he observes:[1]

> The inhabitants of all the districts are savage and warlike, and take such pleasure in war and conflict, that one who loses his life in battle is regarded as happy beyond all others. For those who depart from this life by a natural death they assail with insults, as degenerate and cowardly. (XXIII, 6.44)

The desert dwellers to the south he describes as 'the Saracens ... whom we never found desirable either as friends or as enemies' (XIV, 4.1). To conquer such neighbours by armed force would have been expensive, difficult, and dangerous, and the results neither secure nor useful. Instead, both empires followed what became a classical imperial policy, of wooing the tribal peoples in various ways, and trying to gain, and, as far as possible, to retain their good will, with financial, military, and technical aid, titles and honours, and the like. From an early date, the tribal chiefs – the Greek term was phylarch – both north and south, learnt to exploit this situation to their advantage, leaning sometimes one way, sometimes the other, sometimes to both or to neither. Sometimes the wealth accruing from the caravan trade enabled them to establish cities and kingdoms of their own, with their own political role, as satellites or even allies of the imperial powers. Sometimes these imperial powers, when they felt it safe to do so, tried to conquer the border principalities and subject them to direct rule. More often, they preferred some form of indirect rule or clientage.

The pattern is an ancient one, and no doubt goes back to remote antiquity. The Romans had their initiation into desert politics in 65 BCE, when Pompey visited the Nabatean capital at Petra, now in the Hāshimite kingdom of Jordan. The Nabateans appear to have been Arabs, though their culture and written language were Aramaean. In the oasis of Petra, they had established a flourishing caravan city, with which the Romans found it expedient to establish friendly relations. Petra served as a sort of buffer state between the Roman provinces and the desert, and as a valued auxiliary in reaching towards southern Arabia and the routes to Indian trade. In 25 BCE, the emperor Augustus decided to try another policy, and sent an expedition to conquer the Yemen. The intention was to establish a Roman foothold at the southern end of the Red Sea, and thus open the way to direct Roman control of the route to India. The expedition was a dismal failure, and the Romans never tried again. That is to say, they never again tried to penetrate with military force into Arabia proper, but preferred to rely, both for their trade in peacetime and their strategic needs in wartime, on the caravan cities and the desert border states.

It was this Roman policy that made possible the efflorescence of a succession of Arabian border principalities, of which Petra was the first in Roman times. There were several others, notably Palmyra, the modern Tadmur in southeastern Syria. Palmyra grew up around a spring in the Syrian desert. It was an ancient site, where there had apparently been centres of settlement and trade in earlier times. The Palmyrenes had an emporium at Dura, on the Euphrates, and were thus in a position to operate the trans-desert route from the Mediterranean to Mesopotamia and the Gulf. This gave them a position of some commercial and strategic importance.

North of the two empires, north of the Black Sea and the Caspian, lay the overland route across Central Asia to China, where a situation in many ways similar prevailed. In the last quarter of the first century CE, there seems to have been a revolt of Central Asian tribes in this region against the authority of China, which had claimed a vague general suzerainty. Among the leaders of this revolt were the people whom the Chinese chroniclers called 'Hiung Nu', apparently identical with the Huns of European history. A Chinese general named Pan Chao led an expedition from China into Central Asia, where he crushed the rebellion and drove the Hiung Nu away from the silk route. But this time the Chinese went further, and conquered the regions in later times known as Turkestan, comprising the territory of the present republics of Uzbekistan and its western neighbours. From there, Pan Chao was able effectively to bring the inner Asian silk route under Chinese control. At the same time, he sent an embassy, led by one Kang Ying, to the west to meet the Romans. This mission is reported to have reached the Persian Gulf in the year 97 CE.

These and other military and diplomatic activities from the East may help to explain the policies of the Roman emperor Trajan, who embarked on an active and ambitious programme of expansion in the Middle Eastern region. In 106, abandoning the previous Roman relationship with Petra, he invaded and conquered it. The realm of the Nabateans was now a Roman province, called Provincia Arabia, governed by a legate of the Roman Legion stationed at Bosra. Trajan also established a water route from Alexandria to Clysma, by linking canals and branches of the Nile so that Roman ships could sail from the Mediterranean to the Red Sea. In 107 CE, a Roman embassy was sent to India, and shortly after that, a road was traced from the eastern Syrian borderlands to the Red Sea.

All this, not surprisingly, appears to have alarmed the Parthians, who took the initiative in the war which followed between the two empires. In a campaign which began in 114 CE, Trajan occupied Armenia, one of the main areas disputed between the two empires, made an agreement with the prince of Edessa, an independent Christian ruler, crossed the Tigris eastwards, and in the summer of 116, captured the great Persian city of Ctesiphon, not far from the present site of Baghdad, and even reached the shore of the Persian Gulf. It was surely not coincidental that a major revolt took place in Judaea in this period. After the death of Trajan in 117, his successor Hadrian withdrew from the conquered provinces in the east, but retained the Provincia Arabia.

In about 100 CE, that is to say, on the eve of Trajan's expansion, the position in the Arabian peninsula was roughly as follows. The interior was completely free of any sort of authority, local or external, but was surrounded by a number of smaller states, or rather principalities, which had entered into relationships of various kinds with the empires: in the east with the Parthians; in the west, with the Romans. All these made their livelihoods from the trade routes that crossed by caravan through Arabia to the Yemen, and then by sea to east Africa and to India.

The Roman annexation of Petra marked a serious change of policy, and brought about a collapse of the balance of power as it existed at that time. Later the Romans pursued a similar policy with Palmyra, but that too was modified and Palmyra annexed to the empire at an unknown date. By the second century there are references to a Roman garrison stationed in Palmyra.

The advent of the Sasanids in Persia, and the establishment in that country of a more centralized and much more militant regime, again transformed the situation, this time on the northeastern borders of Arabia, where the Persians too subjugated and absorbed some of the border principalities. About the middle of the third century CE, they destroyed Hatra, an old Arabian centre, and seized parts of the east Arabian along the Gulf coast.

Roman historians record an interesting episode in the third quarter of the third century CE, when a remarkable woman ruler, whom the Romans called Zenobia (probably the Arab name Zaynab), made a final effort to restore the independence of Palmyra. It ended when Zenobia was defeated by a Roman force sent by the emperor Aurelian, and Palmyra was once again firmly incorporated in the empire.

Meanwhile, in the far south of the Arabian peninsula, other important changes had been taking place. South Arabia was very different from the semi-desert north, with cultivated fields and cities ruled by dynastic monarchies. But these monarchies had collapsed and a new regime was established, the so-called Himyaritic monarchy, which had become a battleground for external influences – Persian from the east and Ethiopian from the west. The militant Christian monarchy which had emerged in Ethiopia developed a natural interest in the events on the other side of the Red Sea. Persians were, of course, always concerned to counter Roman or Christian – for them, the two were much the same – influence.

By this time even these remote outposts of Mediterranean civilization were influenced by the general economic decline of the ancient world, and especially by the drying up of trade from the third century CE. One measure of this is the finds of Roman coins, which become fewer and fewer. There are practically none in India dated later than the reign of Caracalla, who died in 217 CE. Between the fourth and the sixth centuries, Arabia seems to have sunk back into a sort of dark age, a time of impoverishment and a bedouinization; that is to say, a decline in such cultivation as existed, of such sedentary centres as had been established, and a consequent extension of camel nomadism. The memory of this time is vividly recalled in early Muslim stories of the period which immediately preceded the advent of Islam.

At least part of the reason for this decline in Arabia must be sought in the loss of interest by both rival imperial powers. During the long period from 384 to 502 CE when Rome and Persia were at peace, neither was interested in Arabia or in the long, expensive and hazardous trade routes that passed through its deserts and oases. Trade routes were diverted elsewhere, subsidies ceased, caravan traffic came to an end, and towns were abandoned. Even settlers in the oases either migrated elsewhere or reverted to nomadism. The drying-up of trade and the reversion to nomadism lowered the standard of living and of culture generally, and left Arabia far more isolated from the civilized world than it had been for a long time. Even the more advanced southern part of Arabia also suffered, and many southern nomadic tribes migrated to the north in hope of better pasturage. Nomadism had always been an important element in Arabian society. It now became predominant. This is the period to which Muslims give the name Jāhiliyya, the Age of Ignorance, meaning by that of course to contrast it with the Age of Light, Islam. It was a dark age not only in contrast with what followed, but also with what went before. And the advent of Islam in this sense may be seen as a restoration and is indeed presented as such in the Qur'ān – as a restoration of the religion of Abraham.

In the sixth century, the century in which Muḥammad was born, everything changed again. The main overriding fact which determined most of the others was the resumption of Perso-Byzantine conflict and the return, after more than a century of peace, to almost continuous war. And in this state of warfare and rivalry between the two empires, Arabia once again emerged as a factor in the struggle, and the inhabitants of Arabia once again enjoyed the experience of being wooed, honoured, and on occasion subsidized by both sides. In peacetime, the most convenient route from the Mediterranean world to the further East was through the river valleys to the Persian Gulf. With a comparatively short overland connection, most of the route was by water, thus making it both cheap and safe as compared with others. But with Byzantium and Persia at war again, all this was changed. The Mesopotamian and Gulf route was, for the Byzantines, far too vulnerable. The Persians could cut it at any time, by military action in time of war, or even by economic pressures at times of what passed for peace between the two empires. Byzantine policy was therefore once again to seek alternative routes beyond the reach of Persian action.

There were, as previously, two major possibilities: the northern steppe and the southern deserts and seas. A resumption of the trans-Asian overland route gave rise to a series of interesting negotiations between the Byzantine emperors and various khans from the steppes of Central Asia. Envoys of Turkish khans began to arrive in Constantinople, and the Byzantine chroniclers tell odd stories of some khans, wiser than the others, who sent embassies both to Persia and to Byzantium. Usually, however, it was the khans who accused the Byzantines of perfidy. The Byzantine historian Menander tells of an incident in 576 CE. A Byzantine embassy presented their credentials to the khan, who reproached them bitterly for dealing at the same time with him and with his enemies. Placing his fingers in his mouth, the khan exclaimed:[2]

> Are you not those Romans, who have ten tongues and one deceit? ... As my ten fingers are now in my mouth, so you have many tongues, using one to deceive me, another to deceive [the Avars] ... You flatter and deceive all peoples with cunning words and treacherous intent, indifferent to those who fall headlong into misfortune, from which you yourselves derive benefit ... It is strange and unnatural for a Turk to lie.

In general, however, patrons and clients, north and south, seem to have understood each other quite well.

By the sixth century the southern route was more important than the northern route, partly because it was possible to get further away from the reach of Persia, and partly because it offered several alternatives. From the early sources it is possible to assemble a fairly clear picture of the policies and actions of the three major parties involved: the Byzantine attempt to open and maintain a line of communication to India free from Persian interference; the Persian attempt to block, prevent, or disrupt such a line of communication; and the action of the various peoples along the line to profit from the situation – to keep the route open, since this was obviously to their advantage, but to prevent the Byzantines from monopolizing or controlling it, and thus reducing their own independent role.

Many of the developments of the time fit into this pattern. One is the reappearance of the frontier states, client principalities on both the Byzantine and the Persian sides. On the Byzantine desert border, there was the Arab principality of Ghassān in roughly the area of Jordan at the present time; on the Persian side, the principality of Hīra. Both were Arab, both touched by Aramaic culture, both Christian, but one was tied politically to Byzantium and the other to Persia.

In about 527 CE the Byzantine emperor Justinian encouraged Ghassān to make war against Hīra. What followed was a war by proxy in what was to become a classical pattern, this time with Byzantium and Persia as principals. The Chief of Ghassān was given high honours. He was declared a Patrician of the Roman Empire, invited to Constantinople, provided with Roman weapons and instructors, and adequate quantities of Roman gold. We are less well informed about what happened on the Persian side, but it seems to have been much the same.

A second significant development in this period was the brief reappearance on the stage of history of the little island of Tiran, also called Yotabe, off the southern corner of the Sinai Peninsula in the middle of the Straits of Tiran. There seems to have been a small settlement of people engaged in the transit trade since early times. It is recorded that in 473 CE a tribal chief from the island visited Constantinople and that others followed, some of whom were seen as friends, others as enemies of the empire. At a certain point the inhabitants of this island are described as Jewish – whether they were old established Jews, converts to Judaism, or newly arrived Jewish settlers from Judaea is not known. Engaged principally in the southward trade, that is, down the Red Sea, they were at first independent and tended to be rather anti-Byzantine. Then in the sixth century when the Red Sea trade became a major concern, the island was brought under Byzantine control and transferred as a matter of convenience to a Ghassanid prince.

The year 525 CE brought a number of interesting developments. The Jews of Tiran-Yotabe were subjugated, but other Jews appeared at the southern end of the Red Sea where the king of the Himyarites was converted to Judaism, thus establishing, for the first time in many centuries, a Jewish monarchy – this time in the southwestern corner of Arabia. There must surely be some connection between the sudden appearance of a Jewish element at both ends of the Red Sea at about the same time, both engaged in the Red Sea trade, and both reportedly following a pro-Persian and anti-Byzantine policy.

Byzantine policy was of course primarily directly against Persia. Byzantine actions were not only anti-Persian; they were also anti-neutralist, designed to eliminate or subjugate local forces and to establish Byzantine supremacy and commercial monopoly from one end of the Red Sea to the other. At the northern end they were well able to handle it themselves with some assistance from their Arab auxiliaries. At the southern end this was beyond their resources, and they met the challenge by bringing Ethiopia into play – a Christian state which allied itself with Byzantium against the Jews in Yemen and the Persians further east who were behind them. At this point, Ethiopia had already become an international trading power with ships sailing eastwards as far as India and with troops on the Arabian mainland. Newly converted, the Ethiopians were fervent in their Christianity and responded eagerly to Byzantine embassies.

Unfortunately for the Ethiopians, they were not able to complete the task assigned to them. They succeeded initially in crushing and destroying the last independent state in southern Arabia, and opening the country to Christian and other external influences, but they were not strong enough to maintain it. They had even tried to advance northwards from the Yemen, and in 507 CE had attacked Mecca, a Yemenite trading post on the caravan route to the north. The Ethiopians failed and were defeated, and a little later the Persians came to the Yemen in their place.

In the early years of the Prophet's life and for a while thereafter, Yemen was governed by a Persian satrap, and the country was wholly under Persian control. The establishment of Persian power at the southern end of the Red Sea represented a major defeat for the Byzantine policy of developing a separate and open trade route to the East. Ironically, the same period saw a development which significantly reduced the importance of the whole issue. For many centuries the manufacture of silk had remained a closely guarded secret in China and the export of silkworms was punishable by death. In 552 CE two Nestorian monks succeeded in smuggling silkworm eggs from China to Byzantium, and by the early seventh century sericulture was well established in Asia Minor. Chinese silk was still valued for its superior beauty and quality, but the Chinese world monopoly was ended.

The sixth century ended with the withdrawal or enfeeblement of both contestants. The Ethiopians were evicted from Arabia and their regime, even in Ethiopia, was much weakened. The Persians managed to hang on for a while, but they, too, were gravely weakened by a disputed succession at home and by great religious problems arising out of conflict within the Zoroastrian faith. The Byzantines had their own problems following the reign of Justinian, notably the great church disputes which convulsed Byzantine Christianity. The last independent centres of power in the Arabian peninsula, the principalities of the south, had disappeared, giving way to successive foreign occupations.

All these changes had considerable effect in the Arabian peninsula. After these events, there were numbers of foreigners in Arabia, colonists, refugees and other groups of outsiders settled in the peninsula and bringing new ways, artefacts, and ideas with them. As a result of the continuing Perso-Byzantine conflict, there were established trade routes passing through Arabia and a significant movement of merchants and commodities. And even in the north, the border states rose again, linked with their imperial patrons, yet remaining part of the Arabian family.

All these external influences produced a number of responses from among the Arabians themselves. Part of the response was material. They learned the use of arms and armour, and the military tactics of the time – a valuable lesson for the events that were to follow. They acquired some of the tastes of the more advanced societies, as the traders brought them commodities which they had not previously known, but which they rapidly learned to enjoy. There was also a certain intellectual and even spiritual response, as the Arabians began to learn something of the religion and culture of their more sophisticated neighbours. They learned about writing, created a script, and began to write their own language. They absorbed new ideas from outside and perhaps most important of all, they began to be dissatisfied with their religion, with the primitive paganism which most of them had followed up to that point, and to seek for something better.

There were several religions within reach. Christianity had made considerable progress. Most of the Arabs of the borderlands, on the Persian as well as the Byzantine side, were Christians, and there were Christian settlers far to the south in Najrān and the Yemen. There were Jews also, especially in the Yemen, but also in various places in the Hijaz. Some of these were no doubt the descendants of refugees from Judaea, others converts to Judaism. By the seventh century, both the Christians and Jews of Arabia were thoroughly Arabized and part of the Arab community. The religions of Persia won few if any converts – not surprisingly, since the Persian religion was too distinctively national to have much appeal to those who were not themselves Persians.

The early Islamic chronicles tell of a group of people known in Arabic as Ḥanīf who, while abandoning paganism, were not prepared to accept any of the competing religious doctrines on offer at the time. They were among the earliest converts to the new religion of Islam.

PART III

The Dawn and Noon of Islam

CHAPTER 3

ORIGINS

The advent of Islam and the story of the founder and his first companions and disciples are known only from the Muslim scriptures, traditions, and historical memories. It was not until some time later that these events came to the attention of the outside world and drew the testimony of independent or external observers. In this Islam resembles Judaism, Christianity, and other great religions of humankind, and presents a similar problem to the historian. Already in medieval times, some pious Muslim scholars, more rigorous than others, questioned the accuracy or even the authenticity of individual biographical and historical traditions, while still accepting without reservation the validity and perfection of the religious message. Modern critical scholarship, subject to no such constraints, has raised many more questions, and until independent evidence in the form of contemporary inscriptions or other documents and records becomes known, much of the traditional narrative of early Islamic history must remain problematic, while the critical history is at best tentative.

For Muslims, the essentials of the story are clear and certain. The mission, struggles and final triumph of the Prophet, the foundation of the Muslim community, the vicissitudes of his followers and successors, are known from scripture and from the transmitted recollections of participants; these form the central core of historical awareness of Muslims everywhere. According to the tradition, the call to Prophethood first came to Muḥammad, the son of 'Abdallah, when he was approaching his fortieth year. On a night in the month of Ramaḍān, it is related, the Angel Gabriel came to Muḥammad as he slept in solitude on Mount Ḥirā' and said, 'Recite!' Muḥammad hesitated, and three times the Angel nearly stifled him until Muḥammad asked, 'What shall I recite?' Then the Angel said, 'Recite in the name of thy Lord who created all things, who created man from clots of blood. Recite, for thy Lord is the most generous, who taught by the pen, who taught man what he did not know.' These words form the first four verses of the ninety-sixth chapter of the Muslim scripture, known as the Qur'ān. This is an Arabic word which combines the meanings of 'reading' and 'recitation'. It denotes the book containing the revelations which, according to Muslim belief, were vouchsafed to Muḥammad by God. After this first message, there were many more which the Prophet brought to the people of his birthplace, urging them to give up their idolatrous beliefs and practices and to worship one single, universal God.

Muḥammad was born, according to tradition, in about 571 CE to a family of the Arab tribe of Quraysh, in the small oasis town of Mecca in the region known as the Ḥijāz, in western Arabia. The greater part of the peninsula at that time consisted of empty desert, broken by a few scattered oases and crossed by a few caravan routes. Most of its people were nomads, who gained their livelihood by raising sheep, goats, and camels, and from time to time by raiding rival tribes, the people of the oases, and those of the borderlands. Some lived by tilling the soil in the few places where this was possible; some by commerce, when events in the outside world brought traders back to the trans-Arabian routes. The renewal of warfare between Rome and Persia in the sixth century was such a time, and a number of small towns along the caravan route between the Mediterranean and the East were able, briefly, to flourish. One of these towns was Mecca.

During the early years of his mission, Muḥammad gained a number of converts, first among members of his own family, and then in wider circles. In time, these new ideas and the new movement inspired by them aroused suspicion and opposition among the leading families of Mecca, who saw the Prophet and his teaching as a threat to the existing order, both religious and material, and to their own pre-eminence. The traditional biography speaks of pressures and even of persecution to the point that some of the converts left home and took refuge on the other side of the Red Sea, in Ethiopia. In the year 622 CE, about thirteen years after the traditional date of the first Call, the Prophet entered into an agreement with emissaries from a small town called Yathrib, in another oasis some 218 miles north of Mecca. The people of Yathrib welcomed Muḥammad and his followers to their town, and offered to make him arbitrator in their disputes and to defend him and those converts who would accompany him from Mecca as they would defend their own people. Muḥammad sent some sixty families of his followers ahead of him, and finally joined them himself in the autumn of the same year. This migration of the Prophet and his followers from Mecca to Yathrib is known in Arabic as the *Hijra*, literally the migration, and is regarded by Muslims as the decisive moment in Muḥammad's apostolate. Later, when a Muslim calendar was established, it was reckoned from the beginning of the Arabian year in which the Hijra took place. Yathrib became the centre of the Muslim faith and community and in time came to be known simply as Al-Madīna – the City. The community was called the *Umma*, a word the meaning of which evolved as did the community itself.

In Mecca, Muḥammad had been a private individual struggling against first the indifference and then the hostility of the rulers of the place. In Medina he himself became ruler, wielding political and military as well as religious authority. Before long, the new Muslim polity in Medina became involved in warfare with the pagan rulers of Mecca. After a struggle which lasted eight years, he crowned his career by conquering Mecca and establishing the Islamic faith in place of the now abrogated idol-worship of his fellow townsmen.

There is thus a crucial difference between the career of Muḥammad and those of his predecessors, Moses and Jesus, as portrayed in the writings of their followers. Moses was not permitted to enter the promised land, and died while his people went forward. Jesus was crucified, and Christianity remained a persecuted minority religion for centuries, until a Roman emperor, Constantine, embraced the faith and empowered those who upheld it. Muḥammad conquered his promised land, and during his lifetime achieved victory and power in this world, exercising political as well as prophetic authority. As the Apostle of God, he brought and taught a religious revelation. But at the same time, as the head of the Muslim *Umma*, he promulgated laws, dispensed justice, collected taxes, conducted diplomacy, made war, and made peace. The *Umma*, which began as a community, had become a state. It would soon become an empire.

When the Prophet died, according to tradition on 8 June 632, his prophetic mission was completed. The purpose of his apostolate, for Muslims, had been to restore the true monotheism which had been taught by the earlier prophets and had been abandoned or distorted; to abolish idolatry, and to bring God's final revelation, embodying the true faith and the holy law. According to Muslim belief, he was the last – the Seal – of the Prophets. At his death the revelation of God's purpose for humankind had been completed. After him, there would be no more prophets and no further revelations.

The spiritual task was thus completed and the spiritual function at an end. The religious function, however, remained – that of maintaining and defending the Divine Law and bringing it to the rest of the world. The effective discharge of this function required the continued exercise of political and military power – in a word, of sovereignty – in a state.

Muḥammad himself had never claimed to be more than a mortal man, the Apostle of God and the leader of God's people, but himself neither divine nor immortal. 'Muḥammad', says the Qur'ān, 'is no more than an Apostle, and Apostles before him have passed away. If then he dies or is killed, will you turn back upon your heels?' (3:138).

The Prophet was dead, and there would be no more prophets. The head of the Muslim community and state was dead, and had to be replaced. In this emergency, the inner circle of the Prophet's followers chose one of their own number, Abū Bakr, one of the earliest and most respected of the converts. The title he used as leader, according to the historiographic tradition, was *Khalīfa*, an Arabic word which, by a fortunate ambiguity, combines the notions of successor and deputy. According to one tradition, he was *Khalīfatu Rasūl Allāh*, the successor of the Prophet of God; according to another, he was *Khalīfat Allāh*, the Deputy of God – a claim of far-reaching implications. At the time of Abū Bakr's accession, it is unlikely that he or his electors had any such notions. But from their act of improvisation came the great institution of the caliphate – the supreme sovereign office of the Islamic world.

The early history of the Muslim caliphate, like that of the Prophet himself, is known principally from Muslim sources, and it is not until some time later that historians of other lands begin to report on the rise and progress of the new state and the new faith. Muslim accounts were orally transmitted for generations before being committed to writing. They are vitiated not only by the fallibility of human memory, less of a problem in a pre-literate society than it would be now, but also, and more significantly, by the many personal, familial, tribal, sectarian, and party disputes that divided the early Muslims and that consequently coloured the different historiographic versions that have come down to us. Even some of the most basic facts, such as the sequence and outcome of battles, may be different in competing versions.

At the Prophet's death, according to the Muslim historians, the religion that he had brought was still confined to parts of the Arabian peninsula. The Arabs, to whom he had brought it, were similarly restricted, with perhaps some extension in the borderlands of the

Fertile Crescent. The vast lands in Southwest Asia, northern Africa, and elsewhere, which in later times came to constitute the lands of Islam, the realms of the caliphs and, in modern parlance, the Arab world, still spoke other languages, professed other religions, and obeyed other rulers. Within little more than a century after the Prophet's death, the whole area had been transformed, in what was surely one of the swiftest and most dramatic changes in the whole of human history. By the late seventh century, the outside world attests the emergence of a new religion and a new power, the Muslim empire of the caliphs, extending eastwards in Asia as far as and sometimes beyond the borders of India and China, westwards along the southern Mediterranean coast to the Atlantic, southwards towards the lands of the black peoples in Africa, northwards into the lands of the white peoples of Europe. In this empire, Islam was the state religion, and the Arabic language was rapidly displacing others to become the principal medium of public life.

Today, more than fourteen centuries after the beginning of the Muslim era, the Arab empire of the caliphs has long since passed away. But in all the countries that the Arabs conquered, except only in Europe in the west and Iran and Central Asia in the east, colloquial Arabic, in a variety of forms, remains the spoken language of the people, and literary Arabic remains the principal instrument of commerce, culture and government. As the language of religion – of scripture, theology and holy law – Arabic spread far beyond the lands of Arabic speech and later beyond the limits of Arab conquest into many regions in Asia and Africa that never knew Arab rule.

The expansion of both the Islamic faith and the Arab empire was much aided by the peoples of the conquered provinces, who in rapidly increasing numbers embraced the one and rallied to the other. In the west, the Berbers of North Africa, after at first posing a fierce resistance to the Arab conquerors, then joined with them in the conquest and colonization of Spain, and later themselves colonized and Islamized many of the black peoples south of the Sahara. In the east, the Persians, their imperial state destroyed and their priestly hierarchy rendered powerless, found structure and meaning in Islam, and helped to bring their new faith to the mixed Iranian and Turkish populations of Central Asia. And in the centre, the predominantly Christian Aramaic-speaking peoples of the Fertile Crescent, and the Coptic-speaking Christian people of Egypt, long subject to the Persian and Byzantine empires, exchanged one imperial domination for another and found their new masters less demanding, more tolerant, and above all more welcoming than the old.

In these countries the transition to Islam and to Arabism proved relatively easy. Arab taxes were lower than those exacted by the Byzantines, especially for Muslims, but also for the general population. The Arab state extended the same legally defined tolerance to all forms of Christianity without concern for the finer points of orthodoxy that had caused so many difficulties for non-orthodox Christians and their Churches under the rule of Constantinople. Jews, who had enjoyed a fair measure of religious tolerance under the Parthians and the pagan Roman emperors, were worse off under the less tolerant Sasanids and Christian Byzantines, and found their position somewhat improved under the Arab Muslim state.

The rulers of the Arab state and the commanders of the Arab armies were mainly townspeople from the oasis towns of Mecca and Medina. But they were not far from their desert origins, and the bulk of the Arab armies that achieved the conquests were desert people. The strategy of the Arabs in their wars of conquest was based very largely on the skilful use of desert power, reminiscent of the use of sea power in the later empires built up by the maritime peoples of the West. The Arabs were at home in the desert; their enemies were not. To them, the desert was friendly, familiar, and accessible; to their enemies, it was a remote and terrible wilderness, full of hardship and danger, which they feared as the landsman fears the sea. The Arabs could use it as a route of communication to send messages, supplies, and reinforcements, as a retreat in times of emergency, safe from molestation or pursuit – and as a road to victory in times of success. The Arab empire had its Suez Canal, too – the desert trail through the isthmus of Suez joining Asia and Africa.

In each of the countries they conquered the Arabs established their main military base and administrative centre in a town on the edge of the desert and the sown. Where suitably placed cities already existed, such as Damascus, the Arabs used them as their capitals. More frequently, they had to build new centres, which became new cities, to meet their strategic and imperial requirements. The most important of these garrison towns were Kūfa and Basra in Iraq, Qomm in Iran, Fusṭāṭ in Egypt, and Qayrawān in Tunisia.

These were the Gibraltars and Singapores, the Bombays and Calcuttas of the early Arab empire. The term by which they are called in Arabic is 'miṣr', plural 'amṣār', an ancient Semitic word which originally seems to have denoted a frontier or limit, and hence a frontier zone or province. The same term incidentally provided the name of Egypt in biblical Hebrew, in Aramaic, and in Arabic. The *amṣār* were of central importance in the government and eventual Arabization of the provinces. In the early days, the Arabs were a small, isolated, dominant minority in the empire which they had created. In the *amṣār* the Arab frontiersmen and their language predominated. The core of each of the *amṣār* consisted of military cantonments, in which the Arab fighter-colonists were settled in their tribal formations. Around that core there grew up an outer town of artisans, shopkeepers and others, drawn from the native population, who ministered to the various needs of the Arab rulers, soldiers and their families. These outer towns grew in size, wealth and importance, and came to include increasing numbers of native civil servants retained in the service of the Arab state. All these perforce learned the Arabic language and were influenced by Arab tastes, attitudes and ideas.

It is sometimes said that the Islamic religion was spread by conquest. The statement is misleading, though the spread of Islam was to a large extent made possible by the parallel processes of conquest and colonization. The primary war aim of the conquerors was not to impose the Islamic faith by force. The Qur'ān is explicit on this point: 'There is no compulsion in religion' (2:256). This was usually interpreted to mean that those who profess a monotheist religion and revere scriptures recognized by Islam as earlier stages of divine revelation may be permitted to practise their religions under the conditions imposed by the Islamic state and law. For those who were not monotheists and possessed no recognized scriptures, the alternatives were harsher, but there were few if any such in the regions ruled by the early Arab conquerors. The conquered peoples were given various inducements, such as lower rates of taxation, to adopt Islam, but they were not compelled to do so. Still less did the Arab state try to assimilate the subject peoples and turn them into Arabs. On the contrary, the early generations of the conquerors maintained strict social barriers between Arab and non-Arab, even when the latter embraced Islam and adopted the Arabic language. They discouraged marriages between Arab women and non-Arab men – though not the converse – and did not admit the new Muslims to full social, economic and political equality with themselves until the revolutionary changes of the second century of Islam put an end to Arab privilege and thereby greatly accelerated the processes of Arabization.

It is the Arabization and Islamization of the peoples of the conquered provinces, rather than the actual military conquest itself, that is the true wonder of the Arab empire. The period of Arab political and military supremacy was very brief, and soon the Arabs were compelled to relinquish the control of the empire, and even the leadership of the civilization which they had created, to other peoples. But their language, their faith, and their law remained – and still remain – as an enduring monument of their rule.

The great change was accomplished, in the main, by the parallel processes of colonization and assimilation. According to a widely accepted view, one of the driving forces of the Arab conquests was the pressure of over-population in the barren Arabian peninsula, and in the early years of the Arab kingdom many Arabs migrated past the fallen defences of the ancient empires into the fertile lands that they had conquered. At first they came only as a ruling minority – an army of occupation with a dominant class of soldiers, senior officials, and landowners. The Arab state took over the state lands of the previous regimes, and also the lands of the enemies of the new order and of refugees who had fled before the conquerors. The Arab government thus disposed of extensive domains, many of which were granted or leased on favourable terms to Arabs. These paid a much lower rate of taxation than the local landowners who remained. The great Arab landowners generally cultivated their estates through native labour and resided in the garrison towns.

It was from these towns that Arab influence radiated into the surrounding countryside, both directly and through the rapidly growing population of native converts, many of whom served in the army. Though the claims of the native converts to economic and social equality were haughtily rejected by those who could claim pure Arabian descent, more and more of these converts accepted the faith of the conquerors and with it their language.

The prestige of the idiom of an aristocracy of conquerors, the practical value of the language of government and commerce, the richness and diversity of an imperial civilization, and perhaps most of all the immense reverence accorded to the sacred language in which the new revelation was written, all helped to further the assimilation by the Arabs of their subject peoples.

The far-ranging military and political changes of the first century of Islamic rule also brought important economic and social changes. The Arab conquests – as is the way of conquests – restored to circulation vast accumulated riches frozen in private, public and Church possession. The early Arab historians tell many stories of rich booty and extravagant expenditure. The tenth-century writer al-Mas'ūdī describes some of the great fortunes accumulated by the conquerors. On the day that the caliph 'Uthmān was killed, according to Mas'ūdī, his personal fortune in cash in the hands of his treasurer was 100,000 dinars (Roman or Byzantine gold coins) and a million dirhams (Persian silver coins). His estates were also valued at 100,000 dinars, 'and he also left many horses and camels'. Al-Zubayr ibn al-'Awwām, one of the first converts to Islam and an important figure in early Islamic history, owned houses in Basra and Kūfā in Iraq and in Fusṭāṭ and Alexandria in Egypt. His house in Basra, says Mas'ūdī, at the present time (332 AH/943–4 CE) still provides lodgings for merchants, commerce, seagoing traders and the like. His property at his death was valued at 50,000 dinars cash, as well as 'a thousand horses, a thousand slaves, male and female, and lands in the cities already mentioned'. Another of the Prophet's Companions, Ṭalḥa ibn 'Ubaydallāh al-Taymī, according to the same source, had a great house in Kūfa and an income from his estates in Iraq that 'amounted to a thousand dinars a day, and some say more; from his estates in the region of al Sharāh, he received more than that. He built himself a house in Medina made with plaster, bricks and teak.' Another early Muslim, 'Abd al-Raḥmān ibn 'Awf, had stables in which 'were tethered a hundred horses, and he owned a thousand camels and ten thousand sheep. At his death, a quarter of his property was worth 84,000 dinars'. When Zayd ibn Thābit died, 'he left ingots of gold and silver that were broken up with axes, in addition to property and estates to the value of a hundred thousand dinars ... When Ya'lā ibn Munya died, he left half a million dinars, as well as debts owed to him by people, landed property and other assets, to the value of 300,000 dinars.'[1]

These and other accounts of the enormous fortunes acquired by the conquerors are no doubt exaggerated, but they paint a persuasive picture of a conqueror aristocracy possessing immense riches, enjoying the opportunities and delights of the advanced countries in which they found themselves, and spending their wealth with abandon.

There were surely many besides Arabs who profited and prospered in the new order. But there were many – including Arabs – who did not, and even among those who prospered, their progress did not always keep pace with their claims and expectations. The historical narratives, the literature, and especially the contemporary poetry reflect the social and political and thus indirectly the economic tensions of the period and the grievances of both individuals and social groups. A conquest and a new regime inevitably displace important groups that have previously enjoyed a monopoly of wealth and power. The impact of this change must surely have been far greater in the eastern, ex-Persian, than in the western, ex-Byzantine provinces. From Syria and Egypt the defeated and dispossessed Byzantine magnates could withdraw to the Byzantine capital and central provinces, leaving their former subject lands and peoples to new masters. No such escape was available to the magnates of the Persian empire, whose imperial capital was in Arab hands and who, with few exceptions, had to stay where they were and find their place as best they could under the new regime. It was therefore natural that the former Persian privileged and governing elements, with their recent memories of imperial domination and their continuing experience of imperial administration, should have contributed significantly to the development of Islamic government and culture – far more so than the residue of population in the long-subject Byzantine cities.

At first the Persian governing classes seem to have made their accommodation with the new regime, and to have retained most of their functions and some of their privileges. But with the consolidation of Arab power, the massive settlement of Arab tribes in Iran, the growth of a population of Iranian Muslims claiming equality as a right with the Arabs, and perhaps most of all the growth of cities, new alignments and therefore new conflicts appeared. In the former Byzantine lands, where city life was old and familiar, change was relatively slight. In the former Persian Empire, much less urbanized, the swift and sudden rise of the Muslim cities brought tension and struggle.

In the early Islamic period, the most dangerous conflicts, offering the most serious threat to the stability of the Arab state and the cohesion of the Islamic community, arose not from the differences between Arab and non-Arab Muslims, still less between Muslims and others, but from the rivalries between Arabs and Arabs – between tribes of northern Arabian and southern Arabian origin; between those who had come early and those who came later; between those who had done well and those who had done less well; between those who were the sons of a free Arab man and wife and those who were the sons of a free Arab father and a foreign concubine. The exercise of the immemorial rights of the victors over the vanquished rapidly increased the numbers of these half-Arabs.

The Arab historiographic tradition presents these conflicts mostly in tribal, in personal, or sometimes in religious terms. All these were no doubt important, but other issues were clearly involved. Continuing and often bitter hostility between different groups of Arabs led to a series of civil wars in which, in time, the growing non-Arab Muslim population became involved, and in which the different factions found religious expressions for their grievances and claims.

The establishment of the Arab empire finally ended the long conflict between Rome and Persia across the Middle Eastern trade routes, and, for the first time since Alexander the Great, joined the entire Middle Eastern region, from Central Asia to the Mediterranean, in a single imperial and commercial system. For some time, both Byzantine gold and Persian silver coins continued to circulate. As a result, exchange rates between the two currencies become an important topic in early Islamic law, and the money-changer a prominent figure in Islamic markets. The new unity and the emergence of a new ruling class disposing of large sums in ready cash surely favoured the growth of both industry and trade. Like the Vikings in medieval Europe, the Arab conquerors in the Middle East spent their money on high-grade textiles, for which the court and aristocracy showed a particular interest. The building of royal palaces and sumptuous private homes, as well as of mosques and other public buildings, in addition to many and varied needs of the well-paid soldiers and settlers, must surely have contributed greatly to this economic development. The discontent in the rapidly growing cities seems to have been due more to resentment than to actual hardship. The half-Arabs, including a fair proportion of men of talent, wealth, and even power, resented their exclusion from the highest levels of society and government. The non-Arab converts, especially the Persians, were offended by the inferior status accorded to them, and demanded the equality which the universalist message of their new faith had led them to expect. If, as in both earlier and later times, the population grew more rapidly than the means of sustaining it, there would also have been a precariously surviving populace of runaway peasants, unskilled labourers, vagabonds, paupers, and semi-criminals. The Arabic sources present a vivid portrayal of this world on the margins of urban society.

All these differences and conflicts, added to the natural strains arising from the vast and swift expansion of the Muslim domains, greatly complicated the task of maintaining and governing the state and empire, and confronted the early caliphs with difficult and, in the event, insuperable problems.

The first four caliphs acceded to office in non-hereditary – in Sunni juristic parlance electoral – succession. They are known as the *Rāshidūn*, 'the rightly guided ones', and the period of their combined reigns is regarded by Sunni Muslims as a golden age, second in sanctity, and in the moral and religious guidance that it provides, only to the lifetime of the Prophet himself. Yet of the four rightly guided caliphs, all but the first died at the hand of an assassin. The second caliph, ʿUmar ibn al-Khaṭṭāb, was killed by a disgruntled Christian slave. The murders of the third and fourth caliphs, ʿUthmān and Alī, were far more portentous, since both were killed by Muslim Arab rebels. Little more than a quarter of a century after the death of the Prophet, his community was riven by fierce dissensions, and his state foundered amid rebellion and civil war – not between conquerors and conquered, not between new and old Muslims, but between Arabs and Arabs.

After the brief reign of Abū Bakr, he was succeeded on his death in 634 by ʿUmar ibn al-Khaṭṭāb, whose ten-year reign was of decisive importance in the formation of the Muslim state and perhaps even more in the collective historical memory of the Muslim people. According to a widely accepted historiographic tradition, ʿUmar is said to have been designated by Abū Bakr on his deathbed as successor. He was in any case immediately recognized and accepted by most of the Companions and ruled without serious opposition. The only dissenters were those who supported the claims of ʿAlī, cousin and son-in-law of the Prophet. For some this claim rested on his personal qualities as a candidate; for others on a kind of legitimate right of succession to the Prophet. The rule of ʿUmar appears, however, to have been accepted by the great majority of the Arabs, and he was able not only to maintain unity but to establish the beginnings of what later became a functioning system of imperial government. The change in authority is symbolized by the adoption of a new title. As well as the title '*khalīfa*', with its connotation of deputy, ʿUmar is said to have been addressed as '*Amīr al-Muʾminīn*', 'Commander of the Faithful', with a more explicit connotation of authority at once political, military and religious. This became and remained the most commonly used title of the caliphs, and was indeed a prerogative of those who held that office, as long as the institution remained in effective existence.

During his lifetime – according to the tradition he was only fifty-three when he was killed – ʿUmar made no provision for the succession. On his deathbed he is said to have appointed a committee – in Arabic *shūrā* – of six of the senior Companions, with instructions to nominate one of their own number as caliph. Their choice fell on 'Uthmān, a member of the great Meccan clan of Umayya, the only representative of the Meccan aristocracy in the inner circle of early converts.

The early caliphs had little force at their disposal – no praetorian guard nor indeed any regular forces. The only armed forces available were the Arab tribal levies, and the caliphs ruled less by armed force than by personal prestige and authority – by the deference due to them as successors of the Prophet, and the respect won for them by their personal characters.

'Uthmān's character did not inspire the same respect as was accorded to his two predecessors. The religious bond, more than a decade after the death of the Prophet, was beginning to weaken, and was further strained by the vigour with which the Meccan aristocracy exploited the opportunities vouchsafed to them by the accession of one of their number to the highest office. The pressure of authority, always irksome to the nomadic tribesman, was becoming intolerable.

'Uthmān became caliph in 644 CE. By the mid-century, Syria and Egypt in the west, Iraq and much of Iran in the east, were already in Muslim hands. At 'the Battle of the Masts' (654–5), the newly created Muslim fleets were even able to win a great naval victory over the Byzantines. The Persian empire was already destroyed. It was time for a pause, and the temporary cessation of warfare gave the tribesmen leisure to reflect on their grievances. Their reflections, and their resulting actions, exploded into a devastating series of inter-Arab civil wars.

The first of these began in 656 CE with the murder of the caliph 'Uthmān by a group of mutineers from the Arab army in Egypt who had come to Medina to place their grievances before him. The mutineers stormed into the caliph's quarters on 17 June 656 and wounded him mortally. Their action, and the struggle which followed, marked a turning-point in Muslim history. For the first time – but by no means for the last time – a Muslim caliph was murdered by his Muslim followers, and Muslim armies fought a bitter war against one another. The mutineers installed 'Alī as caliph.

In the complex and many-sided struggle of the first Islamic civil war, 'Alī ibn Abī Ṭālib, the Prophet's cousin and son-in-law, occupied a key position. As husband of the Prophet's daughter Fāṭima, 'Alī would have had no special claim to attention. Such relationships counted for little in a polygamous society. As the Prophet's kinsman, however, he could, according to the accepted practices of pre-Islamic

Arabia, offer himself as candidate for the succession to at least some part of both the political and religious authority of the Prophet. His personal qualities and standing in themselves made him a strong candidate. In addition, he was able to attract the support of many Muslims who were disappointed with the conduct of the elective caliphs and their henchmen, and who hoped that a new regime, headed by the kin of the Prophet, might bring a return to the true, original message of Islam. They came to be known as the party of 'Alī, *shī'atu 'Alī*, and then simply as the Shī'a.

In January of 661 CE, after a five-year reign of almost continuous struggle, the caliph 'Alī too was murdered, this time not by mutinous soldiers but by a lone assassin, the emissary of a radical religious sect. A second precedent had been set, of far-reaching significance.

Among the various warring factions engaged in the first Islamic civil war, one, that led by Mu'āwiya ibn Abī Sufyān, the governor of the province of Syria, triumphed. Mu'āwiya was in many ways in a strong position. As a member of the Meccan house of Umayya and a cousin of the murdered caliph 'Uthmān, he had the right, indeed the duty, sanctioned by immemorial Arab custom and confirmed by Islam, to demand and exact retribution for the murder of his kinsman. He had been appointed to his post by the caliph 'Umar, and his tenure thus antedated the challenges and rivalries of the last two caliphates. As governor of Syria, on the military frontier between the Islamic and the Byzantine Christian worlds, he commanded a skilled and disciplined army, distinguished by the lustre of the holy war, and strengthened by the experience gained in waging it.

After the murder of 'Alī, his son Ḥasan, to whom some had looked as their new leader, renounced his claim to the caliphate and recognized Mu'āwiya, who had been hailed as caliph in Syria and was now recognized all over the empire. His accession marks a new phase in Islamic history, known as the Umayyad caliphate, in which the succession became in fact, though never in principle, dynastic, and remained within the house of Umayya. There was no rule or right of succession – indeed later Muslim dynasties, no doubt inhibited by the strongly anti-monarchical attitude expressed in the Qur'ān and in the oldest traditions, did not accept a fixed rule of succession, by primogeniture or otherwise. Mu'āwiya set a precedent followed by most later caliphs by nominating his son Yazīd during his own lifetime as heir apparent. The significance of this action is vividly symbolized in a story told by a ninth-century author:

The people gathered in the presence of Muʻāwiya, and the orators rose to proclaim Yazīd as heir to the Caliphate. Some of the people showed disapproval, whereupon a man of the tribe of ʻUdhra ... rose to his feet. Drawing his sword a handspan from the scabbard, he said, 'The Commander of the Faithful is that one!' and he pointed to Muʻāwiya. 'And if he dies, then that one!' and he pointed to Yazīd. 'And if anyone objects, then this one!' and he pointed to his sword.

Muʻāwiya said to him, 'You are the prince of orators.'[2]

The caliphate of the Umayyads lasted for less than a century, and the Arab Islamic historiographic tradition, most of it committed to writing after their fall, deals harshly with them. For the Shīʻa they are usurpers and tyrants, who wrested the caliphate from ʻAlī and his son, the rightful heads of the community, massacred or persecuted his descendants, and rejected or corrupted the authentic message of Islam. Even for Sunni historians writing after their fall, the Umayyads were usurpers and, if not tyrannical, were worldly and irreligious in their purposes and methods. In the classical histories, their reign is described as an interlude of 'kingship' (*mulk*) between the caliphate of the rightly guided rulers who preceded them and that of the divinely approved caliphs who followed them. The Arab historiographical tradition, in general hostile to the Umayyads, pays a kind of tribute to Muʻāwiya's political and diplomatic skill, but even this is a somewhat equivocal compliment.

Modern scholarship has on the whole taken a somewhat more benign view of the Umayyad achievement, and has, in particular, given credit to a succession of remarkable rulers, seen as having maintained the stability and continuity of the Islamic state and society in a time of dangerous and disruptive internal struggles.

The Umayyad caliphs accomplished this task through a series of compromises and interim arrangements which enabled them to preserve a measure of unity, to continue and extend the conquests, and to establish the nucleus of an imperial administration, society and culture. They did this at the cost of some dilution of the pristine Islamic message. The prestige of religious authority and the bond of religious loyalty had been weakened to breaking point by regicide and civil war. The Umayyad caliphs found a substitute by creating what has been called an 'Arab kingdom', and might more accurately be described as an Arab ascendancy. Only true Arabs, those who were of pure Arabian descent on both sides, were admitted to the highest levels of power and privilege. Half-Arabs, sons of an Arab father and of a non-Arab, usually a slave, mother, could ascend part of the way, but were still excluded from the highest levels. Even an Umayyad prince like Maslama, the son of one of the greatest of the Umayyad caliphs and himself an outstanding and successful military commander, was, as the son of a slave woman, excluded even from consideration for the succession.

Below the half-Arabs in the social order came the non-Arab converts to Islam, and below them the mass of non-Muslims, still forming at that time the vast majority of the population. But the non-Arab population, both converted and unconverted, though excluded from political and military command, nevertheless played an important part in Umayyad government. By another of the compromises for which the Umayyads are blamed by a later historiographic tradition, some Islamic precepts in such matters as administration and taxation were tacitly set aside, and a system of government established, both at the centre and the provinces, that relied more and more on the structure, the methods, and above all the personnel of the empires which the Islamic caliphate had overthrown and superseded.

This process did not pass unobserved, and evoked both moral and armed resistance. The latter came from two groups in particular, whose critique of the Umayyad caliphate was expressed in religious terms, and whose organization therefore assumed the form of a sect. One group were the Kharijites, from an Arabic word meaning 'to go out'. Kharijism began with a small party of 'Alī's supporters who seceded from his forces during the first civil war and turned against him. His murderer was one of them, and they continued to oppose the Umayyads and indeed their successors. The Kharijites represented the most extreme form of tribal independence; they refused to accept any authority not deriving from their own freely given and always revocable consent, and insisted that any believer, of whatever birth and origin, could be caliph if chosen by the believers. The Shī'a took the exact opposite point of view, insisting that the caliphate belonged by divine right to the successors of the Prophet in his own family. Both groups were responsible for a number of sometimes dangerous rebellions, seeking to overthrow the existing order and establish a new and more authentically Islamic order in its place.

The second civil war began with such a rising – a relatively minor one in its immediate political and military effects, but of immense religious and therefore historical significance. In 680 CE Husayn, a son of 'Alī and a grandson of the Prophet, led an insurrection in Iraq. On the tenth day of the month of Muḥarram, at a place called Karbalā', Ḥusayn, his family, and his followers met an Umayyad force in battle and were defeated. According to the tradition, some seventy were killed in the battle and its aftermath, the sole survivor being a sick child, 'Alī the son of Ḥusayn, who was left lying in a tent and lived to tell the story. The massacre of Karbalā' became central to the Shī'ite perception of Islamic history, and the tenth day of Muḥarram a major event in the Shī'ite religious calendar. Wherever Shī'ites are to be found, on this day they commemorate the martyrdom of the Prophet's family, the penitence of those who failed to save them, and the wickedness of those who killed them, in religious rituals inspired by the potent themes of sacrifice, guilt and expiation. The doctrinal differences between Sunni and Shī'a Muslims are of minor importance, far less than those that divide the rival churches of Christendom. But the Shī'ite sense of martyrdom and persecution, reinforced by their long experience through the centuries as a minority group under rulers whom they regarded as usurpers, raised a psychological barrier between them and the Sunni state and majority, a difference of experience and outlook, and therefore also of religious and political attitudes and behaviour.

The massacre of Karbalā' speeded the transformation of the Shī'a from a political party to a religious sect, and brought a new bitterness and intensity to the second civil war. Once again the lands of the caliphate were riven by years of internecine warfare in which – an ominous change – others beside the Arabs were becoming involved. Though in the long run the revolt of the 'Alids was the most portentous, it was not, at the actual moment, the most dangerous. Among the many risings and opposition movements confronted by the Umayyad caliph 'Abd al-Malik on his accession in 685, certainly the most threatening was the revolt of the brothers Muṣ'ab and 'Abdallah ibn al-Zubayr. 'Abdallah had proclaimed himself caliph in the Ḥijāz in 683, and was able for a while to extend his power to Iraq and to obtain some measure of recognition in other provinces of the empire. It was not until after his death in 692 that 'Abd al-Malik succeeded in overcoming all opposition and in restoring and reinforcing the power of what was becoming a monarchical state.

Under 'Abd al-Malik (685–705) and under the most notable of his successors, Hishām (724–743), a process which the Arabic historians call 'organization and adjustment' was carried significantly further. The older administrative structures retained from Byzantine and

Persian times were replaced by a new imperial order in which Arabic supplanted Greek and Persian as the official language of administration and accountancy. The Arabic historical tradition attributes the reform to 'Abd al-Malik, and on this point is confirmed by hard evidence. In 694 CE, 'Abd al-Malik issued a new caliphal gold coinage, with far-reaching implications and effects. The minting of gold coins had been a Byzantine prerogative, inherited from the Roman emperors, and there were no other gold coins in the world. The Arabs, until that time, had struck only silver coins, and these were issued in the mints which they found in the former Byzantine and Persian provinces. The coins were much the same as before, with surcharges to indicate the change of rulers. The Arabs had continued to import gold coins from Byzantium. 'Abd al-Malik's gold *dinars* – the name is of course adapted from the Roman *denarius* – were rightly seen as a challenge by the Byzantine emperor, who went to war in protest. The challenge was emphasized and clarified by the inscriptions on these gold coins, consisting of a creed supported by verses from the Qur'ān:

> There is no God but God alone, he has no companion. Muḥammad is the Prophet of God, who sent him with guidance and the religion of truth to make it prevail over all religion. (9:33)
>
> He is God, one, eternal; he does not beget nor is he begotten. (112: 1–3)

These Qur'ānic verses, which directly challenge Christian doctrines, also appear among the inscriptions on the Dome of the Rock, the shrine which 'Abd al-Malik built on the Temple Mount in Jerusalem in the year 72 of the Hijra (691–2 CE). The building and its inscriptions state a religious purpose. New highways, with milestones bearing the caliph's name, illustrate an imperial purpose. The coinage does both. At this time it was clear that a new universal state and a new world religion had arisen to challenge the pretensions of the Byzantine Empire and the Christian mission.

The Dome of the Rock, along with the adjoining Aqṣā Mosque, constituted the first great religious building complex in the history of Islam. It marked the beginning of a new era. The time for borrowing, for adaptation, for improvisation had passed. The Umayyad caliphate was no longer a successor state of Rome and Persia, but a new universal polity. Islam was no mere successor religion of Christianity, but a new universal dispensation. The place, style, and above all the ornamentation of the Dome of the Rock reveal its purpose. The style and scale were surely intended to rival and outshine the Church of the Holy Sepulchre, with the subtle changes needed for Muslim, not Christian, piety. The place was Jerusalem, the most sacred city on earth to both the predecessor religions, Judaism and Christianity.

The choice is significant. Jerusalem is never mentioned in the Qur'ān. Even the name 'Jerusalem' does not figure in early Muslim writings. When the city is mentioned at all – as for example on 'Abd al-Malik's milestones – it is called Aelia, the name imposed by the Romans to desacralize the city and to obliterate its Jewish and also Christian associations. The choice of a site in Jerusalem for the first great Islamic shrine is the more remarkable. The site was the Temple Mount, the scene of major events in both Jewish and Christian sacred history. The actual spot was the rock on which, according to rabbinic tradition, Abraham had prepared to sacrifice his son, and on which in later times the Ark of the Temple had rested. This, 'Abd al-Malik seemed to be saying, was the shrine of the final dispensation – the new Temple, dedicated to the religion of Abraham, replacing the Temple of Solomon, continuing the revelations vouchsafed to the Jews and Christians and correcting the errors into which they had fallen.

The polemical purpose of the shrine is reinforced by the choice of Qur'ānic verses and other inscriptions that decorate the interior. One verse occurs again and again: 'God is one, without partner, without companion.' The rejection of the Christian doctrine of the Trinity is clear, and is made explicit in other inscriptions:

> Praise be to God, who begets no son, and has no partner in [his] dominion: nor [needs] he any to protect him from humiliation: yes, magnify him for his greatness and glory!

Another repeated inscription is the famous *Sura* 112 in its entirety: 'He is God, one, eternal. He does not beget, nor is he begotten, and he has no peer.' Another quotation addresses an explicit warning to the recipients of previous revelations (Qur'ān 3:18–19):

> O people of the book! Commit no excesses in your religion: and say nothing of God but the truth. Jesus Christ, the son of Mary, was indeed an apostle of God... Therefore believe in God and his apostles, and do not say 'Three'. Desist, and it will be better for you, for indeed God is one God, exalted above having a son ...

Yet another inscription emphasizes the warning to the Jews and Christians of the error of their ways (Qur'ān 3:18–19):

God bears witness that there is no God but he, and so too the angels, those who possess knowledge, and stand firm in justice. There is no God but he, the omnipotent, the omniscient. God's religion is Islam ... Let whoever disbelieves in the signs of God beware, for God is swift in reckoning.

The meaning of all this is at once political and religious. Only religion can justify empire. Only empire can sustain religion. Through his apostle Muḥammad and his vicegerent the caliph, God has given a new dispensation and a new order to the world. In this first great religious structure dedicated to the new faith, its worldly head, the caliph 'Abd al-Malik, asserted Islam's connection with the precursor religions, and at the same time made clear that the new dispensation had come to correct their errors and to supersede them.

Similar considerations may have inspired the building of the Great Mosque of Damascus by 'Abd al-Malik's son and successor, the caliph al-Walīd. The tenth-century geographer al-Muqaddasī records an interesting conversation:[3]

> One day I said to my uncle, '[the caliph Al-Walīd] was wrong to squander the wealth of the Muslims on the mosque of Damascus. Had he spent this money to maintain the roads and the water cisterns and to restore the fortresses, that would have been more apposite and more meritorious'. To which my uncle replied, 'Don't you believe it, my boy. Al-Walīd was rightly guided towards an important matter. He saw that Syria, the land of the Christians, was full of beautiful churches of seductive appearance and vast renown, like those of the Resurrection [i.e. the Holy Sepulchre], of Lydda and of Edessa. He therefore gave the Muslims a mosque to divert their attention from these churches, and made it one of the wonders of the world. In the same way 'Abd al-Malik, when he saw the immense and dominating dome of the Church of the Resurrection, feared that it would dominate the hearts of the Muslims, and he therefore erected the Dome which we see on the Rock.'

Perhaps because of this great mosque, and its evocation of Solomon's temple, Jerusalem came to be known for a while as Bayt al-Maqdis, clearly related to the Hebrew *Bayt ha-Miqdash*, the biblical name of the Temple. In time both this name and Aelia were replaced by al-Quds, 'the [city of] holiness' (cf. Isaiah 52:1; Nehemiah 11:1, 11:18, etc.). A Qur'ānic verse (17:1) tells how God took the Prophet on a journey by night from the sacred mosque (in Mecca) to the farthest mosque (in Arabic, *al-Masjid al-Aqṣā*). One early exegetical tradition places 'the farthest mosque' in heaven; another places it in Jerusalem. The latter of these interpretations came to be universally accepted by Muslims. This verse is not included among the inscriptions in the Dome of the Rock. A contrasting tradition, equally early, denied the sanctity of Jerusalem in Islam. According to this tradition, only Mecca and Medina are holy cities, and the veneration of the Temple Mount is a Judaizing error. The argument continued for centuries, and was only settled in favour of sanctity in comparatively modern times.

A wall-painting in Quṣayr 'Amra, a hunting lodge in the Jordanian desert some fifty miles east of Amman, conveys a more directly political message. Probably dating from the early eighth century, it depicts the caliph as seated while the six rulers of the infidels pay homage to him. They are named in both Greek and Arabic script. Four of the names are fairly clear – Caesar, i.e. the Byzantine emperor; Roderic, the last Visigoth king of Spain, defeated by the Arabs in 711; Chosroes, the Persian emperor; and the Negus of Ethiopia. The remaining two figures are defaced beyond recognition, but may perhaps represent the Chinese emperor and a Turkish or Indian prince. Remarkably, these kings are not depicted as humiliated captives, as was common in ancient portrayals of vanquished enemies, but rather as subordinate rulers offering homage. The message this time is not conquest and subjugation – two of the countries, China and Ethiopia, had not been subjugated – but rather the recognition by the rulers of the world of the superiority of Islam and the primacy of the Muslim caliph as the heir of some of them and the overlord of all.

Under the last Umayyads, the caliphs and their advisers tried to rationalize the varied fiscal systems which they had inherited into a new and specifically Islamic system of taxation. The later historiographic tradition assigns a key role to the 'pious caliph' 'Umar ibn 'Abd al-'Azīz, to whom alone it allows the title 'caliph', all the other Umayyads being designated as 'kings'.

But the grievances remained, and those who harboured them were reinforced by the rapidly increasing numbers of half-Arabs and non-Arab Muslims. Even among those who offered no armed resistance and formulated no alternative doctrine, there was a growing feeling, frequently expressed in the literature, that the march of Islamic history had taken a wrong turn, and that the leaders of the community were leading it into sin. It was a passive withdrawal from involvement with the state, the service of which was seen as demeaning and unworthy of a truly pious Muslim.

It was time for revolutionary change. In a profound sense, the advent of Islam had itself been a kind of revolution. The new faith overwhelmed existing doctrines and churches, bringing not a third testament to add to the previous two, but a new scripture to supersede them. The new rulers installed by conquest overthrew an old order – political, ecclesiastical, social – and created a new one in its place. In Islam, as ideally conceived, there were to be no priests, no Church, no kings and no nobles, no privileged orders or castes or estates of any kind, save only for the self-evident superiority of those who accept the true faith to those who wilfully reject it – and of course such obvious natural and social realities as the superiority of man to woman and of master to slave. Even these inequalities were softened and humanized by the new dispensation. In Islam, unlike the ancient world, a slave was no longer a chattel but a person, with a recognized legal and moral status. Women, though still subject to polygamy and concubinage, were accorded property rights not equalled in the West until modern times. Even the non-Muslim, despite some fiscal and social disabilities, benefited from a tolerance and a security in sharp contrast with the lot of non-Christians in medieval and sometimes also in modern Christendom.

In principle, all the Arab warriors shared – though not equally – in the booty and tribute won by conquest. Many of them also sought and obtained further – sometimes conflicting – advantages. There were tribesmen in search of pasturage, oasis-dwellers seeking bigger and better estates, and Meccan merchants eager to exploit the rich commerce of great cities. Much of the complaint against the government of the caliphs, especially of the third caliph 'Uthmān, was that they were more responsive to the needs of these groups than to the needs of Islam.

For a people accustomed to nomadic freedom, all authority was irksome and unfamiliar; the increasing power of the state and of those who controlled it was an affront, a betrayal of the authentic message of Islam.

In the eyes of both the pious and the rebellious, the caliphate had been established to uphold and to spread that message. Its purpose was to serve Islam; its authority derived from the freely given and revocable consent of the Muslims. But for many of them the state, instead of serving Islam, served the interests of small groups of rich and powerful men, who operated – in government and in other fields – by methods that to an increasing and disquieting extent resembled those of the ancient empires that Islam had overthrown and superseded. The issues were crystallized in the debate about the killing of 'Uthmān. According to some, it was a wilful murder, an act of rebellion against legitimate authority, to be punished with the full rigour of the law. According to others, it was not a murder but an execution, the just punishment of one who had misused – the Shī'a would also say usurped – the highest office in the Islamic community and turned it from its true path. This debate, in various forms, continued to affect Muslim political theory and practice through the centuries.

In the early period, the declared issues were the caliphate, that is, who should rule and how, and the restoration – and definition – of authentic Islam.

By a tragic paradox, only the reinforcement of the state could preserve the cohesion of the community, and the Islamic state, as it grew stronger, was obliged to make many compromises on the social and ethical ideas of Islam. Resistance to this process was constant and vigorous; sometimes successful, in the sense that the rebels were able to seize power, but always unavailing, in the sense that in every such struggle the victory, whether of the rebels or of the defenders, led to a reinforcement of the power of the state and a further step towards centralized autocracy in the older Middle Eastern style and away from the Islamic ideal of government. In the course of this resistance, a series of religious sects emerged, differing in the nature of their doctrines and the composition of their support, but alike in their desire to restore the radical dynamism of the Islamic founders. At first, when 'Arab' and 'Muslim' were virtually synonymous terms, the religious struggle was an Arab civil war. Later, as Islam spread rapidly among the conquered peoples, converts began to play an increasing, sometimes a dominant, role in these movements. It is a striking testimony to the universalist appeal and the continuing revolutionary power of the Islamic idea that the great radical movements in the Islamic empire were all movements within Islam and not against it.

After the death of Hishām in 743, four short reigns brought the Umayyad caliphate to a rapid end. A resurgence of tribal feuding, an intensification of both Kharijite and Shī'ite sectarianism, and the emergence of a new and powerful opposition in the east Iranian province of Khurāsān, brought the caliphate to the point where it was challenged even in Syria and ignored elsewhere. The last of the

Umayyads, Marwān II (744–750), was an able ruler, but he came too late to save the dynasty. A new force, a new dynasty and a new era in Islamic history were emerging in the East.

CHAPTER 4

THE 'ABBASID CALIPHATE

On 25 Ramaḍān 129, corresponding to 9 June 747, Abū Muslim, a manumitted Persian slave and the leader of a militant sect, unfurled the black flags of revolt in the eastern Iranian province of Khurāsān. He and his predecessors had already been active for nearly thirty years, denouncing the impious Umayyads and urging the claims of the kinsmen of the Prophet, especially of the 'Abbasids, descendants of the Prophet's uncle al-'Abbās. He found a ready audience. The Iranian Muslim population chafed under the inequalities imposed upon them by Umayyad rule; the Arab army and settlers, half Persianized by long residence, were sharply divided, and pursued their tribal feuds even when the rebel forces were advancing to victory. With chiefly non-Arab but with some important Arab support, Abū Muslim was soon able to seize all Khurāsān and from there advanced westward across Iran towards the old metropolitan province of Iraq. In 749 his armies crossed the Euphrates and defeated another Umayyad force, and in the same year, Abu'l-'Abbās, the leader of the sect, was hailed as caliph by the troops in Kufa with the title of al-Saffāḥ. Further victories in 749 and 750 in Iraq and Syria sealed the fate of the Umayyads, and the authority of the new caliph was soon secure all over the Islamic empire.

This struggle, resulting in the replacement of the Umayyad by the 'Abbasid caliphate, was more than a simple change of dynasty. It was a revolution in Islamic history.

This character of the 'Abbasid victory has long been recognized by both Muslim and Western historians, and both have devoted much effort to explaining it. Some, influenced by national and even racial theories of history, interpreted the accession of the 'Abbasids as a victory of Persians over Arabs – the destruction of the so-called 'Arab Kingdom' of the Umayyads and the establishment of a new Iranian empire under a veneer of Persianized Islam.

At first sight there is some evidence to support this view – the prominence of Persians among both the leaders of the rebellion and the ministers and courtiers of the new regime, and the strong Persian element in 'Abbasid political culture. But subsequent research has obliged historians to modify, in several important respects, such theories of Persian victory and Arab defeat. Shī'ism, seen by some nineteenth-century Western and twentieth-century Iranian scholars as the expression of an 'Iranian National Consciousness', has been shown to be in fact of Arab origin. It was strongest among the mixed population of southern Iraq and was taken into Iran by Arab colonists, who for long provided its main support. The revolt of Abū Muslim was directed against Umayyad rule and Syrian predominance rather than against the Arabs as such. As well as Persians, the pro-'Abbasid movement had many Arab supporters, including several of its leaders and commanders. Though ethnic antagonisms no doubt played some part, and though Persians were prominent among the victors, the movement served an Arab pretender, and established an Arab dynasty. After the victory, many of the high offices of government were reserved to Arabs, Arabic remained the sole language of government and culture, Arabian land remained fiscally privileged, and socially at least, the doctrine of Arab superiority was maintained. What the Arabs had lost was not, as was once thought, the reality of power – this came later – but the exclusive right to the fruits of power, which they were now compelled to share with other people, notably their own half-breed brothers. Under the Umayyads, only those of full Arab parentage on both sides were admitted to the highest offices of the state. Under the 'Abbasids, not only half-Arabs, but Persians and others rose at the caliphal court, where the favour of the ruler, more than noble descent, was the passport to power and prestige. If a term must be set to the Arab Kingdom, it should be put later, with the decline of the Arab warriors from the status of a privileged caste and the rise to power of the Turkish guards in the capital and of autonomous local dynasties in the provinces.

As in so many revolutions, the profounder changes were gradual, and preceded as well as followed the political changes. The last Umayyad caliph, Marwān II, was the son of a Kurdish slavewoman. The first 'Abbasid caliph, al-Saffāḥ, was the son of a free Arab mother, and was for that reason, it is said, preferred to his brother. But that brother, the son of a Berber slavewoman, succeeded him, and, with the regnal title al-Manṣūr (754–775) was in many ways the founder of 'Abbasid greatness. With few exceptions, his successors, and almost all subsequent Muslim dynasts, were the sons of famous, often royal fathers and of nameless, usually foreign, slave mothers.

The larger significance of the 'Abbasid victory may be better judged by the changes that followed it than by the movement that achieved it. The first and most striking change was the transfer of the capital from Syria, where the Umayyads had ruled for a century, to Iraq, the centre of gravity of the great cosmopolitan empires of the ancient Middle East. The first 'Abbasid caliph, al-Saffāḥ, established a temporary capital by the Euphrates. His successor, al-Manṣūr, established a permanent capital in a new city on the west bank of the Tigris. This new city was at an intersection of trade routes, near the site of the old Sasanid Persian capital of Ctesiphon. In a story rich in cultural symbolism, a medieval Arabic author relates that during the construction of one of the great caliphal residences in Baghdad, the builders, on orders from the caliph, made use of some bricks from the ruined palace of Chosroes in Ctesiphon.

The official name of the new capital was Madīnat al-Salām, the City of Peace, but it is usually known by the name of the small town that previously occupied the site – Baghdad. From this city and its neighbourhood, the caliphs of the House of 'Abbās reigned as heads of most of the Islamic world for five centuries – at first as effective rulers of the Empire; later, after a period of rapid political decline, as nominal suzerains, while real power was exercised by other, mostly military, rulers.

The 'Abbasids, like others before and after them who attained power by means of a revolutionary movement, were soon forced to choose between the tenets and objectives of their supporters on the one hand, and the needs of government and empire on the other. They chose consensus and continuity, and had to meet and suppress the angry resentment of some of their more consequent followers. Abū Muslim himself, the architect of 'Abbasid victory, was put to death, as were several of his associates. This choice alienated the radicals and extremists, who thereafter found other outlets. At the same time, it reassured mainstream Muslims and helped al-Manṣūr to meet and overcome the dangers of foreign war and domestic rebellion, and, in a long and brilliant reign, to lay the foundations of 'Abbasid government.

In this task, he was ably seconded by a family that was to play an outstanding role in the first half-century of 'Abbasid rule. The Barmecides are often described as Persians. More precisely, they were Central Asian Iranians, descended from the Buddhist priesthood of the city of Balkh. Shortly after the foundation of Baghdad, Khālid al-Barmakī became the chief minister of al-Manṣūr. Thereafter he and his descendants, as *wazīrs*, developed and directed the administration of the Empire until their fall during the reign of Hārūn al-Rashīd in 803.

The capital had been moved eastward, nearer to the old centres of Iranian civilization. The Arab monopoly of power had ended, and Islamized Iranians were, so to speak, adopted into the ruling elite. The Iranians, with their greater experience of politics, were advancing on all levels of the administration, and the *wazīrs* were firmly ensconced as heads of the whole apparatus of the state, subject only to the supreme authority of the caliph. As a natural consequence, Iranian influences became stronger. Sasanid texts were translated or adapted in Arabic, Sasanid traditions were revived, and Sasanid Persian models were followed both in court ceremonial and government administration. This meant considerable departure from Arab tribal tradition, which for that matter could offer little guidance in either respect. The formation, for the first time in the Islamic state, of a standing army on the Persian model reduced the dependence of the dynasty on the Arab tribal levies and thus further diminished Arab influence in the capital.

In many respects, the early 'Abbasid caliphs maintained and developed the policies of their predecessors, with far less break than was at one time believed. Certain changes, clearly discernible under the late Umayyads, continued at an accelerated pace. The caliph was no longer an Arab 'supershaykh', presiding by the intermittent consent of the Arab tribal chiefs. He was an autocrat in the old Middle Eastern style, claiming a divine origin for his authority, resting it on his armed forces, and exercising it through a vast and growing bureaucracy. Stronger in this respect than the Umayyads, the 'Abbasids were nevertheless weaker than the ancient despots, in that they lacked the support of an established feudal caste and a priestly hierarchy, and were, according to a basic tenet of their faith, subject to a divine law which they could not abrogate nor even emend.

To compensate for this, and to replace the weakening bond of Arab ethnic cohesion, the caliphs laid increasing stress on Islamic identity and conformity, trying to impose on their vast and diverse empire the unity of a common faith and culture. Again following Sasanid precedent, they stressed the religious element in the authority and functions of the caliphate, and, by the patronage and encouragement of approved and compliant theologians, tried to underpin the regime with a class of official exponents of religion – a priesthood in the sociological, though not in the sacerdotal, sense. In pursuit of these aims, the caliphs rebuilt the holy cities of Mecca and Medina, organized the pilgrimage to them from Iraq on a regular basis, and began an inquisitorial persecution of various deviant Muslim sects and especially of Manichaeism, which seems to have attracted many followers in this period. The caliph al-Ma'mūn (813–833) and his successors attempted to impose one doctrine, that of the theological school known as the Mu'tazila, as the official doctrine of the state, and persecuted followers of other teachings. This attempt failed, and when al-Mutawakkil (847–861) needed popular support against the insubordinate Turkish soldiery, he was compelled to abandon and even to suppress the Mu'tazila and to adopt mainstream Sunni views. Sunnism and the Sunni ulema were already strong enough to resist and overcome the attempt by the ruler to impose his will on them in matters of doctrine, even when the ruler was the rightful Sunni caliph. This attempt at an Erastian Islam failed and was not repeated. After al-Mutawakkil, the 'Abbasids adhered, formally at least, to the most rigid orthodoxy, nor did any other dynasty not openly heretical try to dictate doctrine to the Islamic religious institution.

The reign of Hārūn al-Rashīd (786–809) is usually regarded as the apogee of 'Abbasid power, but it is from this time that the first portents of decline are seen. One of them was the rapid collapse, under his successors, of the political authority of the caliphate in the provinces. In the west, Spain and North Africa (756–800) became virtually independent under their own amirs, who conceded a purely nominal recognition of 'Abbasid suzerainty. In 868 even Egypt fell away when the governor, Aḥmad ibn Tulun, a Turkish praetorian sent from Baghdad, made himself independent and extended his rule to Syria. The fall of his dynasty was soon followed by the accession of another Turkish dynasty of similar origin, and thereafter Egypt – except for a very brief interregnum – was never again ruled from Baghdad. The rise of an independent political power in Egypt, often ruling Syria too, created a new No Man's Land between Syria and Iraq, and allowed the Bedouin Arab tribes of the desert fringes to recover the independence they had lost. At times they were even able to extend their activities into the settled lands of Syria and Mesopotamia, and to seize cities and establish transitory dynasties.

In the east, the process of disruption took a somewhat different form. The alliance of the 'Abbasid caliphs with their Iranian supporters was badly shaken by an obscure internal convulsion during the reign of Hārūn, which culminated in the degradation and destruction of the Barmecides and the assumption by Hārūn of the reins of power in his own hands. After his death, smouldering conflicts burst into civil war between his sons, al-Amīn and al-Ma'mūn. Al-Amīn's strength lay mainly in the capital and in Iraq, al-Ma'mūn's in Iran; and the civil war has been interpreted as a national conflict between Arabs and Persians, ending in a Persian victory. It was more probably a continuation of the social struggles of the immediately preceding period, complicated by a regional rather than national rivalry between Iran and Iraq. Al-Ma'mūn, relying upon eastern support, for a while projected the transfer of the capital from Baghdad to Marv, but in the face of the fierce opposition of the people of Baghdad, and indeed of Iraq, decided to return to the imperial city. Thereafter, Iranian ambitions found an outlet in local autonomous dynasties. In 820, Ṭāhir, al-Ma'mūn's Iranian general, became virtually independent in Khurāsān and founded a dynasty. In doing so, he set a precedent for many others who, while for the most part still recognizing the nominal suzerainty of the caliphs as the supreme heads of Sunni Islam, deprived them of all real authority in the regions under their sway.

While the power of the caliphs in the provinces in both east and west was reduced to the granting of diplomas of investiture to the *de facto* rulers, their authority even in the metropolitan province of Iraq was rapidly diminishing. As long as Baghdad retained control of the vital trade routes leading through it, the political fragmentation of the Empire did not impede, and in some respects actually helped, the expansion of commerce and culture. But there were other, growing dangers. A spendthrift court and a bloated bureaucracy created recurring financial crises, aggravated by the loss of provincial revenues and, subsequently, by the exhaustion or loss to invaders of gold and silver mines. The caliphs found a remedy for their cash-flow problems in the farming-out of state revenues, eventually with the local governors as tax-farmers. These farmer-governors soon became the real rulers of the Empire, the more so when tax-farms and governorships were held by army commanders, who alone had the force to impose obedience. From the time of al-Mu'taṣim (833–842) and al-Wāthiq (842–847), the caliphs became the puppets of their own generals, who were often able to appoint and depose them at will.

By the early years of the tenth century, the breakdown of caliphal authority was complete. The event that is usually taken to symbolize this process was the grant to the governor of Iraq, Ibn Rā'iq, of the title *amīr al-umarā'* – Commander of Commanders. The immediate purpose of this title and office was no doubt to assert the primacy of the military commander of Baghdad over his colleagues elsewhere. At the same time it gave formal recognition to the existence of a supreme governing authority besides the caliph, exercising effective political and military power, and leaving the caliph only as formal head of the state and the faith and representative of the religious unity of Islam. Finally, on 17 January 946, came the ultimate degradation, when the Shīʿite Persian house of Būyeh, already rulers of a virtually independent dynastic state in western Iran, invaded and occupied the capital. The caliph was no longer master in his own city. Worse, the supreme head of Sunni Islam was controlled by a Shīʿite, who kept him in place because he was useful. Later, the Shīʿites were replaced by Sunni rulers, but the subordination of the caliph remained.

From this time until the conquest of the city by the Mongols in 1258, the caliphate became a largely titular institution, a formal expression of the unity of Sunni Islam, and a legitimizing authority for the numerous military rulers who exercised effective sovereignty. The caliphs themselves, except for a brief period in the late twelfth and early thirteenth centuries, were at the mercy of these rulers.

The arrival of the Būyids in Baghdad was not only significant as a turning point in the political evolution of the caliphate; it also marks an important moment in what has been called the 'Iranian Intermezzo' in Middle Eastern history. Between the decline of Arab power in the ninth century and the final establishment of Turkish power in the eleventh century, there was an interval of Iranian revival, this time in an unmistakably national form, through Iranian dynasties resting on Iranian support, based on Iranian territory and, most important of all, fostering a revival of an Iranian national spirit and culture in a new Islamic form. The first Iranian Muslim independent dynasty, that of the Tahirids in eastern Iran (821–873), was followed by the Saffarids (867–903) and Samanids (875–999) in the east and by the Būyids (932–1055) and others in the north and west. All these dynasties were Muslim. Some of them were still imbued with Arab Islamic ideals and indifferent to Persian culture, but the course of events and the nature of their support made them willing or unwilling sponsors of an Iranian renaissance. The most active were the Samanids, whose capital at Bukhara was a centre of Iranian cultural revival. Under most of the Samanid rulers, the official language was Persian. They encouraged Persian poets and scholars, and the tenth and eleventh centuries saw the birth of a new Persian literature, written in the Arabic script and profoundly influenced by the Muslim faith and tradition, but distinctively and essentially Persian.

The Būyid period was one of Shī'ite as well as Iranian revival, and the two have often been erroneously identified. The establishment of the 'Abbasid caliphate had led to a major change in Shī'ite claims and leadership. Under the Umayyads, the claims of the Shī'ite pretenders to head the Muslim community and state were based on kinship to the Prophet in the male line — that is, on descent from 'Alī, the Prophet's cousin, rather than from the Prophet himself through his daughter Fāṭima. Claims were thus advanced on behalf of descendants of 'Alī by wives other than Fāṭima, and even on behalf of kinsmen of the Prophet's family through other lines of descent. Such were the 'Abbasids, whose bid for power began in a Shī'ite sect. After the pre-emption of 'Alid claims by their 'Abbasid cousins, greater emphasis was placed on direct physical descent from the Prophet through Fāṭima, and in time this became first the dominant, then the exclusive argument of the Shī'a . The sons, grandsons, and subsequent descendants of 'Alī and Fāṭima were known among the Shī'a as the Imāms. After the death of the sixth Fatimid imam Ja'far al-Ṣādiq in 765, his followers split into two main groups, supporting the claims to the succession of his sons Mūsā and Ismā'īl. The followers of the former recognized Mūsā and his descendants as rightful imams of the Islamic world until the twelfth in line after 'Alī. He disappeared in obscure circumstances and his messianic return is awaited by the so-called Twelver Shī'a to this day. The Twelvers were generally moderate in their doctrines, which differed on comparatively minor points from those of Sunni Islam.

The second group, known as the Ismā'īlīs from their support of Ismā'īl, inherited the extremist doctrines and insurrectionary methods of earlier Shī'ism in the Umayyad period, and applied them to the new, changing realities. The spread of commerce, the rise of industry, the growth of cities, the simultaneous proliferation and militarization of government, the increasing complexity and diversity of society, subjected the loose social structure of the Empire to grave strain, and engendered widespread discontent. The growing sophistication of intellectual life and the clash of cultures and ideas encouraged the rise and spread of sectarian movements which, in a theocratically conceived society, were the natural expression of dissent from the existing order. In the late ninth and early tenth centuries these strains reached breaking point, and the rulers of Islam confronted a series of challenges ranging

The Emperor Constantine, known as Constantine the Great, who ruled from 306 to 337. The first Christian Roman emperor and the founder of Constantinople.

The land walls of Constantinople.

Rock carving near Persepolis depicting the triumph of the Persian emperor Shapur and the defeat and capture of the Roman emperor Valerian, c.259-260.

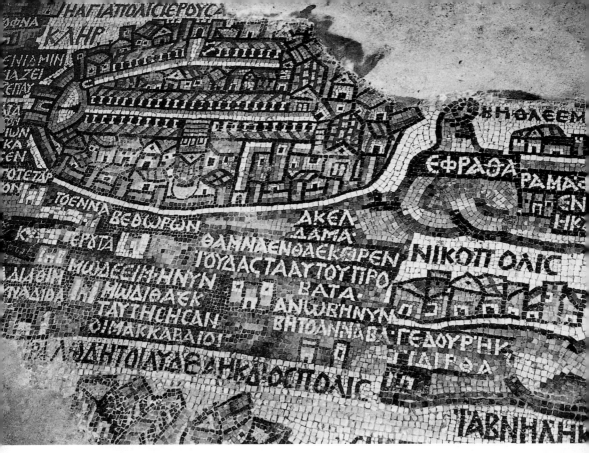

Early Christian mosaic at Ma'daba in Jordan, showing the holy city of Jerusalem and surrounding area.

Medallion commemorating a victory of the Roman emperor Justinian, c.530.

Third-century synagogue, excavated at Dura Europos in Syria.

ستجدني إن شاء الله من الصابرين فلما أس
لما وتله للجبين وناديناه أن يا إبراهيم
قد صدقت الرؤيا إنا كذلك نجزي المحسنين
إن هذا لهو البلاء المبين وفديناه بذبح عظيم
صدق الله العظيم

Hz. İBRAHİM'İN OĞLU İSMAİLİ
KURBAN ADAMA MİSALİ

Abraham prepares to sacrifice his son. In the Muslim version, this is Ishmael, not Isaac.

Muhammad receiving revelation from the Archangel Gabriel (from the *Universal History of* Rashīd al-Dīn, 1307).

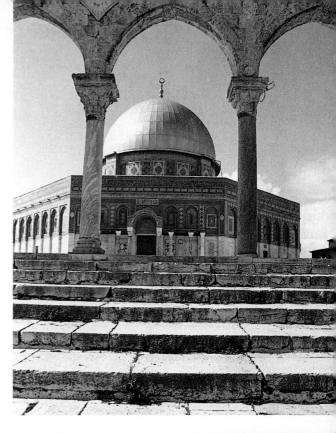

The Dome of the Rock, built by ʿAbd al-Malik on the Temple Mount in Jerusalem in 691–692. The first great religious building in the history of Islam.

A detail from the inscription and decoration inside the dome of the Dome of the Rock.

The Church of the Holy
Sepulchre in Jerusalem.
The original structure,
dating from the time of
Constantine, was several
times destroyed, renovated
and rebuilt. The present
structure dates from the
extensive rebuilding by
the Crusaders after they
captured Jerusalem
in 1099.

Quṣayr ʿAmra, the
little palace of ʿAmra, an
Umayyad hunting lodge
in the Jordanian desert,
some fifty miles east of
Amman.

(clockwise from above left)
Byzantine coin of the emperor
Heraclius (610–641); Umayyad
coin of Muʿāwiya – Caliph
661–680 CE; Umayyad coin of
ʿAbd al-Malik, caliph 685–705,
who introduced Arabic coinage
in 696; ʿAbbasid coin of Hārūn
al-Rashīd, caliph 786–809; an
ʿAbbasid coin.

The monumental 'Tower of Victory' built in the name of Mas'ūd III (1099-1115) in Ghazni in present-day Afghanistan, to celebrate his victory over the Hindu rulers of Kanauj.

The assassination of Nizām al-Mulk, the celebrated chief minister of the Seljuk Sultans, in 1092. He was killed by emissaries of the Assassins, a radical and violent opposition to Sunni Islam. Founded in Iran at the end of the eleventh century, it was extended to Syria in the early twelfth.

from the armed violence of the Carmathians in eastern Arabia and Syria–Mesopotamia and the seditious preaching of the Ismā'īlīs, to the more subtle and ultimately more effective criticism of peaceful moralists and mystics in Baghdad itself. The Carmathian revolts in Syria and Mesopotamia were with difficulty suppressed by the caliphs, and the rebels in eastern Arabia were isolated. In the Yemen, however, the Ismā'īlīs won a more lasting victory and succeeded in establishing themselves in power.

From the Yemen, they sent emissaries to North Africa, where they succeeded so well that in 908 they were able to enthrone the Ismā'īlī pretender, 'Ubaydallāh, as the first Fatimid caliph – so called because of his claim to be descended from the Prophet through his daughter Fatima. The first three Fatimid caliphs ruled only in North Africa, but in 969 the fourth, al–Mu'izz, conquered Egypt, where he built the new city of Cairo as his capital.

For the first time a powerful independent dynasty ruled in the Middle East that did not recognize even the titular authority of the 'Abbasids, but on the contrary founded a caliphate of their own, challenging the 'Abbasids for the headship of the whole Islamic world, and rejecting even the theoretical basis of the Sunni caliphate. In addition to their political, military and religious actions, the Fatimids also pursued a skilful economic policy aimed at diverting the eastern trade from the Persian Gulf to the Red Sea, and thus at the same time strengthening Egypt and weakening Iraq.

The Fatimids rapidly extended their sway into Palestine, Syria, and Arabia, and for a while greatly surpassed in power and influence the Sunni caliphs in Baghdad. The peak of the Fatimid period in Egypt was the reign of the caliph al-Mustanṣir (1036–1094), under whom the Fatimid Empire comprised the whole of North Africa, Sicily, Egypt, Syria, and western Arabia. In 1056–7 a pro-Fatimid general succeeded in seizing even Baghdad itself and proclaimed the sovereignty of the Fatimid caliph from the pulpits of the 'Abbasid capital. He was driven out in the following year, however, and thereafter the power of the Fatimids declined. The breakdown was first noticeable in the civil administration, and led to the rise of a series of military autocrats who exercised their authority in Cairo just as their counterparts had for some time been doing in Baghdad. Deprived of real power, and reduced to the status of helpless puppets of the amirs, the Fatimid caliphs gradually lost the support of the sectaries. Their regime was finally overthrown and Egypt restored to the Sunni allegiance.

The regime of the Fatimids in Egypt at its height differed in a number of respects from those that had preceded it. At the top was the caliph, an absolute monarch, who, according to the beliefs of his followers, was the infallible Imam, ruling by hereditary right transmitted by the divine will through a divinely ordained family. His government was centralized and hierarchic, and was divided into three branches: religious, military and bureaucratic. The last two were in charge of the wazīr, a civilian, under the caliph. The religious branch consisted of a network of missionaries in several grades under a missionary-in-chief, who was an extremely influential political personage. This department was responsible for the higher schools of learning and for the Ismāʿīlī propagandist organization, and seems to have played a role not unlike that of the Party in some modern one-party states. The propagandist branch directed a vast army of agents throughout the eastern provinces still under the nominal control of the ʿAbbasid caliph in Baghdad. The effectiveness of this propaganda can be seen in a number of ways. From Iraq to the borders of India repeated outbreaks attested the activity of the Ismāʿīlī agents, while the intellectual life of Islam shows many examples of the seductive appeal of Ismāʿīlī teachings.

The Fatimid period was also an epoch of great commercial and industrial efflorescence in Egypt. Except for a few periods of famine due to the misbehaviour of the Nile or of military cliques, it was a time of great prosperity. From the first, Fatimid governments realized the importance of trade both for the prosperity of their Empire and for the extension of its influence. The wazīr Yaʿqūb ibn Killis initiated a commercial drive which later rulers followed. The pre-Fatimid trade of Egypt had been meagre and limited. The Fatimids developed plantations and industries in Egypt and began an important export trade of Egyptian products. In addition they created a wide net of commercial connections, especially with Europe and India. In the West they established relations, dating back to their early Tunisian days, with some of the Italian city republics. A great volume of seaborne trade passed between Egypt and the West, and Fatimid fleets controlled the eastern Mediterranean. Further east the Fatimids cultivated important contacts with India, gradually extending their sovereignty southward over both shores of the Red Sea. Much of the Indian trade passed through the Fatimid port of ʿAydhāb on the Sudanese coast. Wherever the Egyptian merchant went, the Ismāʿīlī missionary was not far behind, and soon we find the same ferment of ideas among the Muslims both of Spain and of India.

But the Fatimids failed to win the ultimate victory against the 'Abbasids. After the death of the Fatimid caliph al-Mustanṣir in 1094 their power dwindled, and they were never again able to offer a serious challenge to 'Abbasid supremacy. One cause of their failure was the dissipation of Shī'ite energies in the conflict between the Ismā'īlī and Twelver Shī'a. The latter also had an important following, including several of the local dynasties of Iran. It is ironic that at the moment of the great Fatimid challenge to Baghdad, the 'Abbasids themselves were under the domination of the Twelver Shī'ite Būyid amirs. Despite their Shī'ism, the Būyids made no attempt to install an Alid as caliph – the Twelfth Imam of the Twelvers had disappeared some seventy years earlier – but gave outward homage to the 'Abbasids, retaining them as a Sunni cover for their own power and as an instrument of their policies in the Sunni world.

CHAPTER 5

THE COMING OF THE STEPPE PEOPLES

By the eleventh century, Islamic state and society show many signs of internal weakness. The symptoms are discernible even earlier: the fragmentation of the empire into a series of autonomous regional sovereignties; the dwindling of the power and prestige of the caliphs even in their own capital; the collapse of the whole political and administrative structure elaborated by the Islamic empire on foundations inherited from Byzantium and Sasanid Iran. While the real power of the caliphs and of the Islamic state was lost to military autocrats ruling through their troops, even the religious status of the caliph as head of Sunni Islam was dragged to the lowest level, as great sections of the population followed deviant sects and most of the empire from Iran to Egypt, even including the city of the caliphs itself, fell under the rule of Shī'ite generals and princes.

In economic life signs of deterioration appear somewhat later. The Būyids restored for a while the order and prosperity of the central provinces. The Fatimids inaugurated the age of the greatest prosperity in medieval Egyptian history. But the difficulties were increasing in the east and later also in Egypt. The once profitable trade with China dwindled and died away, partly for reasons arising out of internal conditions in that country. Trade with Russia and the Baltic countries, which had flourished during the eighth, ninth and tenth centuries, diminished and disappeared during the eleventh, while the growing shortage of precious metals helped to stifle commerce even inside the Empire and accelerated the development of a quasi-feudal economy.

In cultural life, the eighth, ninth and tenth centuries had seen a great intellectual expansion. The economic expansion of the time encouraged the growth of cities and of an urban population with leisure, taste and curiosity. The translation of Greek scientific and philosophic literature into Arabic initiated what has been called 'The Renaissance of Islam', while even traditional and Sunni Islam, in reaction against Greek learning and Persian worldly wisdom, renewed and enriched the old Arabic humanities with which it became increasingly identified. This cultural efflorescence was, however, insecure and impermanent. It was a culture of cities, limited to certain sections among the urban leisured classes. Its relations with tradition, and through tradition with the deeper strains of Islamic religious life, remained tenuous and uncertain.

During the eleventh and early twelfth centuries, the weakness of the empire was exposed by a series of almost simultaneous attacks by internal and external enemies on all sides. In Europe, the forces of Christendom advanced in both Sicily and Spain, wresting vast territories from Muslim rule in a wave of reconquest which culminated in the arrival of the Crusaders in the Near East itself. In Africa, a new religious movement among the Berbers led to the rise of a new Berber empire in Spain and North Africa. Further east, the two great Bedouin Arab tribes of Hilāl and Sulaym burst out of Upper Egypt, where they had been living, and swept across Libya and Tunisia, wreaking havoc and devastation from which Arab North Africa never fully recovered. On the northern border of the caliphate, already weakened by Byzantine offensives and Khazar raids in the previous centuries, the Christian Georgians were able to restore a Georgian empire stretching from the Black Sea to the foothills of Daghestan and thence to advance into Muslim territory.

Most important of all in its permanent effects was the wave of invaders from the east – from the Altaic peoples of the great Asian steppes. The Muslims first met the Turks on the eastern borders of the empire, and had for some time been importing them as slaves, especially of the kind trained from childhood for military service and later known as *Mamlūk* – an Arabic word meaning 'owned', to distinguish them from the humbler slaves used for domestic and economic purposes. Occasionally, Turkish slaves appear in the empire under the early 'Abbasids and even earlier, but the first to use them extensively was the caliph al-Muʻtaṣim (833–842), who collected a large force of Turkish military slaves even before his accession, and later arranged to receive a large number annually as part of the tribute from the eastern provinces. Under his successors, the caliphate relied to an increasing extent on Turkish troops and commanders, who in time ousted the Arabs and Persians from military, and therefore from political, hegemony. As the military caste became predominantly Turkish, and as the regimes of Islam became predominantly military, the Turks established a domination that lasted for a thousand years. As early as 868, the first independent dynasty in Muslim Egypt was founded by a

Turkish military slave, and most subsequent regimes in Egypt were of similar origin. In Iran, national dynasties lasted for a while, but the most important and longest-lived – that of the Samanids – came to depend on Turkish soldiers, and was in due course supplanted by one of the most remarkable Turkish dynasties – that of the Ghaznavids (962–1186), founded by a Turkish slave in the Samanid service.

These were, however, single soldiers or groups of soldiers entering the service of Muslim states as slaves or mercenaries and then taking them over. In 960, an event of quite different significance took place – the conversion of the Karakhanids, a Turkish dynasty beyond the frontier of Islam, with their people. Hitherto, conversion to Islam had only been of individuals or groups of individuals. Now for the first time a whole free Turkish people, numbering, according to an Arabic chronicler, 200,000 tents, embraced Islam, forming the first Muslim Turkish kingdom in the lands beyond the Jaxartes. After their conversion, the Karakhanids seem to have forgotten their pre-Islamic Turkish past, and identified themselves to the full with Middle Eastern Islamic civilization.

A distinguishing feature of Turkish Islam, from its very beginning, is the completeness with which the Turks surrendered themselves to their new religion. Partly because of the simple intensity of the faith as they encountered it on the frontiers of Islam and heathendom, partly because their conversion to Islam at once involved them in Holy War against their own heathen kinsmen, the converted Turks sank their national identity in Islam as the Arabs and Persians had never done. There is no Turkish equivalent to Arab memories of the heroic days of pagan Arabia, to Persian pride in the bygone glories of ancient Iran. Save for a few fragments of folk poetry and of genealogical legend, the civilizations, states, religions, and literatures of the pre-Islamic Turkish past were blotted out and forgotten. Even the very name Turk came to be synonymous with Muslim, for Turks as well as for Westerners. In the earnestness and seriousness of their loyalty to Islam the Turks are equalled by no other people. It is therefore not surprising that in time a great Sunni revival began and spread under the aegis of Turkish dynasties.

At the beginning of the eleventh century, the Fatimid caliphate was still a great power, with its rule extending from Egypt into western Arabia and into Syria, where, however, it was forced to share power with local desert-based Bedouin dynasties. In Iraq and western Iran, Iranian dynasties ruled, the most important of them, the Būyids, in the central provinces. In the east, the heritage of the Samanids was divided between two dynasties – the Ghaznavids south of the Oxus, and the Karakhanids north of the Oxus. Both of these were Turkish, but they were very different. The former was a classical Muslim state headed by a Turkish general with a Turkish Mamluk army; the latter was a Turkish state ruled by a khan with his own free Turkish tribesmen.

At about this time, two great migrations of the Turkish peoples transformed the face of the Middle East and for a while of Eastern Europe. Far to the north, in the lands beyond the Jaxartes, lived the Oghuz Turks, and beyond them, in the neighbourhood of the Irtish river, the Kipchaks. These last now advanced from the Irtish to the Jaxartes, displacing the Oghuz, and then moved westwards across south Russia into Eastern Europe where they were variously known as Polovtsi and Kumans. The Oghuz, forced out of their homeland, migrated into Islamic territory. There were several waves of migration, the most important being that known as the Seljuks, after the family that led them. Seljuk and his family seem to have entered Islamic territory in the late tenth century, settled in the province of Bukhara and embraced Islam. With the armies which they assembled, the sons of the house of Seljuk served various Muslim dynasties, the last of whom were the Ghaznavids. From these they parted company, and in the struggle against them they swiftly won power. The grandsons of Seljuk, Tughrul and Chagri, led Turkish armies into Khurāsān, crushing the Ghaznavids and seizing their chief cities.

It was not long before they began to act on their own behalf. In 1037, prayers were recited in their names in the mosques of Marv and Nishapur. They soon overran the rest of eastern Iran, and then marched westwards, leading a growing army of Turks to the conquest of western Iran. Finally, in 1055, Tughrul led his army into Baghdad, seizing the city from the last of the Būyid amirs. A new empire had arisen in Islam. By 1079, the Seljuks had wrested Syria and Palestine from local rulers and from the declining Fatimids, and, succeeding where the Arabs and Persians alike had failed, they conquered from Byzantium the greater part of Anatolia, which became, and remained, a Muslim Turkish land.

The Seljuk conquests created a new order in the Middle East, most of which was now united under a single authority for the first time since the early 'Abbasid caliphate. The Seljuks were Sunni Muslims, and retained the caliphs as nominal rulers, even strengthening their position in two important respects – first, by extending the area under their suzerainty, and then by eliminating the sectarian regimes that had denied even their titular headship of Islam. But the real sovereigns of the Empire were the Seljuk Great Sultans, who had swept away the petty sovereignties into which it had been divided and had met and defeated both the Byzantine and the Fatimid enemies in the west. The title 'sultan', adopted by Tughrul after his conquest of Baghdad in 1055, is often attributed by chroniclers to earlier rulers like the Būyids and Ghaznavids, who exercised a non-caliphal sovereignty. The Seljuk sultans appear, however, to have been the first to have used the title officially and inscribed it on their coins. The title has remained in use ever since for the holder of supreme power.

In the second half of the eleventh century, the Seljuk Great Sultans ruled over a united Empire, comprising almost the whole of the lands of the caliphate in southwest Asia, with the addition of Anatolia. After the death of the third Great Sultan, Malikshah, in 1092, civil war broke out between his sons, and the process of political fragmentation, which had been interrupted by the Seljuk conquest, was resumed, this time under different branches or officers of the Seljuk family. The most important were the Seljuk monarchies of Kirman, Iraq, Syria and Anatolia, all owing a tenuous allegiance to the Great Sultan, who resided in Khurāsān.

It was during this period of weakness and dissension that, in 1096, the Crusaders arrived in the Levant. For the first thirty years, the disunity of the Muslim world made things easy for the invaders, who advanced speedily down the coast of Syria into Palestine, and established a chain of Latin feudal principalities, based on Antioch, Edessa, Tripoli and Jerusalem. But even in this first period of success the Crusaders were limited in the main to the coastal plains and slopes, facing the Mediterranean and the Western world. In the interior, looking eastwards to the desert and Iraq, the reaction was preparing. The Seljuk princes who held Aleppo and Damascus were unable to accomplish very much, and the real strength of the movement came from further east. In 1127, Zangi, a Turkish officer in the Seljuk service, seized Mosul, and in the following years gradually built up a powerful Muslim state in northern Mesopotamia and Syria. His son, Nūr al-Dīn, took Damascus in 1154, creating a single Muslim power in Syria and confronting the Crusaders for the first time with a really formidable adversary.

The issue before the two sides was now the control of Egypt, where the Fatimid caliphate was tottering towards final collapse. A Kurdish officer called Ṣalāḥ al-Dīn – better known in the West as Saladin – was sent to Egypt, where he served at the same time as wazīr to the Fatimids and as representative of the interests of Nūr al-Dīn. In 1172, he abolished the Fatimid caliphate, restored the titular supremacy of the 'Abbasid caliphs in Egypt, and established himself as effective ruler while professing a somewhat ambiguous allegiance to Nūr al-Dīn. After Nūr al-Dīn's death in 1174, Saladin seized Muslim Syria from his heirs as a preliminary to launching a *jihād* against the Crusaders in 1187. By his death in 1193, he had recaptured Jerusalem and expelled the Crusaders from all but a narrow coastal strip. It was only the break-up of Saladin's Syro-Egyptian empire into a host of small states under his successors which permitted the Crusading states to drag out an attenuated existence for another century, until the reconstitution of a Syro-Egyptian state under the Mamluks in the thirteenth century brought about their final extinction, along with that of the other states of Syria.

In Anatolia, the Turkish occupation seems to have been accomplished by migrating tribes rather than by any deliberate action on the part of the Great Seljuks. After the conquest, however, the Seljuk prince Suleymān ibn Kutlumush was sent to organize the new province, and by the end of the twelfth century his successors had built up a strong Turkish monarchy in Anatolia with its capital in Konya (the ancient Iconium). Under the rule of the Anatolian Seljuks, which in various forms lasted until the beginning of the fourteenth century, central and eastern Anatolia gradually became a Turkish land. Masses of Turkish immigrants from further east entered the country and a Turkish, Muslim civilization replaced Greek Christianity.

Meanwhile, the Seljuk states in the east, weakened by constant dissension and strife, faced new external and internal enemies. In the north-east, another steppe people, the Kara-Khitay, appeared on the frontiers of Islam. They were immigrants from China, of Mongol stock, forerunners of a deadlier enemy yet to come. Towards the middle of the twelfth century they conquered Transoxania from the Karakhanids and set up a vast empire stretching from the Oxus to the Yenisei river and the borders of China. A *jihād* declared against these infidel invaders led to the defeat and flight of the Seljuk sultan Sinjar in 1141, at the Battle of the Katvan Steppe. Echoes of this disaster for Muslim arms even reached faraway Christian Europe, and encouraged the flagging spirits of the Crusaders. Revolts among the nomadic

Turkish tribes accelerated the decline of Seljuk power, and after the death of Sanjar in 1157, his crumbling realm broke up into a number of small states, most of them ruled by former Seljuk officers. Even the caliph in Baghdad for a while succeeded in reasserting his independence and religious authority and in maintaining a sort of ephemeral caliphal state in the ancient capital of Sunni Islam. Further east, the Turkish governor of Khwarezm, the province south of the Aral Sea, started a new but short-lived empire which for a while seemed about to inherit the territories and powers of the Great Seljuks.

This period of Turkish immigration and of the consolidation of Turkish political and military supremacy also saw certain significant changes in government, in economic and social life, in culture and in religion.

In their administration, the Seljuks relied largely on Persians and on the well-entrenched Persian bureaucracy. One of the most notable figures of the period was the great minister Niẓām al-Mulk, who developed and systemized the trend towards feudalism that was already inherent in the tax-farming practices of the immediately preceding period. The misuses of the previous era became the rules of a new social and administrative order, based on land instead of money. Land was granted to or taken by officers, who in return furnished a number of armed men. These grants carried rights not merely to a commission on the collection of taxes, but to the actual revenues themselves, and the state was forced to maintain its income by imposing a growing series of tolls and levies, in addition to the land and poll taxes authorized by the Holy Law.

Social upheaval in such a period of change was inevitable. The Iranian aristocracy found itself displaced and pauperized by the emergence of a new Turkish military ruling class. Landowners were hard hit by the appearance of new non-resident overlords. Minted money became far less common, and the merchants and artisans suffered in consequence.

The chief opposition movement was again the Ismāʿīlī Shīʿa, but in a new and radically altered form. After the death of the Fatimid caliph al-Mustanṣir in 1094, the Ismāʿīlīs split into two groups, one recognizing his younger son and successor on the throne of Cairo, the other proclaiming its allegiance to an elder son who had been set aside and then put to death in Alexandria. The Persian Ismāʿīlīs, led by Ḥasan-i Ṣabbāḥ, rejected the new Fatimid caliph and severed connections with Cairo. At the same time they elaborated a revised form of their faith and embarked on a new campaign of radical and violent opposition in the Seljuk dominions. The followers of the 'New Preaching', as the reformed Isma'ilism of Ḥasan-i Ṣabbāḥ was known, are usually called 'Assassins'. This name is derived from the Arabic word hashish, probably in reference to the strangeness of their behavior. The modern European meaning of the word derives from their political tactics.

In 1090 Ḥasan-i Ṣabbāḥ obtained control of the inaccessible mountain fastness of Alamut in northern Persia. Here, and in similar bases established in Syria in the following century, the Grand Masters of the sect commanded bands of devoted and fanatical followers, waging a campaign of terror and 'assassination' against the kings and princes of Islam in the name of a mysterious hidden Imam. The emissaries of the Grand Masters carried out a series of daring murders of prominent Muslim statesmen and generals, including the Niẓām al-Mulk himself in 1092. The terror of the Assassins was not finally exorcized until the Mongol invasions of the thirteenth century, after which Isma'ilism stagnated as a minor heresy.

The activities of the Assassins were the last serious attempt by the Shī'a to overthrow the Sunni caliphate and the establishment. Meanwhile a great Sunni revival had been taking place which in time affected every aspect of Muslim life, thought and letters. Its roots may be sought far back in the past. The religious institution had long since disentangled itself from the state and had jealously guarded its prerogatives in the fields of doctrine, law, education and social institutions, developing according to its own inner logic and only indirectly affected by the needs and pressures of state and government. Though this brought some advantages, it also involved a dangerous failure of co-ordination. The tension between religion and the state was much worsened when the victory of the army commanders in the multipartite struggle for supreme power reduced the connection between state and subject to one resting only on force and concerned only with taxation. The gulf was further widened when the military caste ceased to be of the same ethnic origin as the population and became separate and distinct, and when supreme political authority was held by sectaries who denied the basic political precepts of orthodoxy. The removal of the last moral and personal links between ruler and ruled, in a theocratically conceived society, led to a profound crisis in the Islamic religion. Government was left to soldiers and sectaries, administration to a scribal class deriving much of its cultural and professional ethos from pre-Islamic sources. Even in the religious field itself, deviant sects offered seductive alternatives to Sunni teachings and gained wide support, especially in the cities.

The Sunni revival began in the early eleventh century in Khurāsān, which under the Sunni Turkish Ghaznavids was the only important area of the Muslim world not under Shīʿite rule. Determined but unsuccessful attempts were made by the Shīʿites to win over Maḥmūd of Ghazna (r. 999–1030), who instead gave his support to the Karrāmī sect. These, though themselves accused of heresy, were the spearheads of an anti-Shīʿite Sunni revival. From the Ghaznavids, the mission was taken over by the Seljuks, who carried the Sunni revival westwards to Baghdad and beyond. Their capture of the city was regarded by the Sunnis as a liberation from the Shīʿite Būyids.

The purposes of the Sunni revival, conscious or unconscious, were, briefly, three: to overthrow the Shīʿite regimes and restore the caliphate; to reformulate and disseminate a Sunni answer to the Shīʿite challenge of ideas; and, most difficult of all, to integrate the religious institution into the political life of Islam.

The first of these was almost completely accomplished. In the east, the Būyids and other Shīʿite dynasties were overthrown and the political unity of Sunni Islam restored. After the suppression of the Fatimid caliphate in 1171, prayers were recited in the name of the Sunni caliph of Baghdad over all the lands of Islam from Central Asia into Africa. Even the militant Assassins, though not overcome, were contained in their mountain fastnesses, and their attempt to overthrow the Sunni order defeated. The military strength, political tenacity, and religious seriousness of the Turks which had made these things possible also gave the Islamic world the strength to meet and defeat the infidel, to conquer Anatolia for Islam and to repel the attack of Western Christendom.

The struggle against the Shīʿite heresy was carried through with conspicuous success. It began in Khurāsān, under the wing of the Sunni political resurgence. In the early eleventh century, Sunni divines and jurists began to organize orthodox colleges called *madrasa*, in imitation of the Ismaʿīlī mission schools in Cairo and elsewhere, in which the Fatimids had trained the religious propagandists of their cause. After the Seljuk conquest, Niẓām al-Mulk established a *madrasa* in Baghdad, and others soon appeared in cities all over the Empire. The *madrasa* system was extended by Saladin and his successors to Egypt. In these theological colleges, Sunni teachers formulated and disseminated a Sunni reply to the doctrines that had come first from the colleges and missions of Fatimid Egypt, and later, in a more radical form, from the secret emissaries of the Assassins.

The Sunni victory was almost complete. Shīʿism, of both kinds, had been discredited by the weakness and misgovernment of the late Būyids and Fatimids. On the level of dogmatic theology, the final and authoritative Sunni formulations of the Ashʿarī and Māturīdī schools ousted Shīʿi dogmatics among all but small minorities. On the level of popular piety, much of the emotional content of Shīʿism was transferred to Sufism, which, while expressing the intuitive and mystical religion of the masses as against the cold dogmatism of the orthodox state and hierarchy, nevertheless remained within the Sunni fold.

In the course of time, the religious institution not only recovered, but actually greatly improved on the position which it had held in the early Islamic state. A new Sunni bureaucracy, trained in the *madrasa*, replaced the scribal class of earlier times, and the men of religion, with their own recognized hierarchy and their own jealously guarded preserves, acquired for the first time an established and authorized position as one of the pillars of the social and political order. The ancient dichotomy of religious and political authority, of faith and power, of law and opportunism, was retained and indeed institutionalized, in the parallel sovereignties of caliph and sultan. But the religious establishment had made significant gains.

Turkish Islam was dedicated from the start to the defence or advancement of the faith and power of Islam, and never lost this militant quality. It was born on the eastern frontier against heathendom, was carried to the western frontier against Christendom, and took control of the caliphate at a time when Islam itself had to be defended against the threefold attack of the Eastern heathen, the Western Christian, and the internal heretic. This long, bitter and ultimately successful struggle could not fail to affect Islamic society and institutions in the age of Turkish dominance. Under Seljuk rule, a deep religious earnestness begins to affect the whole structure of government and administration. It is most obvious in the increased power and prestige and better organization of the Sunni hierarchy, and in the growing stress laid on religious education and personal piety even for government officials. The religious institution had codified its doctrines, increased its cohesion, extended its influence both with the people and the state. Its final integration into the structure of political authority was to follow under the Ottoman sultans.

Meanwhile a new external threat to Islam, more deadly than any yet, was in preparation. Far away in the north-eastern corner of Asia, the Mongol prince Temujin had, after a bitter struggle, united the warring nomadic tribes and made himself master of Mongolia, with the title of Jenghiz Khan. In the spring of 1206, Jenghiz summoned all the Mongol tribes to a great assembly by the sources of the Onon river. There he unfurled before them the white banner with the nine horsetails, and they reaffirmed their loyalty to him as their khan. The mighty Mongol empire had begun.

During the following years the remaining Mongol and pagan Turkish peoples, even the forest tribes of southern Siberia, were forced or terrified into submission, and Jenghiz Khan was ready to launch the steppe peoples on a vast career of conquest. By 1218, with northeast Asia at his feet, he was ready to turn his attention westward. Under the command of his general Jebe Noyon, Mongol troops invaded the country of the Kara-Khitay, and, by occupying all the lands up to the Jaxartes, became the neighbours of the Muslim Turkish Shah of Khwarezm. In the new year, at the border town of Utrar on the Jaxartes, by order of the Khwarezmian governor, a caravan from Mongolia was pillaged, and the merchants, some 450 in number, most or all of them Muslims, were put to the sword.

The vengeance of Jenghiz Khan was swift and overwhelming. In 1219 he led his armies across the Jaxartes into the lands of Islam – by 1220 the cities of Bukhara and Samarqand and all Transoxiania were in their hands. In the following year the Mongols were ready for the next step. Crossing the Oxus without difficulty, they swept on to the capture of Marv and Nishapur and the conquest of eastern Iran.

The death of Jenghiz Khan in 1227 brought a brief respite, but soon the new khan was ready to resume the attack. In 1230 a fresh offensive was launched against the broken remnants of the Khwarezmian state and army. By 1240 the Mongols had conquered western Iran, and invaded Georgia, Armenia, and northern Mesopotamia. In 1243 they met and overwhelmed the forces of the Seljuk sultan of Anatolia.

In the middle of the century, a new move westward was planned and executed. The Mongol prince, Hülägü, a grandson of Jenghiz, crossed the Oxus with orders from the Great Khan, now ruling from Peking, to conquer all the lands of Islam as far as Egypt. Within a few short months, the long-haired Mongol horsemen thundered across Iran, overcoming all resistance and crushing even the Assassins, who in their castles had withstood all previous attackers.

Finally, in January 1258, the Mongol armies converged on the city of Baghdad. The last caliph, al-Musta'sim, after a brief and futile attempt at resistance, pleaded in vain for terms or for mercy. The city was stormed, looted and burnt, and on 20 February 1258, the Commander of the Faithful, together with as many members of his family as could be found, was put to death. The House of 'Abbās, for almost exactly five centuries the titular heads of Sunni Islam, had ceased to reign.

The destruction of the great historic institution of the caliphate, even in its decay still the legal centre of Islam and symbol of its unity, was the end of an era in Islamic history, not only in the outward forms of government and sovereignty, but in Islamic civilization itself, which, after the transformation wrought by the last great wave of invasion from the steppe peoples, flowed in new channels, different from those of the preceding centuries. But the immediate moral effects of the destruction of the caliphate were probably not as great as has sometimes been suggested. The caliphate had long since ceased to exist as an effective institution, and the Mongols did little more than lay the ghost of something that was already dead. To the real organs of political and military power, the disappearance of the caliphate made very little difference. In all Islamic states, the sultanate had acquired the recognition of the jurists and of the religious institution, and sultans began to arrogate to themselves religious titles and prerogatives formerly reserved to the caliphs.

In another respect, too, the effects of the Mongol conquest have been exaggerated – in the extent and magnitude of the damage done by them. At one time, Mongol destruction was blamed for the decay of classical Islamic civilization and indeed for all the economic, social, cultural and political failings of the Middle East ever since. This view has been abandoned or substantially modified by most modern historians, as closer study of the past, and more direct experience of war and devastation in the present, have softened the judgements of a more innocent age. It is now agreed that the destructive effects of the Mongol conquests were neither as great, as lasting, nor even an extensive, as was once thought. The immediate blows of the Mongols, though no doubt trivial by modern standards, were certainly crushing, and whole areas were devastated, depopulated and destroyed. But Egypt, which by that time had become and has ever since remained the chief centre of Arabic culture, was never conquered by the Mongols, and was thus only indirectly affected. Syria suffered only raids, and after the decisive defeat of the Mongols by the Mamluk army of Egypt at the battle of 'Ayn Jālūt in 1260 it was incorporated into the Egyptian sultanate and protected from Mongol attack. Anatolia was long overshadowed and in many ways reshaped by the Mongol presence in Iran, but was still able to cradle the last and greatest of all Islamic empires. Iran, indeed, was hard hit – but even here, by no means the whole country was affected. In the south, the local dynasties submitted voluntarily to the Mongols, and their cities, not looted by the invaders, continued to flourish. Fars, the ancient Persis, once again became a focal centre of Persian national life, and the city of Shiraz, some thirty miles from the ancient seat of Persepolis, saw a rich flowering of Persian culture in the post-Mongol period. Outstanding figures of the time include the poets Sa'dī (1184–1291) and Ḥāfiẓ (c. 1320–1389), the astronomer Qutb al-Dīn (d. 1310), and the architect Qawām al-Dīn (d. 1439), the builder of the Gawhar Shād Mosque in Mashhad, which many regard as the greatest achievement of Iranian architecture.

Even in those parts of Iran which were actually overrun, recovery was rapid. After the initial shock of the conquest, the Mongol khans gave Iran a period of relative political stability, encouraged the reconstruction of town life, industry and trade, fostered what they considered useful sciences, and, after their conversion to Islam in 1295, even Islamic literature and learning. In the fourteenth century, Muslim khans were already raising magnificent buildings for Islamic worship. In one respect the Mongol conquests actually helped to infuse new life into the faltering civilization of the Middle East. Just as the first Arab conquerors, by uniting for the first time in one state the civilizations of the eastern Mediterranean and of Iran, inaugurated a new era of fruitful social and cultural contact, so now the Mongols united, for the first time under one dynasty, the civilizations of the Middle East and of the Far East, with immediate and beneficial effects both for trade and culture. At the same time they opened the door to new and mutually advantageous contacts with Europe, as many Europeans availed themselves of the opportunity offered by the presence of non-Muslim rulers in the Middle East to explore the overland routes to China. A good example of the fruits of these contacts between different civilizations is the *Jāmiʿ al-Tawārīkh* – the 'Assembly of Histories' – by the Persian historian, Rashīd al-Dīn (1247–1318). Rashīd al-Dīn was a Jewish convert to Islam, a physician, scholar and wazīr, who was entrusted by the khans Ghazan and Öljeitu with the task of compiling a universal history. He assembled a team of collaborators, including two Chinese scholars, a Buddhist hermit from Kashmir, a Mongol specialist in tribal tradition, and a Frankish monk, as well as some Persian scholars, and with their aid, he wrote a vast history of the world from England to China. Incidentally, in attempting a universal history going beyond their own civilization, Rashīd al-Dīn and his patrons anticipated Europe by half a millennium.

In one area the Mongol invasions did indeed cause permanent damage: Baghdad and Iraq never again recovered their central position in the Islamic world. The immediate effects of the invasion were the breakdown of civil government and the consequent collapse of the elaborate irrigation works on which the country depended for its prosperity, even for its life. Whereas in Iran order and prosperity were restored once the new regime was firmly in control, in Iraq ruin was unchecked. The Mongol rulers of Iran set up their capital in Azerbaijan, where Tabrīz, their residence, grew into a great and wealthy city. Iraq now became an outlying frontier province, abandoned to the destructive inroads of the Bedouin, who moved into the breaches made by the Mongols and, unlike them, did not pass on, but stayed. Henceforth, the valley of the Tigris and the Euphrates, cut off from the Mediterranean countries in the west by a frontier of sand and steel, outflanked in the east by the rise of the Persian centre to which it was subordinated, could no longer serve as a channel for East–West trade, which moved northwards and eastwards to Anatolia and Iran, westwards and southwards to Egypt and the Red Sea, leaving Iraq and the fallen city of the caliphs to centuries of stagnation and neglect.

In the period following the destruction of the caliphate, a division became clear in the Middle East between two great cultural zones. In the north was the zone of Persian civilization, with its centre in the plateau of Iran, extending westwards into Anatolia and beyond to the lands conquered in Europe by the Ottoman Turks, eastwards into Central Asia and the new Muslim Empires of India. In these countries, Arabic remained the language of religion and the religious sciences, law, tradition, theology, but Arabic literature was little known. Literary and artistic life was dominated by the traditions of Muslim Iran, which had begun during the 'Iranian Intermezzo', continued under the Turkish dynasties, and achieved a new renaissance under the Mongols and their successors. In Iran itself, Persian remained the spoken as well as the cultural language. To the east and west of Iran, in Central Asia and Anatolia, new languages and literatures appeared among the Turks, which were nourished and deeply influenced by the Persian classics.

South of the Iranian zone were the old Arabic-speaking centres of civilization, the derelict province of Iraq, and the new centre of Egypt with its extensions westwards and southwards into the continent of Africa. In these lands, despite some Persian influences in art and more especially in architecture, Persian language and literature were little known, and literary culture continued along the lines of the old Arabic humanities.

Politically, the Turk and the Mongol were everywhere dominant. Turkish or Mongol dynasties ruled all the countries from the Mediterranean to Central Asia and India, and even the Syro-Egyptian empire of the Mamluks was for long maintained and defended by a ruling class of imported Mamluks of Turkish stock, mainly from the Kipchak country north of the Black Sea. Later they were supplemented, even in some respects supplanted, by Circassians and others from the Caucasus.

In this age of growing cultural diversity and political conflict between the two zones, the chief unifying factor was religion, especially in the new Sufi form that had been spreading since the great compromise between mysticism and orthodoxy achieved by al-Ghazālī in Seljuk times. The Sunni revival of the eleventh century had gone far to revive and reunite Islam, but its task was not completed. The countryfolk and the nomads remained outside, and the latter were of great importance in an age when civil government was collapsing and whole peoples were on the move. The Turkish tribes in particular were deeply affected by Sufism. They had first been converted to Islam by wandering monks and mystics, mostly Turkish, whose faith had little in common with the complex dogmatism of the schools. The compromise of al-Ghazālī prepared the way for the interpenetration of mysticism and theology. The shock of heathen conquest and rule drove the theologians and the people into each others' arms. Henceforth, both Sufi and dogmatist professed the same orthodox Sunni religion, although with considerable variation of worship and belief, and not infrequent conflict.

Since the thirteenth century, the characteristic expression of religious life for the mass of the people has been the Sufi brotherhood. Sufism became the binding force of Islamic unity, the main expression of religious sentiment and loyalty. In time it became a source also of intellectual culture, and sometimes even of political power. The dynasties that ruled in Turkey and Iran, the two rival powers that competed for the mastery of the Islamic Middle East at the beginning of the modern age, were both deeply affected in their origins by Sufi ideals and organizations.

CHAPTER 6

THE MONGOL AFTERMATH

In the centuries following the Mongol conquests and the destruction of the caliphate, three major power centres emerged in the Muslim Middle East: Iran, Turkey, and Egypt. The first was ruled by a line of Mongol khans, at first pagan, later converted to Islam, but still retaining a Mongol identity and important elements of Mongol tradition. The second, ruled by Turkish, Muslim princes, for a while endured Mongol overlordship, and was profoundly marked by the culture of Mongol Iran. The third, ruled by Mamluk, mostly Turkish, sultans, successfully resisted Mongol invasion, but submitted in many ways to the influence of the current masters of the world. Two other Mongol khanates on the margins of the Middle East, in Russia and Central Asia, played some role in the politics of the Mongol world and, especially after their conversion to Islam, in the politics of the Middle East.

The main centre of power was at first Iran. After the conquest of Baghdad Hülägü withdrew into the northwest, whence for the next eighty years or so he and his line ruled over Iran and the surrounding countries. The Mongol khans of Iran were called Il-Khans – territorial rulers – in token of their subordination to the Great Khans in Mongolia, whose supremacy they recognised. On the whole, Iran was quietly and peacefully governed by the Il-Khans, who before their conversion gave equal tolerance and opportunity to men of all faiths. The main external activity of the Il-Khans was the attempt to extend their conquests westwards. In Anatolia, they humbled the Seljuk sultans and were content with an occupation zone and the vassalage of the Anatolian princes. The struggle against the Mamluk sultanate was more momentous. In 1259, Hülägü set forth from Tabriz on a new campaign. He advanced through Armenia and Upper Mesopotamia, and, turning southwards into Syria, took Aleppo and Damascus. But in September 1260, at a place called 'Ayn Jālūt, 'the spring of Goliath', in Palestine, a Mongol advance raiding party met and was utterly defeated by a Mamluk army from Egypt, commanded by a Kipchak Turk called Baybārs. The army of Egypt at once reoccupied all Syria.

Thereafter the Mongols made many further attempts to invade Syria, but were always thrown back by the Mamluks.

This period saw a series of interesting but inconclusive diplomatic missions between the Mongols and Christian Europe, the purpose of which was to plan a war on two fronts against the common Islamic enemy. They produced no result, however, and meanwhile Baybārs, now Sultan of Egypt, countered this projected alliance by forming his own alliance with Berke Khan, of the Mongol successor-state in Russia. Berke, who had made himself independent, had embraced Islam, and his realm, later known as the Khanate of the Golden Horde, was becoming a Muslim state with a predominantly (Kipchak) Turkish population.

The conflict between Iran and Egypt continued for some decades, even after the conversion of Ghazan Khan to Islam. A final peace was agreed in 1323. By this time, the kingdom of the Il-Khans was subjected to the same disruptive factors as its predecessors, and after the death of the Il-Khan Abū Sa'īd in 1336, Iran was again split into a number of small states ruled by local dynasties. They were of short duration. Timur, surnamed Lang (the Lame), in Europe known as Tamerlane, had made himself ruler of the Mongol fief of Central Asia. In 1380, already master of Transoxania and Khwarezm, he invaded Iran, and in the next seven years conquered the whole country. He twice defeated the khan of the Golden Horde, raided India, annexed Iraq from the local dynasty that ruled it, and then overran Syria and exacted homage from the Mamluk sultan. In 1394 and 1400, he invaded Anatolia and in 1402 inflicted a crushing defeat on the Ottomans at the battle of Ankara, capturing the Ottoman sultan Bayezid. He died in 1405 while preparing an invasion of China.

Timur Lang was born in a Turkicized, Islamized tribe of Mongol origin. Of modest social background, he married a princess of the house of Jenghiz Khan, a claim to greatness proudly inscribed on his tomb in Samarqand. He led mixed Mongol and Turkish armies, in which the former were the dominant element but the latter the great majority. Unlike the earlier Mongol rulers, Timur was, or claimed to be, a pious Muslim, and despite enormous destruction was careful to show due deference to the places and personnel of the Islamic faith. His conquests were, if anything, more destructive than those of Hülägü, and represented the last convulsion of the Altaic invasions. With his death, the great movement of the steppe peoples that had begun in the tenth century and had transformed the Middle East seems to have come to an end – though the infiltration of tribes continued, and, what is more important, the seepage of nomads already in the Middle East into the structure of urban life and civilization.

Timur was a great conqueror, but no empire-builder. After his death, his vast possessions fell apart. In Anatolia and Syria, the Ottomans and Mamluks resumed their sway. In western Iran, Mesopotamia and eastern Anatolia, two clans of Turkomans, known as the Black Sheep and the White Sheep, succeeded in establishing control. Only in eastern Iran and Transoxania did the line of Timur continue to rule. Their capitals, Bukhara, Samarqand, and especially Herat, were centres of a brilliant civilization. The age of the Timurids was one of great achievement in art, architecture, science, and in literature in both the Persian and eastern Turkish languages. For the latter, this is the great classical age, when works were written that had a lasting influence on the cultural development of all the Turkish peoples from Constantinople to the Far East and India.

In the Arabic-speaking countries, the centre of gravity had finally moved from Iraq to Egypt. The disorganization and weakness of Iraq and its remoteness from the Mediterranean, across which both the invaders and the traders of the following period were to come, ruled that country out as a possible base of Muslim power in the age of the Crusades. The alternative was Egypt: the other trade route, and the irrigated valley of a single river which, by its very nature, demanded a single centralized government. Egypt served as base for the wars of reconquest which in time ejected the Crusaders from the Near East; Egypt provided the resources for the Mamluks to repel the armies of the Il-Khans and save most of the Arab world from Mongol invasion.

By the middle of the thirteenth century, the Ayyubid dynasty, founded by Saladin, was losing control, and effective power was in the hands of the Turkish Mamluks. The final crisis of the Ayyubid sultanate in Egypt came in 1250, when the sultan died during the crusade of King Louis IX of France. In this crisis, the stability of the Muslim state and army was maintained by the presence of mind of the dead sultan's concubine, Shajar al-Durr (literally, Tree of Pearls), who kept his death a secret and issued orders in his name until his son Turan Shah arrived from Mesopotamia. Turan Shah was soon able to surrround, defeat and capture the Crusader army, and King Louis saved himself and some of his followers only by surrendering what he had captured and paying a large indemnity. The Mamluks, led by Baybārs, now turned on Turan Shah and murdered him. Still trying to maintain an appearance of

Ayyubid legitimacy, they proclaimed Shajar al-Durr as sultan. This gesture did not reconcile the Ayyubid princes of Syria to the overthrow of their dynasty in Egypt, and the new female 'sultan' was soon confronted by a coalition of princes demanding her removal. Even the caliph in Baghdad, though not directly involved in these matters, protested against the enthronement of a woman – a former inmate of his own harem, whom he had sent as a gift to the sultan of Egypt. The caliph lent his support to the Syrian Ayyubid princes, and ordered the Mamluks in Egypt to choose a sultan. According to an Egyptian chronicler, he wrote to them: 'If there is not a man left among you whom you can appoint, tell us and we shall send you one.'[1]

In 1260, after a period of confusion following the death of the last Ayyubid, the Mamluk general Baybārs, fresh from his victory over the Mongols, made himself sultan. Like Saladin, he united Muslim Egypt and Syria into a single state, this time more permanently. He defeated the external enemies of that state, both from east and west, and began the elaboration of a new social order. Saladin had symbolized the return of Egypt to Sunnism by formally recognizing the suzerainty of the 'Abbasid caliph in Baghdad. Baybārs brought the caliphate to Cairo, by welcoming an 'Abbasid refugee fleeing from the Mongol conquerors of Baghdad, and installing him as the first of what became a line of shadow caliphs. This shadow caliphate evoked only a limited response. The so-called Cairo caliphs were completely helpless and powerless, being in fact little more than minor Court pensioners with purely ceremonial duties to perform on the accession of a new sultan. Their caliphate ended in 1517, when Egypt was conquered by the Ottoman Turks who silently allowed it to pass into oblivion.

The Mamluk system of Baybārs and his successors was quasi-feudal, and was an adaptation of the Seljuk system brought into Syria and Egypt by the Ayyubids. It was also profoundly influenced by the Mongol example and by Mongol emigrants from the east who sought a career in Egypt. Even in this bastion of Islamic resistance, Mongol prestige stood high, and the Mamluks for a while imitated Mongol arms and tactics, even Mongol dress and manners.

A Mamluk officer received a grant of land for life or some shorter period. He did not normally reside on his estates, but in Cairo or in the chief town of the district where his fief lay. He was interested in revenue rather than possession. The system therefore developed no chateaux or manors or strong local authorities of the Western feudal type. There was no 'subinfeudation', and even the division of the land in Egypt into fiefs was not permanent, being subject to a periodic territorial refount.

The Mamluks themselves were bought slaves, trained and educated in Egypt. At first they were mainly Kipchak Turks from the northern shores of the Black Sea; later they included Mongol deserters and men of other races, chiefly Circassians, with occasional Greeks, Kurds and even some Europeans. But Turkish or Circassian remained the language of the dominant class, many of whom, including some sultans, could hardly speak Arabic. The Mamluk state as developed by Baybārs and his successors was based on a highly elaborate dual administration, civil and military, both sides controlled by Mamluk officers with civilian staffs. Until 1383 the Mamluk sultans followed one another in more or less hereditary succession. Thereafter, in the second or Circassian Mamluk sultanate, the throne was held by the strongest commander. On the death of a sultan, his son succeeded as formal head during an interregnum while the real succession was decided.

The trade with Europe, and particularly the trade between Europe and the further East via the Near East, was of vital importance to Egypt, both in itself and for the customs revenues derived from it. During periods of strength, Mamluk governments protected and encouraged this trade, which brought Egypt some prosperity. But the Mongol threat, warded off by Baybārs, was not yet averted. In 1400–1 the Turco-Mongol forces of Timur ravaged Syria and sacked Damascus. Plague, locusts and the depredations of the unleashed Bedouin completed the work of the departed Mongols, and the Mamluk sultanate suffered a blow to its economic and military strength from which it never fully recovered.

In the fifteenth century, economic and financial difficulties brought a new fiscal policy aimed at extracting the maximum possible amount of money from the transit trade. The method adopted was the monopolization of the chief local and transit products. The rising prices that resulted helped to provoke a European response, with far-reaching effects on the economic life of Egypt.

Under the rule of the Seljuk sultans of Konya, or Rūm, central and eastern Anatolia had been gradually transformed into an Islamic state, an integral part of the Islamic civilization of the Near and Middle East. The political independence of the frontiersmen and tribesmen who had conquered and colonized the country was curbed by the growth of the centralized Seljuk monarchy; their faith was subjected to the scrutiny and control of a hierarchy of theologians. Muslim bureaucrats and literati, jurists and divines, merchants and artisans moved into the newly colonized territories, bringing with them the old, high, urban civilization of classical Islam, impressing on the country the traditional patterns of Islamic life and polity.

The shock of the Mongol invasion shattered the Seljuk state beyond repair. After dragging out an attenuated existence for some half-century, it finally disappeared at the beginning of the fourteenth century. With the collapse of the central state authority and the irruption into Anatolia of new waves of Turkish nomadic migrants, fleeing before the Mongols, the war on the frontier was resumed. In religion the dervishes, in military and political life the warriors in the frontier marches, became the dominant elements in western Anatolia in the late thirteenth and fourteenth centuries. A new wave of expansion against Byzantium extended Turkish and Muslim rule to the whole of western Anatolia.

Among the principalities that shared the new conquests, one grew into a vast and mighty empire. It took its dynastic name from its eponymous founder Osman, whose career, according to tradition, spanned the first quarter of the fourteenth century. The name Ottoman, by which the dynasty and the empire they governed are commonly known, commemorates his achievement. Its position in the far west, on the borders of Byzantine Bithynia and on the edge of the defences of Constantinople, gave this principality greater tasks and greater opportunities, and thus attracted support from elsewhere. Osman and his successor carried on incessant border warfare against the Byzantines. In 1326 they took Brusa, which became the capital of their rapidly growing state. In 1354 Ottoman forces crossed the Dardanelles into Europe, and within a few years conquered Gallipoli and then Adrianople, which became and for almost a century remained their main base in Europe. A series of victories against the Serbs and Bulgars, notably at the battles of Maritza (1371) and Kosovo (1389), brought a large part of the Balkan peninsula under Ottoman rule, and reduced most of the rest to vassalage. This inaugurated further rapid victories in Macedonia, Bulgaria and Serbia. Each war of conquest in Europe was preceded by an expansion, twice by peaceful means, in Anatolia, which strengthened the home base of Ottoman power.

The Ottoman arrival on the European scene was not only military. No sooner had they established themselves than they were approached by the Genoese, at war with their commercial rivals the Venetians, with a request for military help and an offer of financial aid. 'The Genoese', says the contemporary Byzantine historian Kantakouzenos, '... promised vast sums of money and that this good deed should be inscribed forever in the hearts of the Senate and peoples of Genoa.'[2] With the conclusion, in 1352, of a first Ottoman–Genoese commercial treaty, one of the basic themes of European and Middle Eastern history was reaffirmed.

The fourth Ottoman sovereign, Bayezid I (1389–1401), succeeded to considerable possessions in both Europe and Asia. He was a man of far-reaching ambition, who sought to impose a new character on his realm. Turning his attention eastwards, he overcame the Turkish emirates one after another and incorporated all Anatolia under his rule. The Ottoman rulers used the title 'Sultan', in a general sense, almost from the beginning. Bayezid made it more specific, by asking the 'caliph' in Cairo for recognition as 'Sultan of Rūm'. This revival of the old title of the Seljuk sultans of Anatolia implied a claim to the old Islamic monarchy in Anatolia, perhaps even to the Islamic Empire in the Middle East. A crushing victory won at Nicopolis in 1396 over the chivalry of Western Europe, sent to liberate the Balkans, still further encouraged Bayezid in his ambitions. But he encountered – perhaps provoked – a greater conqueror than himself. After his defeat and capture by Timur at the decisive battle of Ankara in 1402, Bayezid committed suicide in captivity. The Ottoman possessions were reduced to those which he had inherited, and were moreover threatened by a ruinous civil war between his sons, followed by a dangerous revolt, probably social in origin, inspired and led by dervishes. It was not until 1413 that Mehmed I had overcome his brothers, and for some years more he and his successor had to face rebellions from various quarters.

Mehmed's reign was thus mainly concerned with restoring and consolidating the Ottoman state, but under his son, Murad II (1421–1444 and 1446–1451), great and significant changes took place. Territorial expansion was resumed and great victories won in Europe against the Greeks, Serbs, Hungarians and Crusaders. In Anatolia, too, most of Bayezid's former acquisitions were recovered. Thereafter, there was a period of peace and consolidation, during which the Ottoman sultans began to maintain a real Islamic court and to patronize poets, writers and Muslim scholars. Of particular interest is the appearance in the literature of this period of a Turkish national consciousness. Murad encouraged this and even composed poetry. During his reign the history and legends of the Oghuz were studied and incorporated in the historical tradition, and the story first appeared linking the Ottoman royal house with Turkish tribal tradition and legends and tracing its descent from Oghuz Khan. These new ideas of court and dynasty were sustained by the emergence of a core of trusted generals and counsellors, increasingly aware of and devoted to the principle of the Muslim dynastic state, and loyal to the Ottoman house.

They were immeasurably strengthened by the inauguration, towards the end of the fourteenth century, and more regularly from about 1430, of the *devshirme*, the levy of boys from among the Christian population for recruitment into the Ottoman army and state service. The system is well described by the sixteenth-century Ottoman historian Sadeddin (known as Hoca Efendi), cited here in the translation by the seventeenth-century English scholar William Seaman:[3]

The most renowned King . . . entering into consultation with his Ministers of State, the result hereof was, that for the time to come, there should be choice made, of valiant and industrious youths, out of the children of unbelievers, fit for the service, whom they should likewise innoblize, by the faith of Islam; which being a means to make them rich and religious, might be also a way to subdue the strongholds of the unbelievers. In prosecution hereof, there were severall persons deputed by the king, for this businesse; with order to collect in severall Countreys, about a thousand of the unbelievers children, whom they should discipline and train up in the way of Auxiliaries . . . they by this means being conversant with Religious people, and continuing in the service of Single worshippers: the light of Islam may penetrate their hearts, and they may be cleansed from the pollution of false worship: likewise their desires fixed upon that which is of worth, and their hopes placed upon degrees of advancement; they may perform with faithfulness, their duties, and services. Their wages were ordained to be at first, one Asper a day, and so to be augmented, according to their abilities, and merits: and they were commonly known by the name of Janissarie [that is, the new army]. Those valiant men in expeditions of warre, and fighting of battels have been so skilfull that by their assistance, the Most renowned Kings have gotten much fame. Likewise they having by their worthy services attained to Eminent advancements; others in contemplation hereof (with their hearts, and soules) were desirous, and did petition to have their children accepted: so that by this means, there were in a short time some thousands of unbelievers made glorious by the faith of Islam.

By this means, the energies of the Christian population and the spirit of the march warriors were both harnessed to the service of the

Ottoman dynasty, and a solution was found to the pressing problems of associating, in harmonious collaboration, the army, which was still dominated by the traditions of the border, and the state, which was evolving along orthodox Islamic patterns, as modified by the political and religious changes of the Seljuk and following periods.

In the Ottoman state the Islamic religious institution reached its maturity, and achieved its final integration into the Sunni polity. Islam was now represented by a real institutional structure – a graded hierarchy of professional and academically trained men of religion, with territorial jurisdictions and defined functions and powers, under the headship of a supreme religious authority recognized as the highest instance of the Holy Law. The Ottomans made what was perhaps the only really serious attempt, in a Muslim state of high material civilization, to establish the Holy Law of Islam as the effective law of the land. They gave to its scholars and its judges a status, authority, and power such as they had never known before.

In 1451, Murad was succeeded by his son Mehmed II. The new sultan inherited an empire that was still divided into two parts. Anatolia was by now old Islamic territory, absorbed into and reshaped by the civilization of Middle Eastern Islam. Rumelia – the European provinces – was newly conquered, still a frontier march, profoundly affected by the ideals and habits of the frontiersmen and the eclectic and mystical faith of the dervishes. Between the two – between the old and new capitals in Brusa and Adrianople – a new link was needed. On 29 May 1453, two years after the sultan's accession and seven weeks after the siege began, the janissaries made the final assault on the crumbling walls of Constantinople. The last Constantine was killed fighting among his troops; the crescent was raised above the dome of Hagia Sophia, and the sultan took up residence in the imperial city.

CHAPTER 7

THE GUNPOWDER EMPIRES

With the conquest of Constantinople, for so many centuries the coveted goal of Muslim arms, the last piece had fallen into place. Sultan Mehmed II, henceforth known as *Fatih*, the Conqueror, had sealed the union of the two continents, Asia and Africa, that formed his inheritance, and of the two traditions, Islam and the frontier, that had moulded them. The principality of the frontier fighters had become an empire; its chief, an emperor. This victory established the Ottoman sultanate as the spearhead of Islam pointing to the West, and brought it immense prestige within the Islamic world.

The remainder of Mehmed's reign was devoted to a series of military campaigns on both his European and Asian frontiers. In Europe, Ottoman armies subjugated the last Greek despotates in the Morea, made Serbia and Bosnia Ottoman provinces, and conquered several of the Greek islands. In Asia, they took Amasra from the Genoese, Sinope from its Muslim amir, and Trebizond from its Greek emperor. Significantly, the sultan refused to be drawn further east or to fight against Muslim sovereigns. When challenged by Uzun Ḥasan, a Turkoman ruler in eastern Anatolia and Mesopotamia, he defeated him in battle in 1473, but made no attempt to follow up his victory. In a conversation quoted by the sixteenth-century historian Kemalpashazade, the sultan explains his reasons. It was proper to punish Uzun Ḥasan for his temerity; it would have been wrong to destroy his line, for 'to seek the destruction of ancient dynasties of the great sultans of the people of Islam is not good practice'.[1] More to the point, it would have distracted the sultan from the serious business of the *jihād* in Europe.

The Ottoman sultans could not, however, afford to neglect the Muslim lands beyond their southern and eastern borders, where important changes were taking place. One of these was the manifest decline of the Mamluk sultanate which had ruled Egypt and Syria since the mid-thirteenth century. In a sense, the Egyptian sultanate had, in its last years, become a kind of Arab Byzantium. In the north and in the east, on the plateaux of Anatolia and Iran, among the Turks and the Persians who had taken over the political and cultural leadership of Islam, new states and societies were appearing, and a new civilization was developing, expressed mainly in the Persian and Turkish languages. In Egypt and Syria, despite great and mounting influences from the east, the old order survived. The earlier Islamic culture in its Arabic form entered on its long silver age. Mamluk soldiers defended the realm and saved the Nile Valley from invasion. Egyptian and Syrian scribes and scholars, many of them sons and descendants of the Mamluks, maintained and operated the state, and at the same time preserved, interpreted, and by so doing, enriched the heritage of classical Islam.

The Syro-Egyptian sultanate had already been weakened by a complex of causes both internal and external – the devastating war against Timur, the drying-up of resources through financial malpractice and economic dislocation, the impact of plague, drought, and famine, and the breakdown of the Mamluk order and society.

The final blows came from outside, from the west and from the north. The first was economic, caused by the coming of the Portuguese to eastern waters. By opening direct sea lanes between Europe and India, the Portuguese outflanked Egyptian commerce. The long-term effects of all this were not as great as was at one time believed, and the sixteenth century saw a considerable revival of the trade through the Levant. The immediate effects, however, were serious, and presented the Mamluk sultan Qansawh al-Ghawri (1500–1516) with a crisis of declining trade and falling revenue. Encouraged by Venice, he sent an Egyptian fleet to India. After some initial successes, they were defeated by the Portuguese, who then began a systematic destruction of Muslim merchant shipping in the Indian ocean. Some Portuguese vessels even ventured into the Persian Gulf and the Red Sea.

The second – the death blow – was military. Relations between the Mamluk and Ottoman sultanates had for some time been reasonably friendly. They deteriorated during the second half of the fifteenth century. Between 1485 and 1490 the two states fought an inconclusive war in which the Mamluks on the whole fared rather better than the Ottomans.

But the military balance was changing rapidly, to the Ottoman advantage. A crucial new factor was firearms – handguns and cannon – which the Ottomans adopted readily, extensively and with great effect. The Mamluks, in contrast, were very reluctant to adopt these new weapons. Unlike the Ottoman lands, Mamluk domains were poor in metals, which had to be imported. But more serious than any practical difficulty was the social and psychological attitude of the Mamluk amirs, who clung to the 'lawful' and 'honourable' weapons of the past and despised firearms and those who used them as unworthy and unchivalrous. In their last years, the Mamluks made some desultory efforts to introduce firearms. They were assigned to specially raised units consisting of black slaves, of the native-born sons of the Mamluks, and even of a kind of militia including locally recruited artisans and miscellaneous foreign mercenaries. They had little effect, and the mounted lancers, swordsmen, and bowmen who were the flower of the Mamluk army were hopelessly outclassed by the musket-armed infantry and the artillery of the Ottomans.

But before launching the final attack on the Mamluks, the Ottomans had to face another and far more dangerous Muslim enemy. Half a century after the conquest of Constantinople, the Ottoman position was challenged not by a Christian but by a Muslim rival, the new Safavid dynasty of the shahs of Iran. They were brought to power by a radical Shī'ite movement, and, for the first time in centuries, created a united and powerful state embracing the whole area between the Mediterranean lands and the approaches to Central Asia and India. The establishment of a new, militant power in Iran, inspired by radical Shī'ite doctrines and based in the northwestern area near the Ottoman borders, was seen in Turkey as both a threat and a challenge, and gave a religious character to this renewal of the age-old rivalry between the rulers of the Anatolian and the Iranian plateaux. There were still millions of Sunni Muslims in Iran, perhaps a majority. There were still at least hundreds of thousands of Shī'ites in the Ottoman lands who might be suspected of sympathizing with the new Shī'ite regime to the east. Both the Ottoman sultan and the Safavid shah were for one another heretics and usurpers beyond the pale of toleration. The Safavid threat to the Ottomans was rendered at once more acute and more intimate by the Turkish origin of the Safavid family and their extensive support in Turkish Anatolia.

The Ottoman reaction to the perceived threat began early. In 1502 Sultan Bayezid ordered the deportation of Shī'ites from Anatolia to Greece, and mobilized his forces along the Iranian frontier. In 1511 the Ottomans faced a dangerous Shī'ite revolt in central Anatolia. In the following year, the ageing sultan abdicated in favour of his son Selim I (1512–1520), known as 'Yavuz Selim' (Selim the Grim). It did not take long before the rivalry and hostility between Sultan Selim of Turkey and Shah Ismā'īl of Iran broke out into open warfare. It is ironic that in the increasingly angry correspondence between the two monarchs that preceded the outbreak of hostilities, the sultan wrote to the shah in Persian, the language of urbane, cultivated gentlemen, while the shah wrote to the sultan in Turkish, the language of his rural and tribal origins.

The war ended with a decisive but not conclusive Ottoman victory. On 23 August 1514, on the plain of Chaldiran, near the border between the two empires, the Ottoman janissaries and artillery inflicted a crushing defeat on the Iranian forces, and on 7 September the sultan occupied the Iranian capital, Tabriz. Like his predecessor Mehmed II, Sultan Selim did not pursue his victory eastwards, but withdrew to Turkey, leaving the shah defeated and weakened, but still ruler of a Shī'ite state in Iran. A long and bitter struggle between the two empires followed, in which the bloody repression of the Shī'ites in Turkey and of the Sunnis in Iran watered their mutual hate and fear with the blood of martyrs.

The resulting struggle was for both the leadership of Islam and the control of the Middle East. It was waged not only on the battlefield but also in a war of propaganda between the Sunni and Shī'ite faiths of which the Ottoman sultan and the Safavid shah were respectively the champions. The struggle ended with a limited victory for the Ottomans, who were able to contain but not to destroy the empire of Iran. This success opened the way for the next stage – the absorption into the Ottoman realms of the Arabic-speaking countries to the south. In a short, sharp war in 1516–17, the Ottomans overthrew the tottering Mamluk sultanate which had dominated Egypt, Syria, and western Arabia for two and a half centuries and brought these lands under their rule. From these newly acquired possessions Ottoman sovereignty or suzerainty was extended in several directions – westwards across North Africa as far as the border of Morocco, southwards down both shores of the Red Sea in Africa and Arabia, and eastwards into the waters of the Indian Ocean and, later in the sixteenth century, to Iraq, which the Ottomans after a protracted struggle were able to take from its Iranian rulers and thus bring Ottoman arms to the Persian Gulf. The Ottoman sultans now ruled over the two holy cities of Mecca and Medina and the Arab heartlands of Islam. The one added greatly to their prestige; the other, to their responsibilities.

With the Persians tamed and the Mamluks conquered, the Ottomans were now prepared to resume their major task, the war in Europe. By the reign of Süleyman the Magnificent (1520–1566), the empire was at the peak of its power. In 1526, at the decisive battle of Mohacs, the Ottomans shattered the army of the kingdom of Hungary. Kemal-pashazade celebrated the Ottoman victory in quasi-epic rhymed prose:[2]

> With flashing swords like burning flames they charged the doomed but stout-hearted infidels, in glorious squadrons resembling tulip-strewn mountains. In a festival of battle, they were at once dyed red like goblets of wine, their heads like the flower of the Judas tree, their eyes like shining cornelian, their hands like coral.... [the battle continued] until the rim of the heavenly hippodrome was tarnished by the bloodstains of sunset.... the evil-doing [Hungarian] king ... advanced into the battlefield, amid a cloud of dust that shrouded both east and west ... undaunted by the fire of guns and muskets, with a stout heart impervious to fear, he led a charge of his headlong cavalry, charging at one bound against the janissaries, the bravest of brave soldiers ... he reached the batteries, where the musketeers greeted him with a deadly hail of fire that withered the flowers in the garden of the evildoing enemy's unavailing existence....

After a long and desperate struggle, the king is finally defeated:

> At the Sultan's command, the janissary musketeers fired volleys against the enemy ... and in an instant sent hundreds, or rather thousands, of them straight to Hell ... the scroll of [the king's] time was folded, the circuit of his days of command was concluded, the record of his transient life was sealed with the loss both of this world and of the next.

After this victory, Süleyman's armies advanced across Hungary, and in 1529 for the first time laid siege to Vienna. In the east, Ottoman fleets challenged the Portuguese in the Indian Ocean. In the west, control of North Africa brought Muslim naval power to the western Mediterranean and even, on raids, to the Atlantic Ocean and the coasts of Western Europe. Once again, the advance of Islam offered a mortal threat to Christendom. The Crusade was finished; the *jihād* had begun again. Richard Knolles, the Elizabethan historian of the Turks, was expressing the common feeling of Europe when he spoke of the Turkish empire as 'the present Terror of the World'.

The sixteenth century saw the high-water mark of the Turkish tide, and the beginnings of its ebb. In Central Europe, the first unsuccessful attempt to take Vienna inaugurated a century and a half of bloody and inconclusive struggle, which ended with the second failed siege of Vienna in 1683. This time the Turkish defeat was total and final. In the east the Ottomans, from bases in Egypt and a little later in Iraq, asserted their naval power in both the Persian Gulf and the Red Sea, and for a while established Ottoman governors in Yemen and in the horn of Africa. At one point they even sent a contingent of Ottoman artillerymen to Southeast Asia to help local Muslim rulers against their European Christian enemies. But it was to no avail. Even the Ottoman fleets were no match for the Portuguese and other Western warships, and despite local help from Muslim rulers the Ottomans were compelled to abandon South and Southeast Asia to the rising maritime powers of Western Europe.

In the Mediterranean, the Ottomans suffered their first major defeat in the naval battle of Lepanto in 1571. Lûtfi Pasha records that as grand vizier he had raised the question of naval power with Sultan Süleyman the Magnificent, and had told him: 'Under the previous sultans there were many who ruled the land, but few who ruled the sea. In the conduct of war at sea the infidels are superior to us. We must overcome them.'[3] The Turks did not overcome them, but it was some time before the consequences were clear. The Battle of Lepanto was celebrated all over Christian Europe as a great victory. It was, however, far less important than the defeat and destruction of the Ottoman fleets in Asian waters. Before long, the Ottomans were able to restore their naval power in the Mediterranean and to protect their European conquests from attack. A Turkish chronicler records a conversation between the grand vizier Sokollu Mehmed Pasha and the Sultan Selim II (1566–1574) about the building of a new fleet to replace the ships destroyed at Lepanto. The sultan asked about the cost, and the grand vizier replied: 'The might of our Empire is such that if it were desired to equip the entire fleet with silver anchors, silken rigging, and satin sail, we could do it.'[4]

The fleet was indeed rebuilt, albeit with less luxurious equipment, and Muslim naval power from Near Eastern and North African bases continued to dominate the Mediterranean, and to venture into the Atlantic, well into the seventeenth century. Though the real power of the Islamic world in relation to Christian Europe had already declined in significant respects, that decline was still hidden from the sight of Christians and Muslims alike by the imposing panoply of Ottoman military might.

In the mid-sixteenth century Busbecq, ambassador of the Holy Roman Empire at the court of Süleyman the Magnificent, expressed deep misgivings about the survival of Christian Europe under the threat of overwhelming Ottoman power, and noted:[5]

> Persia alone interposes in our favour, for the enemy, as he hastens to attack, must keep an eye on this menace in his rear ... Persia is only delaying our fate; it cannot save us. When the Turks have settled with Persia they will fly at our throats, supported by the might of the whole East; how unprepared we are I dare not say.

The Ottomans did not, however, 'settle with Persia'. They continued to struggle with their eastern neighbour and rival until the early nineteenth century, by which time neither Turkey nor Persia was in any position to threaten the West.

The rulers of Iran, like the Mamluk sultans of Egypt, viewed firearms with distaste, and at first made little attempt to adopt them in their armed forces. Like the Mamluks, they were taught the error of their ways on the battlefield by the Ottoman musketeers and gunners. Unlike the Mamluks, they lived to fight another day, and to apply the lessons that they had learned. In the course of the sixteenth century, but still more in the seventeenth, the shahs of Iran took steps to acquire handguns and artillery pieces and to re-equip their forces with them. As in both earlier and later times, the kings of Islam were always able to find Christian European manufacturers, merchants and experts to supply, equip and train their forces and even some European soldiers of fortune to lend or sell their services. Their principal sources of supply appear to have been Venice, Portugal, and England.

Despite their initial reluctance, the Persians very rapidly acquired the art of making and using handguns. A Venetian envoy, Vincenzo di Alessandri, in a report presented to the Council of Ten on 24 September 1572, observes:[6]

> They used for arms, swords, lances, arquebuses, which all the soldiers can use; their arms are also superior and better tempered than those of any other nation. The barrels of the arquebuses are generally six spans long, and carry a ball a little less than three ounces in weight. They use them with such facility that it does not hinder them drawing their bows nor handling their swords, keeping the latter hung at their saddle bows till occasion requires them. The arquebus is then put away behind the back so that the one weapon does not impede the use of the other.

This picture of the Persian horseman, equipped for the almost simultaneous use of bow, sword and firearm, aptly symbolized the complexity of the changes that were taking place. In the course of the sixteenth and the seventeenth centuries, the rulers of Persia, however reluctantly, made increasing use of handguns, and equipped significant numbers of their troops with these weapons. Like the Ottomans, though to nothing like the same extent, they also deployed siege artillery. Their use of field artillery, however, was limited and on the whole ineffective.

The most remarkable among the successors of Shah Ismā'īl was Shah 'Abbās (1587–1629). His first major task was to build a new infantry and artillery, after the Ottoman model. In this he was much helped by two English brothers, Anthony and Robert Shirley, who went to Iran in 1598 with twenty-six followers and remained in the Persian service for a number of years. 'Abbās's first task was to halt the Uzbeks of Central Asia, who had invaded and conquered a number of towns in the eastern provinces of Iran. To free himself for this purpose, he made peace with the Ottomans, abandoning Georgia and Azerbaijan, including the former Safavid capital of Tabrīz. After a successful campaign against the Uzbeks and the recovery of the lost provinces in the east, he turned his attention again to the west. In 1603 his armies recaptured Tabrīz, and went on to win further victories and capture new territory, including much of Iraq which had previously been lost to the Ottomans. Another major event of his reign was the appearance, in 1616, of the English East India Company, operating out of Surat in India. The Portuguese, who until then had had a virtual monopoly of Western trade in Iran, tried unsuccessfully to stop the English intrusion, and in 1622 the English merchants helped a Persian army to recapture the Persian Gulf port of Hormuz which the Portuguese had held since 1514. This achievement of the Persian army was celebrated in an epic poem composed for the occasion.

The reign of Shah 'Abbās, sometimes known as 'the Great', was in many ways the peak of the Safavid period. The commercial rivalries of the Western powers – Portuguese, Dutch, and English – in the Persian Gulf and the Indian Ocean offered advantages which the shah was quick to see and exploit. In 1597 Shah 'Abbās transferred the capital again. It had previously been transferred from Tabrīz to Qazvīn, and he now moved it to the more centrally located city of Isfahān, from which he could supervise operations against both his eastern and western enemies, the Uzbeks and the Ottomans. The many buildings erected or rebuilt in Isfahān during his reign give the city a lasting beauty, and give colour to the proud claim of its inhabitants, '*Isfahān nisf-i jehān*' ('Isfahān is half the world').

After his death, the Safavid dynasty declined rapidly to its fall. The Ottomans recovered Baghdad and other territories recaptured by Shah 'Abbās; the eastern neighbours of Iran, Afghans as well as Uzbeks, resumed their depredations; perhaps most portentous for the future, the first Russian mission arrived in Isfahān in 1664, while the Cossacks began to raid the Caucasian frontiers.

In the meantime, changes of far-reaching importance had been taking place in the north. In 1480 the tsar Ivan the Great of Moscow was finally able to throw off what Russian historians call 'the Tatar yoke' and to end all tribute and dependence. Like the Spaniards and Portuguese in the West, but with far greater success, the Russians, having ended the Muslim domination of their country, set out to pursue their former masters into their own lands. In 1552, after a long and hard struggle, they captured the Volga Tatar capital at Kazan, which became and remained part of the Russian realm. From there they advanced down the Volga, and in 1556 seized the Caspian port of Astrakhan. The Russians now controlled the entire course of the Volga river and had gained a foothold on the Caspian Sea. They had overwhelmed most of their Muslim enemies on their way southwards, and were encroaching on Ottoman and Crimean Tatar territory. The Ottomans were aware of this danger, but their attempts to counter it were unavailing. An expedition to recapture Astrakhan, and a plan to dig a canal between the Don and Volga rivers and move Ottoman fleets from the Black Sea to the Caspian, came to nothing. For a while, the Tatar khans of the Crimea were able to ward off Russian encroachments and maintain their allegiance to the Ottoman sultans as suzerains. For the time being, the Black Sea remained under Turkish and Tatar control, and an important trade was carried on between the Crimea and Istanbul, notably in foodstuffs and in East European slaves.

But the Russian advance continued. In the course of the seventeenth century, Astrakhan served as a base for further Russian expansion at the expense of the independent Muslim states of northern Caucasia. In due course it became the administrative centre of a Russian imperial province dominating the whole area between the mouths of the Don and Volga rivers. In 1637 the Don Cossacks, acting independently, seized the Turkish naval fortress of Azov, near the Black Sea. They held it for several years against Turkish naval and military attack and then offered it to the Russian tsar, who after careful consideration decided to refuse this gift rather than risk a full-scale war with the

Ottoman Empire. The Russian road to the Black Sea was not yet open, but it was clearly marked.

As early as 1606, the Treaty of Sitvatorok between the Holy Roman Emperor and the Ottoman sultan marked another significant change. This treaty was negotiated and signed on an island in the river that formed the frontier between the Habsburg and Ottoman empires. This was no longer, as in the past, a truce dictated by the victors in their own capital, but a treaty negotiated between equals on the frontier. The change is symbolized by the first use, in the Turkish text of the treaty, of the sultan's own title, *Padishah*, for the Habsburg monarch, hitherto contemptuously described in Turkish documents as 'the king of Vienna'. During the early stages of the Ottoman advance into Europe, there were no treaties in the proper sense, and very little negotiation. The state of war between the advancing power of Islam and its infidel enemies, conceived as a perpetual religious duty, was from time to time interrupted by truces, which the victorious Ottomans dictated in Istanbul to their defeated foes. The Treaty of Sitvatorok thus marked a significant change in concept and procedure, reflecting a change in the realities on the ground.

The seventeenth century began with a grudging concession of equality; it ended with an unequivocal admission of defeat. The change in the political and military balance of power between the Muslim and Christian worlds was slow and gradual, and it was some time before its lessons were seen, understood, and applied. The economic disparity was even less immediately apparent; but it was more profound and, in its effects, more decisive. After the oceanic voyages of discovery, the main centres of European commerce and, ultimately, power, shifted from the Mediterranean to the Atlantic, and from central and southern Europe to the maritime states of the West.

In their dealings with the Islamic states in the Middle East and elsewhere, the Westerners enjoyed considerable advantages. Their ships, built to ride the Atlantic gales, were bigger and heavier than those of the Muslim powers of the Mediterranean and the Indian Ocean. Designed by shipbuilders and operated by navigators trained to face the challenge of the Atlantic, they were more manoeuvrable than the Muslim fleets. They had a double advantage: in war they could carry more guns; in peace they could carry larger cargoes and travel greater distances at lower costs. As the maritime powers of Western Europe began to colonize the tropical and subtropical territories in Central America and in South and Southeast Asia, they were able to raise a wide variety of crops previously unknown or unavailable in Europe. With these, and with their own internal economic development, fuelled by the inflow of American bullion, and new possibilities of credit far beyond anything in Middle Eastern experience, they could now offer a wide range of commodities in Middle Eastern markets.

No less important than the changes in the terms of trade was the increasing difference in economic culture. During the sixteenth century and after, producer-directed economies and mercantilist policies enabled European trading companies and the governments that protected and encouraged them to concentrate their economic energies and expand their commercial activities in a manner and to a degree not previously known in the consumer-oriented societies of the Ottoman Empire and other Islamic states. The range and scope of their commercial activities were enormously increased when West Europeans established themselves in India and Indonesia, not just as merchants but as rulers, and through the exercise of naval power were able to control the trade in spices and other vital commodities between Asia and Europe from both ends.

But the change in the balance of economic power between the two worlds cannot be attributed entirely to the rise of the West. Some part at least of the causes of the relative decline in Muslim power must be sought in internal changes.

In the first half of the sixteenth century, the classical Ottoman system was at the height of its glory, and it is small wonder that contemporary European observers saw in it the very model and exemplar of an efficient, centralized absolutism. If some of them, loyal to the entrenched privileges of the old European order, saw in the sultanate a terrible example of arbitrary and capricious power, there were others who looked forward to the new European age of enlightened royal despotism in the nation state and saw in Turkey a paradigm of disciplined, modern monarchy.

By an irony of history, at the very time when Machiavelli and other European political thinkers were contrasting the weakness of the French king with the might of the Turkish sultan, processes were beginning in both countries which in time would reverse the roles of the two monarchs. In France, the magnates would become courtiers, the autonomous regions administrative districts, and the king would grow in power and authority over all his subjects and all his realm until he could indeed say 'L'état c'est moi.' In the Islamic empires, the same Arabic word 'sulṭān' had denoted both the state and the sovereign; but there the courtiers became magnates, the provinces principalities, the slaves of the imperial household its masters, and the 'lord of the world' the puppet of his army, his office, and his household.

When Süleyman the Magnificent was invested with the sword of Osman in 1520, he became master of a perfect machine of absolutist government, ruling over an empire that stretched from Hungary to the borders of Persia, from the Black Sea to the Indian Ocean. True, he was subject to the unalterable provisions of the Holy Law, but the Holy Law itself conceded him almost absolute power, and its authorized exponents were the firm prop of his authority among the people. The government and the army – the men who ruled and the men who fought – were his personal slaves; privileged and immune as against the mass of the people, but totally without rights as against the will of their sovereign. The regular replacement of the old cadres by new intakes of slaves of humble origin forestalled the growth of a hereditary aristocracy at the centres of power – while at the same time the feudal gentry, bound to the sultan by revocable, functional fiefs, were nevertheless secure enough in their holdings to ensure the prosperity of agriculture and the well-being of the countryside.

To the Ottoman Empire, the great challenge of the sixteenth century, which forced Europe to enter upon new paths of economic and political development, presented no difficulty and therefore no stimulus; alone among the states of Europe, Turkey already possessed the territory, the manpower, the resources, the centralized control to organize and finance the new apparatus of war. While the peoples of Europe entered upon an age of feverish endeavour and advance, the Turks could relax, remain stationary – and eventually fall back.

The Ottoman historians date the decline of the Empire from the death of Süleyman the Magnificent, and it is indeed in the second half of the sixteenth century that the first signs of breakdown in the Ottoman institutional structure begin to appear. They are discussed in a remarkable series of memorials, written by Ottoman statesmen and officials, and extending from the late sixteenth century to the last days of the Ottoman Empire.

One of these signs, to which the memorialists frequently allude, was the decay of the sipahi class – the feudal gentry who had been the backbone of the Ottoman state in its early days and remained an important element for long after. There were several factors that contributed to their decline. One was the sultan's preference for professional 'slave' troops over feudal levies, as being at once more efficient and less independent. Another was the technological advance in warfare, which required the formation of more and more specialized long-service regiments, of gunners and bombardiers and sappers and miners, and reduced – though it did not end – the importance of the feudal cavalry.

The Ottoman timar, or military fief, was revocable, transferable, and conditional upon military service. Though it was usual in practice to confirm the heir of a sipahi in the possession of his father's fief, this was not a right and depended on his ability to perform military service. Sipahis could be, and frequently were, transferred from one fief to another, or from one province to another. Towards the end of the sixteenth century, it became increasingly common to terminate fiefs on the death or transfer of the holder, and incorporate the land into the sultan's domain. The land registers from the sixteenth century onwards show a steady decrease in fief land, and a corresponding increase in domain. This was especially marked in Asia, rather less so in Europe.

As the feudal cavalry decayed, the standing army increased rapidly, and so too did the cost of maintaining it. This was no doubt one of the main reasons for the seizure of vacant fiefs. To secure a quick and easy cash return, the sultan did not administer the revenue of these lands directly, but farmed them out on various kinds of leases and concessions. These were all of a monetary and not a military nature. Some were tax-farms, others were usufructuary assignments. At first they were for a brief term; later the practice spread of granting the tax-farmer a life interest which, by abuse, became heritable and alienable. The system spread rapidly all over the Empire. Not only crown lands were affected. Many fiefs were granted, as apanages, to dignitaries or favourites at court, who exploited them in the same way, and eventually many even of the sipahis farmed out the revenues of their timars.

The economic and social power derived from the permanent local control of tax-farms and leases produced a new propertied, influential class in the provinces, which soon began to play a prominent part in local affairs. This class interposed itself between the government and the peasantry, and intercepted much of the revenue. In theory, they only held possession as lessees or tax-farmers, but as the government, through growing weakness, lost control of the provinces, these new landowners were able to increase both the extent of their holdings and the security of their tenure. In the seventeenth century, they even began to usurp some of the functions of the government.

The name by which they are known in Ottoman history is '*a'yān*,' usually translated 'notables'. The term '*a'yān*' had been in use since early times in the general sense of provincial or local notables, usually merchants. It now came to denote a definite social group or class of old and new landlords, exercising important political functions. At first these were resisted as a usurpation, but amid the financial and administrative strains of the eighteenth century, the central government found it expedient to delegate more and more of the conduct of provincial affairs, including even the running of provincial towns, to the *a'yān*, who begin to resemble a freeholding landed gentry.

While these developments were taking place in the position of the feudal cavalry and in the countryside of which they had been the mainstay, the slave establishment too was undergoing radical changes. These are usually dated from the second half of the sixteenth century, when the first clear indication appears of a change in the policy of recruitment. The corps of janissaries was a closed and privileged corporation, enjoying great power and bound together by a strong *esprit de corps*. At first they were recruited exclusively from Christian captives and slaves, mainly by the *devshirme*. Joining the mystical fraternity of the Bektashiyya, with which the janissary corps had been associated since its foundation, these recruits became a dedicated, celibate soldiery, with no home other than their barracks, no families other than their comrades. Janissary officers were allowed to marry, and so too were elderly soldiers in retirement or on garrison duty. In the words of the *Kavānīn-i-Yenicheriyān* – the regulations of the janissary corps:[7]

> From time immemorial it has been unlawful for janissaries to marry; only officers married and also private soldiers who were old and definitely unfit for service and then only on application to the Sultan. The state of a janissary is a state of celibacy, and for that reason barracks were built for them.

The decline of the corps may be dated from the time when it began to recruit by inheritance and by purchase. At first these new methods supplemented the *devshirme*; eventually they supplanted it entirely. The first breach was a consequence of the increasing practice of marriage by janissaries. Already common under Süleyman the Magnificent, it was recognized as a right by Selim II on his accession, and thereafter a substantial proportion of the janissaries, private soldiers as well as officers, were married men living with their families.

Marriage also meant children, and it was natural that fathers who belonged to privileged groups should try to obtain the same privileges for their sons. In 1568 Selim II, after repeated demands, agreed to allow the janissaries to enter their sons on the army payrolls as cadets. As boys they received rations and a small allowance, and were in due course enrolled as full members of the corps. These new janissaries – the 'sons of slaves', as they were called, to distinguish them from the real 'slaves' – were neither as carefully selected nor as rigorously trained as the products of the *devshirme*. By 1592 they constituted the majority of the corps.

Once a breach had been made in the rigid system of slave recruitment, it collapsed altogether. During the war with Iran towards the end of the sixteenth century, the corps was in effect thrown open to all and sundry, irrespective of origin or status, who could buy their way on to the payrolls. 'In the reign of the late Sultan Murad Khan [1574–1595]', says the historian Selaniki Mustafa,[8]

> ... a vile rabble of contemptible interlopers entered the respected household and, through bribery, the regiments of janissaries, armourers and gunners were opened to peasants, to farmers who have abandoned their farms, to Tat, Chepni, Gypsies, Jews, Laz, Russians, and townspeople ... When these joined the ranks, tradition and respect disappeared entirely; the curtain of reverence of government was riven, and in this way men with neither aptitude nor experience of affairs came and sat in the seats of power. ...

The complaint became a common one, and is repeated by the memorialist Koçu Bey, who laments that in his day (the early seventeenth century) all kinds of riff-raff were joining the janissary corps – 'men whose religion and faith were unknown, townsmen, Turkomans, Gypsies, Tats, Kurds, foreigners, Laz, nomads, muleteers, camel-drivers, porters, syrup-makers, highwaymen and pickpockets and other kinds of rabble, so that order and discipline have been ruined, and law and tradition have gone. . .'[9]

Koçu Bey, himself recruited by the *devshirme* from Goritsa in Macedonia, was deeply distressed at this degradation of the corps, and reminded the sultan that he had no need to fill his armies with such riff-raff: 'In Bosnia and Albania there are still men ... with brave and stout-hearted sons. . .'

But it was too late. The hasty and haphazard recruitment, brought about by the military and financial stresses of the late sixteenth century, initiated a process of rapid change which, within a very short time, transformed the entire nature of the corps of janissaries. With the abandonment of the *devshirme* and the admission of free-born Muslims, the corps became a hereditary corporation with extensive and jealously guarded privileges, both individual and collective. Accession was primarily by inheritance, but also by purchase, and there were not a few merchants and craftsmen who bought, for themselves and their descendants, a place on the janissary payrolls. Still nominally the slaves of the sultan, the janissaries were often his masters; still nominally soldiers, they degenerated into a kind of armed rabble, ready enough to fight in the streets in the interests of their corporative privileges or in response to religious or palace instigation, but of little use against a disciplined enemy in the field.

The abandonment of the *devshirme* also had an immediate and extensive effect on the palace school of pages, from which the imperial household and the high officers of state were recruited. To some extent the dwindling supply of captives and renegades from Europe could be made good by importing slaves from the Caucasus. Caucasian women had always been appreciated in the harems of the Middle East, and Caucasian men-slaves had also played a role of some importance, notably in the later phase of the Mamluk sultanate of Egypt. In the Ottoman Empire, however, their role had been a minor one, and they had been overshadowed, in the slave establishment and army, by their colleagues of Balkan and other European origin. Towards the end of the sixteenth century this began to change, and men of Caucasian origin – Georgians, Circassians, Chechens and Abaza – begin to figure more prominently in the ruling elite of the Empire. The first grand vizier of definitely Caucasian slave origin seems to have been Hadim Mehmed Pasha, a palace eunuch of Georgian birth who held office for some four months in 1622–3. Thereafter, Caucasians became more numerous, and in the seventeenth and eighteenth centuries there are many of them among the generals, governors, and ministers of the Empire.

The clash of factions in the capital took many forms, and the alignments were constantly changing. The struggle does, however, seem to have revolved between two poles – at the one end the grand vizierate, supported by the freeborn men of the bureaucracy and much of the religious hierarchy; at the other the palace and the harem, with their vast network of influence, and their graduates, slave or free, scattered through the whole apparatus of imperial administration.

The clash between Christian Europe and Ottoman Islam has often been compared with the confrontation in our own day between the free world and the Soviet Union. The comparison is not without merit. On both occasions, the West was threatened by a militant and expanding polity and society, impelled by the twin imperial attributes of appetite and a sense of mission, and exalted by a dogmatic belief in perpetual struggle ending in inevitable victory. But the comparison should not be pushed too far. In this earlier confrontation, exaltation and dogmatism existed on both sides, and greater tolerance on the Turkish side. In the fifteenth and sixteenth centuries, the movement of refugees – of those who, in Lenin's vivid phrase, 'voted with their feet', was from West to East and not, as in our day, from East to West. The flight of the Jews, expelled from Spain in 1492, to Turkey is well known, but was by no means unique. Other groups of refugees, dissident Christians persecuted by the dominant Churches in their own countries, as well as Jews, found refuge in the Ottoman lands. When Ottoman rule in Europe came to an end, the Christian nations they had ruled for centuries were still there, with their languages, their cultures, their religions, even, to some extent, their institutions, intact and ready to resume their separate national existence. The same cannot be said of those Muslims who remained after the ending of Turkish rule in the Balkans and of Moorish rule in Spain.

Refugees were not the only European beneficiaries of Ottoman rule. The peasantry of the conquered provinces also found their lot in many ways improved. Ottoman imperial government brought unity and security in place of conflict and disorder. There were important social and economic consequences. In the course of the wars of conquest, a large part of the old hereditary landowning aristocracy was destroyed, and their ownerless estates granted as fiefs to Ottoman soldiers. In the Ottoman system, however, a fief was basically a grant of the right to collect revenues. It was, theoretically at least, for life or for some shorter period, and was forfeit when the holder ceased to perform military service. It carried with it no hereditary rights and no seigniorial jurisdiction. The peasants, on the other hand, usually enjoyed what was in effect a form of hereditary tenure, protected by Ottoman usage from both fragmentation and concentration of ownership. They thus had greater freedom on their farms than under their previous Christian rulers. The taxes they paid were modestly assessed and humanely collected in comparison with the practice of previous and also of neighbouring regimes. This security and prosperity did much to reconcile them to other, less attractive aspects of Ottoman rule, and account in large measure for the long tranquillity that reigned in the Ottoman provinces until the explosive irruption of nationalist ideas from the West.

As late as the nineteenth century, European visitors to the Balkans comment on the well-being and contentment of the Balkan peasantry, which they compare favourably with conditions in parts of Christian Europe. The contrast was far more striking in the fifteenth and sixteenth centuries, the age of the great peasant revolts in Europe. Even the much-condemned *devshirme* levy had its positive aspects. By this means the humblest villager could rise to the highest and most powerful offices in the state. Many did so and brought their families with them – a form of social mobility impossible in the aristocratic societies of contemporary Christendom.

The Ottoman Empire affected Europe in a number of ways. For long it was feared as a dangerous enemy – a fear that long survived the danger. For merchants, manufacturers, and later financiers, it was a rich and increasingly open market, and for many also – and here, too, there is a parallel with the modern confrontation – it exercised a powerful fascination. The disaffected and the ambitious were attracted by Ottoman opportunity, and many whom Europe called 'renegades' and whom the Muslims called '*muhtadī*' ('those who have found the true path') made brilliant careers in the Ottoman service. Downtrodden peasants looked hopefully to the enemies of their masters. Martin Luther in his 'Admonition to prayer against the Turk', published in 1541, gave warning that the poor, oppressed by greedy princes, landlords and burghers, might well prefer to live under the Turks rather than under Christians such as these. Even the defenders of the established order were impressed by the political and military efficiency of the Turkish empire at its height. A significant proportion of the vast literature produced in Europe on the Turkish menace deals with the merits of the Turkish order and the wisdom of imitating it.

On the night of 5–6 September 1566, Sultan Süleyman the Magnificent died in his tent during the siege of Szigétvár in Hungary. It was a moment of crisis. The battle was still in progress, the issue uncertain, the heir to the throne far away. The grand vizier resolved to keep the sultan's death secret. Süleyman's body was partially embalmed and carried in a litter for three weeks, until word came that the new sultan, Selim II, was safely installed in Istanbul. Only then was the secret of Süleyman's death revealed.

The dead sultan, commanding armies from behind the curtains of his litter, was a symbol. The new sultan, a drunken incompetent known in Turkish annals as 'Selim the Sot', was a portent of the declining fortunes of the state and empire. The Ottoman armies had withdrawn from Vienna, the Ottoman fleets from the Indian Ocean. For some time, the imposing façade of Ottoman military might concealed the real decline of Ottoman power. In Istanbul, an able and ruthless sultan, Murad IV (1623–1640), and later two brilliant grand viziers, the Albanian Mehmed Köprŭlŭ and his son Ahmed, who between them held office from 1656 to 1678, were able to stop the rot at home and even to win some victories in the field. In 1683, under the leadership of a new grand vizier, Karamustafa Pasha, brother-in-law of Ahmed Köprŭlŭ, they were even able to make a second attempt to capture Vienna.

But it was too late, and this time the Ottoman defeat was decisive and final. Instead of the strength, it was now the weakness of the Ottoman state that posed a problem for Europe. That problem came to be known as 'the Eastern question'.

PART IV

Cross-Sections

CHAPTER 8

THE STATE

According to Muslim tradition, the Prophet Muḥammad sent letters from his home in Arabia to the kings and princes of the infidels, informing them of his apostolate and summoning them to embrace Islam. Many rulers, governors, and bishops are cited as receiving such letters, but the most important of them are named as 'Caesar' and 'Chosroes', that is to say, the emperors of Byzantium and of Persia, who between them divided the Middle East.

'Caesar' was, of course, the emperor in Constantinople, the successor of the emperors in Rome and, since Constantine, the ruler of a Christian empire. The nature of the imperial dignity as perceived under the new dispensation was set forth by Agapetus, deacon of the Church of Holy Wisdom – in Greek Hagia Sophia, in the West commonly known by its Italian name, Santa Sophia. In an address to the Emperor Justinian in about 530 CE, he said:[1]

> Having a dignity which is set above all other honours, sire, you render honour above all to God, who gave you that dignity; inasmuch as He gave you the sceptre of earthly power after the likeness of the heavenly kingdom, power to the end that you should instruct men to hold fast the cause of justice, and should punish the howling of those who rage against that cause; being yourself under the kingship of the law of justice and lawfully king of those who are subject to you.

In pagan Rome, the emperor was king, priest and even, in a sense, god. After the conversion to Christianity the sovereign no longer claimed divinity, and the Christian emperors came to recognize a boundary – though not a separation – between the imperial and priestly functions, between *imperium* and *sacerdotium*. The distinction between politics and religion or, in modern language, between State and Church, is implicit even in the Gospels, where the founder of Christianity is quoted as enjoining his followers to 'render unto Caesar the things which are Caesar's, and unto God the things which are God's' (Matt. 22:21). It was apparently the Emperor Justinian who drew a clear distinction between the two. In the preface to his sixth *novella*, addressed by the emperor to the Patriarch of Constantinople and dealing with the ordination of bishops and other clergy, the emperor states:[2]

> The greatest blessings of mankind are the gifts of God which have been granted us by the mercy on high – the priesthood and the imperial authority. The priesthood ministers to things divine; the imperial authority is set over, and shows diligence in, things human; but both proceed from one and the same source, and both adorn the life of man.

The earlier Byzantine rulers still used such Roman titles as Imperator, Caesar and Augustus. Later the emperors were commonly designated by two Greek terms, *'basileus'*, 'monarch,' and *'autokratōr'*. To emphasize the nature of their sovereignty, the emperors issued their decrees 'in the name of the Lord Jesus Christ', *'en onomati tou Despotou Iēsou Khristou'*. In Byzantium, the emperor usually bore the ultimate responsibility for Church as well as State, and it was his duty to approve and impose the 'right opinion' – the Greek term, taken from Plato, is *'orthē doxa'* – as defined by the ecclesiastical authorities.

In the early centuries, the emperors in Constantinople saw their mission as universal. As rulers of the one imperial realm, and heads of the one true religion revealed by God, it was their task to bring the imperial peace and the Christian faith to all the world. Byzantine ceremonial gives the emperor the title of *kosmokratōr*, ruler of the world, and even *khronokratōr*, ruler of time. Among the insignia and emblems of universal imperial sovereignty, none was more potent than the gold coin, the *solidus* or *denarius*, which for many centuries was struck only in the name of the Roman Caesar or the Byzantine *autokratōr*, and which was known and recognized all over the world.

The conflicts and chaos of the third century left the Byzantine emperors ruling a smaller realm with a weakened and impoverished military and administrative apparatus. The reforms of Constantine, continued and completed by his successors, restored both the strength and the efficiency of the imperial government and enabled it to survive the dangers and the defeats that were to come. The new organization affected both the capital and the provinces. At the centre, the administration was divided into a number of departments staffed by professional civil servants, and dealing with such matters as defence and state security, chancery and foreign policy, and of course finance. The provinces of the empire were reduced in size and therefore increased in numbers, and were grouped into four major prefectures, each headed by a praetorian prefect. These had very considerable powers and a large measure of independence in both fiscal and military matters, but were personally responsible to the emperor.

The effectiveness of the new system depended very largely on the military organization. In the new system, there was a regular army – mobile and highly trained – attached to the person of the emperor, and at his disposal to deal with either domestic rebels or foreign enemies.

The most important of these enemies was, of course, the ruler of Persia, the only rival claimant to imperial authority. In an inscription of 260 CE proclaiming his victory over the Romans, the Persian ruler Shapur I describes himself as follows:[3]

> I, lord Shapur, worshipper of Mazda, King of Kings of Iran and of non-Iran, of the race of the gods, son of the worshipper of Mazda the Lord Ardashir, King of Kings of Iran, of the race of the gods, grandson of Papak ... I am ruler of the land of Iran.

Shapur had indeed won a great victory over the Romans, but in the centuries that followed, while the Roman state was reorganized and strengthened, the state in Iran was gravely weakened.

The reign of Chosroes I (531–579 CE), known as 'Anushirvan' ('the Great Soul'), marked the climax of a period of revolutionary struggle and change. Under his father and predecessor Kavadh (448–496; 499–531), a kind of communistic movement led by a religious rebel called Mazdak, possibly a Manichaean, arose and was for a while protected by the king, perhaps as a weapon against the feudal nobles. Chosroes restored order and relative calm. Suppressing the Mazdakites, he tried to reorganize the state, government, and army. In this, he achieved some initial success, and a period of military strength followed.

But the empire was basically weakened. Its feudal structure was broken and replaced by a military despotism with a permanent paid army. The privileged classes retained their freedom from taxation, but became increasingly dependent on the king, and life centred more than ever before around the court. The process of change, however, was still incomplete. The ancient spirit of independence persisted, and after Chosroes the nobles again threatened the crown. Even the military commands tended to become fiefs during the foreign wars and civil strife of the sixth century. A new kind of military feudalism, dominated by generals, emerged from these struggles, but was given no time to consolidate.

When, in the early seventh century, the Muslim Arabs invaded Iran, the central authority was disintegrating; hereditary territorial princes ruled the provinces, and after the initial defeat of the imperial armies, they were conquered one by one and their territories absorbed into the realm of the caliphs. The social and political crisis of the last Sasanid century was paralleled by religious upheavals. A series of Zoroastrian heresies, notable among them Manichaeism and its various offshoots, challenged the priestly and royal establishment. Though never entirely successful, these movements undermined both the cohesion and the authority of the Zoroastrian religious establishment.

Such was the Sasanid system encountered by the Muslims – and the model on which some of the political institutions of the 'Abbasid caliphate were based. Its characteristic feature was despotism, tempered by deposition and assassination, and maintained by elaborate rituals and ceremonials which fascinated the Arab conquerors. It also left another heritage, bureaucratic and clerical. The survivors of the old Persian feudal nobility had become militarily inefficient and even insignificant. The aristocratic families, however, retained power and influence through the bureaucracy; the skills and attitudes of the Persian patrician scribal class were to reappear in Islamic times.

The Persian theory of kingship was basically religious. The Sasanids, in contrast to the Parthians, had introduced a kind of state Church, which in turn sanctified the royal power, and took an active part in social and political life. It was run by a minutely regulated hierarchy, under the supreme authority of the High Priest, exercising not only spiritual but also worldly authority, with lands, tithes, and privileges. The higher ranks of the priesthood also belonged to the aristocracy, and thus formed a kind of *noblesse de robe*.

Sasanid Persia was an eminently aristocratic society, in which status derived wholly from membership of the closed upper classes. As well as the defects, it also had the merits of such a society, notably a tradition of chivalry and courtesy generally lacking in the Greco-Roman world.

The aristocratic basis of the Persian polity had already been gravely weakened by the convulsions of the sixth century CE. It was fatally undermined by the democratization brought by Islam.

A comparison between the two states defeated by the Arabs – Byzantium and Persia – may be instructive. Geographically, there is a striking resemblance between the two. Each of the two empires had its main base on a high plateau in which the dominant language and culture – Greek and Christian in Anatolia, Persian and Zoroastrian on the high plateau of Iran – were those of the dominant imperial people. Both controlled adjoining territories inhabited by peoples whose language and religious beliefs were different from their own. Byzantine subjects in Syria, and Persian subjects in Iraq, were primarily Aramaic-speaking Christians. In Syria, the Byzantines also faced opposition from dissident groups within the churches, groups which gradually established their own separate hierarchies, identities, and liturgical usages.

The most dramatic difference was in the situation of the two imperial capitals. Constantinople was on the far side of the Anatolian plateau, safe behind its high walls. All the Arab attempts to conquer the city failed, and the empire was able to regroup its forces, and to survive for centuries more. The Sasanid capital was at Ctesiphon in Iraq, on the near side of the Iranian plateau. It was lost in the first wave of assault in 637, and thereafter the Persian magnates with their separate armies had no centre around which to rally and recover.

In the course of their expansion, the Arabs encountered two very different imperial state traditions, the Roman and the Persian, and they were profoundly yet differently affected by both of them. There is also an important difference between the Arab Muslim invaders and those other waves of invasion, earlier and later, that engulfed the great empires. The Germanic peoples who invaded the territories of the Western Roman Empire encountered a polity and a religion, the Roman Empire and the Christian Church, each with its own institutions, hierarchy, and law. The invaders, in principle at least, accepted both, and tried to achieve their own aims within the dual structure of Roman and Christian polity. The Western emperor became a puppet of his barbarian masters, but they still found the game of puppetry worth playing, and even when the Western empire finally collapsed of inanition, a new 'Holy Roman Empire' was in the course of time created in Germany. The Arab invaders of Persia and Byzantium behaved very differently, abolishing even – or rather especially – the forms of the old order and creating their own sovereign institution. But the later invaders who entered – and conquered – the realms of Islam from the East followed a pattern much closer to that of the Germanic people in Europe. The Turks and, after their conversion, even the Mongols, preserved the institutions of the Islamic faith and the structure of the caliphate and sultanate, and turned them to their own use. Like Latin in the West, Arabic and Persian in the East were preserved and even cherished by the new masters.

Muslims, like others, governed, collected taxes, and made war. Far more than others, they involved their religion in all these activities. Between the Christian and the Muslim experience in particular, there was a profound difference. For three centuries, until the conversion of Constantine, Christians were a minority, subject always to suspicion and often to persecution by the state. During this time, they developed their own institutions, which became the Church. Muḥammad, the founder of Islam, was his own Constantine. During his lifetime, Islam became a political as well as a religious allegiance, and the Prophet's community in Medina became a state with the Prophet himself as sovereign – ruling a place and a people. The memory of his activities as ruler is enshrined in the Qur'ān and in the most ancient narrative traditions which constitute the core of historical self-awareness of Muslims everywhere.

For the Prophet and his companions, therefore, the choice between God and Caesar, that snare in which not Christ but so many Christians were to be entangled, did not arise. In Muslim teaching and experience, there was no Caesar. God was the head of the state, and Muḥammad his Prophet taught and ruled on his behalf. As Prophet, he had – and could have – no successor. As supreme sovereign of the religio-political community of Islam, he was succeeded by a long line of caliphs.

It is sometimes said that the caliph was head of State and Church, pope and emperor in one. This description in Western and Christian terms is misleading. Certainly there was no distinction between *imperium* and *sacerdotium*, as in the Christian empire, and no separate ecclesiastical institution, no Church, with its own head and hierarchy. The caliphate was always defined as a religious office, and the caliph's supreme purpose was to safeguard the heritage of the Prophet and to enforce the Holy Law. But the caliph had no pontifical or even priestly function, and he belonged neither by education nor by professional experience to the ulema. His task was neither to expound nor to interpret the faith, but to uphold and protect it – to create conditions in which his subjects could follow the good Muslim life in this world and prepare themselves for the world to come. And to do this, he had to maintain the God-given Holy Law within the frontiers of the Islamic state, and to defend and, where possible, extend those frontiers, until in the fullness of time the whole world was opened to the light of Islam. In Muslim historiography, the early conquests are designated by an Arabic word, *futūḥ*, literally, 'openings'.

The caliph had various titles, which symbolize the different aspects and perceptions of the office. Theologians and jurists usually speak of him as the imam, the leader, with the primary meaning of leader in prayer, of the Muslims. His political and military authority is denoted by the term '*amīr al-mu'minīn*', usually translated 'commander of the faithful'. This was the most frequently used title. The term '*khalīfa*' was commonly used by historians, and often appears on the coinage. In theory, and for the first few centuries after the Prophet in practice, there was one Muslim community, ruled by one state, and the caliph was head of it. The titulature of sovereignty in Islam, unlike that of Christendom, does not normally make use of territorial or ethnic designations. There are no equivalents to the kings of England, of France, of Spain, or other realms in the West. During the great wars between the sultan of Turkey and the shah of Iran in the sixteenth century, these were titles which each applied to the other to belittle him, and never to himself. Each in his own realm was the representative of God on earth and the ruler of the Muslims. His opponent was a dissident, a rebel, at best a local potentate.

The key questions that confronted the early Muslims in the formative years of the caliphate were: Who is to be caliph? How is he to be chosen? What are his duties? What are the extent and limits of his powers? Can he be deposed? Who is to succeed him? All these questions were intensively discussed and, at times, bitterly disputed among the jurists and theologians, arguing the principles of religious law and doctrine, and citing the practical experience of the early caliphate. The Shī'a maintained that the caliphate should be hereditary in the line of the Prophet, and therefore that all the caliphs, except only for the brief rule of 'Alī and of his son Ḥasan, were usurpers. The more generally accepted view of the Sunni Muslims was that the caliphate was elective, and any member of the Prophet's tribe, Quraysh, was eligible. The Sunni jurists envisaged a form of election based on the choice of a new chief in an ancient Arabian tribe. Neither the composition and numbers of the electorate nor the procedure of election were ever authoritatively defined. Some jurists required the concurrence of all competent electors, but without defining their competence. Some spoke of a quorum, five, three, two, or even one elector. The next stage was to accept that the one elector might be the reigning caliph who could thus nominate his heir apparent.

These teachings and arguments reflect the acceptance, however reluctant, by pious jurists of political realities. The evolution of the caliphate as an institution may be divided into four periods. The first is that known to modern historians as the patriarchal, to Sunni Muslims as the 'rightly guided' caliphate. All four caliphs of this first period were chosen in some manner by their predecessors or colleagues; none succeeded by hereditary right. But the patriarchal caliphate ended in regicide and civil war, and with it the experiment in elective sovereignty. Thereafter the caliphate became, in practice even if not in theory, hereditary in two successive dynasties, the Umayyads and the 'Abbasids. The elective principle remained strong enough to prevent the emergence and acceptance of any regular rule of succession, such as the primogeniture of the European monarchies. In most other respects, the system and style of government became more and more like the ancient empires which the Muslims had conquered, and less and less like the Prophet's community in Medina.

The power wielded by the early caliphs was very far from the despotism of their predecessors and of their successors. It was limited by the political ethics of Islam and by the anti-authoritarian habits and traditions of ancient Arabia. A verse attributed to the pre-Islamic Arabic poet ʿAbīd ibn al-Abraṣ speaks of his tribe as 'laqāḥ', a word which, according to the ancient commentators and lexicographers, denotes a tribe that has never submitted to a king. ʿAbīd's proud description of his people makes his meaning clear:[4]

> They refused to be servants of kings, and were never ruled by any
> But when they were called on for help in war, they responded gladly.

The ancient Arabs, like the ancient Israelites depicted in the books of Judges and Samuel, mistrusted kings and the institution of kingship. They were, indeed, familiar with the institution of monarchy in the surrounding countries, and some were even led to adopt it. There were kings in the states of southern Arabia; there were kings in the border principalities of the north; but all these were in different degrees marginal to Arabia. The sedentary kingdoms of the south used a different language, and were part of a different culture. The border principalities of the north, though authentically Arab, were deeply influenced by Persian and Byzantine imperial practice, and represent a somewhat alien element in the ancient Arab world. Even among the tribes the royal title was not entirely unknown. The earliest surviving inscription in the Arabic language, a funeral inscription of 328 CE, found at Namāra in the Syrian borderlands, commemorates Imru'l-Qays ibn 'Amr, 'king of all the Arabs, who wore the diadem and subjugated Asad and Nizār and their kings'. The epitaph ends with the claim that no king until this time 'had attained what he had attained'.[5] The king commemorated in the epitaph probably reigned in one of the border principalities.

The pre-Islamic history of Arabia is little known and is encrusted with all kinds of myths and legends. The Arab historical tradition preserves the recollection of one attempt to establish a monarchy – the short-lived kingdom of Kinda, which flourished in the late fifth and early sixth centuries CE. The realm of Kinda disintegrated, and the general attitude of the Arabians, sedentary as well as nomadic, was hostile to monarchy. Even in Mecca, an oasis town, the Arabs preferred to be led by consensual chiefs rather than commanded by monarchs. This mistrust of monarchy is in general reflected in the Qur'ān and in the traditions. The Arabic word 'malik' (king) occurs as one of the divine epithets and as such is of course endowed with sanctity. But when applied to human beings it usually has a negative connotation. Thus, for example, it is commonly used in the Qur'ān of Pharaoh, the prototype of the unjust and tyrannical ruler (18:70, 79). In another passage, the Queen of Sheba, in a conversation with Solomon, remarks that 'When kings enter a city, they pillage it and make its nobles destitute. Thus do kings' (28:34). The early Muslims were well aware of the nature of imperial monarchy as practised in their own day in Byzantium and in Persia, and believed that the state founded by the Prophet and governed after him by his successors the caliphs represented something new and different. They were the more resentful of what they saw as attempts to transform the religious leadership of Islam into a new empire. The early ninth-century author al-Jāḥiẓ, in a tract justifying the supersession of the Umayyads by the 'Abbasids, lays the blame on Muʿāwiya:[6]

> Then Muʿāwiya installed himself in power and made himself sole ruler against the other counsellors and the community of the Muslims, both the Helpers [Medinese] and the Migrants [Meccans], in the year which they called 'the year of reunion'. But it was not the year of union, rather the year of division and force and oppression and violence, a year in which the imamate became like the kingdom of Chosroes and the caliphate like the tyranny of Caesar.

Al-Jāḥiẓ is a little premature in attributing these changes to Muʿāwiya.

But he depicts with accuracy the process which took place under the late Umayyads and, ironically, was brought to completion by the 'Abbasid caliphs whose cause al-Jāḥiẓ was trying to defend.

The reference to 'counsellors', literally members of the '*shūrā*', is significant, and recalls early Islamic and indeed pre-Islamic traditions. In the pre-Islamic Arab tribe, the chief, known as sheikh (Arabic *shaykh*) elder, or *sayyid*, lord or master, assumed and held his office for as long as he retained the freely given consent of 'those who bind and loose', i.e. those senior and respected tribesmen who would appoint and might dismiss a chief. He functioned as a sort of first among equals, an arbitrator in disputes. Only in battle was he granted and allowed to exercise genuine command. In performing his duties, whether in war or in peace, he was expected to apply the inherited customs of the tribe.

The choice of a new tribal chief, even if in practice often limited to the members of one family, was not bound by any rule of succession. The chief of the tribe was usually chosen from among the members of a single family seen as noble. Often this family was holy as well as noble, and the descendants of a sheikhly family might enjoy the hereditary custodianship of a local shrine or sacred object. The choice was personal, and was made for personal qualities – the ability to evoke and retain loyalty. The tribal chief maintained himself by prestige rather than by authority. With the advent of Islam, the already existing anti-monarchical, anti-dynastic attitudes were reinforced by an anti-aristocratic sentiment expressed in the Islamic belief in the brotherhood and equality of believers, and the rejection of any primacy save that of religious or personal merit. Through all the many subsequent changes in the caliphate as it actually existed, the doctrine of elective succession remained enshrined in Sunni theory and jurisprudence, and the fiction of election, which increasingly took the form of the nomination by a ruler of his own successor, was preserved through the later caliphal dynasties.

The early Muslims clearly regarded the caliphate as an enlarged and expanded version of the same kind of authority – as a kind of super sheikhdom, no longer of a single tribe, but of the united tribes that formed the political community of Islam, in which the Islamic faith and law successively supplemented, adapted, incorporated and supplanted tribal custom. At a time of expanding and almost continuous warfare, the function of command, already present in the older system, assumed a new importance.

One of the functions of the tribal chief was to preside over the *majlis*, sometimes also known as the *jamāʿa*, a meeting or council of the notables of the tribe. The primary meaning of *majlis* is a place where one sits; that of *jamāʿa* is a gathering or assemblage. The *majlis*, in ancient Arabia, seems to have functioned as a kind of oligarchic council where the chief, with the assistance of the notables, dispensed justice, made political decisions, received visitors, heard poets, and presided over discussions on topics of current concern. This practice survived into the early caliphate, when it came to be more precisely regulated by etiquette and ceremonial. With the increasing size of the caliphal empire and the increasing complexity of its political life, the old-style *majlis* was no longer adequate. The caliph Muʿāwiya, in seeking support for his nomination of his son Yazīd as heir apparent, sent and received delegations (*wafd*) to win over the influential leaders of the Arab tribes. In this he achieved enough success to ensure Yazīd's succession, but not enough to save him from the need to win a civil war in order to confirm it. The classic case of the choice of a successor by a form of consultation was the celebrated *shūrā*, appointed by ʿUmar on his deathbed. This procedure, though deemed classic, was not repeated.

Two verses in the Qurʾān, 3:153 and 42:36, are frequently cited as imposing a duty of consultation on rulers. Muslim authors contrast consultation with arbitrary personal rule, commending the one, deploring the other. The case for consultation is supported by a considerable body of material – by traditionists recording the precept and practice of the Prophet, by commentators elaborating on the references to consultation in the Qurʾān, and by numerous later writers in Arabic, Persian, and Turkish belonging to both the legal and scribal traditions. In general, the ulema urged the need for consultation with ulema, while officials were more insistent on the importance of consulting officials. But while consultation was recommended and arbitrary rule deplored, the one was not enjoined nor the other forbidden. And the trend of events was towards greater, not lesser, personal authority for the sovereign or his agents. The increasingly authoritarian character of government and the disappointment of successful revolutionaries is vividly expressed in a passage quoted by several classical authors. A certain Ṣudayf, a supporter of the ʿAbbasids, is cited as complaining of the changes resulting from the fall of the Umayyads and the accession of the ʿAbbasids to the caliphate: 'By God, our booty, which was shared, has become a perquisite of the rich. Our leadership, which was consultative, has become arbitrary. Our succession, which was by the choice of the community, is now by inheritance.'[7]

Some kind of public assembly was continued even under the most autocratic of rulers. Caliphs of various dynasties held public sessions, at which representatives of different social orders were admitted to the presence of the ruler, or of some high-ranking official acting for him, and allowed to present petitions. Poets and scholars in search of patronage might also gain admittance and thus further their careers. These procedures gave influence and sometimes even power to those – chamberlains and others – who could control access. By Ottoman times, the imperial council (*divan-i humayun*) had become an institution. In the early fifteenth century if not earlier, the sultan presided regularly over a council of the pashas. Between the death of a sultan and the arrival of his successor, the *divan* could, exceptionally, be held by the pashas on their own. Mehmed II seems to have been the first sultan to give up the practice of presiding in person, and relinquished this function to the grand vizier. According to an anecdote related by the Ottoman historians, the reason for this change was that one day a peasant with a grievance came to the *divan* and said to the assembled dignitaries: 'Which of you is the sultan? I have a complaint.' The sultan was offended, and the grand vizier suggested to him that he might avoid such embarrassments by not appearing in person at the *divan*. Instead he could observe the proceedings from behind a grille or screen.[8]

Whatever the truth of this anecdote, the withdrawal of the sultan is confirmed by the rules of procedure promulgated by Mehmed II. These state clearly that the sultan sits behind a screen. This practice continued until the time of Süleyman the Magnificent, who ceased to attend the meetings of the *divan* even in this form. During the sixteenth century, the *divan* met regularly four times a week, beginning at daybreak, and dealt with a whole range of government business. The morning was normally devoted to public sessions and especially the hearing of petitions and complaints, which were adjudicated by the relevant member of the *divan* or by the grand vizier himself. At about noon, the mass of petitioners and other outsiders withdrew, and lunch was served to the members of the *divan*, who then proceeded to discuss what business remained. Contemporary descriptions make it clear that the council was purely consultative: the final responsibility rested with the grand vizier, and beyond him with the sultan. In dealing with specific questions the grand vizier might seek information and possibly advice from the relevant member of the *divan*, but not from the *divan* as a whole. Military matters were referred to the aga of the janissaries, naval matters to the *kapudan* pasha, legal matters to the chief judges, and so forth.

The more elaborate and institutional aspect of the Ottoman council may be, in some part, a reflection of the fuller and better information available for the Ottoman period, but in part also it represents a general change. After the coming to the Middle East of the steppe peoples, first the Turks and then the Mongols, we begin to find references for the first time in Islamic history to regular and permanent consultative councils. The Mongol rulers of Persia are reported as having adhered to the practice of convening a great council of high dignitaries, presided over by the vizier. This body, known in Persian as the *dīvān-i buzurg*, the great *divan*, may be based on the Mongol tribal council, *kurultay*. Such a council continued to exist under the post-Mongol rulers of Persia, and its functioning is attested by both Persian and external sources. In Mamluk Egypt, too, there seems to have been some kind of supreme council of high-ranking amirs; under the later Mamluks, however, references to it become extremely rare.

In the Ottoman Empire, in addition to the *divan-i humayun*, which had a prescribed membership, fixed times of meeting, and a regular order of business, there were also meetings of another kind, called *meshveret* (consultation), from the same Arabic root as the word *shūrā*. This term was not used of the *divan*, but of *ad hoc* meetings and gatherings of military and other dignitaries convened by the sultan or grand vizier to consider a specific problem. There are frequent references to such *meshverets* in the course of the Balkan wars in the fifteenth century. They continued through the sixteenth and seventeenth centuries, and became very frequent during the crises of the late eighteenth century. An early Ottoman historiographic tradition even ascribes the founding of the Ottoman dynasty to a *meshveret*. According to this version, the beys assembled in a *meshveret* to choose a leader: 'After much discussion they chose Osman bey and asked him to become their chief. He accepted.'[9] This may or may not be an authentic account of the birth of the Ottoman state. But even if it is a myth, the fact that early Ottoman chroniclers should have chosen such a myth and enshrined it in the dynastic historiography is itself of some significance.

As the autocratic powers of the 'Abbasid caliphate increased, the personal power of the caliphs in Baghdad diminished, and from the tenth century onwards the Commanders of the Faithful, once the unchallenged rulers of all Islam, found themselves successively deprived of effective command in their provinces, their capital, and finally even their palace.

The process began in the more distant provinces of the far-flung Muslim empire, and eventually affected all but the immediate environs of the capital. For a while the caliphs were able to maintain the authority of the central government in the provinces by a kind of separation of powers, whereby government, finance and communications were placed in the hands of different chiefs, all of them reporting directly to Baghdad. The governor of the province was responsible for the armed forces and for the maintenance of order on the frontiers and in the cities. The intendant of finances was responsible for the collection of taxes and tributes and for the remission of the proceeds, after defraying local expenses, to the department of finance in Baghdad. The postmaster was responsible for the maintenance of the imperial courier service and for the submission of regular reports on events to the director of posts and intelligence in the capital. Central control was weakened and often ended when one of them, usually the governor, succeeded in winning over the other two, and in turning his governorship into an autonomous, or even hereditary principality.

By the tenth century, almost the whole of the former Islamic empire consisted of such hereditary principalities, according token recognition to the caliph in Baghdad, mentioning his name in the Friday prayer and sometimes on the coinage, but otherwise independent in all significant respects. With the rise of the Fatimids, who called themselves caliphs and challenged the 'Abbasids for the headship of the whole world of Islam, even the fiction of suzerainty was abandoned. It was restored after the fall of the Fatimids, but lost most of what little importance it had retained with the destruction of the remnants of the 'Abbasid caliphate by the Mongols in 1258. For a while, a line of shadow caliphs was maintained by the Mamluk sultans of Egypt, but that, too, ended with the Ottoman conquest in 1517.

The real rulers were no longer the caliphs, but the military commanders known as the amirs, and, from the early tenth century, the 'Amir of Amirs' (Amīr al-Umarā'). The form of the title is significant, and is clearly an echo of the usage of pre-Islamic Iran, where the commander-in-chief was the commander of commanders, the high priest was the priest of priests, and the emperor himself was the king

Crac des Chevaliers, seized by the Crusaders in 1099, rebuilt after the earthquakes in 1201 and 1202, and finally recaptured by Muslim forces in 1271.

Saladin's *minbar* (pulpit) from Aleppo, now in the Al-Aqsā mosque, Jerusalem. By his death in 1193, Saladin (Ṣalāḥ al-Dīn) had recaptured Jerusalem from the Crusaders.

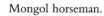
Mongol horseman.

Jenghiz Khan tells the people of Bokhara that he has been sent as a punishment from God. By the time of his death in 1227, most of eastern Iran was in Mongol hands.

In 1258 the Mongols stormed and looted Baghdad and put to death the last caliph in that city. Baghdad never recovered its position in the Islamic world.

The tomb in Samarqand of Timur Lang (the Lame), known in Europe as Tamerlane. After his death in 1405 his vast possessions fell apart.

(above) Sultan Bayezid I (1389–1402), known in Ottoman history as 'the Thunderbolt'.
(right) Sultan Murad II (1421–1444, 1446–1451).

The castle of Rumeli Hisar, built by Mehmed II in 1452, in preparation for the final siege of Constantinople.

Sultan Mehmed II (1444–1446, 1451–1481), known as the Conqueror.
Portrait by Bellini.

(above) The mosque, now museum, of Aya Sofya, Istanbul. Formerly the Byzantine church of the holy wisdom (Hagia Sophia), to which Mehmed II added four minarets.
(below) The mosque of Sultan Ahmed, Istanbul, also called the Blue Mosque. Built 1609–17.

The helmet of Shah ʿAbbās, whose reign
(1587–1629) marked the peak of Safavid power.

The army of Süleyman the Magnificent
(1520–1566) crosses the River Drava in
Hungary. In 1526 at the battle of Mohacs,
Süleyman destroyed the Hungarian army.

Ottoman galleys in the Black Sea, early
seventeenth century

Spanish galleon, sixteenth century.

Ottoman military parade. On the right, on horseback, are the Lieutenant of the Aga of the Janissaries and the Bashchaush or Chief Pursuivant, an important functionary of the Court.

Janissary musketeers. The sleeve-like hats and long-barrelled muskets are characteristic of the corps.

of kings, or *shāhanshāh*. By the mid–tenth century, even the title 'king'
(*malik*) appears in inscriptions and on coins used by rulers to describe
themselves. The first to use this title were some of the new Iranian
dynasties that rose to power at that time. They were followed by the
Seljuks, by the descendants of Saladin, and lesser dynasts. The use of
this title did not, apparently, indicate a claim to equality with the caliph
or, later, with the sultan. It served, rather, to assert a local sovereignty
under the loose suzerainty of a supreme imperial ruler elsewhere. In
this it was roughly equivalent to the contemporary use of the title
'king' by various monarchs in Europe under the nominal supremacy
of the Holy Roman Emperor.

The reason for the choice of this royal title among the many
possibilities offered by the rich lexical resources of the Arabic language
is not difficult to guess. The first to use this title ruled in lands of
Iranian culture, where the monarchical traditions of ancient Iran were
still very much alive. Iranian-style court etiquette and even titulature
had strongly affected the court of the 'Abbasid caliphs themselves,
through the influence of high officials of Iranian background, and the
translation of old Iranian treatises on court etiquette and ceremonial.
These influences were all the stronger in the capitals of the new
principalities that were arising on the actual territory of Iran. The old
Iranian title 'shah' was still too alien and too heathen to be adopted by
Muslim rulers, but its Arabic equivalent, '*malik*', served in its place.
The title '*malik al-mulūk*' (king of kings), which appears a little later,
is an obvious echo of the ancient Persian '*shāhanshāh*'. This title is
specifically condemned by an early tradition, according to which the
Prophet said that no man should call himself 'king of kings', since only
God can be so described. The title was nevertheless used by rulers of
the Būyid, Ayyubid, and later dynasties. The meaning was clear. If the
masters of the provinces were kings, the master of the capital was a
king of kings.

In this way, from the provinces to the centre, a new system of
imperial authority was emerging, associated with that of the caliph
but usurping most of his authority in political and military affairs.
The process was completed by the mid–eleventh century, with the
establishment of the dominion of the Seljuk Turks over most of
southwestern Asia, and the creation by them of what came to be
known as 'the Great Sultanate'.

'*Sulṭān*' in Arabic is an abstract noun, meaning authority and rule,
and was used from early times to denote the government, or more

generally, the authorities. In a society where state and ruler were often synonymous terms, it came to be applied to the holder as well as to the function of political authority, and was used informally of ministers, governors, and even on occasion of the caliphs themselves, Fatimid as well as 'Abbasid. By the tenth century it had become a common designation of independent rulers, and served to distinguish them from those who were still appointed and – with increasing rarity – dismissed by a superior. This use, however, remained informal. It first became official in the eleventh century, when the Seljuks adopted it as their chief regnal title. In Seljuk usage, the word acquired a new sense and embodied a new claim, no less than supreme political sovereignty over all Islam, parallel and at least equal to the religious primacy of the caliph. A Seljuk view of their position is clearly expressed in a letter of 1133 CE, from the Seljuk sultan Sanjar to the caliph's vizier:[10]

> We have received from the lord of the world . . . the kingship of the world, and we receive this by right and inheritance, and from the father and grandfather of the commander of the faithful . . . we have a standard and a covenant.

Sovereignty, in other words, belongs to the house of Seljuk, given by God and ratified by the caliph as religious authority. Like the caliphate, the sultanate was unique and universal. Just as there was only one caliph to serve as religious head of Islam, so there could be only one sultan responsible for the order, security and government of the Islamic empire. This perceived division of authority between the caliphate and the sultanate became so well established that when, during a period of Seljuk weakness, a caliph attempted to exercise some independent political power, the sultan and his spokesman protested against what they now regarded as an infringement of sultanic prerogatives. The caliph, they said, should busy himself with his duties as *imām*, as leader in prayer, which is the best and most glorious of tasks, and is the protection of the rulers of the world; he should leave the business of government to the sultans, to whom it was entrusted.[11]

Muslim writers on statecraft and politics were well aware of the emergence of this dual sovereignty. The awareness is naturally clearest in the writings of those whose experience of politics was practical. It can, however, be detected even in the works of theologians and jurists. Neither group saw this dichotomy in terms of the old Christian–Roman division between *imperium* and *sacerdotium*, still less in terms of the modern separation between religious and secular. The sultanate, no less than the caliphate, was conceived as a religious institution, maintained by and maintaining the Holy Law, and the relations between the state and the ulema became much closer under the Seljuk sultans and their successors than they had ever been under the caliphs. Nor could the caliph and his followers in any sense be described as a clergy. As seen by medieval Muslim, and especially Persian, authors, the real distinction is between two kinds of authority, one prophetic, the other monarchical, but both religious. The Prophet is sent by God, with the task of promulgating and establishing God's law. The polity which the Prophet establishes is a divine one. But human polity must be ruled by a monarch who gains, maintains, and exercises his authority by political and military means. This authority enables him to give orders and punish transgressors independently of – though not contrary to – the law of God. There is no need for a Prophet in every age, and there has been none since Muḥammad, nor will there be any more; but there must always be a monarch, for without a monarch order would give way to anarchy.

The relationship between religious orthodoxy and political stability was well understood and frequently expressed. It is summed up in a dictum often cited by Muslim authors, sometimes as a piece of old Persian wisdom, sometimes even as a saying of the Prophet: 'Islam (or religion) and government are twin brothers. One cannot thrive without the other. Islam is the foundation, and government the guardian. What has no foundation, collapses; what has no guardian, perishes.' The sultan would choose and appoint the caliph himself and then swear allegiance to him as head of the community and embodiment of the principle of Sunni unity. The distinction between the two offices might be described in Walter Bagehot's terms as one between the 'dignified' and the 'efficient' parts of the government – between those which, in Bagehot's words, 'excite and preserve the reverence of the population' and those 'by which it, in fact, works and rules'. Bagehot was speaking of the British constitution and the relationship between the monarchy and Parliament, but his distinction applies very well to the medieval Islamic situation. The caliph represented authority, the sultan power. The sultan empowered the caliph, who authorized him in return. The caliph reigned but did not rule; the sultan did both.

For a while, the Seljuk sultanate was maintained and respected as a single, universal Sunni institution. With the break-up of the Seljuk sultanate, the title 'sultan' was more widely and more commonly used, and in time became the normal Sunni title for anyone who claimed to be a head of state and did not recognize any suzerain. By the beginning of the sixteenth century there were three major states in the Middle East. Two, Turkey and Egypt, were ruled by sultans; the third, Iran, by shahs. After the Ottoman conquest of Egypt in 1517, the last of the 'Abbasid shadow caliphs was sent from Cairo to Istanbul, whence he returned as a private citizen some years later. Thereafter there were no caliphs, and the Ottoman sultans, as well as their lesser imitators elsewhere, ruled alone as supreme sovereigns in their domains, each sultan his own caliph. The very word 'caliph' became one of the numerous titles which sultans added to their titulature. It retained little or nothing of its old significance until it was revived, in quite different circumstances, in the late eighteenth century.

From early times the government of the caliphs and of the sultans was underpinned by a bureaucratic apparatus of increasing magnitude and complexity. The surviving documents of the early caliphate make it clear that provincial administration, at least, was still carried on much as before the conquests, with the old bureaucracies, Persian in Iraq and Iran, Christian in Syria and Egypt, continuing to man the offices, keep records and collect taxes much as before. The principal difference was that they now remitted the proceeds to the new Arab government. The Arabization and standardization of governmental practice, and the creation of a central, imperial administration, seem to have been largely the work of the later Umayyad caliphs. The Arab historiographic tradition attributes to the caliph 'Umar the initiative to create a central registry, or *dīwān*, the primary purpose of which was financial – to record incoming money, to register those entitled to receive stipends, and to ensure that the distribution was promptly and fairly made. The Umayyad caliph 'Umar II is reported to have tried to delay the growth of bureaucracy. According to an early administrative historian, one day the caliph's secretary asked him for more papyrus:[12]

> 'Umar replied, 'Sharpen your pen and write less. It will be more swiftly understood.' The caliph also wrote to another official, who had written asking for papyrus and complaining that he had very little of it. 'Cut your pen fine and your words short, and make do with what papyrus you have....'

Such policies could at best delay the growth of bureaucracy, and the replacement of papyrus by paper greatly speeded its proliferation. Detailed records in archives survive only from the Ottoman period, but enough is known of earlier periods – from chronicles, from bureaucratic literature, and from a not inconsiderable number of surviving documents – to give a fairly good idea of how these bureaucracies functioned.

As in modern states, the administration was divided into departments, known in 'Abbasid times as *dīwān*, each with its own assigned task. The two most important were the departments of chancery, concerned with correspondence, and of finance, concerned with the assessment and collection of revenue. Other important departments were those of the army, of public works, of internal security, of domain lands, of royal slaves and freedmen, of the courier service, including intelligence, of pious foundations, and of charities. These were differently organized under different regimes and in different periods. They were in general grouped around the three main concerns of correspondence, money, and the armed forces. There were also supervisory *dīwāns*, whose function was to exercise control over the others. A *dīwān* of 'inspection of grievances' acted as a kind of court of appeal, rather like the medieval English court of chancery, on issues not fully covered by the Holy Law.

The head of the entire governmental apparatus under the caliph, or later the sultan, was the vizier (in Arabic *wazīr*). The word means 'one entrusted with a burden or duty', and might be Arabic in origin. It could also be derived from or influenced by some earlier Persian term. The office appears to have been an 'Abbasid innovation, one of many adapted or imitated from Sasanid usage. Under the caliphs, the *wazīr* was the head of the entire administration, both chancery and finance. Apart from the early period, when *wazīrs* were appointed from a single, noble family of east Iranian origin, the *wazīrs* tended to come from the scribal class, and rose through the bureaucratic hierarchy. The *wazīr*, as chief of the administration, was usually chosen from among the heads of the *dīwāns*. The office was essentially civilian, and the *wāzīr* rarely, if ever, took part in military operations.

The rise of the military amirs led to a decline in the importance of the *wazīr*. The Būyids maintained their own *wazīr* as chief secretary and intendant of finances, but he, like his master, was also a military officer. The wazirate reappears in a new form under the sultans, and acquires a new importance. The sultans were men of the sword, often illiterate and ignorant of the languages, Arabic and Persian, in which government business was conducted. This gave the office of *wazīr* a new lease of life. It ended, however, with the Seljuk sultanate. Under their successors control of the bureaucracy, as of everything else, was in the hands of military officers. In Mamluk Egypt, the chief of the bureaucracy was the *dawādār*, literally the ink-holder, a high military functionary. Under his direction a large and important bureaucracy emerged, which was responsible for conducting the business of government under the Mamluk sultans and, in no small measure, for ensuring its long survival.

The Ottoman sultans appointed a number of viziers from among their military commanders, the chief of whom, known in Europe as the grand vizier, exercised very extensive powers over civil, military, and even judicial affairs. The emoluments of the Ottoman grand vizier were commensurate with his power and responsibilities. Lûtfi Pasha, who served as grand vizier under Süleyman the Magnificent, notes that in his day the annual income of the grand vizier amounted to about two and a half million aspers, 'which, thank God, is in the Ottoman state a sufficient bounty'.[13] Lûtfi Pasha tells us that when he was grand vizier he spent one and a half million on the expenses of his kitchen and his suite and half a million on charity, leaving half a million in his personal treasury. The Safavid shahs of Iran also employed a chief official of comparable status and functions.

A large part of government administration was concerned with finance – that is to say, with revenue and expenditure. In the Ottoman period, and especially from the sixteenth century onwards, extensive archives, both central and regional, have been preserved, and from these it is possible to construct a detailed picture of the Ottoman financial system. For the earlier Islamic empires, however, the archives, which undoubtedly existed, have not survived, and the historian therefore has no detailed, day-to-day evidence comparable with that available for the Ottoman Middle East and even from the medieval West. There are, however, many documents – some of them in small archival collections, others preserved by chance and haphazard but nevertheless in considerable numbers. Thanks to these and to the vast amount of information provided in historical, geographical, juridical and above all bureaucratic literature, the historian can observe in some detail the workings of medieval Islamic financial institutions.

Under the early 'Abbasids finance, like every other aspect of administration, was the direct responsibility of the *wazīr*. In later times, a more specialized functionary emerged, concerned specifically and exclusively with financial matters. Under the Persian and Turkish regimes he came to be known as the *defterdār*, a title which literally means keeper of registers, and might approximately be translated as intendant of finances.

The prescriptions of Islamic law and the practice of most Muslim governments required the maintenance of two separate treasuries, one general, the other designated as 'special' (*khāṣṣa*), both under the authority of the intendant of finances. The division between them is sometimes unclear, and there are indications that the second was sometimes drawn upon to make good the deficits of the first. The two principal charges on the general treasury were the maintenance of the military units stationed in the capital and the expenses of the sovereign's court. A text from the reign of the caliph al-Ma'mūn gives a figure of six thousand dinars per day.

While the general treasury was thus concerned to defray expenses incurred by the sovereign as supreme military and political chief, the responsibilities of the 'special' treasury consisted primarily of expenses incurred by him in his capacity as religious head of the Muslim community. The 'special' treasury thus had to meet the costs of the pilgrimage to Mecca, the upkeep of the frontier fortresses needed for the *jihād*, the salaries of qāḍīs and other religious functionaries charged with upholding and enforcing the Holy Law, the maintenance of the courier system, as well as such other charges as the ransom of captives, the reception of ambassadors, and the distribution of largesse to poets and other suitable beneficiaries.

In principle, the revenues of the state derived from the Islamic taxes – that is to say, those specified by Holy Law. These were the *kharāj*, the land tax; the *jizya*, poll tax, paid by non-Muslims; and the *zakāt*, or *'ushr*, literally tithe, paid by Muslims. The proceeds from these taxes were allocated to the general treasury. It became increasingly common practice for them to be supplemented by a variety of duties, tolls, and other imposts collectively known as *mukūs*. These were deplored or even condemned by the jurists, but were nevertheless universally collected by Muslim rulers. The resources of the 'special' treasury consisted of the private estates and revenues of the caliph, supplemented by fines, confiscations and escheat.

Revenues were assessed and collected both in cash and in kind. In the former Sasanid territories, Iraq and Iran, as also in their eastward extensions into Central Asia and northwest India, the unit of currency was the silver dirham. In the former Byzantine territories, that is to say in the Levant and in Egypt, as also in western and southwestern Arabia, the unit of currency was the gold dinar. The rate of exchange between the dinar and the dirham naturally varied according to the prices of gold and silver. Theoretically, the dinar was equivalent to ten dirhams. Descriptions of official accounting show, however, that the rate varied considerably, and that the dirham sometimes fell to twenty or even more to the dinar.

The sources preserve several tabulations of net revenues received in the imperial capital after the deduction for whatever was needed to defray provincial and local expenses. The earliest of these dates from the reign of al-Hādī (785–786 CE). Another, slightly later, comes from the reign of Hārūn al-Rashīd (786–809 CE). Some other lists dating from the times of later caliphs illustrate both continuity and change. The figures show an income from the eastern provinces in the neighbourhood of 400 million dirhams, and from the western provinces of about 5 million dinars.

In addition to revenues in cash, the surviving lists enumerate the taxes or tributes assessed and collected in kind. Those from Sind, for example, included 3 elephants, 4,000 waist-wrappers, 1,000 pairs of sandals, and 400 maunds of aloes wood. The revenue for Qūmis included 2,000 ingots of silver and 40,000 pomegranates; from Fārs, 150,000 ratls of pomegranates and quinces, 30,000 bottles of rose water, and 15,000 ratls of preserved fruits. From Isfahān came honey and wax, 20,000 ratls of each; from Sijistān, 300 checquered garments and 20,000 ratls of sugar; from Armenia, 20 embroidered carpets, 58 ratls of variegated cloth, and 20,000 ratls, ten thousand each, of two kinds of salted fish. From Syria and Egypt, long accustomed to Roman and then Byzantine methods of tax extraction, the deliveries in kind are much less significant. In general, the deliveries in kind seem to have consisted mainly of foodstuffs, followed by clothing and other textiles. Live deliveries included horses, mules, falcons, and slaves.

Later listings show a decline in revenues. Payments in kind are gradually eliminated, being replaced by money payments. The latter also dwindled, to some extent because of economic changes, but also through the interception of an ever-increasing proportion of the revenues by provincial rulers, army commanders, and tax-farmers. A summary of revenues from the reign of al-Muqtadir from the year 918–19 CE gives a net income from all provinces of 14,501,904 dinars, including 1,768,000 from the state lands. This listing appears to enumerate all the revenues actually received, even including confiscations and tolls not specified in earlier accounts.

After the decline of the ʿAbbasid caliphate and the break-up of its administration, figures become both infrequent and unreliable, and it is not until the Ottoman period – and the Ottoman territories – that full fiscal information is available. A budget of the financial year 1669–70 may serve as an example. The figures are given in aspers (Turkish *akçe*), originally a small silver coin roughly corresponding to the classical dirham, later a money of account with changing equivalents in hard currency. According to the budget of this year, the total revenue of the Ottoman state was 612,528,960 aspers, including land-tax, poll tax, miscellaneous tolls, fees and levies, escheat, and revenues of tax farms. The expenditure for the same year was 637,206,348 aspers, of which 398,392,602 went for the armed forces and war materials; 180,208,403 for the palaces; 5,032,512 for the sultan's household and the offices of the central government; and the remaining 44,572,831 for miscellaneous other expenses. Like the earlier listings, they are divided by tax and by region. Unlike the earlier listings, they do not enumerate deliveries in kind as part of the tax revenues. There are, however, extremely detailed lists of foodstuffs – type, quantity, etc. – delivered to the imperial kitchens, and materials delivered to the imperial workshops 'apart from payments in cash'.

There is a contradiction in Muslim attitudes to the state. On the one hand, according to religious doctrine, it was a divinely ordained institution necessary to the maintenance of order and the fulfilment of God's purpose. On the other hand, it was commonly viewed as something evil, contaminating to those who participated in its work, dangerous to those who became in one way or another involved. According to a saying dubiously attributed to the Prophet, government and paradise cannot be combined. In other words, the business of government necessarily involves evil-doing and sin. Sometimes such views are attributed even to those engaged in government. A *wazīr* in ninth-century Baghdad is quoted as saying: 'The basis of government is jugglery. If it works, and lasts, it becomes policy.'[14] One story tells of a discussion at the court of the caliph al-Manṣūr as to the true nature of happiness. The caliph himself was asked how he would define a truly happy man, and he answered, 'I don't know him, and he doesn't know me.' The meaning is clear: the less one has to do with government, the happier one is likely to be. The same duality is visible in the pastoral image of government which Islam shares with other religions. On the one side, there are many religious texts in which the caliph or sultan is depicted as the shepherd of his subjects, who are his flock, and for whom he is answerable to God. The reverse side of the pastoral image is expressed in a remark attributed to 'Amr ibn al-'Āṣ, the Arab conqueror of Egypt. When Caliph 'Uthmān proposed to maintain him as military governor of Egypt while putting another in charge of the revenue, 'Amr refused, saying, 'That would be as if I were to hold the horns of the cow while he milked it.'[15]

A broad spectrum of different medieval Muslim perceptions of the nature and purpose of government are illustrated in some maxims on statecraft collected by an early ninth-century Arab writer of *belles-lettres*:[16]

> Islam assigns four things to government: justice, booty, the Friday prayer, and the *jihād*.
>
> Islam, the government, and the people, are like the tent, the pole, the ropes, and the pegs. The tent is Islam, the pole is the government, the ropes and the pegs are the people. None will do without the others.
>
> Chosroes said: 'Do not stay in a country which lacks these five things: a strong rule, a just judge, a fixed market, a wise physician, and a flowing river.'
>
> 'Umar ibn al-Khaṭṭāb said: 'He alone is fit to rule, who is mild without weakness and strong without harshness.'

Perhaps the most eloquent statement of the classical Islamic ideal of statecraft is contained in the remark attributed to an unnamed king concerning his subjects: 'In their hearts I stored respect untainted with hate, and love untainted with disrespect.'

CHAPTER 9

THE ECONOMY

The economic and social history of the Middle East in pre-modern times has been little explored, and is in consequence little known or understood. The principal reason for the relatively backward state of historical studies in this field as compared with other fields, notably medieval European history, is to be found in the problem of documentation. The states of medieval Western Europe evolved into the states of modern Europe, and their archives, often still required for practical purposes, were preserved until modern times, when they became a precious resource for the historian. The states of the medieval Middle East, with one exception, the Ottoman Empire, were overthrown and destroyed by internal upheavals and external invasions, and their archives, no longer serving any current need, were neglected, dispersed and lost.

Until the spread of Western influence and administrative methods in the twentieth century, the Ottoman Empire was the one state which had continued from late medieval times into the early twentieth century with no abrupt political and administrative discontinuity. Its records were therefore more or less intact. The Ottoman archives, like those of many European states and principalities, survived the dangerous transition from the age when archives were kept only for practical use to the new age when they were preserved for historical study. Research in these archives has already thrown a flood of light on the history of the Middle East in the Ottoman period, and has even illuminated some dark places in the preceding centuries. The Ottoman archives are of daunting difficulty and immensity, and much work remains to be done before the study of Middle Eastern history, and in particular of social and economic history, can reach the level of proficiency already established as normal in other, more fortunate, fields.

Nevertheless, on the basis of the information already available, a tentative outline of the evolution of the Middle Eastern economies and societies is possible. This may also help to clarify the changing political structures which they supported.

Since the most ancient times, agriculture has always been, and over the greater part of the area still remains, overwhelmingly the most important form of economic activity. The vast majority of the inhabitants derive their livelihood from it, and the state, until comparatively recent times, drew the greater part of its revenues from their labours.

Middle Eastern agriculture was traditionally of two types. The first, and more important, was that of the river-valley economies: the Nile valley, the Tigris–Euphrates valley, and the two rivers of Central Asia, the Oxus and the Jaxartes. In some other parts of the Middle East, agriculture depends on rainfall, as in the Syrian valleys, along the Syro-Palestinian coastlands, and in parts of Iran and most of what is now Turkey. This type of agriculture was more difficult, and produced lower yields than the river-valley type. In the Middle East, it was poor and undeveloped, even by comparison with the rainfall agriculture of other parts of the world such as Western Europe and China.

A notable feature of the region as a whole is the lack of forests and consequently of timber. In biblical times, the cedars of Lebanon provided building materials for the temple in Jerusalem. But already by the Islamic Middle Ages, the Middle East was importing timber from Africa and, more especially, from India and Southeast Asia, from which tropical hardwoods, invaluable for building, were brought.

The most important crop was of course cereals. The earliest seem to have been barley, millet, and some primitive forms of wheat. By early medieval times, wheat predominated. It still does at the present day. At an unknown date, rice was introduced from India, and its cultivation can be followed through Iran and Iraq to Syria and Egypt. At the time of the Arab conquests in the seventh century, we are told that the conquerors encountered rice in Iraq, and from early accounts it would seem that it was a complete novelty to them.

An Arab narrator who participated in the conquest of the region of Basra tells a curious story:[1]

Some Persian pickets whom an Arab force surprised in the marshes took flight, leaving behind them two baskets, one containing dates, and the other what they afterwards learned to be unhusked rice. The Arab commander told his men: 'Eat the dates, but leave this other thing, for it must be poison which the enemy has prepared for you.' They therefore ate the dates and avoided the other basket. But while they were eating, one of their horses broke loose and started to eat the rice. They were about to slaughter the horse, so that they could eat it before its flesh was also poisoned, but the horse's owner told them to wait, and said that he would see to it in due course. The following morning, finding that the horse was still in excellent health, they lit a fire under the rice and burned off the husks, and their commander said: 'Pronounce the name of Allah over it and eat.' 'And they ate of it, and they found it a most tasty food.'

Under Arab rule, the cultivation and consumption of rice progressed further westwards. Other cereals are mentioned, notably sorghum. Other food crops included leguminous pulses – beans, peas, lentils, chickpeas, and the like – a staple in many parts of the Middle East to the present day, notably in Egypt.

Oleaginous plants were of course very important, oil being required for food, lighting, and toiletries of various kinds, especially soap. The chief oil-bearing plant was the olive, which in parts of the Middle Eastern and North African area was the major crop. Oil was also extracted from a wide range of oil-seeds. A crop introduced from further east and carried westwards during the period of Arab-Muslim rule was sugar, that is the sugar cane. In Persia it was known by two names: 'sheker' and 'qand'. Both words survive in modern English. Sugar was little known in the Greco-Roman world and was used, if at all, for medicinal purposes. When necessary, food and drink were sweetened with honey. During the Islamic Middle Ages, the cultivation and refining of sugar spread to Egypt and North Africa, and sugar became one of the major exports of the Islamic Middle East to Christian Europe. The cultivation of sugar and the plantation system by which it was ensured were carried from North Africa to Muslim Spain, thence to the Atlantic islands, and eventually to the New World.

Spices were grown in many parts of the Middle East, and were also imported in great quantity from South and Southeast Asia. They also figured prominently among Middle Eastern exports to the Western world, until the west European maritime powers first opened and then dominated a direct sea route to Asia, bypassing the Middle East. In a hot climate, before the invention of modern refrigeration, food perished rapidly. To preserve it, food, especially meat, was salted and pickled in various ways, and many spices and condiments were needed to make it palatable.

Fodder crops were basic in a society relying very largely on animals for transport as well as meat, and industrial crops were required for light clothing in a region where wool and leather, the commonest clothing materials in colder climates, were often unsuitable. Three of these were of special importance. Flax has been cultivated in the Middle East since remote antiquity, especially in Egypt, as is attested by linen wrappings on mummies. Cotton was one of the many crops introduced from further east, and seems to have come from East Asia. Within the region, it is first recorded in Persia, whence it moved steadily westwards. The mulberry provided sustenance for the silk-worm, and from the sixth century onwards was cultivated in the Middle East. Persian and Syrian silks were especially appreciated. Dye crops and scent plants of various kinds helped to complete the turn-out of the well-dressed individual.

Another industrial crop was of the greatest importance – papyrus, a reed from the banks of the Nile which provided the principal writing material of the eastern Mediterranean world until the advent of parch-ment and then of paper.

Fruits and vegetables were also widely grown. In earlier times, the most important fruits were vines, figs, and dates. The vine, grown not only for fruit but also for wine, appears to have been much more widely cultivated before the advent of Islam than after. Dates were a staple in oasis and semi-desert areas. Most of the other fruits cultivated in the Middle East were of eastern origin, from Persia and beyond, such as the peach and the apricot. Vegetables like spinach, aubergine (i.e. eggplant), and artichoke are still known in the West by the Persian or Arabic names with which they were introduced.

Citrus cultivation has a curious and somewhat obscure history. In most Middle Eastern languages nowadays, the orange is called 'Por-tugal' – in Arabic '*bortaqal*', in Turkish '*portakal*', with equivalent terms even as far east as Afghanistan. Indeed, the sweet orange, long familiar in India and China, was introduced to the Middle East by Portuguese merchants at the beginning of the sixteenth century. Citrus fruits were, however, known in the Persian Empire long before the advent of Islam, and both Persian and Talmudic sources make mention of an edible citron, the *turunj* (whence Hebrew *ethrōg* and Arabic *utrūja*) and of a small, bitter fruit with attractive flowers, which was used for ornamental, cosmetic, and some culinary purposes, chiefly for sherbets and seasoning. It was known in Persian as *nārang*, whence Arabic *nāranj*. In Portugal and elsewhere in the West, the sweet, edible fruit was called by derivatives of this name. The *nārang* is already mentioned by the ninth-century Arab poet Ibn al-Mu'tazz, who likens it to the cheeks of a young girl. The same poet also mentions lemons, which were probably introduced from India at this time. The cultivation of the lemon and the lime spread rapidly across the Middle East and into Europe, where both fruits are still known by their Perso-Indian names.

They were no doubt brought from the Far East to the Middle East by Muslim caravan-traders, and from the Middle East to Europe by the Crusaders and their commercial companions.

The Portuguese and other West Europeans were certainly responsible for the introduction to the Middle East of previously unknown American plants, notably tobacco, maize, potatoes, and tomatoes. The Turkish historian Ibrahim Pechevi, writing in about 1635, is quite specific:[2]

> The fetid and nauseating smoke of tobacco was brought in the year 1009 [1600–01 CE] by English infidels, who sold it as a remedy for certain diseases of humidity. Some ... pleasure-seekers and sensualists ... became addicted, and soon even those who were not pleasure-seekers began to use it. Many even of the great ulema and the mighty fell into this addiction.

Two other plants of non-Middle Eastern origin were, in more recent times, to have an important impact on the economic and perhaps still more on the social life of the region. An early medieval Arab traveller, describing to his readers the wonders of the mysterious land of China, has a strange tale to tell:[3]

> The king has the exclusive right to the income from salt and from a herb which they drink with hot water. It is sold in every city at high prices, and it is called *sakh*. It has more leaves than a clover and is slightly more scented, but is somewhat bitter. Water is boiled and then poured on it ... The total receipts of the public treasury come from poll-tax, salt, and from this herb.

A little later, another writer, the famous al-Bīrūnī, writing in the early eleventh century, gave a fuller description and some information about the cultivation and use of tea in China and Tibet. Tea drinking appears to have been introduced to Iran by the Mongol conquerors in the thirteenth century. It did not, however, become widespread, nor is there evidence of the habit having travelled any further west. The large-scale switch to tea drinking in Iran occurred in the early nineteenth century, when it was reintroduced from Russia. The extensive cultivation of tea did not begin until the twentieth, when it was encouraged by rulers in both Iran and Turkey, no doubt to reduce dependence on coffee, which they could not grow. Tea cultivation remained of relatively minor importance, mainly for local consumption and a small export surplus. A major tea-drinking area is the western Maghreb, where tea is first mentioned in about 1700. It was introduced and sold by French and English merchants who brought it from the East, and saw Northwest Africa as a useful extension to their European markets. Prepared with mint leaves, it has become the national drink of Morocco.

Over the area as a whole, a far more important beverage was coffee. According to most of the evidence it originated in Ethiopia, and may indeed take its name from the Ethiopian province of Kaffa, where the coffee plant still grows wild. From Kaffa it was introduced in the fourteenth or fifteenth century to Yemen. According to an Egyptian writer, 'at the beginning of this [the sixteenth] century, the news reached us in Egypt that a drink called "*qahwa*" had spread in the Yemen, and was being used by Sufi shaykhs and others to help them stay awake during their devotional exercises...' The writer goes on to explain that coffee was brought back to Yemen by a traveller to Ethiopia who found it in common use there.[4]

> After he had returned to Aden he fell ill, and remembering [*qahwa*] he drank it and benefitted by it. He found that among its properties was that it drove away fatigue and lethargy, and brought to the body a certain sprightliness and vigour. In consequence, when he became a Sufi, he and other Sufis in Aden began to use this beverage.... Then the whole people – both the learned and the common – followed his example in drinking it, seeking help in study and other vocations and crafts, so that it continued to spread.

It did indeed spread. By 1511, coffee drinking is already attested in the holy city of Mecca, and from there, thanks no doubt to returning pilgrims and merchants, the habit was carried westwards to Egypt and Syria and the central Ottoman lands and eastwards to Iran, where coffee remained the major beverage until the early nineteenth century. Unlike tea, for which the Western world had direct access to better, cheaper, and more plentiful sources of supply in India and China, coffee was and for some time remained a Middle Eastern monopoly.

The earliest European references to coffee, coffee drinkers, and coffee-houses, are somewhat disdainful. A Venetian envoy in Istanbul, Gianfrancesco Morosini, writing in 1585, remarks of a coffee-house which he visited:

> All these people are quite base, of low costume and very little industry, such that for the most part they spend their time sunk in idleness. Thus they continually sit about, and for entertainment they are in the habit of drinking, in public, in shops, and in the streets, a black liquid as boiling

hot as they can stand which is extracted from a seed they call 'Cavee'.

An English visitor, George Sandys, who traveled in Turkey in 1610, is even more disparaging. 'There [in their coffee-houses] they sit chatting most of the day and sippe of a drinke called "*Coffa*" . . . as hot as they can suffer it: black as soote, and tasting not much unlike it. . . .' Nevertheless Europeans acquired the taste both for coffee and for the coffee-house, and coffee, mainly produced in the Yemen, rapidly became a major item in the list of Middle Eastern exports to Europe. For the Egyptian merchants, who were losing the once profitable spice trade, coffee – with a growing European market – was a useful substitute. The first coffee-house in Europe was opened in Vienna after the second Turkish siege. It belonged – with exclusive rights – to an Armenian, who requested this privilege as a reward for his services to Austrian intelligence behind the Turkish lines.

It is easy to understand why tea and coffee became so popular in the Middle East, and why the tea-house and the coffee-house became important social centres. Islam, unlike Christianity and Judaism, bans alcoholic drinks. In general, this ban was far from totally effective, and there is no lack of evidence in poetry and narrative of widespread drinking and even drunkenness. But drinking was of necessity clandestine, or at least decently concealed – behind the high walls of a private home, or among the non-Muslim subjects of a Muslim state who were not affected by the ban. In classical Arabic and Persian poetry, the Christian monastery and acolyte and the Zoroastrian mage became the poetic symbols of the tavern and the tavern-keeper. But these indulgences, even when tolerated, were of necessity discreet, and there was nothing in the life of the medieval Muslim cities to correspond to the tavern and its equivalents in the West. The coffee-house and the tea-house filled this void. Before long, complaints are heard that the coffee-house has become a centre of slander, sedition, and, worst of all, gambling.

Techniques of cultivation in the region were, and remained, rudimentary. The simple wooden, wheelless plough of antiquity has remained in use from ancient times until, in some regions, even the present day. It is often used without a mould-board, and yoked to oxen or to mules, sometimes to buffaloes, but not normally to horses. In the rich river-valley societies no great effort was required to get bountiful harvests, sometimes even two or three crops in a year, and there was therefore no incentive, such as those which drove people in poorer and harsher climates with heavier soils, to technological invention.

There may perhaps be another reason for the lack of technological innovation; that is the absence, in these societies, of two characteristic European phenomena – the monastery, where educated and dedicated men devoted themselves to the growing of crops, and, later, the educated farmer. The type of the English country gentleman, for example, who studied at the university and then worked and managed his own farm, applying a trained mind to the problems of agriculture, had no equivalent. Educated gentlemen in the Middle East, with few exceptions, did not bother with farming. Farmers were not educated. The combination of intellectual discipline, technical skill, and actual involvement in agriculture needed to produce technological improvement was, in general, lacking.

Though the contribution of the classical Islamic period to the technology of agriculture – apart from irrigation – was small, farmers and merchants of the Islamic Middle East nevertheless enormously enriched the range and variety of crops, and especially of food crops. The movement westwards of some of the produce of eastern and southern Asia had already begun in the pre-Islamic empires, and crops of East Asian origin were being cultivated in ancient Persia and in Iraq, where their presence is attested in middle Persian and Talmudic writings. Further west they appeared, if at all, as expensive and exotic luxuries. The peach, for example, was known as such in ancient Rome, and its modern name derives from the Roman term '*persicum malum*' ('the Persian apple'). The Islamic conquests for the first time created a single political and economic unit extending from Europe in the West to the borders of India and China in the East. Muslim soldiers and travellers in Central Asia, Muslim seamen and merchants who sailed from the Persian Gulf to India and beyond, must surely have played an important part in the discovery and dissemination of these new crops. The movement westwards in Islamic times from Iran to the Fertile Crescent and North Africa and Europe includes rice, sorghum, sugar cane, cotton, watermelons, aubergines, artichokes, oranges, and bananas, as well as a wide range of food, fodder, and fibre crops, spices and condiments, and other plants required for both medicinal and cosmetic purposes. Medieval Muslim travellers describe an astonishingly wide range of crops, each with many subvariants. An account of the North African coast written in about 1400 CE speaks of sixty-five kinds of grapes, thirty-six kinds of pears, twenty-eight kinds of figs, and sixteen kinds of apricots.

Where Middle Easterners really showed their skill was in irrigation – in the organization and maintenance of an elaborate system of dykes and reservoirs and canals to preserve and distribute the floodwaters of the great rivers. This was of course the work not only of farmers, but of technocrats and bureaucrats. Some historians have seen in the centralized irrigation works of the river-valley societies the nucleus of the modern bureaucratic state and the command economy.

Harvesting was usually with reaping hooks to avoid loss of grain, and the crop was ground with mortar and pestle by hand or with millstones operated by slaves or by beasts of burden. This can still be seen in some parts of the region.

In Egypt fertilizers were unnecessary, since the Nile with its alluvial deposits refertilized the soil every year. They were lacking in most other places where they were needed, and this often gave rise to serious exhaustion of the soil. In Iraq this process was accentuated by salt deposits brought down by the rivers. These were drained in times of peace and good order, and allowed to accumulate in times of trouble. In general farmers seem to have worked on a biennial system, cultivating land and letting it lie fallow in alternate years, except in the river valleys, where the rivers provided sufficient water.

Erosion had long been a problem, even in antiquity. It became so again during the Middle Ages and in modern times. Whenever there was a breakdown of civil order, the nomads came out of the desert into the cultivated land, and the result was an extension of the desert at the expense of the sown.

This could happen in several ways. Defences were necessary to keep back the desert. When the civil order broke down, the defences broke down, and the desert encroached. There was also a more visible element of destruction – the goat. Unlike the sheep, which crops the grass, the goat tears it out, often thereby removing the topsoil or weakening it so that it can be blown away. The goat also eats the bark of trees, which then perish, thus again opening the plains to the winds and the removal of the topsoil. Because of these and other factors, there has been extensive soil erosion in much of the region, so that if we compare the cultivated areas of modern times to those revealed by archaeological evidence in earlier times, the difference can be very striking. Ibn Khaldūn, writing in the fourteenth century, describes how even in his day, 'ruin and devastation prevail' in North Africa, where in the past there was 'a flourishing civilization, as the remains of buildings and statues, and the ruins of towns and villages attest.'[5]

Fiscal and other evidence would suggest an overall decline in agricultural yield and in the revenues from agricultural yields from late Roman times onwards. This process appears to have been well advanced at the time of the Arab invasions. After a brief recovery it continued in later medieval Islamic times. There are a number of indications of this decline. The archaeological evidence – the abandoned wells and farms, the broken-down terraces, the derelict villages in many parts of the Middle East and North Africa – is confirmed by literary and documentary evidence of a decline in output and a consequent decline in revenue. This change was accompanied by a decline in population and a flight from the villages to the towns, usually attributed to the burden of taxation, the exactions of the moneylenders, and similar troubles.

Certainly an important factor in the overall decline in agricultural output was the low esteem in which the cultivation of the earth and those engaged in it were held by government, the upper classes, and to some extent even religion. Islam was born in a caravan city, and its Prophet belonged to a merchant patriciate. After his death, his followers conquered a vast empire which they ruled and exploited from a network of garrison cities in all the provinces. These rapidly became centres of Islamic culture and learning, while the countryside for long remained faithful to the older, pre-Islamic religions. In time even the peasantry were converted and assimilated to Islam, but the old stigma remained, and with the creation of new Muslim empires in India and the Balkans, the same pattern was re-created of Muslim townsfolk ruling non-Muslim peasants. Among the traditions attributed to the Prophet, there are many in praise of commerce, few that show respect for agriculture. In the same spirit, the *sharī'a*, the Holy Law, is primarily concerned with the lives and problems of city-dwellers, which it examines and discusses and regulates in minute detail. It gives remarkably little attention to the concerns of the peasantry, other than the payment of taxes. The situation was surely worsened by the increasing tendency towards the state direction of the economy, and the control of agricultural land by military officers with no great knowledge of agriculture and no great interest in the long-term prosperity of their domains.

Much of the region consists of semi-arid lands, too poor for agriculture or even for grazing large cattle, but sufficient to support sheep and goats. In addition to meat, wool, and hides, these provided yoghurt and cheese, essential components of Middle Eastern diet. A nomadic herding culture had existed in the region for millennia, and together with the first rudimentary agriculture made possible the beginnings of civilization. Camel nomadism can also be traced back to prehistoric times; it remains central to the Bedouin economy and way of life, and provides a major means of transport in both peace and war. Horses in ancient Arabia were few in number, but were highly honoured and known by name and pedigree. After the rise of Islam, Arab breeders, using Persian and Byzantine and later Berber bloodstock, were able vastly to increase their herds, and make extensive use of steppe grazing grounds. Horses and ponies were of primary importance among the nomadic peoples of the Eurasian steppe. Farm animals, kept for food or work, or as pets, were few. The pig, so important in the husbandry of other civilizations, was excluded by the taboo which Islam shared with Judaism. Some historians have even argued that the pig set the geographical limits of Islamic expansion, when the Muslim conquerors reached Spain, the Balkans, and western China. Despite centuries of Muslim rule in these lands, the Muslim faith did not take root among their pig-rearing and pork-eating peoples. Poultry were bred for meat and eggs, and for the latter, poultry farmers in Egypt (and perhaps elsewhere) devised a new technique that startled the first Westerners who encountered it. The French traveller Jean de Thevenot, who visited Egypt in 1655, observes:[6]

> The first of these extraordinary things I saw at Caire, was the artificial way of hatching Chickens; one would think it a Fable, at first, to say that Chickens are hatch'd, without Hens sitting upon the Eggs; and a greater, to say, that they are sold by the Bushel: Nevertheless both are true, and for that effect, they put their Eggs in Ovens, which they heat with so temperate a warmth, which imitates so well the natural heat, that Chickens are formed and hatched in them. . . . They heat them with a very temperate heat, only of the hot ashes of Oxen and Camels-dung, or the like, which they put at the mouth of each Oven, and daily change it, putting fresh hot dung into the same place. . . . Many think that this cannot be done but in Aegypt, because of the warmth of the Climate; but the Great Duke of Florence having sent for one of these Men, he hatched them aswel there as in Aegypt: The same also (as I was told) had been done in Poland.

As Thevenot notes, this method, also known as incubation, was introduced to Europe and later widely practised.

In Western Europe, agriculture and stock raising have been closely associated, often, indeed, in the same hands. In the Middle East, there is an immemorial separation and conflict between the peasant and the nomad. Agriculture and stock raising were separated and usually opposed. A peasant might have a few animals for immediate domestic purposes, but in the main, raising animals, whether for transport or for food, was the work of the nomad. This division of labour led frequently to a conflict of interests harmful to both. The conflict between them appears right at the beginning of one of the oldest Middle Eastern historical narratives that we possess – in the story of Cain and Abel. One of the brothers brought a burnt animal offering; he was a stock raiser. The other brought the fruits of the earth; he was a cultivator. The Pentateuchal God favoured the nomads. He accepted the burnt offering and rejected the fruits of the earth, whereupon Cain, the peasant, murdered Abel, the nomad. More often in Middle Eastern history it has been the other way round, and it is the peasants who have suffered from the depredations of marauding nomads. All the cultivated lands of the Middle East are within easy reach of deserts inhabited by nomads ready to take advantage of any sign of weakness in the defences established by the civil authority. And beyond the northern and southern borders of the civilized lands, in the Eurasian steppes and the Arabian desert, there were nomad principalities and kingdoms waiting to become empires.

Both agriculture and stock raising provided the raw materials for industry, and especially for the major industry of the Middle Ages, textiles. The importance of textile exports to Europe is attested by the many textile names of Middle Eastern origin – from places, e.g. muslin (from Mosul), damask (from Damascus), or technical terms, like gauze (*qazz*), mohair (*mukhayyar*), taffeta (Persian *tāftah*). Textiles manufactured and exported included tapestries, cushions, and other furnishings, as well as clothing. While the peasants brought flax and cotton, the nomads provided wool and hides. Another important raw material, timber, was in short supply and consequently expensive, being mostly imported.

Minerals were of course of major importance. These included stone, clay, and the like, which could be collected, and metal, which had to be mined. Gold, silver, and unalloyed copper were already being mined in the Middle East in prehistoric times. Bronze was being made in eastern Mesopotamia by the third millennium BCE, in Egypt in the second. Tin was being imported from the faraway 'tin islands', that is to say Cornwall, while iron came from several places in the north: Armenia, Transcaucasia, and what is now eastern Turkey. Many of the mines of the Middle East were already exhausted in antiquity, and the Muslim states came to rely increasingly on imports from their remoter provinces and from yet further away.

Some mines remained, principally on the outskirts of the region in Armenia, in Iran, in Upper Egypt, and the Sudan, but very few in the central lands of the Middle East, that is, the Fertile Crescent, and Egypt. Gold and silver had to be brought from elsewhere. The search for these metals, and the routes by which they were transported, often had a significant influence on the course of events. One of the richest sources of gold for the Islamic world was the mines of Africa, particularly in the 'Allāqī area south of Aswān, in the border region between Egypt and the Sudan. Undoubtedly one of the main incentives for the Islamic advance south of the Sahara was the quest for gold and slaves. Silver was found in a number of places, principally in the former Sasanid territories.

Industrial techniques were and remained rudimentary. With few exceptions, the only source of energy was human and animal muscle. Some minor automata were invented and used, but principally as toys. Apart from these, the only machines were the mill and the missile launcher. Mills, driven by both wind and water, are attested from early times, and remained in use to the present day. They were, however, very few in number compared with even the early medieval West, and were used only for irrigation and for grinding corn, not for industrial purposes. The other machine was the catapult and similar devices used in warfare to hurl pots filled with incendiary liquids against enemy cities on land and ships at sea. Until the importation of guns and gunners from Europe in the late Middle Ages, these were operated by tension, by torsion, or, in the most sophisticated phase, by the use of balances, that is, the movement of weights and counter-weights. This made it possible to hurl larger projectiles with greater force over greater distances than was possible by earlier methods. Other weapons of war – swords, daggers, shields, armour, and artillery (meaning such things as mangonels and ballistas) – had an important place both in industrial production and as a commodity in international trade.

One obvious reason for the lack of progress in the generation of energy is the absence of suitable raw materials – of anything comparable with the firewood and charcoal and coal of Western Europe, or the water power available from so many rivers and waterfalls. There was of course petroleum, but the secret of its extraction and use lay far in the future. In ancient and medieval times, it was obtained only by natural seepage. In Zoroastrian Persia, it was used to maintain the sacred flame in the temples. In the Byzantine and the Islamic empires, it was used principally to make explosive mixtures for weapons of war.

After clothing, shelter was the most universal need, and many industries developed to supply materials for the construction, furnishing, and adornment of private and public buildings. The needs of city-dwellers included pots and pans and other utensils, soaps and scents and unguents, and of course writing materials: ink, parchment, papyrus, and later paper.

Transportation, which in other civilizations was an important stimulus to industrial production, was of less importance in the Islamic lands. Perhaps because of the shortage of wood and metals, wheeled vehicles were rarely used, and few roads were made for them. From time to time, wheeled carts are mentioned, described, and even depicted, but were clearly seen as something unusual. In the fourteenth century, Ibn Baṭṭūṭa, who travelled from his native Morocco across the Middle East to Central Asia, encountered wheeled carts among the Turkish peoples of the steppe, and thought it remarkable enough to mention and describe them. As late as the eighteenth century, the French traveller Volney observed:[7]

> It is noteworthy that in the whole of Syria no wagon or cart is seen; this is probably due to the fear lest they should be seized by the government's men, and a heavy loss should be suffered in a moment.

Transportation was normally by pack animals or by water. The camel, domesticated in the second millennium BCE, can carry up to 1200 pounds, cover 200 miles in a day, and travel for 17 days without water. Camels could not be used everywhere. In the moist climate of the Balkans, great numbers, brought from Anatolia and Syria to transport Ottoman supplies and ordnance, sickened and died, impeding the Ottoman advance. But in the dry climate of the Middle East, these beasts were certainly far more cost-effective than would have been any system of carts and roads. And even the humble mule or donkey served quite adequately for the transportation of goods and persons over shorter distances. Water transport was, however, quite another matter, and from early times there was a large-scale development of shipbuilding, both for the Mediterranean and for the eastern seas, as well as for the inland waterways. Historians of Rome have calculated that it cost more to cart wheat seventy-five miles in the Roman Empire than to transport it by sea from one end of the Mediterranean to the other. Something of the same sort must have been true also in Islamic times.

The usual form of manufacture, especially for textiles, was domestic, the artisan working in his own home, perhaps with his family or in a small workshop. Manufacturing was primarily for community, family, and local needs, not for international trade, and only a few commodities, the most important being carpets, reached that level. Sometimes industrial organization developed on a larger scale. There are, for example, documents from medieval Egypt indicating that flax workers were employed by an entrepreneur for a daily wage. Similar arrangements are attested for sugar refining, another important Egyptian industry. The state also intervened in many ways in industry, sometimes by providing encouragement through its patronage, sometimes even by investment of money by rulers, and sometimes through the establishment of state industrial monopolies.

The most important of these was *ṭirāz*. In classical Arabic the word denotes a kind of brocade or embroidery, the wearing or granting of which was a royal prerogative. It was worn only by rulers or by those persons on whom rulers wished to bestow a mark of honour. The *ṭirāz* became a system of honours and decorations. Because of this special status the manufacture of *ṭirāz* was, in the early centuries, a jealously guarded state monopoly. *Ṭirāz* workshops were state-owned, and their directors were state employees. Later it became more diffused. War production, too, was sometimes state-controlled, for example the building of warships and the making of certain types of weapons.

From time to time the state also intervened in economic life to fix prices. This practice goes back to antiquity, and in particular to the reign of the Roman emperor Diocletian, who seems to have been the first to try to fix prices on a grand scale. Despite a *ḥadīth* attributed to the Prophet that 'Only God can fix prices' – an eloquent statement of *laissez-faire* economics – Muslim authorities frequently tried to fix what medieval economists called 'a fair price'. Such policies almost invariably failed. Some rulers went beyond price-fixing to monopolization. In late Mamluk Egypt in particular, governments seemed to have reasoned that if they could earn so much a year by taxing the pepper trade, they could earn even more by taking it over entirely, and thus having all the profits instead of just what they could exact from the pepper merchants. One ruler in particular, the Mamluk sultan of

Egypt Bārsbāy (1422–38 CE), carried the policy of state monopolies to extremes. The resulting disruption of the transit trade was one of the main motives which led the Portuguese to set out on their journey around Africa.

In industry, as in so much else, one of the major developments of the Islamic period was the harmonious blending of traditions and techniques from different regions, from the ancient civilizations of the eastern Mediterranean world on the one hand, and the Iranian world on the other, which achieved a new beauty in Islamic pottery. In the thirteenth century, the great Mongol invasions for the first time brought east and west Asia under a single rule, and opened the Middle East, especially Persia, to the tastes and styles of the Far East.

The pursuit and extraction of precious metals both encouraged and facilitated the development of a far-flung system of distribution and exchange. The simultaneous use of two coinages, gold in the former Byzantine territories and silver in the former Sasanid territories, led to the development, in effect, of a bimetallist economy and of a system of monetary exchanges. The need to conduct large-scale trade over vast areas produced a class of money-changers, functioning in almost every major commercial centre, and ultimately to the development of a ramified and sophisticated system of banking.

The circumstances of the medieval Islamic world were uniquely favourable to the development of long-range, large-scale commerce. For the first time ever, a vast region of ancient civilizations, from Morocco across North Africa to the Middle East and as far as – and later beyond – the borders of India and China, was united in a single political and cultural system, for a while even under a single central authority. The Arabic language, in universal use at least as a medium of international and inter-regional communication, was understood from one end of the Islamic world to the other, and provided a subtle, rich and sophisticated medium of communication.

'God has permitted buying and selling', says the Qur'ān, 'and forbidden usury ... those who [after warning] revert to usury are doomed to everlasting hellfire ...' (2:275). The ban on usury, strongly expressed in the Qur'ān, is further emphasized in both traditions and commentaries, one of which even lays down that a single act of usury is worse than thirty-three acts of fornication. This ban has always been taken seriously by Muslims, and to this day makes banking and investment difficult for the truly devout. The overwhelming majority of theologians and jurists interpret the ban as applying to any interest, not just excessive interest – a rule which, strictly applied, would have prevented the development of credit and thus of large-scale commerce. In this as in many other matters, merchants and jurists devised procedures – the technical term is '*ḥīla sharʿiyya*' ('legal device') – whereby, while formally respecting the law, they were able to organize credit, investment, partnerships, and even banking.

One of the basic obligations of the Islamic religion, the pilgrimage to Mecca (*ḥajj*), which every Muslim is required to perform at least once in his lifetime, contributed greatly to the development of long-distance commerce. The *ḥajj*, held every year, brought together great numbers of Muslims from every part of the Islamic world to share in the same rites and rituals at the same holy places, and certainly helped to create and maintain a sense of common identity.

The Islamic world had its local traditions, often very vigorous, but there was, almost from the start, a degree of unity in the civilization of the cities – in values, standards, and social customs – that was without parallel in medieval Christendom. 'The Franks', says Rashīd al-Dīn, 'speak twenty-five languages, and no people understands the language of any other.'[8] This was a natural comment for a Muslim, accustomed to the linguistic unity of the Muslim world, with two or three major languages serving not only as the media of a narrow clerical class, like Latin in Western Europe, but as the effective means of universal communication, supplanting local languages and dialects at all but the lowest levels. With a degree of physical as well as social and intellectual mobility unparalleled in ancient and medieval times, the Islamic world developed a far-flung network of communications by both land and water.

Both kinds of travel were hazardous, the one threatened by bandits and brigands, the other by pirates. Both were slow and arduous. Both were expensive, though travel by sea or waterways was far cheaper. For all these reasons, long-range commerce was, in the main, limited to a narrow range of commodities of sufficiently high price to justify the risks of such enterprises.

Foodstuffs, therefore, so important a commodity in more modern commerce, were of limited importance in earlier times. They were generally cheap and needed to be transported in bulk. They were not therefore worthwhile. The costs were too high, the profits too low, the risks too great. The production of food for consumption was almost entirely local. Long-range commerce was primarily concerned with three types of merchandise, which because of their rarity and high cost could justify the risks and rigours of distant journeys by ship and caravan. They consisted primarily of essential minerals, of slaves, and of luxury goods.

Foodstuffs could usually be grown locally with only minimum dependence on imports. Gold, silver and iron could not, and had to be imported, at whatever cost.

The large-scale, long-range commerce in human beings was, in the main, a development of the Islamic period, and was due, by a sad paradox of history, to the humanizing effect of Islamic legislation. In the ancient empires, even in early Christian times, the vast slave population was for the most part recruited locally. The supply was always replenished in a number of ways: by the enslavement of criminals and debtors, by the 'adoption' as slaves of children abandoned by their parents, and by those who sold their own children or even themselves into bondage. All this was ended with the Islamic conquests and the gradual application of Islamic law. According to the principle formulated by the Muslim jurists and generally respected by Muslim rulers, the natural condition of humankind is freedom. Freeborn subjects of the Muslim state, whether Muslims or followers of one or other of the permitted religions, could not be enslaved either for debt or for criminal offences other than armed rebellion. Abandoned children must be presumed to be free unless they could be proved to be slaves. The children of slave parents were born and remained slaves unless and until they were manumitted. Free persons could only be enslaved if they were infidels captured in a holy war. In such a case, both they and their families were lawful booty and became the property of their conquerors. The recruitment by natural increase to slave parents within the empire was never sufficient for the insatiable needs of Middle Eastern society, and a vast traffic therefore developed in newly enslaved infidels brought from beyond the imperial frontiers. The price of slaves, especially of young female slaves, was high, and despite the perishable character of this merchandise the trade was well worth the risks. The price of young male slaves could be greatly increased by castration to meet the demand for eunuchs to serve in palaces, in the wealthier homes, and in some religious sites. The law of Islam forbids mutilation, and eunuchs were therefore 'manufactured' on the frontiers before entering Islamic territory.

Slaves came from three main areas: from Europe, from the Eurasian steppe, and from Africa. Occasionally slaves are mentioned from further afield – from India, China, and elsewhere – but these were few and exceptional. The regular supply of slaves from medieval to modern times came from these three main groups. The Slavic peoples of Central and Eastern Europe from whom, indeed, the English word 'slave' is derived, provided an important part of the slave population of Muslim Spain and North Africa. In the Middle Ages they were supplied mainly by West European slave merchants and intermediaries. In Eastern Europe, the Ottomans, advancing into the Balkans, were able to cut out the middlemen and get their Slavic slaves direct from the source. A smaller but not unimportant supply of West European slaves was provided by the activities of the Barbary corsairs, who by the seventeenth century extended their raids from the Mediterranean shores and shipping to the Atlantic coasts and sea-lanes. In 1627 they raided Iceland, and carried off 242 captives for sale in the slave market of Algiers. On 20 June 1631 Barbary corsairs raided the fishing village of Baltimore, in Ireland. A report sent at the time to London lists the Baltimore people 'carried away' by the raiders, with their wives, children and maidservants – 107 persons in all, to which were added forty-seven 'captured from other sources'. A contemporary witness, a French priest named Father Dan, describes their arrival at their destination:[9]

> It was a piteous sight to see them exposed for sale at Algiers, for then they parted the wife from the husband, and the father from the child; then, say I, they sell the husband here, and the wife there, tearing from her arms a daughter whom she cannot hope to see ever again.

In the same period, the Tatar rulers of Eastern Europe raided the villages of Russia, Poland, and the Ukraine, and each year carried off thousands of young slaves – 'the harvest of the steppes' – who were shipped to Istanbul and sold in the cities of the Ottoman Empire. This traffic continued until the late eighteenth century, when it was ended by the Russian annexation of the Crimea in 1783.

The second major group of slaves were the Turks of the Eurasian steppe who from early Islamic times were recruited by capture and purchase in the lands extending from north of the Black Sea to the borders of China and Mongolia. These constituted the main body of white slaves in the eastern Islamic world in the Middle Ages, and were used especially for military purposes. With the Islamization of the Turkish steppe, such recruitment was no longer possible, but a new source was found in the Caucasian lands from which Georgian and Circassian slaves, both male and female, were imported in great numbers for a variety of services in the Ottoman and Persian lands. This source too was substantially blocked with the Russian conquest of the Caucasus in the first quarter of the nineteenth century.

The third and most lasting slave trade was that which brought black slaves from Africa south of the Sahara. Black slaves appear occasionally in Roman times, especially in Egypt, where they had been known since remote antiquity. But in general they were the exception rather than the rule. The massive importation of black slaves dates from the advance of the Muslim armies into the African continent. The slaves came by three main routes: from East Africa, by sea, through the Red Sea and the Persian Gulf to Arabia and Iran and beyond; from the Sudan by caravan down the Nile valley to Egypt; from West Africa northwards across the Sahara to all the lands of the Mediterranean littoral from Morocco to Egypt. This source of supply, too, was for a while blocked by the establishment of European colonial rule in most of tropical Africa. These black slaves were used for a variety of purposes – agricultural, industrial, commercial, and above all domestic. Though black slaves are encountered in agriculture, for example in drainage projects in Iraq, in mines, notably in the salt and gold mines of Nubia and the Sahara, and in some forms of manufacturing, the medieval Islamic economy, unlike that of the ancient world, was not primarily based on slave labour.

Finally, there was the traffic in luxury goods, items of small bulk, light weight, high cost, and great value.

By far the most important of these were textiles, especially valuable textiles such as silk and silk brocade. In late Roman, Byzantine, Persian, and early Islamic times, silk was of considerable political as well as commercial importance. Often the importation of silk, and later the manufacture of silk, were royal monopolies. As silk robes of honour were also from time to time granted to barbarian princelings, the silk trade could also have some diplomatic significance. The importation of silk from the East for a time constituted a major theme in the political and military history of the areas through which it passed.

Another major commodity was incense, brought, along with other aromatics, from southern Arabia and points further east. Because of its universal use in the temples of the Greco-Roman world and later in Christian churches, incense was a commodity of major importance. Some modern historians have even described it as the oil trade of the ancient world – it helped to make the wheels go around, but in a figurative rather than a literal sense.

Islam has no use for incense in its rituals and worship, and after the advent and spread of the new faith this commodity became far less important in the Islamic world, though there was a continuing demand for it in Christian Europe. Rather more important, after the decline in the incense trade, was the trade in spices, and above all pepper, coming from the Malabar coast. There was a substantial market both in the Muslim lands and beyond for pepper and other spices and condiments, and the merchants who dealt in these commodities were a wealthy and highly respected community.

Precious stones also had the advantages of light weight and high cost. The same is true of such other items as ivory, rare and precious woods, and even rare animals, which in Roman times were imported in considerable numbers for the circus.

In the high Middle Ages the commerce of the Islamic Middle East was in every way ahead of that of Europe – richer, larger, better organized, with more commodities to sell and more money to buy, and a vastly more sophisticated network of trading relations. By the end of the Middle Ages, these roles were reversed. The Middle Eastern trade was not, as was once thought, ended by the voyages of discovery and the arrival of the Portuguese in Asia – it is now well known that the trade continued for more than a century after Vasco da Gama arrived in India. Nor was the decline in the Middle Eastern trade caused by the transoceanic discoveries, the economic effects of which were a consequence, not a cause, of changes in the Middle East. It is remarkable that the Portuguese, a small nation in a small West-European country, were able to establish a naval and commercial presence and for a while even domination in the East; it is even more remarkable that the great Middle East powers – Mamluk Egypt, Ottoman Turkey, Safavid Iran – were unable to muster either the economic strength to compete with them or the naval strength to defeat them. The Discoveries must surely have accelerated the decline of Middle Eastern trade. They did not cause it, and the historian must seek causes elsewhere.

This decline was not limited to the Islamic lands. A similar process can be observed in the remaining Byzantine territories and even, to a lesser extent, in Mediterranean Europe, notably Italy, where the once-great commercial states were outperformed by the rising economies of northwestern Europe. Nor can the decline be attributed simply to Islamic religious attitudes or to the working of the Holy Law. Their presence did not prevent an earlier flourishing of commerce; their absence did not save Byzantium and Italy.

Some material factors are readily identifiable. The exhaustion, or loss to invaders, of mines and precious metals left the Islamic states short of money at precisely the time when their European competitors were finding new sources of gold and silver in the Americas. The Black Death and other natural disasters had affected both Christendom and Islam, but the Islamic lands had suffered more from destructive invasions, especially those of the Mongols in the East and the Hilālī Bedouin who devastated North Africa.

Perhaps even more destructive in the long run than external invasions were political changes at home and the increasing domination of the state by military aristocracies with little concern for commerce and little interest in production. Even the Mediterranean sea trade had been taken over by the Italian cities – without conquest, without pressure, simply by more active and more effective commercial methods. Apart from a few products like sugar and later coffee, Middle Eastern agriculture and industry were no longer able to provide an exportable surplus of commodities, and Middle Eastern traders had to depend increasingly on the transit trade between Europe and the further East. The diversion of that trade was therefore a far greater blow than it might otherwise have been. Meanwhile, technological, financial and commercial advances in Western Europe provided Western traders with the means, the resources and the skills to dominate Middle Eastern markets, to which their access was, if anything, facilitated by the unity and stability achieved by the Ottoman Empire. Ottoman armies ruled the land, and Ottoman fleets for a while dominated the seas; but the European merchant, quietly and peacefully, captured the markets.

CHAPTER 10

THE ELITES

In Islamic civilization, as in every other known to history, a distinction existed and was recognized between some limited, more or less privileged groups, and the undifferentiated remainder of the population. In classical Arabic usage, they were usually denoted by the terms *khāṣṣa* and *ʿāmma*, two Arabic words meaning 'special' and 'general'. Islam is in principle egalitarian, recognizing no superiority of one believer over another by birth or descent, race or nationality, or social status. Like its sister religions, classical Islam assumed a basic inequality between man and woman, freeman and slave, believer and infidel, and enforced the inferior status of the latter by the rules of the Holy Law. Apart from these established and recognized inequalities, Islamic law and doctrine recognize no distinction between believers. Only piety and good deeds can confer honour, since piety and good deeds outrank wealth and power and noble birth alike.

In practice, however, those who were fortunate enough to possess wealth and power or even learning usually wished to pass these assets on to their children, and there was thus a tendency, inevitable in all human societies, towards the formation of hereditary privileged groups. Until Ottoman times, few political regimes lasted long enough to establish and preserve an entrenched aristocracy; most of the regimes of medieval Islam were overthrown by upheaval from inside or, much more frequently, by conquest from outside. The new rulers, with their kinsmen, their henchmen, and their supporters, then duly formed a new aristocracy of wealth and power. A conquest gave obvious advantage to those who shared an ethnic origin with the conquerors, but with two exceptions such privileges were of brief duration. The two exceptions were the Arabs, who created and for a while governed the Islamic polity, and the Turks, who, from the later Middle Ages until modern times, established a near monopoly of political sovereignty and military command. And both, in time and in different ways, merged their original ethnic identities – the Arabs into the Arabized mass of the indigenous population, the Turks into the multinational governing and administering elite of the Ottoman Empire.

There is only one context in which social ranking is discussed by the doctors of the Holy Law, and that is in connection with the principle of *kafāʾa*, which might be roughly translated as equality of birth and social status in marriage. This principle is not a recognition of any sort of aristocratic privilege. It does not forbid unequal marriages, and the jurists are far from unanimous on what constitutes inequality. The purpose of the rule is to protect the honour of respectable families by enabling them, if they wish, to stop unsuitable marriages. The principle of *kafāʾa* may be invoked by the father or other legal guardian of a woman to prevent her from contracting a marriage without permission, or to annul it if it is contracted without permission or with permission fraudulently obtained, provided there is no child or pregnancy. It may be invoked to restrain a woman from marrying a man who is below her in social status, and thus dishonouring her family. There was no objection to a man marrying a woman of lower status, since the woman, in the view of the jurists, is in any case inferior, and no social damage could therefore result from such a marriage.

The jurists differ considerably on how equal status is to be defined. For some, the rule is concerned only with religion, and is intended to protect a pious women from being married against her will to an impious man. In all other respects, according to the great jurist Mālik ibn Anas, 'All the people of Islam are equal to one another, in accordance with God's revelations'.[1] But for another school of jurists, perhaps influenced by the hierarchic notions and practices of pre-Islamic Persia, *kafāʾa* was concerned with other matters besides piety and character. These include pedigree, profession, financial status, and – for the children or grandchildren of converted unbelievers or manumitted slaves – the date when their families became Muslim or free.

Clearly, the distinction between *khāṣṣa* and *ʿāmma* was not simply economic – a distinction between those who possess and those who do not possess. The theme of the poor gentleman and the rich parvenu is as familiar in Islamic literatures as in any other. But equally clearly, sustained poverty over generations was not compatible with membership of the *khāṣṣa*. Nor was the difference primarily one of birth, origin, and status, though again these had their place in the definition. Being born to a *khāṣṣa* father and brought up in a *khāṣṣa* home created at least a presupposition of *khāṣṣa* status. And, as in other times and places, social distinctions could outlast the economic and political realities that gave rise to them. When real power and wealth have gone, a sentiment of social superiority may still remain. Occupation was obviously important, and indeed medieval Muslim writers devote some attention to the classification of different trades, crafts, and professions with indications of their place in the social order.

Education too could be a determining factor, and was of special significance in a society which accorded divine status to its scripture, revered the language in which that scripture was written, and esteemed those who could use it with elegance. First one, then two, finally three languages – Arabic, Persian, and Turkish – defined the cultural identity of the major regions of Middle Eastern Islam and gave to their educated classes a remarkable degree of cultural and moral unity. While the 'general' populations used a multiplicity of local languages and dialects, the khāṣṣa was united by a common literary language, a common classical and scriptural tradition, and through them a common set of decencies and conformities – rules of behaviour and politeness. In earlier times, notably in 'Abbasid Baghdad and Fāṭimid Cairo, adherence to the dominant faith was not a necessary condition of membership of the elite, and we hear of Christian and Jewish poets, scientists, and scholars moving in the same circles as their Muslim colleagues – not only as colleagues, but as friends, partners, pupils, and teachers. Later, at least partly because of the religious struggles both at home and abroad, attitudes became harsher, and the non-Muslim communities, though still enjoying that measure of tolerance prescribed by Muslim law, were gradually separated and isolated from the main Muslim community. By late medieval and early modern times, while non-Muslim physicians and other specialists were still employed, often at the highest levels, social and even intellectual communication between people of different religions was greatly reduced.

The literary and documentary evidence that has come down to us from earlier times derives almost in its entirety from the khāṣṣa, and it was therefore inevitable that the record of the past, and modern historical writing based on that record, should in the main reflect the interests, activities, and concerns of the khāṣṣa. Only in recent years have scholars begun to study the life of the unprivileged commonalty – the peasants, the artisans, and the urban poor. While some fascinating documents have survived from the Middle Ages, this study is in the main limited to the Ottoman period, from which alone detailed archival records have survived.

Literary evidence for the study of Islamic history – books, letters, and other documents – derives overwhelmingly from two major social groups, the bureaucracy and the men of religion. The institution of bureaucracy dates back to very ancient times, and may indeed have originated in the Middle East. It arose in response to certain practical needs, and in particular of organizing and maintaining the irrigation systems in the river valley societies. Already during the second half of the fourth millennium BCE, the pharaohs of the old kingdom of Egypt drained swamps, extended irrigation, built towns, and conducted external trade by land and sea to bring Egypt the timber and minerals she needed. The development of government and administration, and the building of palaces and temples, required some system of accounts and records. To meet this new need, the specialized 'mystery' of writing came into being, and with it a new social class of clerks and scribes, and the revolutionary possibility of recording, accumulating, and transmitting knowledge. Bureaucracy flourished in Egypt through successive changes of regime and even civilization – the pharaohs, the Hellenistic monarchs, the Romans, the Christian Byzantines, the Arabs, and their various Muslim successors. A similar progression may be seen in Iraq and Iran, where a bureaucratic tradition dating back to the Babylonian and ancient Persian monarchies survived into Sasanid times and after them under the Muslims caliphs and sultans. Their prototype was Ezra the scribe, whose skills and functions are described in the book of the Hebrew Bible that bears his name.

Certain persistent features characterize all these bureaucracies. Perhaps the most important and enduring is that this form of government is continuous and is conducted in writing. Letters and accounts are an essential part of administration; writing and ciphering are essential skills for those who work there. A considerable proportion of classical Islamic literature was written by scribes for scribes, and reflects both their ethos and their professional interests and concerns. This literature portrays a bureaucracy which is functionally demarcated and hierarchically ordered. Each official has a task for the performance of which he is authorized by some higher authority. His function is defined, his authorization limited. Within the system there is what one might call a chain of command, which is also a ladder of promotion. Each knows approximately what lies ahead of him, and what he needs to do in order to achieve the coveted promotion. This kind of hierarchy also involves supervision and control, and brings into play the important principle of accountability.

Among the defining characteristics of a bureaucracy are its methods of recruitment and payment. Characteristically, the scribe is a salaried employee. His emoluments come to him not by inheritance, not by the ownership or control of some revenue-producing asset, not as a perquisite of his status. He neither owns nor possesses his source of income, nor is he the recipient of any kind of grant. He is paid a wage for doing a job. In the better organized and more successful bureaucracies, he is paid in cash. In times of financial stringency, rulers sometimes paid their officials in the form of grants – a sure prescription for administrative breakdown.

In the course of the millennia Middle Eastern bureaucracies, through many changes of government, religion, culture, and even script and language, show a remarkable persistence and continuity. In the centuries between the rise of Christianity and the rise of Islam, the administrative systems were Hellenistic in the western half, Persian in the eastern half of the region. West of Iraq, in the lands under Roman and later Byzantine rule, the business of administration was carried on in Greek, not Latin, and appears to have maintained the practice of the Hellenistic monarchies. Fortunately for the historian, the special conditions of Egypt – centralized administration, a fair degree of stability and continuity, and a dry climate – made possible the preservation of great numbers of administrative documents which have survived to the present day. These enable the historian to follow, with a degree of detail impossible in other regions, the administrative processes of Roman, Byzantine, and Islamic Egypt, and to see how this bureaucracy worked and sometimes changed. While there is no comparable documentary evidence from the Syrian regions, such literary evidence as is available tends to confirm the hypothesis that much the same was happening there as in Egypt. There too, a Roman, then Byzantine, bureaucracy carried on the daily business of government in Greek, keeping its accounts and filing its correspondence in the Greek language. Many, if not indeed most of the employees were Hellenized natives rather than Greeks. By the time of the Islamic conquest, they were overwhelmingly Christian.

Climatic pressures and political discontinuities combined to prevent the survival of any comparable body of documents from the Persian Empire. But external testimony from both the Hebrew Bible and the Greek authors portrays a busy and professional chancery operating under the ancient Persian emperors, while later Muslim sources attest the existence of an elaborate registration of fiscal and other financial affairs. The preparation of bound volumes in codex form, into which records were copied and preserved for future reference, may indeed have originated in the Persian administration. Papyrus, in common use in Roman and Byzantine offices, did not lend itself to the codex form, and papyrus registers as well as books were usually kept in rolls. Parchment and vellum were more convenient and more durable, and were extensively used in early Christian times to make books which began to assume something like the modern shape. In the Persian Empire, they were also used to make record books which, surviving into Arab times, were often consulted by the new masters. The introduction of paper made the keeping of registers general in Islamic lands.

Perhaps the most astonishing example of bureaucratic continuity is the situation after the Arab Muslim conquests of the seventh century. The Persian Empire ceased to exist, and vast lands were wrested from the Byzantines and incorporated in a new Arab Islamic empire. And yet, in spite of these changes, the record of the Egyptian papyri makes it clear that as far as the day-to-day business of government was concerned, nothing changed. The Egyptian Christian officials continued to collect the same taxes according to the same rules, to write the same administrative documents, even dating them by the old Egyptian Christian era, exactly as they had done before. The ultimate destination of the revenues changed; everything else remained the same. It is only gradually, in the course of more than a century, that the documents show real change taking place in the bureaucracy. It is not until comparatively late that bilingual papyri begin to appear, written in both Greek and Arabic. Then, in the course of time, there are more Arabic, fewer Greek documents, until, by the late eighth century, Greek entirely disappears, and only Arabic papyri are found. From literary evidence, it seems likely that much the same was happening in Syria and Iraq, and also in the East, where Arabic replaced the old Persian script and language.

Even this change did not mean that the old bureaucrats were being dismissed and replaced. Long after the arrival of the Arabs, the old bureaucratic families preserved their craft mysteries, and especially their secret systems of keeping accounts. Many stories are told in the Arabic chronicles of how, when the Arabs came as conquerors, they tried to take over the government but couldn't, because nobody could read the accounts except the accountants, and no one could deal with correspondence except the clerks in the office. And so, the stories relate, perforce the Arabs had to give way, and though they were the unchallenged political and military masters of the empire, they had to leave the old clerks still doing their job. By the second century of the Muslim era, Arab rulers, after considerable effort, had finally succeeded in imposing the Arabic language on their staffs, and introducing some measure of unity between the different provinces of the empire. But even this did not necessarily mean that the old bureaucratic families had been ousted – merely that they had mastered the Arabic language. Many adopted Islam along with the new language, but by no means all, and as late as the thirteenth and fourteenth centuries CE, there are still bitter complaints from pious Muslims in Egypt who say that Copts, that is to say Christians, are still running the administration and collecting the taxes, and that an honest Muslim can't get a fair chance in his own country.

This extraordinary persistence of bureaucratic tradition was both a cause and a consequence of the existence of great bureaucratic or scribal families. Traditional historiography focuses largely on the caliphs and sultans, the military commanders and provincial governors, the great political and military figures whose names dominate the pages of history. But at least as much attention is due to other people whose names are rarely mentioned by the chroniclers, and who can only be detected, if at all, with difficulty from a study of the documents – the heads of departments, the chiefs of chancery, the intendants of finances, the assessors and collectors of taxes, and their various underlings, who from generation to generation and from century to century kept the business of government going, often establishing dynastic traditions which made them, in effect, a kind of bureaucratic nobility or aristocracy. An early eighth-century bureaucrat, in a letter addressed to his fellow bureaucrats, speaks with pride of their role in the maintenance of both state and society:[2]

God ... made you secretaries in the most distinguished positions, men of culture and virtue, of knowledge and discernment. By your means the excellences of the Caliphate are well-ordered, and its affairs uprightly maintained. By your counsel God fits government to the people, and the land prospers. The king cannot do without you, nor can any competent person be found, save among you. You are, therefore, for kings the ears with which they hear, the eyes with which they see, the tongues with which they speak, the hands with which they strike.

The natural desire of bureaucrats, like other holders of position and power, to transmit their advantages to their children, had important consequences in the sphere of education. The Muslim empires do not seem to have developed a system of recruitment by public examination – like printing and gunpowder, this was a Chinese invention which did not reach the Islamic world until it was introduced from the West. Recruitment was by apprenticeship. At a suitable point, a bureaucrat might introduce his son or nephew or other protégé to the office, where he would begin work in a fairly humble capacity, initially without pay, and gradually work his way up the ladder. This continued into modern times, and patronage, the ability to nominate, to appoint, even to recommend, has been a powerful political weapon in the region. In this as in other areas, the patron–client relationship is one of the most important and most effective in the whole society.

In the bureaucracy, unlike some other forms of activity, patronage and protection were not enough. The apprentice also needed specialized skills and a level of education which would enable him to acquire them. There was thus an important link between the bureaucratic and learned elements in society – not as close as in medieval Christian Europe, but not unimportant, and increasing in the later Middle Ages.

With two different literate and educated classes, the medieval Islamic world developed two different kinds of literature and learning. One of them, called *adab*, consisted of poetry, history, *belles-lettres*, and a wide range of works illustrating what a man of culture was expected to know and appreciate. The other, called *'ilm*, literally 'knowledge', was the domain of the ulema, and consisted primarily of the religious sciences – the Qur'ān and its interpretations, the traditions of the Prophet, the lives and precedents of the Prophet and his companions, and, deriving from these, the sister sciences of theology and law.

In time, the Byzantine and Persian administrations were gradually modified, adapted, assimilated, Arabized, and Islamized. A new phase began with the invasions from the steppe, when first the Turks and later the Mongols established their domination in the Middle Eastern Islamic world, and the world of Islam was riven by religious conflicts – between Sunni and Shī'a, between 'Abbasids and Fāṭimids, between moderates and radicals within each of these groups. During this period there was a noticeable change in the training, ethos, and general outlook of the bureaucracies. Far greater stress was laid on Islam, and especially on Islamic law and practice, in their education and training.

More and more, they tended to be the products of a religious education provided by men of the ulema class.

The bureaucrats, known as scribes (in Arabic '*kātib*'), formed a numerous, powerful, and self-conscious group in Islamic society. They had their own special attire, a kind of cloak called the *darrā'a*, and their own supreme chief, the vizier, who was head of the administration under the caliph or sultan. Before the militarization of government, he took precedence over all other dignitaries, and was preceded, on ceremonial occasions, by his emblem of office – an inkpot.

It is often said that Islam has no priesthood. This is certainly true in the theological sense. There is no ordination in Islam, no priestly function, no sacraments which only an ordained priest can perform. In principle, anyone with the necessary knowledge can lead in prayer, preach in the mosque, or officiate at weddings and funerals. In principle, there is no priestly mediation between God and the believer. And since there is no priesthood, there could in principle be no priestly hierarchy, no higher or lower ranks of clergy, no bishops or cardinals, no synods or councils. Some men might devote their lives to pious pursuits, but they were expected to earn their livelihood in some other way, through an honourable occupation such as handicraft or commerce. In this, the Muslim position was very different from that of Christians, and much closer to that of the Jews, who after the destruction of the Temple and the dissolution of its priesthood accepted no new priesthood, and perceived the rabbis only as teachers and as jurists. A well-known saying in *The Ethics of the Fathers*, a rabbinic work probably compiled in the third century CE, warns those who learn and teach the Torah: 'Do not make it either a crown with which to shine, or a spade with which to dig.' Similar dicta may be found in Muslim writings.

The realities were, of course, somewhat different, and both rabbis and ulema in time lost their amateur status. As the law became more extensive and more complicated, full-time experts were needed to administer it and adjudicate. As the corpus of religious literature grew from the scriptural nucleus to embrace a vast range of commentaries, interpretations, and systematizations, its study again required full-time specialists. There was no ordination, but both Jews and Muslims developed systems of certification, whereby after pursuing a prescribed course of study a student might be granted a certificate by his teacher or teachers, attesting that he was a full-fledged scholar and specialist in the religious sciences. And since theologians and even theological students need to eat, some system had to be devised to provide for their material needs. It remained true that there was no priesthood in Islam, but a class of professional, academically qualified men of religion emerged whom it might not be inappropriate to call a clergy. Like the scribes, they had their own distinguishing garb, the most important part of which was the turban. This became and has remained their emblem and perquisite.

The ulema ranged from the humble officiant in the village or neighbourhood mosque to important legal dignitaries such as the *qāḍī* and the *muftī*. In Islam, it will be recalled, there is in principle only one law, that revealed by God. Law therefore ranks as one of the religious sciences, and its professional exponents are part of the ulema class. These include the *qāḍī*, a judge appointed by the ruler to administer the Holy Law, the *muftī*, a jurisconsult called upon to give rulings or opinions on disputed questions of law, and the *muḥtasib*, a government-appointed inspector of markets and morals whose task is defined by the oft-repeated Qur'ānic injunction, incumbent on all Muslims, 'to command good and forbid evil' (3:104, 110; 22:41, etc.). Until the nineteenth century, there were no advocates – a function and profession previously unknown to Muslim jurisprudence.

In the early centuries of Islamic history, the relationship between the state and the ulema was distant, even at times one of mutual suspicion. For the truly pious, the state was a necessary evil, but one with which good men would not become involved. The service of the state was demeaning and in a sense even sinful, since the revenues of the state were obtained by extortion, and anyone who received a salary from the state was a participant in this sin. It became a commonplace in the biographies of pious and learned men that the hero of the narrative was offered an appointment by the state and refused it. The offer established his fame, the refusal his integrity. The *qāḍī* was of course appointed by the state – but the *qāḍī* became a figure of ridicule in Islamic folklore and popular religion. The *muftī*, being independent, was more highly esteemed. His status was conferred upon him through a kind of co-option by preceding *muftīs*, and his emoluments came from fees or pious foundations. In general, the ulema and their institutions relied very heavily on pious foundations – the Arabic term is *waqf*, an endowment in mortmain for some pious purpose – for their upkeep.

In the unofficial and unarticulated separation of powers which evolved between the state and the ulema, the former usually conceded the exclusive competence of the latter in all that pertained to the Holy Law. This recognition, coupled with their aloofness from the state, gave them – especially those not holding public functions – immense moral authority. In Islam, Holy Law regulates most social and personal relations, and this gave to its authorized exponents an extensive and pervasive role in society. The mass of the people depended on them for guidance, or even for decisions, on a wide range of matters including, especially, marriage, divorce, and inheritance.

This relationship, or rather lack of relationship, between the men of religion and the state raised serious practical difficulties. The ulema evolved their own doctrine of political rights and duties, which the rulers of the empire found, in most respects, politically impracticable. Rulers often found it necessary to seek the support of the ulema; when they did, they were sometimes asked, as a condition of that support, to apply an ideal system based on a sanctified and mytho-logized past. For Sunni ulema, this meant the precedents of the four righteous caliphs supplemented by those of the Umayyad caliph 'Umar II. For Shī'a ulema, only the precedents of the Prophet himself and of the caliph 'Alī were valid, and the other, so-called 'righteous' caliphs were not righteous at all.

The withdrawal of the ulema from political life was never, of course, complete, but a kind of truce or *modus vivendi* was gradually established between the two sides. The rulers recognized the Holy Law in prin-ciple, avoided open contravention of its rules, especially in matters of ritual and social morality, and from time to time consulted ulema and raised them to positions of authority. The ulema, on their side, tried to avoid too close an involvement with the public authorities. When one of them accepted a position of authority, he did so with becoming reluctance, and was looked at askance by the more pious.

The result of this relationship was that the ulema tended to be split into two groups. One consisted of the very devout, regarded both by their colleagues and by the mass of the population as the upright and incorruptible custodians of the truth; the other group, which might be called either compliant or realistic, comprised those ulema who accepted public office and by so doing forfeited much of their moral authority. Such a situation, when the less conscientious and less scru-pulous of the ulema entered the service of the state while the more conscientious and pious avoided it, had harmful effects both on the state and on religion. Popular sympathy was clearly with those who avoided the service of the state, and many of the recommendations in pious literature amount to a demand for a virtual boycott of the public service.

The twelfth and thirteenth centuries brought significant changes. This was a time of major religious struggles which, for a while, seemed to threaten the very survival of the Islamic faith and community. Islam was assailed by both internal and external enemies – from the West, from the East, and from within. Before these dangers there was a closing of ranks, a drawing together of previously separated or even opposed elements in Muslim society. The servants of the state, both military and civil, became more concerned with religion; the religious classes, less hostile to the state.

An important part in this drawing-together of government and religion and the men involved in them was played by the *madrasa*, a kind of seminary or college which became the major centre of Muslim higher education. In the early period, primary and secondary instruction was provided at, or in association with, mosques, and by the ninth and tenth centuries CE, there were even centres of higher learning attached to some mosques, principally but not exclusively in the religious sciences. Such centres were endowed by both rulers and private individuals. Some of the larger centres were also provided with libraries, which were available to students and scholars. There were also semi-public libraries which contained books on non-religious subjects such as mathematics, medicine, chemistry, philosophy, and music. In the early ninth century, the 'Abbasid caliph al-Ma'mūn founded the famous 'house of wisdom' in Baghdad, the first of many academies of higher learning. It was probably modelled on the older academy of Gondeshapur in Persia, a centre of Hellenistic sciences and especially of medicine, founded by Nestorian Christians who sought refuge under Sasanid rule from Byzantine religious persecution, and itself probably modelled on the older Greek schools of Alexandria and Antioch.

The *madrasa* in its classical form appears to date from the eleventh century, when the first of what became a great number was founded. Others followed, all over the Islamic world. Sometimes the *madrasa* was attached to a mosque, sometimes the *madrasa* was independent, with its own small place of worship – a kind of chapel – attached to it for the convenience of its professors and students. Later it was much more like an organized college with a syllabus and timetable of study, a permanent faculty in receipt of stipends, and funds and facilities for student support. Like the cathedral schools which arose in medieval Europe, the *madrasas* were concerned primarily with instruction in religion and law, the two being in Islam different aspects of the same whole. But later, like the colleges and universities of the West, they came to play a major part in the formation of the educated class generally.

As the servants of the state began to show a new and profounder religious earnestness, so too the professional men of religion became more willing to enter the service of the state. In the Ottoman Empire – in part, no doubt, inspired by the Christian ecclesiastical organization which the Ottomans encountered in the lands they had conquered – the Islamic men of religion became part of the apparatus of govern- ment. Both the *qāḍīs* and *muftīs* were government-appointed and assigned to a region in which they had jurisdiction, and which it would not be inappropriate to call a diocese. At this stage, the men of religion became a third branch of imperial govenment alongside the bureaucracy and the military, with their own hierarchy headed by the *sheykh al-Islam*, the chief *muftī* of the capital, whom one might, without too much distortion, call the primate of the Ottoman Empire.

Inevitably, as the ulema moved nearer to the state, they moved further away from the people, and lost much of the influence which they had previously enjoyed. For the mass of ordinary Muslims, their place was taken by the Sufi sheykhs, who represented a rather different form of religiosity. From late medieval times, the Sufis were organized in brotherhoods, each dedicated to a different mystical way. The leaders and members of these brotherhoods, sometimes known as 'dervishes', supplied much that was lacking in conventional Islam. Dervish meet- ings and rituals offered spiritual sustenance and communion and, on occasion, solidarity and help in the struggle for human needs.

Medieval Muslim writers often divide society – by which they apparently mean those who run society – into two main groups: the men of sword and the men of the pen. The first were obviously the military; the second comprised both the bureaucratic and religious classes. There were, however, some others who, while living by the exercise of intellectual or literary skills, do not quite fit into either of these two groups. Such, for example, were the physicians, who figure prominently in the historical and biographical literature, sometimes as medical advisers to the ruler, sometimes through their work in the many hospitals which flourished in the Islamic world, sometimes for the research that they conducted and the books that they wrote. The theory and practice of medieval Islamic medicine derived in the main from Hellenistic sources, but the Muslims added a great deal to it, and in the high Middle Ages the level of medical knowledge and practice in the Islamic world was far above anything known in Europe.

By early modern times, however, they had fallen badly behind. A few European medical treatises were translated. In the fifteenth and sixteenth centuries some European refugees, mostly Jewish, went to practise medicine in Islamic lands. In the seventeenth and eighteenth centuries a number of Ottoman Christians went to Europe to study medicine and returned to practise in their homelands. But it was not until the nineteenth century that some of the more vigorous reforming rulers sent students to European medical schools and established new medical schools with foreign teachers in their own countries, and thus rescued the practice of medicine from the old Hellenistic–Islamic tradition which had survived with little change since the Middle Ages.

Another important group of men of the pen – or more precisely, of the spoken word – were the poets. Even the most minor of potentates would maintain at least one poet to sing his praises in verses which could be easily memorized and rapidly disseminated. More powerful rulers would maintain a whole corps of court poets acting as a kind of ministry of propaganda. Poetic eulogists also plied their trade with wealthy private individuals, celebrating births, marriages, and other events. In an age when there were no mass media, poetry and the poet could fulfil an important function in the publication of news and the projection of a favourable image.

If the poet took care of the ruler's current image, the historian was responsible for the image he projected to posterity. In medieval times, historians, unlike poets, were neither freelancers nor palace employees. Most of them belonged either to the bureaucratic or to the religious classes. It is probably for this reason that they were able, under the caliphs, to maintain a high standard of independence and freedom of expression. Later it became customary for rulers to appoint their court historians as well as their court poets, and in the Ottoman Empire this was formalized in the high office of Imperial Historiographer. The holder of this office, to which he was appointed by the sultan, had as his primary duty to continue the work of his predecessors in chronicling the history of the empire. This office, maintained over centuries, survived until the final years of the Ottoman Empire, and the last of the imperial historiographers became the first president of the Ottoman Historical Society.

There were, of course, other professions – astronomers and astrologers, artists and calligraphers, architects and engineers – but most of these, increasingly in the later centuries, were attached in one way or another to the ruling institution by which they were employed. By Ottoman times, the professions of architecture and engineering were almost exclusively military.

In the Middle East, as everywhere else in the world, rulers maintained armed forces, sometimes to repel external invaders, always to maintain public order at home and defend the authority of the state.

Under Roman rule, defence and policing were ensured by the Roman legions, with the assistance of locally raised auxiliary forces. The numbers were remarkably small. Even in Syria, near the Persian border and the most heavily policed of the eastern provinces, the Empire never stationed more than four legions in peacetime, as contrasted with eight in the German borderlands in Europe. These numbers were, of course, increased in wartime, and legions might be transferred or reinforced to meet special needs. The Armenian wars of 58–66 CE and the Jewish rebellion of 66–70 CE brought several important changes, notably the transfer of the tenth legion, the Fretensis, from northern Syria to Jerusalem, where it became the permanent garrison in the newly-constituted Roman province of Judaea.

The legions recruited only Roman citizens, but with the gradual extension of citizenship to the provincials, it became possible for many of these to enlist. The evidence indicates that in Asia Minor and the Levant as elsewhere in the Empire, locally recruited legionaries might serve in the region but not in their country of origin. The legions were assisted, particularly in their police work, by auxiliary troops. Some of these were the more or less Romanized troops of Roman client-rulers; others were formed and recruited by the Romans themselves, including specialized units such as the *Alae Dromedariorum*, or camel-riders, and the mounted archers. The service of Arab tribesmen from the desert borderlands in these units gave them a direct knowledge and experience of the skills and methods of warfare that were to stand them in good stead at the time of the Islamic conquests. Police duties were normally entrusted to an auxiliary cohort; their name survives in the Arabic term '*shurṭa*', used to denote the police forces of the caliphate and later Islamic regimes.

The Persian Empire was a formidable military power, and a worthy rival of Rome. The peasant infantry contributed by the feudal lords was not rated highly by its Roman opponents, but the mounted mercenaries and the auxiliary forces raised among the warlike frontier peoples were another matter. The core of the army was recruited from the nobility; the Persian cataphracts, mail-clad horsemen armed with lances and bows, were among the most redoubtable military forces of their time. The famous mounted archers of the Parthians, with their hit-and-run tactics, were known and feared in Rome. Another major innovation in the armies of Persia was the stirrup, which vastly increased the power and thrust of the mounted, armoured lancer, and made him, in a sense, the battle-tank of early medieval warfare.

During the reign of Chosroes I (531–579 CE), the Persian Empire underwent major changes, especially in its military organization, which now became less feudal and more professional. Soldiers received pay and equipment allowances, and were subject to long and arduous training and strict discipline. Instead of a single supreme commander, the *Eranspahbadh*, who combined the functions of Minister of Defence, Commander-in-Chief, and, where necessary, negotiator of peace, the army was now placed under a hierarchy of generals, military governors, and officers. Chosroes' armies won some successes. They ended the civil war at home; they pacified the frontier zones; they drove the Ethiopians from Yemen, ended the threat of the Hephthalite Huns, and, in the war against Byzantium, invaded Syria and sacked Antioch. They could not, however, withstand the assault of the Arab Muslims.

In pre-Islamic Arabia, the notion of a standing, professional army, separate from the main body of adult males, like the notion of monarchy with which it was associated, was alien and repugnant. In the northern borderlands, there were petty kings whose people sometimes served in Byzantine or Persian auxiliary formations. It is likely that the more sophisticated states of the sedentary south also had professional men in arms of one sort or another. But for most of northern and central Arabia, the army was simply the tribe in arms, mobilized for raiding or warfare.

The earliest Muslim historical narratives portray a significantly changed situation. The Prophet and his successors ruled more than a tribe – they were heads of a religio-political community comprising men of different origins and sometimes previously conflicting allegiances. They were almost continuously at war – first against the pagan Quraysh, and then, after the death of the Prophet, in the wars of conquest. These last in particular, extending over a long period and

a vast area, inevitably led to increasing specialization and pro-
fessionalization. The Arabic sources reveal a growing awareness of a
new and, in central and northern Arabia, unprecedented distinction
between combatants and non-combatants, and among the former
between long-term specialists and short-term amateurs or auxiliaries.
According to the principle later formulated by the Muslim jurists, the
obligation of *jihād* fell on every able-bodied male Muslim in defence,
on the community as a whole in attack. This latter no doubt reflected
the situation during the conquests, when each tribe was called upon
to supply its quota of fighting men, most of the quota being normally
met by volunteers.

Even those who formed the long-term nucleus of the Muslim
armies were not yet full-time professional soldiers. When not engaged
in warfare, they could and often did pursue other avocations. With
few exceptions, they did not live in barracks away from their families.
War was, however, their principal occupation and their main source
of livelihood. The means to provide for this livelihood was supplied
in generous measure by the booty obtained during the wars of
conquest.

With the partial exception of Syria, which under the Umayyad
caliphs became the metropolitan province of the empire, the Arab
armies were installed in camps which eventually became garrison
cities. Such were Basra and Kufa in Iraq, Fusṭāṭ in Egypt, Qayrawān
in Tunisia, and Qomm in Persia. In Syria, the Arab soldiers were
settled in military districts each held by and maintaining an army
corps. They were, from north to south, Ḥimṣ, Damascus, Jordan, and
Palestine, all of them being based on the old Byzantine territorial
divisions. The Arab troops of Syria were used in seasonal campaigns
on the Byzantine frontier and also for large-scale expeditions such as
the attack on Constantinople. With their higher level of experience
and proficiency, and with a higher level of regular pay, they began to
assume the character of a permanent army – the standing army of the
Syria-based Umayyad caliphs. No comparable organization existed
among the Arab military settlers in Iraq and Egypt, where the soldiers
reverted to the status of a tribal militia, with a tribal distaste for regular
military service.

The 'Abbasids continued the same system, with the difference that
the Syrian standing army was replaced by one drawn from Khurāsān,
the east Iranian province from which the 'Abbasids had risen to power,
and which remained for long the mainstay of their military support.

This brought a change of major importance. The armies of the caliphate were at first overwhelmingly Arab, and there was no attempt to recruit the local population of Syria or Egypt, who in any case during the centuries of Roman and Byzantine rule had long since lost any desire or aptitude for the profession of arms. The situation was very different in the eastern, former Iranian provinces of the empire. The Iranians, unlike their western neighbours, had not just changed one imperial master for another. They still had recent memories of their own imperial greatness and their own martial traditions, and it was natural that once they had embraced the new faith of Islam, they should feel entitled to a major role both in its government and in its armies. The same was true, although in a somewhat different way, of the unsubdued Berber population of the former Roman provinces in North Africa, which also passed under Arab rule.

From an early date, the Arab war chiefs began to bring their *mawālī*, non-Arab converts attached as clients to their tribes, into the army, albeit in subordinate positions and with lower pay. These began to assume an increasingly important role, particularly on the frontiers, where the warlike frontier peoples contributed greatly to the further advance of Muslim arms. North African Berbers formed a major part of the Arab Muslim armies that conquered Spain. The peoples of northern Iran and Central Asia did much to bring their new faith to their unconverted kinsmen beyond the imperial frontier.

But these, even at the time of their greatest early successes, were frontiersmen, auxiliaries, not part of the imperial army, and they were kept far from the imperial capital. The arrival of the 'Abbasid Khurāsānī forces in Iraq marked a major change. The Khurāsānīs were, in principle, Arabs, but they had lived in Khurāsān for generations, intermarried with Iranian women, and acquired many Iranian ways. Before long, they included authentic Iranians from eastern Iran.

The 'Abbasids gradually abolished the military pensions automatically paid to Arabs listed on the muster rolls. From the tenth century, men received pay only if they were actually serving in the army. Troops were of two kinds: full-time professionals receiving pay, and volunteers for a single campaign paid out of the booty.

The Khurāsānī guards of the 'Abbasid caliphs lasted no longer than the Syrian standing army of their Umayyad predecessors, and after barely a century of 'Abbasid rule, they were superseded and replaced by a new kind of army recruited on an entirely different basis – one that was to shape the military and therefore political future of the Islamic states for a thousand years or more.

Neither the slave in arms nor the barbarian auxiliary was new. For a while, ancient Athens was policed by a corps of armed Scythian slaves, the property of the city. Some Roman dignitaries had armed slave bodyguards, normally of barbarian origin. In recruiting soldiers from the 'martial races' near or even beyond the imperial frontiers, the rulers of the Muslim empire were doing what the Romans, the Persians, and the Chinese had done long before them, and what the Western empires were to do centuries later. But the military history of the Muslim states shows something new and distinctive – the slave soldier constituting the slave army, commanded by slave generals, and eventually – the ultimate paradox – serving slave kings and dynasties.

The logic of the system was well observed and explained by Paul Rycaut, an English visitor to Turkey in the mid-seventeenth century.[3] In contrast to Western princes, who are served by men who are raised up because of their 'Family, Lineage, and Condition', Rycaut wrote,

[The Turk] ... loves to be served by his own, such as to whom he hath given Breeding, and Education, and are as obliged to employ those parts in his service which he hath bestowed; whose minds he hath cultivated with wisdom and virtue, as well as nourished their bodies with food, untill they arrive to a mature Age, that renders the profit of his care, and expence; such as these he is served by, whom he can raise without envy, and destroy without danger.

The Youths then that are designed for the great Offices of the Empire ... must be such as are ... taken in War, or presented from remote parts ... the Policy herein is very obvious, because [they] will hate their Parents, being educated with other Principles and Customs; or coming from distant places have contracted no acquaintance, so that starting from their Schools into Government, they will find no Relations, or Dependencies on their Interests, than that of their Great Master, to whom they are taught, and necessity compels them to be faithful.

The institution, clearly, was designed to solve one of the recurring problems of every autocratic ruler – how to find reliable and trust-worthy military and civilian servants without thereby creating a power-ful and cohesive element in the state which might curb or even end his power. Other rulers in other times and places found different solutions to this problem. The answer adopted from early times by Muslim rulers was to create armies of long-term professional soldiers, men of alien origin captured and enslaved in childhood and owing no allegiance or loyalty other than to the service for which they were trained and formed. As aliens from remote provinces or from beyond the frontiers, they had no affinities and no kinship with local or subject populations, with whom they could barely communicate. Physically removed and culturally alienated from their own families and backgrounds, they had no cousins or kinfolk on whom they could call. And since each generation of slave soldiers was replaced not by its sons but by a new intake of slaves from far away, they were precluded from forming a new military class which might become an aristocracy and challenge the sovereign power of the autocratic ruler.

The system was not perfect. Sometimes slaves formed ethnic solidarity groups, or even regiments based on their place or tribe of origin. Sometimes, especially in the Ottoman Empire, slaves kept in touch with their families and places of origin, and, if they rose to positions of power and profit, brought their kinsfolk to share these advantages. Slave soldiers, like other men, were anxious to make suitable provision for their sons, and though they were rarely able to admit them to the military, they were often able to find them other places in the religious and bureaucratic professions. Indeed, some of the great scribal and religious families of late medieval times originated in this way.

But by and large, the system worked extraordinarily well. It created the powerful armies which enabled the Middle Eastern Islamic world to defeat and eject the Crusaders and to contain and halt the far more dangerous Mongols. Only in one respect did the slave regiments consistently disappoint the monarchs who formed and owned them. In principle, the slave soldier had no loyalty but his sovereign. In practice, his loyalty was to the regiment and to the officers who commanded it. Before long, military commanders, themselves of slave origin, became the real masters of the provinces and even of the capital, where they dominated the by now powerless caliphs. In the end, the slave commanders themselves became monarchs, sometimes founding their own, mostly short-lived dynasties, sometimes, as in late medieval Egypt, carrying the principle of slave recruitment and succession even to the sultanate itself.

There are references to slave soldiers even in the early Islamic period, but these are individuals, for the most part freedmen who were, so to speak, recruited by their masters or former masters. The introduction of the slave regiment is usually ascribed to the 'Abbasid caliph al-Mu'taṣim, who reigned from 833 to 842 CE. His regiment was composed of Turkish slaves caught young in the steppe lands beyond the eastern frontiers of Islam, and trained from boyhood to military service. Within a remarkably short time, the fighting and garrison forces of most Muslim rulers consisted of slaves, and the slaves were principally Turkish. In the far western lands of Islam, in North Africa and Spain, there was some recruitment of Slavic slaves from Europe, as long as this was feasible. Occasionally, especially in Morocco and in Egypt, black slaves were recruited for military service. But most of the slave soldiers were Turkish, until, with the Islamization of the Turks themselves, this ceased to be legally possible, and Turkish rulers drew their slave soldiers from the non-Muslim peoples of the Caucasus and Balkans.

Changes in methods of warfare and especially the introduction of firearms in time made the old-style slave army obsolete. The last of the great slave armies, the Ottoman Janissaries, survived until the early nineteenth century, but ceased to recruit slaves at the beginning of the seventeenth century. Even so, the old custom did not entirely die out. Black military slaves were extensively used by Egyptian rulers in the nineteenth century. In 1863, when the ruler of Egypt sent an Egyptian expeditionary force to Mexico to help his friend the French emperor Napoleon III, most of its members were black slaves recruited by capture from the regions of the Upper Nile.

By any economic definition, the principal sources of wealth and of the kind of power that wealth can give were land and trade. Members of all the different ruling elites – bureaucratic, military, religious, even royal – usually invested at least part of their capital in one or the other or both.

From the beginning, Islamic teaching took a favourable view of commerce. The earliest prescriptive statements are in the Qur'ān itself, notably in the approval of trade and the ban on usury. Other passages concern the lawfulness of honest trading, and touch on such matters as the use of fair weights and measures, the honest payment of debts, the fulfilment of contracts, and the like (Qur'ān 2:194, 275ff., 282ff.; 4:33; 6:153; 42:9–11). The Qur'ānic approval of commerce as a way of life is confirmed in a large number of sayings attributed to the Prophet and to some of his Companions in praise of the honest merchant.

Some sayings go even further, and defend the luxuries in which the honest merchant may deal – such as silks and brocades, jewels, and male and female slaves. According to one tradition, the Prophet said, 'When God gives wealth to a man, he wants it to be seen on him.'

Even more striking is a story told in an early Shī'ite work about the imam Ja'far al-Ṣādiq. The imam, it is said, was once reproached by a disciple for wearing fine apparel while his ancestors had worn rude, simple garments. The imam is quoted as replying that his ancestors had lived in a time of scarcity, while he lived in a time of plenty, and it was proper to wear the clothing of one's own time.[4]

These certainly apocryphal traditions clearly represent an attempt to justify luxurious living and the trade in luxury goods in response to the strain of asceticism often expressed in Islamic writings. Muḥammad al-Shaybānī (d. 804) argues that earning a livelihood is not merely permitted, but is an obligation for Muslims. Man's primary duty, he says, it to serve God. But in order to do this properly, he must be adequately fed, housed, and clothed. This he can only achieve by working and earning money.[5] Nor – the author points out – need he limit himself to providing the bare necessities of life, since it is also permissible to buy and use items of luxury. The point made by al-Shaybānī and several later authors is that money earned by trade or handicrafts is more pleasing in God's eyes than money received from the government, whether for civil or military service. One of the greatest of classical Arabic authors, al-Jāḥiẓ (d. 869), goes even further. In an essay entitled 'In praise of merchants and in condemnation of officials', he stresses the security, dignity, and independence of merchants in contrast with the uncertainty, humiliation, and sycophancy of those who serve the ruler, and he defends the piety and learning of merchants against their detractors. God Himself, he argues, showed His approval of commerce as a way of life when He chose a merchant community for His final prophetic revelation. No less a figure than al-Ghazālī (d. 1111), one of the major Islamic theologians of the Middle Ages, included in his writings a portrait of the ideal merchant and a defence of commerce as a way of preparing oneself for the world to come.

In a predominantly agricultural economy, the ownership or control of land was of major social and political importance. Landowners did indeed form an important group in classical Islamic society. The word, however, needs redefinition in its Middle Eastern context. The independent smallholder of the type known in Western Europe and elsewhere, exists in the Middle East, but for most periods he was rare and atypical. Independent smallholding does not easily flourish where agriculture depends largely on artificial irrigation – in need of central direction, and therefore easily subjected to central control. In most of the region, the common pattern is one of large landowning, of which there are several different types. Modern writing on agrarian conditions in the Middle East, both past and present, often uses such terms as 'feudal' and 'fief'. But these are specifically Western European terms, with meanings derived from the local history of Western Europe. The use of these words to denote the very different social and economic phenomena of the Middle East is at best a loose analogy, and can be very misleading.

There were several legal forms of tenure by which a landowner could either own or hold his land. One, termed *'milk'* in Islamic law, is roughly equivalent to the English term 'freehold'. In the Ottoman period – the first for which we have detailed records – it is found principally in cities and the areas immediately around them. Apart from building land, it consisted chiefly of vineyards, orchards, and vegetable gardens.

This form of tenure was rare in the countryside or in villages, where most agricultural land was held by large landowners, theoretically on some form of grant from the state. The earliest such grant in Muslim times, given by the first caliphs, was in principle a cession to an individual Muslim of publicly owned lands, that is to say lands acquired by the newly created Arab state in the course of the conquests. Such lands were of two main types – the domain lands of the previous states, that is, former state property of the Byzantine and Persian regimes, and lands abandoned by their former owners. When the Arabs conquered the Levant, Egypt, and North Africa, many of the Byzantine magnates fled, abandoning their estates, which became state property and were assimilated to the former state property. In addition, the so-called 'dead lands', that is, uncultivated and unused lands, could also be granted in this way.

Lands of these types, all of them at the disposal of the state, were allotted to individuals with what was, in effect, a permanent and irrevocable grant. Given for life, it was both alienable and heritable, and was not conditional on either service or status. But the recipient of such a grant was required, in accordance with Islamic law, to pay a tithe to the public treasury on his land, while he himself collected taxes from the inhabitants. The difference between what he collected from the peasants and what he paid to the state constituted his income from the grant.

This system, similar to and probably derived from the Byzantine *emphyteusis*, continued for a while, but it came to an end with the cessation of the wave of conquests. It was then replaced by another and much more common arrangement, which was not a grant of land, but rather a delegation of the fiscal rights of the state over land. In this system, the state granted to an individual the right to collect taxes from an area, usually in lieu of pay from the public treasury, in return for services – more and more commonly, military services. In principle, military officers and other servants of the state were paid salaries in money, but as cash became increasingly scarce in state treasuries, the practice grew and spread of paying officers by grants of this kind. The recipient of such an assignment of taxes had to arrange for their collection. He did not, of course, pay taxes to the state; he collected the taxes for himself in lieu of the pay which the state owed him.

Such a grant was, in principle, functional, given in return for a service rendered. If the recipient of the grant for any reason ceased to render this service, the delegation of fiscal rights was terminated. These grants were not, like those of the early caliphs, irrevocable and permanent. Such a grant was in principle temporary, limited, and revocable if the condition on which it was given ceased to operate. It was neither alienable nor heritable, but was personal to the grantee. By abuse, however, it frequently became permanent, alienable, and heritable. Likewise, by abuse it was often retained even when services were no longer rendered. It was at this point that the system began in some respects to resemble the feudal order of medieval Europe.

The differences, however, remained greater than the resemblances. The grantee had nothing like the seigneurial rights of a European feudal magnate of the Middle Ages. He had no rights over the inhabitants of the area to which his grant applied, other than the right to collect taxes, which of course also meant the right to use such force as might be necessary to collect taxes. But unlike the Western lord of the manor, he did not dispense justice; he did not grant smaller fiefs within his fief; nor, in principle, did he maintain a private army of his own retainers, though in later times this was not unusual. Unlike the Western feudal lord, he did not usually reside in the area of his grant, still less rule it as a quasi-independent principality.

In another kind of arrangement, more a contract than a grant, the state assigned the taxes due from a region or an estate or a group of some kind, in return for an agreed lump sum. In such an arrangement, the state and its agents were no longer involved directly in the assess-

ment and collection of taxes. These tasks were delegated to an inter-
mediary who might be a tribal chief, the head of a religious community,
or an entrepreneur buying a tax-farm for profit. Such tax-farms could
be bought from the state, or from military and other grantees holding
assignments of revenue from the state. The tax-farmer was bound to
remit the agreed sum to the treasury or other party with whom he
had made the agreement. What he collected and how he collected it
was his own business. The state was represented, if at all, by a tax-
commissioner who was a supervisor rather than a participant in the
process. Either the state or a private owner would have had a natural
interest in the long-term prosperity of the land. The tax-farmer was
concerned in the first instance to recover his investment, and then to
make a profit on it. Tax-farms were normally contracted on an annual
basis.

In times of uncertainty and of violent change – and there were
many such – there was a tendency for the unit of a grant of land or
revenue to grow larger. Sometimes this would happen when a large
and powerful landowner extended his protection to smaller or weaker
neighbours less able to defend their holdings in times of trouble.
Sometimes this even happened voluntarily, as when a small landowner,
beset by troubles in a period of civil war, invasion, and the breakdown
of order, sought the help of a powerful neighbour, and in return for a
guaranteed income, assigned his rights to him. This kind of protection
gradually solidified into a virtual takeover by large landowners of
smaller landowners' holdings. From time to time, more radical changes
took place, when a regime and its supporters were ousted and a new
regime installed, whether by conquest or by successful rebellion.
Sometimes when this happened, the existing territorial and fiscal units
were maintained, though with new beneficiaries. More often the
units were all brought back under the control of the state and then
redistributed in a different way to new beneficiaries.

In general, the dividing line between private land and leased state
land was far from clear. In periods of strong state control, there was a
tendency for the power of the state to grow at the expense of the
private landowner. In times of political weakness and consequent
decentralization, there was a tendency for the individual to usurp the
powers and sometimes even the property of the state. In such times,
for example in the late seventeenth and eighteenth centuries, even
tax-farms could be transformed into hereditary holdings, for most
purposes indistinguishable from freehold. The term 'usurpation' was

sometimes applied both ways – to state lands becoming private, and to private lands becoming state.

Like 'feudalism', such Western words as 'gentry' and 'nobility' are of questionable value when applied to Middle Eastern society. There are, however, from time to time, clear signs of the formation of a hereditary landowning class which held property in one form or another, theoretically as freehold, lease, grant, or even tax-farm, and managed to pass this property from father to son. The general tendency of Muslim rulers was to try to prevent, interrupt, or reverse this process, preferring a situation in which all power, all wealth, and all authority derived directly from the state rather than from inheritance or from an assured and accepted social position. Autocratic rulers often tried to destroy or uproot such elements as depended, not on their goodwill, but rather on inherited wealth, such as landowners, or on public acclaim and recognition, such as the ulema and at times a provincial gentry. Such self-sustaining groups formed and survived when the royal authority was for one reason or another weak; they were undermined and often destroyed, or at least replaced, when the royal authority was strong, especially after a new conquest.

This continuing struggle can be traced through Islamic history. In modern times, it would seem, the struggle was finally decided in favour of the autocratic state, and against the social forces which might have limited it. This happened because of the introduction of modern technology and, in particular, of modern communications and weapons. With these, the long-standing, practical impediments to centralized autocracy were finally overcome. In the traditional systems, the powers of the ruler, though in principle absolute, were in effect restricted by a whole series of intermediate authorities and powers. With the abrogation of these powers and the elimination of these authorities by modernization, the power of the ruler is without limit or constraint, and even the pettiest of modern dictators has greater control than even the mightiest of Arab caliphs, Persian shahs and Turkish sultans. The traditional restraints on tyranny have gone. The search for some new or renewed form of limitation continues.

CHAPTER 11

THE COMMONALTY

It is often said that Islam is an egalitarian religion. There is much truth in this assertion. If we compare the principles and to a large extent even the practice of Islam at the time of its advent with the societies that surrounded it – the stratified feudalism of Iran, the caste system of India, the privileged aristocracies of both Byzantine and Latin Europe – the Islamic dispensation did indeed bring a message of equality. Not only did Islam not endorse such systems of social and tribal differentiation; it explicitly and resolutely rejected them. The Qur'ān is quite specific:

> O, people. We have created you from one male and one female, and we have made you into peoples and tribes so that ye might know one another. Indeed the noblest among you in the sight of God is the most God-fearing. (Qur'ān 49:13)

The actions and utterances of the Prophet, and the revered precedents of the early rulers of Islam as preserved by tradition, speak over-whelmingly against privilege by descent, by birth, by status, by wealth, or even by race, and insist that rank and honour are determined only by piety and by merit in Islam.

Such ideas were not without precedent. According to a well-known passage in the New Testament, 'There is neither Jew nor Greek, neither bond nor free, there is neither male nor female; for ye are all one in Christ Jesus' (Gal. 3:28; cf. similar statements in 1 Cor. 12:13, Col. 3:11). And even earlier the Book of Job proclaims the common humanity of master and slave (Job 31:15).

But for Jews, Christians, and Muslims alike, common humanity does not prevent the establishment and maintenance of certain basic differences between human beings. The passage quoted from Galatians was not understood as abolishing or even downgrading, ethnic, social and gender differences, but rather as asserting that they conferred no religious privilege. The religious dividing line – between believer and unbeliever – is clearly drawn in the last three words of the saying. All three religions insist of the value and autonomy of the individual, and the importance of every soul in the eyes of God. All three insist that piety and good deeds outrank wealth and power and noble birth. But while they agree in principle on the equality of human beings, historically they have all limited the full enjoyment of their equality in effect to those who possessed four necessary characteristics – to free, adult, male co-religionists. That is to say, enshrined in all three religions has been the presumption that the slave, the child, the woman and the unbeliever are in significant respects inferior. In all three religious traditions there are rules on how these inferiorities arise, and how, if at all, they may be ended. The slave may be freed by his master; the unbeliever may free himself of his unbelief by embracing the true faith; the child will in due course attain adulthood. Only the woman was, in the traditional religious world view, irredeemably fixed in her inferiority.

For believers in all three faiths, unbelievers are so by their own choice. There are, however, important differences among the three religions in the definition and perception of unbelief and the status of the unconverted unbeliever. There is less difference concerning the other categories. Women and children are born as such, and there was no way that this status could be acquired. All three religions recognized slave birth – the servile status of the child born to a slave parent. Judaism and Christianity, conforming in this to the general practice of ancient laws, recognized a number of ways in which free persons could be enslaved. Islamic law and practice, from an early stage, severely restricted the enslavement of free persons, limiting it in effect to non-Muslims captured or conquered in a war.

In all four categories of social inequality there is also an intermediate status, differently defined in the three religions. Between free and slave, there is the freedman – the former slave who, though legally free, still owes certain duties and obligations to the former master who freed him. Between the child and the adult, there is the adolescent, a category of limited legal but considerable social significance. Between the male and the female there is the eunuch, who alone can move freely between male and female space. And between the true believer and the unbeliever, there are those who have some part of God's truth but not the whole of it.

It is in this last category that the most significant differences among the three religions appear. For the Jew, the other, the outsider, is the gentile – a classification that has more in common with the Greek notion of barbarian than with the Christian and Islamic concept of the unbeliever. The barrier can be crossed; a barbarian can be Hellenized; a gentile can be Judaized; and when this happens they are accepted as members of the community (Lev. 19:33–4). But the change is not expected, still less required. Hellenes and Jews agree that outsiders could attain merit, even as defined in Hellenic and Judaic terms, without becoming Hellenic or Judaic. The righteous of all peoples, according to rabbinic teaching, have a place in Paradise. For Christians and Muslims, in contrast, those who do not share their beliefs, and who resist attempts to convert them, are deniers of God's word, or at least of a major part of it. They are therefore liable to penalties and disabilities in this world and to eternal damnation in the next.

All three adult inferiors, the slave, the woman and the unbeliever, were seen as performing necessary functions, though there were occasional doubts about the third. There were, however, important differences between them. The unbeliever's inferiority was voluntary – a Muslim might say wilful – and he could at any time end it by a simple act of will, that is by embracing Islam, after which all doors would be open to him. The status of the slave could also be changed, and the slave become a freedman, but this could only be done by legal process and, moreover, depended on the will of the master and not of the slave himself. Women were the worst off of all – they could not change their sex, nor could any authority change it for them.

There was another important difference among the three. Slavery, in the Islamic lands, was more often domestic than economic, and slaves as well as women thus had their place in the family and in home life. The rules regulating slavery were seen as part of the law of personal status, the inner citadel of the *sharīʿa*. The position of the non-Muslim, on the other hand, was a public rather than a personal matter, and was in consequence differently perceived. The purpose of the restriction was not, as with the slave and the woman, to preserve the sanctity of the Muslim home, but to maintain the supremacy of Islam in the polity and the society which the Muslims had created. Any attempt to challenge or modify the legal subordination of these groups would thus have challenged the free, male Muslim in two sensitive areas – his personal authority in the Muslim home, his communal primacy in the Muslim state. A whole series of radical movements of social and religious protest appeared within the Islamic world from early medieval times onwards, which sought to overthrow the barriers that from time to time arose between high-born and low-born, rich and poor, Arab and non-Arab, white and black, since all such barriers were regarded as contrary to the true spirit of Islamic brotherhood. It is the more noteworthy that none of these movements ever questioned the three sacrosanct distinctions establishing the subordinate status of the slave, the woman, and the unbeliever.

The humanizing influence of Islamic teachings was in some ways diminished by two other developments – the influence of the Roman and Persian usage which the Arabs found in the conquered provinces, and, perhaps even more, the rapid increase in the number of slaves acquired by conquest, tribute, and purchase. Slaves were subject to serious legal disabilities. They were precluded from any office involving jurisdiction over freemen. They could not give evidence. They counted for less than freemen in that the penalty for an offence against a slave was half the penalty for the same offence against a free person. Slaves did however have some, though few, civil rights in matters of property, inheritance and treatment. Islamic law lays down that the slave is entitled to medical attention, food, and support in old age. A *qāḍī* could order an owner to manumit his slave for failure to carry out these obligations. Slaveowners were enjoined to treat their slaves humanely and not overwork them. The slave could marry, with the consent of his master. In theory he could even marry a free woman, though this seems to have been rare. A master could not marry a slave woman unless he freed her. Slaves could be manumitted by a whole variety of different procedures specified by law.

In the year 31 AH (651–62 CE), according to the Muslim historiographic tradition, the Arab armies in Egypt fought against the Nubians to the south and made an armistice with them by which Muslims and Nubians agreed that each would not raid the other. In return for this, the Nubians undertook to provide a certain number of slaves every year to the Muslims, who in turn would deliver quantities of meat and lentils to the Nubians. The treaty is said to have provided for the delivery, by the Nubians, of 360 slaves a year. The final version of the treaty included this specific provision:[1]

> Every year you shall deliver three hundred and sixty head of slaves to the Imam of the Muslims. They shall be slaves of good quality of your country, without defect, both male and female, neither extremely old nor children under age. Those you shall deliver to the governor of Aswān. If you harbour a runaway slave of a Muslim or kill a Muslim or a *dhimmī* [protected non-Muslim] or attempt to destroy the mosque which the Muslims have constructed in the centre of your city or withhold any of

the three hundred and sixty slaves, then the truce and the security shall be abolished and we shall revert to hostility until God decides between us and He is the best judge.

Some sources add another forty slaves for the personal use of the governor. Although the authenticity of this treaty is questionable, it was accepted by most jurists, and was used to justify a mutually convenient arrangement whereby Nubia remained outside the Muslim empire but tributary to it. Muslim law strictly prohibited enslavement and mutilation within Muslim territory, and thus restricted the domestic supply of slaves and eunuchs. Both, however, could be imported, as slaves and eunuchs, from outside the Muslim lands, and Nubia served as a convenient channel.

Slaves served many different purposes. The Islamic world was not, like the Greco-Roman world, primarily a slave-based economy. Its agriculture depended largely on free or semi-free peasants, its industries on free artisans. There were some exceptions. Slaves, most of them black Africans, appear in large numbers in certain economic projects. From early Islamic times there are reports of gangs of black slaves employed in draining the salt flats of southern Iraq. Poor conditions led to a series of slave risings. Other black slaves were employed in the gold mines of Upper Egypt and the Sudan, and in the salt mines of the Sahara.

In the main, however, slaves were used either for domestic or for military purposes. The former served in palaces and homes, shops and markets, shrines and mosques, and were mainly of African origin. The latter served in increasing numbers in the armies of Islam. These were predominantly though not exclusively white.

Slave women of every ethnic origin were acquired in great numbers to staff the harems of the Islamic world – as concubines or as menials, the two functions not always clearly differentiated. Some slave girls received education. Some were trained as performers – singers, dancers, and musicians. A few even have an honoured place in literary history. These belong to the elite rather than to the commonalty. The same may be said, with even greater force, about the slave women of the royal or imperial harem, who, as the favourites, or still more the mothers, of the reigning sultans, were sometimes able to play a decisive if largely hidden role in the course of public affairs.

The institution of slavery survived and indeed flourished until modern times. It was abolished in the colonial empires in the nine-teenth century, in the independent states of the region in the twentieth.

In general, the advent of Islam brought an enormous improvement in the position of women in ancient Arabia, endowing them with property and some other rights, and giving them a measure of pro-tection against ill treatment by their husbands or owners. The killing of female infants, sanctioned by custom in pagan Arabia, was outlawed by Islam. But the position of women remained poor, and worsened when, in this as in so many other respects, the original message of Islam lost its impetus and was modified under the influence of pre-existing attitudes and customs. Polygamy remained lawful, but was limited to four wives. In practice, it seems to have been rare except among the rich and powerful. Marriage was, however, commonly and lawfully supplemented by concubinage. An unmarried slave woman was at the disposal of her owner. A free woman could own male slaves, but had no such rights over them. The jurists defined the position of woman in society primarily by her function in the family – as daughter, sister, wife or mother, rather than as a person in her own right. She had some compensations. In a few property matters, she was equal to a man. For religious offences, she was subject to lesser penalties, for example to imprisonment and flogging instead of execution for the crime of apostasy. But this, in the eyes of the jurists, was a mark of inferiority rather than a privilege. And like the *dhimmī* and the slave, a woman was subject to certain formal inferiorities in law. In inherit-ance, for example, or in testimony in a lawsuit, she was valued as half a man.

Tolerated unbelievers were called *dhimmī*, or *ahl al-dhimma*, 'the people of the pact'. This was a legal term for the tolerated and protected non-Muslim subjects of the Muslim state. They consisted, in effect, of Christians, Jews, and in the East, Zoroastrians. The *dhimma*, which determined their status, was conceived as a pact between the Muslim ruler and the non-Muslim communities, and was thus essentially a contract. The basis of this contract was the recognition by the *dhimmīs* of the supremacy of Islam and the dominance of the Muslim state, and their acceptance of a position of subordination, symbolized by certain social restrictions and by the payment of a poll tax (*jizya*) to which Muslims were not subject. In return, they were granted security of life and property, protection against external enemies, freedom of worship, and a very large measure of internal autonomy in the conduct of their affairs. The *dhimmīs* were thus significantly better situated than slaves,

(right) Ottoman palace festivities, part of an album by the early eighteenth-century artist Levni. Among the guests are European ambassadors, recognizable not only by their costume but also by the chairs provided for them.

(far right) Early Islamic wood carving from the original Al-Aqsā mosque, Jerusalem. In the Middle East, wood was rare and precious and therefore worthy of artists' attention.

The fourteenth-century bowl from Mamluk Egypt, known as the 'Baptistery of St Louis'. This huge copper basin is inlaid with silver figures and decoration.

Detail from the Baptistery of St Louis.

Silk prayer rug from Tabriz.

Astrolabe made in Cairo in 1236, engraved brass inlaid with silver and copper. The astrolabe was used by astronomers and astrologers throughout the Islamic world.

Taqī al-Dīn (Turkish Takiyeddin), Chief Astronomer of the Ottoman Court and, from 1577, director of the newly-built observatory. Muslim scientists in the Middle Ages had made major contributions to the development of astronomy.

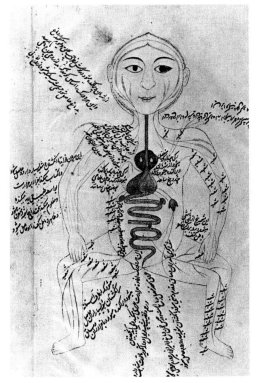

Illustration from a seventeenth-century Persian medical text.

The Shah mosque, Isfahan. One of a group of outstanding buildings of late sixteenth
and early seventeenth-century Isfahan, the capital of Safavid Shah ʿAbbās (1588-1629).

The vestibule of the
madrasa Chehār
Bāgh, Isfahan. The
madrasa (college)
was the cornerstone
of the medieval
Muslim system of
higher education.

Shah ʿAbbās receiving
an ambassador. Wall
painting from the
Chihil Sutūn pavilion
in Isfahan, late
sixteenth century,
rebuilt 1706.

Banquet scene with men drinking coffee, Turkey, late sixteenth century. The first coffee-houses in Istanbul were opened in 1555 by two Syrians.

Turkish merchants in the seventeenth century. The three figures represent an Anatolian, a man dressed for protection against rain, and a Turkish merchant.

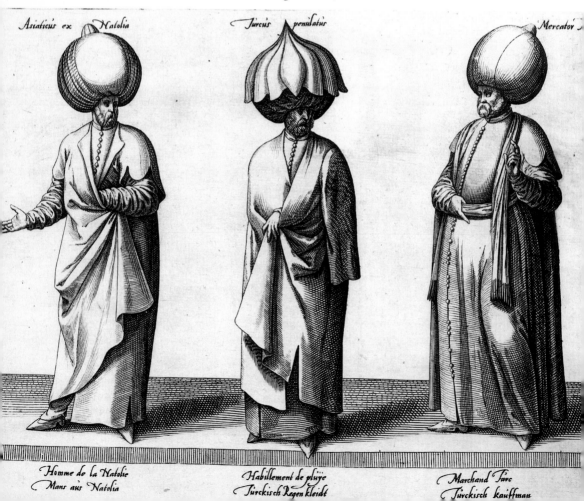

Asiaticus ex Natolia   Turcus penulatus   Mercator

Homme de la Natolie   Habillement de pluye   Marchand Turc
Mans aus Natolia   Turckisch Regen kleidt   Turckisch kauffman

Hasan Ağa (Samson Rowlie), an Englishman who became Treasurer and confidant of the Ottoman High Admiral, Uluç Hasan Pasha, in the sixteenth century. Many European Christians entered the Ottoman service, most of them embracing Islam. In Christendom they were known as renegades, in the Ottoman lands as *Muhtedi*, literally one who has found the true way.

A Jewish doctor (on the right) and merchant, Istanbul, 1574, by an anonymous artist. Jewish refugees fleeing persecution in Christian Europe settled in great numbers in the Ottoman Empire in the sixteenth century.

Dervishes, from a seventeenth-century book drawn by Turkish artists for the Venetian ambassador.

Dragoman (i.e. an interpreter), eighteenth century. Dragomans were employed by the Ottoman government and by most of the foreign embassies. The Chief Dragoman of the Sublime Porte was an important functionary, virtually in charge of Ottoman foreign relations.

Persian hunting scene. Hunting in Persia and Turkey long retained an important social, cultural and even military function.

Smoking scene in a Turkish coffee-house, 1850s. Tobacco was introduced from America by English merchants at the beginning of the seventeenth century. First the use and then later the cultivation of tobacco spread rapidly in the Ottoman lands.

but in important respects worse off than free Muslims. The *dhimmī* communities had their own rules concerning women. Jewish law, as interpreted and applied in Islamic lands, permitted polygamy but prohibited and punished concubinage. Christian law – in all communities – prohibited both, and offenders were liable to excommunication and other penalties.

The legal rules regulating the inferiority of the slave, the woman and the unbeliever did not always conform to the high moral and religious principles of Islam. But at the same time, the social realities of all three were sometimes better than the legal rules. The *dhimmīs* were inferior to Muslims, but we find *dhimmīs* enjoying great wealth, exercising economic power, and even on occasion political power, though this is rare. Woman were inferior to men, but we find women exercising authority in the home, in the market, and in the palace. Slaves are inferior to freemen, but through the centuries of Islamic history we find ever-growing numbers of slave soldiers, slave commanders, slave governors, and even slave monarchs.

In most periods of pre-modern Islamic history, the status and position of the non-Muslim subjects was rather better than that prescribed by the legal rules. The frequent re-enactment of these rules in itself shows that the restrictions which they prescribe were not regularly or strictly enforced. In general, the *dhimmī* seem to have fared better under Sunni than under sectarian rulers. Under most of the caliphs and sultans, both Jews and Christians played some part in the government of the Islamic empires, and particularly in the administrative services. In general, there seems to have been no strong feeling against such employment. There were occasional campaigns against Christian civil servants, and a few outbreaks of violence, but there are rare, and usually the result of what was seen as an excessive and offensive exercise of power by *dhimmī* officials.

Dhimmīs remained, however, inferior, and were not allowed to forget their inferiority. They could not testify before Muslim courts, and like slaves and women they counted for less than Muslims in matters of compensation for injury. They were not free to marry Muslim women under pain of death, though Muslim men were free to marry Christian or Jewish women. They were subject to restrictions on their dress, on which they were required to wear distinguishing signs; their mounts – they were not allowed to ride horses, but only donkeys or mules; and their places of worship – according to the law, they could repair old ones but not build new ones. Although these restrictions were not always strictly enforced, they could always be invoked. While the *dhimmīs* often acquired great wealth, their exclusion from the social and political advantages which normally accrued from such wealth forced them to achieve political purposes, if at all, by intrigue, with damaging effects both on the *dhimmīs* themselves and on the Muslim polity and society.

In the Islamic states, from early until later times, the free, male Muslim enjoyed a considerable measure of freedom of opportunity. The Islamic revelation, when it was first carried by the conquerors to countries previously incorporated in the ancient empires, brought immense and revolutionary social changes. Islamic doctrine was strongly opposed to hereditary privileges of all kinds, even including, in principle, the institution of monarchy. And although this pristine egalitarianism was in many ways modified and diluted, it remained strong enough to prevent the emergence of either brahmins or noblemen, and to preserve a society in which merit and ambition might still hope to find their reward. By later Ottoman times, this egalitarianism was somewhat restricted. The abolition of slave recruitment for government service had closed the main avenue of upward social mobility, while the formation and persistence, in the most enduring of all Muslim monarchies, of such ensconced privileged groups as the notables and the ulema restricted the number of openings accessible to newcomers. In spite of this, however, it is probably true that even at the beginning of the nineteenth century a poor man of humble origin had a better chance of attaining to wealth, power and dignity in the Ottoman Empire than in any of the states of Christian Europe, including post-Revolutionary France.

It is a charge often levelled at historians that their enquiries are concerned only with the possessors of wealth, power and learning; that though they may pretend to write the history of nations, countries and eras, they are in fact writing only of a few thousand privileged persons, and disregarding the great mass of the people. This accusation is largely true. Yet the historians are not at fault. Unlike writers of fiction and other imaginative literature, the historian is limited by the evidence at his disposal. Until comparatively recently, and in some countries even until the present day, writing was the perquisite of those same possessors of power, wealth, and learning, or of persons employed by them. It is in consequence they, and for the most part they alone, who have left the books, the documents, the inscriptions, and other traces from which the historian seeks to reconstruct the record of the past.

But there are exceptions. In recent years, historians have sought, by laboriously piecing together odd scraps of information from here and there, to achieve some insight into the history and experience of the silent masses. For the Greco-Roman world, for Christian Europe, to some extent for the Ottoman Empire, the study of the history of the lower classes has made some progress. For the history of medieval Islam, however, the task has barely been begun. There has been some study of the city, and of various elements of the urban population, most of it concerned with economic rather than social history. A few brief articles here and there, a few chapters in books mostly devoted to other subjects, make up the sparse bibliography of scholarly literature devoted to the daily life of the common people of medieval Islam. From the late fifteenth century onwards, the vast resources of the Ottoman archives, both imperial and provincial, provide a surprising wealth of evidence on the everyday life of ordinary people in the cities and even in the villages. For medieval times the task is more difficult but not impossible. There are no archives comparable with those of the Ottoman Empire or of the European states, but documents have survived in significant numbers, most of them in Egypt. From these, supplemented and interpreted in the light of literary evidence of various kinds, it is possible to achieve some insight into the lives of the *'āmma*, the common people, as contrasted with the *khāṣṣa*, the special people or the elites.

The picture that emerges is one of an extremely diverse and active urban population. The major components of this population were the artisans and craftsmen – masters, journeymen, apprentices, at varying economic levels. Many were organized in guilds, sometimes though by no means always ethnically or religiously homogeneous, and sometimes even occupying their own separate quarter of the city. The political, military and religious establishments as such formed part of the *khāṣṣa*, but all three had their lower-ranking, worse-paid elements, who by their standard and manner of life belonged with the masses rather than with the elite. Order was maintained by a variety of police forces, some of them military units belonging to the army, most of them locally recruited from among the town population. Such were the *'asas*, the night watch, and the *aḥdāth*, a kind of militia recruited principally from the young apprentices.

These various police forces had no easy task. A small number of

Arabic texts have survived that give us an insight into the manners, mores and even language of the submerged underworld of medieval Islam. Its inhabitants were of many kinds. Some were simply criminals – thieves, tricksters, confidence men and assassins. Some were entertainers – tumblers, jugglers, dancers, performers of many kinds, among whom we may include itinerant preachers and professional storytellers. Some might be described as quacks, who provided what was probably the only kind of medical attention available to the mass of the population, whom they served, at once, as doctors, dentists, apothecaries, and psychiatrists. Some dealt in magic, astrology, amulets, and the like. Some were pedlars, providing the cheap and simple goods which were needed by the mass of the population, and which alone they could afford to buy. These, along with the quacks, served an important economic and social function analogous to those of the merchants and of the highly respected physicians among the privileged classes. Perhaps the most visible group – certainly that which is given most attention in the sources – were the beggars. These performed a necessary religious function, providing the opportunity for the pious to discharge the religious duty of almsgiving. In plying their craft, they resorted to an astonishing range of tricks and devices, which are lovingly elaborated in the sources. The vagabonds of medieval Europe are no doubt more richly documented and have been more thoroughly studied. But those of medieval Islam are not undeserving of attention.

In Arab culture, even the beggars have their poetry. A tenth-century vaunt in the grand classical style proclaims:[3]

> For we are the lads, the only lads who really matter, on land or on sea.
> We exact a tax from all mankind, from China to Egypt,
> And to Tangier; indeed, our steeds range over every land of the world.
> When one region gets too hot for us, we simply leave it for another one.
> The whole world is ours, and whatever is in it, the lands of Islam and the
>   lands of unbelief alike.
> Hence we spend the summers in snowy lands, whilst in winter we migrate
>   to the lands where the dates grow.
> We are the beggars' brotherhood, and no one can deny us our lofty pride.

A special category were the brigands and bandits, who inevitably flourished at times and in places when rich caravans travelled by difficult and lonely mountain and desert trails. Some were simply criminals, and were regarded and treated as such. Others, perhaps because they expressed some recognizable social protest, were admired, and sometimes became the object of popular and even literary cults. Such, for example, were the so-called 'brigand poets' (su'lūk, plural sa'ālīk), who flourished in ancient Arabia. The sa'ālīk were outcasts, living outside the tribal system, and with none of the protection that that system afforded. They produced a distinctive type of poetry, which won the admiration of literary historians in both medieval and modern times. Very different were the bands of brigands known as jelâli, who ravaged Ottoman Anatolia, especially in the sixteenth and seventeenth centuries. Recruited from discharged soldiers, landless peasants, unemployed graduates of the religious schools, and other discontented elements, they won fame and success, and some of their leaders are commemorated in the folklore and the folk-poetry of Anatolia.

Historical memory has been less kind to other types of resistance, which it has preferred either to condemn or to forget. Such, for example, are the occasional revolts of slaves against their masters. Notable among these were the East African slaves employed in agricultural projects in Iraq in the early Middle Ages, who rose several times in revolt. Their most important rebellion lasted fifteen years, from 868 to 883 CE. They defeated several imperial armies, and for a while seemed to offer a serious threat to the caliphate in Baghdad. A somewhat grotesque rebellion of slaves against slaves is recorded as taking place in Egypt in 1446 CE. In that year, the chroniclers tell us, some five hundred black slaves tending the horses of their Mamluk masters in pasturages outside Cairo obtained arms and rose in revolt. The Egyptian historians tell us that they established a miniature state and a court of their own. Their leader was called 'sultan' and installed on a throne; his principal followers were given the titles of the chief officers of the Mamluk sultan's court. They survived by raiding caravans and were eventually overcome as a result of internal quarrels between rival claimants to the 'sultanate'.

Far more threatening to the Islamic social and political order was a series of popular revolts, with programmes that were usually expressed in religious terms but were often driven by social and economic discontents. The Kharijites, protesting against the increasingly autocratic character of the Muslim state, drew much support from the nomads, Arabs and others, for whom any authority was seen as an encroachment on their personal freedom and dignity. The Shī'a, by putting forward the claims of the descendants of the Prophet to the caliphate, impugned the legitimacy of the actual holders of that office, and thus provided an expression for the grievances and an outlet for the anger of those who felt themselves to be oppressed or dispossessed. Some of these movements – the 'Abbasids in the eighth century, the Fāṭimids in the tenth century, the Safavids in the sixteenth century, actually gained power and, inevitably failing to satisfy the expectations they had aroused, drove their more resentful followers to still more extremist movements. Even the Sufi brotherhoods, usually more pacific, sometimes became involved in extensive and dangerous risings, with popular support.

Contrary to popular beliefs, medieval Islam was a civilization of cities, not of the countryside or the desert. Its historiography, its literature, its laws discuss urban problems and reflect urban conditions. Not until Ottoman times do we have archives from which it is possible to study the day-to-day life of the peasantry; not until very recent times do we find much literature depicting the life of the peasants – still less, peasant literature. A fair amount is known about such matters as technology and irrigation, land use and land tenure and the like, but very little about the peasants who for most of Middle Eastern history constituted the vast majority of the population.

Peasants – those who actually cultivate the land, as distinct from those who enjoy the fruits of their labours – are the silent ones. Their views and their feelings are for the most part not reflected in the literature and documents which provide most of our information about the history of the region. From time to time people of peasant origin emerge from the background and find their way into the higher strata of society, becoming merchants or ulema or landowners, or officers of the state or of the armed forces; but when that happens they cease, for the most part, to be peasants and to reflect a peasant point of view. Only a few bandit and rebel leaders seem to have remained in touch with their people, but these too are little known. Even in modern times, with all the means of communication available now but lacking in earlier times, it is still extraordinarily difficult to find out what the peasants really think in these countries. Folklore, folktales, folk literature, and proverbs are still probably the best evidence of what peasants thought and felt. The Ottoman archives, with their endless and detailed records of complaints, disputes, investigations and decisions, provide virtually the only evidence on how peasants lived.

Beyond the countryside – but in most Middle Eastern countries never very far away – was the desert, inhabited by nomadic tribes who eked out a livelihood by raising animals for food, clothing and transport, with occasional additions obtained by raiding. Nomad Berbers in northwest Africa, Bedouin Arabs in North Africa and southwest Asia, nomadic Turkish and Iranian tribes on the plateaux of Anatolia and Iran and in Central Asia, remained an important element in the economy, and therefore also from time to time in the polity. Because of the characteristic Middle Eastern separation between agriculture and stock-raising, the nomads remained economically necessary, and were thus able to preserve their distinctive way of life despite the continuous efforts of the various governments that ruled the cities and the countryside to bring them under control. Sometimes when governments were strong, the nomads were relatively quiet. At other times, when government was weak, the nomads became more independent and assertive, raiding the oases and the villages, pillaging caravans, and grazing their cattle on what were once farmlands. Sometimes, inspired by some new religious teacher preaching a return to authentic Islam, they were able to invade and conquer the settled country, and establish new kingdoms and dynasties.

CHAPTER 12

RELIGION AND LAW

Since the establishment of the Islamic Empire in the mid-seventh century, Islam has been the dominant religion in the Middle East. At first it was the religion only of a small minority of conquerors, settlers, and rulers, while the vast mass of the population in both the former Persian and former Byzantine lands remained faithful to their old religions. In the course of time – precisely when and how are still not clear – Muslims became a majority, and in most of the region have remained so, in steadily increasing proportion, to the present day. Only in one region were non-Muslims forbidden to live. According to traditional accounts, the Caliph ʿUmar decreed that in the Holy Land – which for Muslims meant Arabia, the homeland of the Prophet – only one religion, Islam, should be permitted, and Christians and Jews were therefore required to leave. Even this did not apply to southern Arabia, where Christianity survived for some centuries, and Judaism to the present day.

Elsewhere, the destinies of the non-Muslim communities under Muslim rule or influence varied greatly. On the fringes of the Islamic Empire, some countries – Georgia and Armenia in the north, Ethiopia in the south – retained their Christian character, some of them even their independence. In the Fertile Crescent and Egypt, the Christian Churches, despite the steady erosion of their numbers, continued to flourish and even derived some advantage from the removal of the Byzantine preoccupation with defining and imposing correct belief. In North Africa, in contrast, Christianity died out. Jewish communities, well established in the eastern, central, and western provinces alike, were accorded a status similar to that of the Christians – a considerable improvement on their experience under Christian rule. The Zoroastrians, lacking both the encouragement of powerful friends abroad enjoyed by the Christians and the bitter skill in survival possessed by the Jews, fared badly. Some fled to India, where a small community of them, known as Parsees, remains to the present day. In Iran, orthodox Zoroastrians dwindled to a tiny minority. Deviant and dissident Zoroastrian groups, less dependent on the power of the state and the discipline of an established priesthood, fared rather better, and played a role of some importance in the social, cultural and even political history of Iran in the early centuries of Muslim rule. One of the most notable of these groups consisted of the followers of Mani, whose beliefs survived vigorous persecution at the hands of Zoroastrians, Muslims and Christians alike in both the Middle East and Europe, and continued to attract followers from all three faiths.

In the heartlands of the classical caliphate, in southwest Asia and northern Africa, a civilization grew up which was in many ways profoundly influenced by the ancient cultures of the region and enriched by the contributions of the non-Muslim minorities. It was, however, in the profoundest sense, an Islamic civilization, with a distinctive and recognizable character affecting its philosophy, its science, its literature, its arts and its way of life, clearly discernible even in the inner life of the non-Muslim communities.

'Islam' is an Arabic word, usually explained by Muslims and others as meaning 'surrender', that is to say, the surrender of the believer to God. The active participle of the same verb, 'Muslim', means one who performs the act of surrender. It seems likely that in early times the word also conveyed another notion, well attested in Arabic and other Semitic languages – that of entirety. The Muslim was thus one who gave himself entirely to God alone, to the exclusion of others, that is to say a monotheist as contrasted with the polytheists of seventh-century pagan Arabia.

As perceived by the Muslim tradition, the mission of Muḥammad was not an innovation but a continuation – a new and this time final phase in the long struggle between monotheism and polytheism. For Muslims, Muḥammad was the Seal of the Prophets, the last of a long series of divinely appointed apostles, each of whom had brought a book of revelation. Such were the Torah, the Psalms and the Gospel brought by the prophets Moses, David, and Jesus. Muḥammad was the last and greatest of them, and the book he brought, the Qur'ān, completes and supersedes all previous revelations. Thus, in the Muslim perception, both Judaism and Christianity had been true religions at the time of their advent, earlier phases in the same sequence of missions and revelations. These revelations were, however, rendered obsolete by the apostolate of Muḥammad. Whatever truth they contained was incorporated in his message. What was not so incorporated was not true, and was the result of the distortion and corruption of these earlier scriptures by their unworthy custodians.

The word 'Islam' is used today with a number of different meanings. For Muslims, strictly speaking, it denotes the one true faith which has existed since the creation of the world, and in this sense Adam, Moses, David, Jesus and others were all Muslims. More commonly – since adherents of earlier phases in the sequence of revelations had survived under other names – the term Islam is restricted to the final phase, that of Muḥammad and the Qur'ān. But here again there is some variation of meaning. In the first instance the term 'Islam' denotes the religion taught by the Prophet himself through the Qur'ān and through his own precept and practice as transmitted and recorded by subsequent generations. Through this process, it came to denote the whole complex system of theology, law and custom as elaborated by these later generations on the basis of what was taught by the Prophet and what was ascribed to him. In this sense it includes the great structure of the Holy Law, which Muslims call *sharī'a*, and the corpus of Islamic theology which Muslims call *kalām*. In a still wider sense, the word 'Islam' is often used, especially by non-Muslims, as the equivalent not of Christianity but of Christendom, and denotes the whole rich civilization that grew up under the aegis of the Muslim faith and society. In this sense the word denotes not what Muslims believed or were expected to believe, but what they actually did – in other words Islamic civilization as known to us from history and as existing at the present time.

The word 'mosque', in various forms and by different routes, has reached all the languages of Christendom as a designation for the Muslim place of worship. It derives from the Arabic '*masjid*', which means literally a place of prostration, that is to say the place where worshippers prostrate themselves or more precisely kneel before God. It is not, however, the Muslim equivalent of the Christian church or ecclesia. The mosque is a building, a place of worship, often also of meeting and study, and no more. The term in Muslim usage has never designated an institution with its own separate structure and hierarchy, laws and jurisdiction. In the earliest Islamic period it was hardly even a building – just a place where the believers gathered together for communal prayers. These could also be performed in private houses, in public places, in the open air, and frequently, in the very earliest period of the conquests, in places of worship built to serve the various religions of the conquered, and either shared or taken over by the conquerors. In this way the Arab conquerors first shared and later took over and adapted the Church of St John in Damascus and, many centuries later, transformed the great cathedral of Santa Sophia in Constantinople into an imperial mosque. This was accomplished outside the building, by mounting a crescent on the dome and adding four minarets, one at each corner, from which the muezzins could proclaim the unity of God and the apostolate of Muḥammad, and inside the building by removing Christian images and symbols, or by covering them with Qur'ānic verses and other Islamic texts.

The interior of the mosque is simple and austere. There is no altar and no sanctuary, since Islam has no sacraments and no ordained priesthood. The imam has no priestly function, but is only a leader in prayer. Any Muslim who knows the ritual may perform the task, though in practice the imamate usually became a permanent, professional office. Inside the mosque the two chief foci are the *minbar* and the *mihrāb*. The first is a kind of raised pulpit used in the larger mosques during the Friday prayer. The *mihrāb* is a niche in the *qibla* wall, showing the direction of Mecca, towards which all Muslims turn in prayer. It is usually placed in the centre of the wall, and determines the axis of symmetry of the building. Muslim public prayer is a disciplined, communal act of submission to the Creator, to the one universal and immaterial God. It has no place for drama or mystery, no use for liturgical music or poetry, still less for votive art. Sculpture in particular is rejected as blasphemy verging on idolatry. In their place, Muslim artists used abstract and geometrical designs and based their decorative schemes on the extensive and systematic use of inscriptions. The names of God, the Prophet and the early caliphs, the Muslim declaration of faith, and verses or even whole chapters of the Qur'ān are used to decorate the walls and ceilings of the mosque. For Muslims, the text of the Qur'ān is divine, and to write or read it is an act of worship. Many different styles of writing are used, and in the hands of the great masters the art of calligraphy can achieve an intricate and recondite beauty. These decorative texts are the hymns and fugues and icons of Muslim devotion; they are a key to the understanding both of Muslim piety and of Muslim aesthetics.

The most familiar and characteristic outward feature of the mosque is the minaret, usually a separate structure, from the top of which the muezzin (Arabic *mu'adhdhin*) summons the faithful to prayer. It typifies both the unity and variety of the Muslim world. Everywhere it serves the same religious and social purpose, soaring above the crowded alleys and markets, a signal and a warning to the believers. But at the same time each of the great regions of Islam has its own style of minaret, often preserving the remembered outline of some earlier structure, not always a religious one – the step-towers of Babylon, the church steeples of Syria, the lighthouses of Egypt.

In another sense, the Islamic mosque was the successor of the Roman forum and of the Greek *agora* – the centre of the Muslim polity and society, especially in the new garrison towns. The *minbar* of the mosque served as a platform not only for the preacher and leader in prayer, but also for the promulgation of important announcements and decisions, such as the appointment and dismissal of officials, the installing of new rulers or governors, the announcing of news of war and conquest and other important events. In the garrison cities, the mosque, the government offices such as they were, and the military cantonments together formed a sort of citadel, and it was often the ruler or governor himself who made important announcements from the pulpit. From early times it was the custom for the speaker in the pulpit to hold a sword or a staff in his hand to symbolize the sovereignty of Islam – a sword if the place had been taken by assault, a staff if it had been surrendered on terms.

With the increasing complexity of Muslim government and society, the political role of the mosque was reduced but never entirely eliminated. Major appointments, for example the accession of a new caliph, were still proclaimed from the pulpit, and the weekly sermon, the *khuṭba*, including the bidding prayer in which the names of the ruler and governor were mentioned, retained its political importance. Mention in the *khuṭba* was one of the recognized tokens of political authority in Islam – for a ruler, of sovereignty; to a suzerain, of allegiance. Omitting a suzerain's name from the *khuṭba* was a declaration of independence.

A frequently quoted verse from the Qur'ān enjoins the Muslims to 'obey God, obey his Prophet, and obey those in authority over you' (4:59). This verse was interpreted as conferring authority equal to that of the Qur'ān itself on the traditions, *ḥadīth*, concerning the actions and utterances of the Prophet who, according to Muslim belief, was divinely inspired not only in the revelation which he brought but also in all that he did and said. The oral tradition concerning the precept and practice of the Prophet was handed down for generations and later committed to writing in great collections, a few of which are regarded by Muslims as reliable and authoritative. Already in medieval times Muslim scholars questioned the authenticity of some of these traditions; modern critical scholarship has done so in a much more radical form. The standard collections are still, however, revered by most Muslims as second only to the Qur'ān. The two together form the basis of the Holy Law of Islam, *sharī'a*. This magnificent structure of laws, lovingly elaborated by successive generations of jurists and theologians, is one of the major intellectual achievements of Islam, and perhaps most fully exemplifies the character and genius of Islamic civilization.

Towards the end of the eighteenth century a Muslim visitor to England, Mīrzā Abū Ṭālib – one of the first to have left a written account of his impressions – described a visit to the House of Commons, and his astonishment when it was explained to him that its functions and duties included the promulgation of laws and the fixing of penalties for wrongdoers. Unlike the Muslims, he explained to his readers, the English have not accepted a divine law revealed from heaven, and were therefore reduced to the expedient of making their own laws 'in accordance with the necessities of time and circumstance, the state of affairs, and the experience of judges'.[1]

In principle, the Islamic legal system was totally different from that which the traveller found and described in England. For Muslims the sole valid law was that of God made known through revelation, manifested in the Qur'ān and *ḥadīth*, and then amplified and interpreted through the work of the later jurist-theologians. Where the law itself is seen as enacted by God and promulgated by the Prophet, jurists and theologians follow different branches of the same profession. Since the doctors of the Holy Law were not state officials but private persons, their rulings were not formally binding, nor were they unanimous. The *qāḍī*, appointed by the state, administered justice in his court. His task was to apply the law, not to interpret it. That function belonged to the *muftī*, a jurisconsult whose opinions or rulings, called *fatwā*, from the same root, could be cited as legal authorities though not as law.

In principle the *sharī'a* covered all aspects of Muslim life – public and private, communal and personal alike. Some of its provisions, especially those relating to marriage, divorce, property, inheritance and other matters of personal status, acquired the character of a normative code of law which the faithful were expected to obey and which the state took measures to enforce. In other aspects the *sharī'a* was more like a system of ideals towards which both individuals and the community were to aspire. The political or constitutional provisions of the *sharīʿa*, dealing with the conduct of government, fell somewhere between the two, in different times and places closer to the one or to the other.

Muslim jurists divide the *sharīʿa* into two main parts. Of these, one is concerned with the minds and hearts of the believers, that is to say with doctrine and morality; the other with external acts in relation both to God and to man, that is to say with worship, on the one hand, and with civil, criminal, and public law on the other. The purpose of the law was to define a system of rules, the observance of which would enable the believers to live a righteous life in this world and to prepare themselves for eternal bliss in the next. The principal function of the Islamic state and society was to maintain and enforce these rules.

In reality the difference between Islamic and Western legal practice was less stark than Mīrzā Abū Ṭālib's comments would suggest. While the *sharīʿa* admitted no human legislative power in the Islamic state, in practice Muslim rulers and jurists during the more than fourteen centuries that have passed since the mission of the Prophet encountered many problems for which revelation provided no explicit answer, and found answers to them. These answers were not seen or presented as enactments or as legislation. If they came from below, they were called custom. If they came from above, they were called regulations. If – as happened most frequently – they came from the jurists, they were called interpretation, and the jurisconsults of Islam were no less skilled than lawyers in other societies in the reinterpretation of sacred texts. But in one respect Mīrzā Abū Ṭālib was certainly right. The making of new law, though common and widespread, was always disguised, almost furtive, and there was therefore no room for legislative councils or assemblies such as formed the starting-point of European democracy.

Despite the restraining effect of the unchangeable text of the Qur'ān and of the accepted corpus of *ḥadīth*, Muslims managed to a remarkable extent to modify and develop their laws in accordance with the principle laid down by the jurists that 'the rules change as the times change'. Two factors were of particular importance in this development: the discretionary powers of the ruler and the consensus of the learned.

As defined by the Sunni jurists, the Islamic state was a theocracy, with God as the sole source of sovereignty, of legitimacy and of law, and the ruler as his instrument and representative – in the words of a title used by caliphs and sultans, 'the shadow of God on earth'. In practice, Muslims realized from an early date that in order to keep the affairs of state running, even pious Muslim rulers needed to exercise powers, make rules, and inflict punishments, not indeed in opposition, but often in addition to those laid down by divine law. These powers were denoted by the Arabic word '*siyāsa*' and its equivalents in other Muslim languages. *Siyāsa*, which in its primary meaning denotes the training and management of horses, and in its present day usage means policy or politics, was used in medieval and in Ottoman times to denote the discretionary powers of the ruler other than those conferred upon him by the Holy Law, and then more particularly the punishments, sometimes specifically capital punishment, imposed under that discretionary power. The necessity of both kinds of authority came to be recognized even by the doctors of the Holy Law, and by Ottoman times the sultans promulgated elaborately structured sets of rules known as *kānūn*, regulating the affairs of a province, a department of state, or of the monarchy and central government themselves. A *kānūn* could in no way supersede or abrogate *sharī'a*, but it could amplify and update the provisions of the Holy Law by drawing on local custom and on the edicts of the current and previous rulers.

In promulgating and enforcing such rules and regulations, Muslim sovereigns, especially the more devout and committed among them, such as the Ottomans, required the support or at least the acquiescence of the ulema. In earlier times the more pious and respected among these tended to keep aloof from the state and avoid the spiritual contamination that might result from state service. But from the eleventh century onwards, new threats both at home and abroad drew rulers and ulema together. Under the Seljuks and still more under the rule of the Ottomans and their contemporaries elsewhere, the ulema, especially those concerned with the law, became much more involved in the business of the state, and in a sense became part of the apparatus of government.

Even so, they never became a Church, and Islam never produced an orthodoxy in the Christian sense of that term. In Islamic history there are no councils or synods to define truth and denounce error, no popes, prelates or inquisitors to declare, test, and enforce correct belief. The ulema, the theologians and jurists of Islam, may as individuals or in schools or even, in later times, as holders of public office, formulate dogma and interpret scripture, but they form no constituted ecclesiastical authority to lay down a single orthodox dogma and interpretation, deviation from which is heresy. There was thus no Church to impose one approved form of belief. There were attempts by the state to do so, but they were rare and mostly unsuccessful.

There is, however, one universally accepted test of right belief, and that is the *ijmāʿ*, the consensus of believers, which in modern terms might be described as the climate of opinion among the learned and the powerful. The theoretical basis for this consensus is a saying attributed to the Prophet: 'My community will not agree upon an error.' This was understood to mean that divine guidance, after the death of the Prophet, passed to the Muslim community as a whole, and what that community accepts and applies is, by that very fact, correct Islamic doctrine and practice. Sunni jurists usually accepted the principle that pious and learned men might differ in good faith within certain limits while remaining within the fold. It was in this way that they justified the coexistence and mutual tolerance of the different schools of *sharīʿa* law, four of which, the Ḥanafī, Shāfiʿī, Mālikī and Ḥanbalī schools, have survived into modern times and share the entire Sunni world of Islam between them. Difference and change were authorized and indeed facilitated by this doctrine of *ijmāʿ*.

Such a consensus, varying from time to time and from place to place, may seem intangible and inconstant compared with other more structured and more authoritarian systems. In the earliest Islamic times this was indeed so, and wide scope was left to human reasoning and individual opinion, known in the technical language of the *sharīʿa* as *ijtihād*. In time, however, the range of variation was gradually reduced and ultimately limited, in effect, to questions that were minor, marginal, local, or – an important exception – new. From about 900 CE a consensus emerged among Sunni, though not Shīʿi jurists, that all outstanding issues had been resolved, and that in consequence 'the gate of *ijtihād* was closed'. There were, however, always new problems. Examples include coffee, tobacco, and firearms in the early modern period, and many more at the present time. Some jurists have indeed argued for a reopening of the gate. The Shīʿa never agreed that it was closed, and their ulema are indeed known as *mujtahid* – one who exercises *ijtihād*. They were not, however, noticeably more innovative than their Sunni colleagues.

Through the interaction of consensus and the permissible exercise of independent judgement, a great body of rules for correct behaviour and belief – the nuclei of Islamic law and theology – came into being and gained almost universal acceptance. The guiding principle in its formation was respect for tradition – for the Sunna. In ancient Arabia, this meant ancestral precedent, the normative custom of the tribe. In the earliest Islamic times the Sunna was still a living, growing tradition of the community, developed by the actions and policies of the first caliphs and the companions and successors of the Prophet. By the second Islamic century, a more traditionalist point of view prevailed. The Sunna was equated with the practice and precept of the Prophet himself, as transmitted, so it was believed, by the relaters of authentic traditions, and was held to override all but the Qur'ān itself. With the general acceptance of this view and of the body of traditions that were put forward, with varying plausibility, as recording precedents of the Prophet, the role of opinion and therefore of consensus was reduced, though never entirely eliminated. In place of *ijtihād* the ulema relied increasingly on *taqlīd*, unquestioning acceptance of established doctrines. In this way a kind of Islamic orthodoxy emerged, not in the Christian sense of correct doctrine certified as such by constituted ecclesiastical authority, but rather in the more limited sense of a generally accepted core of traditional practice and doctrine, departure or deviation from which might be condemned, according to circumstance, as an error, a crime, and/or a sin.

Those who accepted this orthodoxy were called Sunnis, a term which implied loyalty to a community and acceptance of its traditions, rather than belief in an officially defined dogma and submission to ecclesiastical authority. The same communal and social implications can be seen in the various technical terms used by Muslims to denote deviation from the Sunna.

Perhaps the nearest Muslim approach to the Christian concept of heresy is the term '*bid'a*', innovation. Observance of tradition is good, and it is by this that Sunni Islam is defined; departure from tradition is *bid'a*, and is bad unless specifically shown to be good. The extreme traditionalist view is well summed up in a saying attributed to the Prophet: 'The worst things are those that are novelties. Every novelty is an innovation, every innovation is an error, and every error leads to Hellfire.' The gravamen of a charge of *bid'a* against a doctrine was not, primarily, that it was false but that it was new – a breach of custom and tradition, respect for which is reinforced by the belief in the finality and perfection of the Muslim revelation.

There is thus an important distinction between the Christian notion of heresy and the Muslim notion of *bid'a*. Heresy is a theological transgression, a wrong choice or stress in doctrine. Innovation is a social more than a theological offence. The same is true of two other reproaches – *ilḥād*, deviation, i.e. from the right path, and *ghuluww*, excess, from an Arabic root meaning to overshoot, to go beyond the limit. The latter term occurs in a Qur'ānic verse addressed primarily to Jews and Christians: 'O people of the book! Commit no excess in your religion, and say nothing of God but the truth' (Qur'ān 4:171). Here the term clearly refers to Christian beliefs which Islam regards as 'excessive'. Later, *ghuluww* was more commonly used of Muslim errors.

Some diversity of opinion within the community is seen as harmless and even beneficial. According to a saying attributed to the jurist Abū Ḥanīfa, the founder of the Ḥanafī school of law, and later to the Prophet himself: 'Difference of opinion within my community is God's mercy.' There were different schools of *sharī'a* law, each with its own principles, textbooks, and judiciary, yet living in mutual toleration. While most of their differences were ritual, there were some even concerning matters of doctrine. But there must be limits. Those who carry their divergence to excess, *ghuluww*, are known as *ghulāt*, singular *ghālī*, or as deviants – *malāḥida*, singular *mulḥid*. In the view of many theologians they may not even be considered as Muslims.

Characteristically, the theologians differ on where to draw the line. Most theologians agreed to exclude the radical and extremist Shī'a groups, such as the Ismā'īlīs, from the Islamic fold. But most Muslim societies were willing to tolerate them and even accord them the status of Muslims, provided that they did not engage in socially disruptive or politically seditious activities. This unorthodox tolerance is still extended at the present day to such marginal groups as the 'Alawis and the Druze in the Levant, and the Ismā'īlīs in a number of Muslim countries. The situation regarding the so-called moderate Shī'a, by far the most important non-Sunni group in Islamic history and in the present-day Islamic world, is somewhat more complex.

Heresy is not a category of Muslim theology and therefore not of Muslim law. The self-styled Muslim who fails to comply with even the minimal requirements of the theologians faces a far graver charge, that of unbelief or even of apostasy. Muslim theologians were ready enough to hurl charges of innovation or excess or deviation against doctrines of which they disapproved, but they were usually reluctant to pursue these charges to their logical conclusion. To denounce a doctrine and those who held it as non-Islamic meant that these persons, nominally Muslim, were apostates, subject to the utmost penalty of the law. The sectarian, though some of his beliefs might in time be extruded by the consensus from the mainstream of Islam, remained a Muslim, still entitled before the law to the status and privileges of a Muslim in society, in property, marriage, inheritance, testimony and the holding of public office. If captured in war or even in rebellion, he was to be treated as a Muslim, that is to say he was not subject to summary dispatch or enslavement, and his family and property were to be protected by the law. Though a sinner, he was not an unbeliever, and might even aspire to a place in the world to come. The vital barrier in Islam lay not between Sunni and sectarian, but between sectarian and apostate. Apostasy was a crime as well as a sin, and the apostate was damned both in this world and the next. His crime was treason – desertion and betrayal of the community to which he belonged, and to which he owed loyalty. His life and property were forfeit. He was a dead limb to be excised.

Charges of apostasy were not unusual, and in early times the terms 'unbeliever' and 'apostate' were commonly used in religious polemic. 'The piety of theologians', says al-Jāḥiẓ (d. 869) 'consists of hastening to denounce dissidents as unbelievers.'[2] Ghazālī (d. 1111) speaks with contempt of those 'who would constrict the vast mercy of God to his servants and make Paradise the benefice (waqf) of a small clique of theologians'.[3] In fact such accusations had little practical effect. The accused were for the most part unmolested, and some even held high offices in the Muslim state. As the rules and penalties of Muslim law were systematized and more regularly enforced, charges of apostasy became rarer. Few theologians were both willing and able to invoke the penalties for apostasy against those whose beliefs differed from their own. Even so determined an opponent of all innovations as the Syrian jurist Ibn Taymiyya (d. 1328) preferred a sort of quarantining of suspect groups of individuals, followed if needful by admonition and in bad cases by coercive action. Only when a bid'a was extreme, persistent, and aggressive were its followers to be put beyond the pale of the community of Islam and ruthlessly extirpated.

The absence of a single, imposed, dogmatic orthodoxy in Islam was due not to an omission but to a rejection – the rejection of something that was felt by Sunni Muslims to be alien to the genius of their faith and dangerous to the interests of their community. But Muslims, like followers of other religions, did not always follow their own principles, or even obey their own scriptures. There are examples, from both classical and Ottoman times, of rulers seeking to impose a particular form of Islam or even forcibly to convert their non-Muslim subjects.

There were times when holders of 'deviant' beliefs were coerced to conform, and tortured or killed if they persisted. In general, however, both tolerance and intolerance are in a sense structural – defined by law. Tolerance may not be extended to those who deny the unity or existence of God – to atheists and polytheists. These, when conquered, must be given the choice of conversion or death, which latter might be remitted to slavery. Tolerance must be extended to those who reach the required minimum of belief – that is, those who profess what Islam recognizes as a revealed religion with authentic scriptures. This tolerance is subject to their acceptance and observance of certain fiscal and other disabilities. Tolerance may in no circumstances be extended to the apostate, the renegade Muslim, whose punishment is death. Some authorities allow the remission of this punishment if the apostate recants. Other insist on the death penalty even then. God may pardon him in the world to come; the law must punish him in this world.

There are two versions of the last words of al-Ash'arī (d. 935–6), one of the greatest of medieval Muslim dogmatists. According to one version, his last words were: 'I testify that I do not consider any who pray towards Mecca as infidels. All turn their minds in prayer towards the same object. They differ only in expression.'⁴ According to the other version, he died cursing the errors of the Mu'tazila. Whichever of these versions may be true of al-Ash'arī, there can be no doubt that the first is a more authentic expression of the general attitude of Sunni Islam towards correct belief. The profession of Islam – inscribed on coins, cried from the minarets, repeated in prayers every day – is that God is one and Muḥammad is his Prophet. The rest is detail.

The *shahāda*, or declaration of faith (literally, testimony), is the first of the five pillars of Islam. The second is prayer, and more particularly the *ṣalāt*, the set ritual prayer to be offered with prescribed words and motions five times every day at sunrise, midday, afternoon, sunset, and evening. The Muslim may at any time offer *du'ā'*, a personal, spontaneous prayer, not bound by any rules or rituals. But *ṣalāt* is an obligation of all adult Muslims, both male and female. The worshipper must be in a state of ritual purity, in a ritually clean place, and must face in the direction of Mecca. The prayer itself consists of the *shahāda* and some passages from the Qur'ān.

Muslims, like Jews and Christians, set aside one day in the week which is, so to speak, sanctified for public prayer (Qur'ān 62:9–11). The Muslim Friday, like the Jewish Saturday and the Christian Sunday, was a day of public and communal prayer. Unlike the Jewish and

Christian sabbath, however, it was not a day of rest but rather – as the Qur'ān indicates and subsequent history confirms – a day of heightened public activity in the markets and elsewhere. The notion of a weekly holiday from work was not, however, unknown. The practice is occasionally mentioned during the Middle Ages, becomes more common in Ottoman times, and is almost universal in Muslim lands at the present day.

The third pillar of Islam is pilgrimage, the *ḥajj*. At least once in his lifetime every Muslim is required to undertake a pilgrimage to Mecca and Medina. This is not, like the pilgrimage to Jerusalem for Jews and Christians, a meritorious option. It is a religious obligation. The pilgrimage takes place every year between the seventh and tenth days of the month of Dhu'l-Hijja, and culminates in the great festival of sacrifices and the circumambulation of the Ka'ba, the cube-shaped building in the centre of the great Mosque of Mecca. Containing the revered Black Stone, it is known as the House of God (*Bayt Allah*) and is, for Muslims, the holiest place in the holy city.

The social, cultural, and also economic effects of the pilgrimage throughout Islamic history have been of immense importance. Every year since early times, Muslims from all parts of the Islamic world, of many races and of very different social backgrounds, have left their homes and travelled, often over vast distances, to take part in a common act of worship. These journeys were quite different from the collective migrations of tribes and peoples in Antiquity and in the Middle Ages. Each pilgrimage is voluntary and individual. It is a personal act, following a personal decision, and resulting in a wide range of significant personal experience. This level of physical mobility, unparalleled in pre-modern societies, has from early times involved important social, intellectual and economic consequences. The pilgrim, if wealthy, was often accompanied by a number of slaves, whom he might sell on the way to pay the expenses of his journey. If he was a merchant, he might combine his pilgrimage with a business trip, buying and selling commodities in the places through which he passed, and thus learning to know the products, markets, merchants, customs and practices of many lands. If he was a scholar, he might take the opportunity to attend lectures, meet colleagues, and acquire books, thus participating in the diffusion and exchange of knowledge and ideas.

The needs of the pilgrimage – the commands of the faith reinforcing the requirements of government and commerce – helped to maintain a network of communications between the far-flung Muslim lands. The experience of the pilgrimage gave rise to a rich literature of travel, bringing information about distant places and – perhaps most important – a heightened awareness of belonging to a larger whole. This awareness was reinforced by participation in the common rituals and ceremonies of the pilgrimage in Mecca and Medina, and the sense of communion with fellow Muslims of other lands and peoples. The physical mobility of significant numbers of men, and often women, and the resulting social mobility, made the medieval Islamic world very different from the stratified, rigidly hierarchic society and intense local traditions that existed within the comparatively small area of European Christendom. The Islamic world was vast and diverse, but it achieved a degree of unity, both in perception and in reality, that was never attained in medieval, still less in modern Christendom. The pilgrimage was not the only factor making for cultural unity in the Islamic world, but it was certainly one of the most effective. This institution – the most important agency of voluntary, personal mobility before the age of the great European discoveries – must have had profound effects on all the communities from which the pilgrims came, through which they travelled, and to which they returned.

The fourth pillar of Islam, according to the traditional reckoning, is fasting. During Ramaḍān, the ninth month of the Muslim year, all adult Muslims, men and women, are required to fast from sunrise to sunset. The aged, the sick and the very young may be exempted; those on a journey or engaged in *jihād* may postpone the fast.

The fifth and last of the five pillars is the *zakāt*, a financial levy paid by Muslims to the community or to the state. Originally a charitable contribution collected from the believers for pious purposes, it was in time converted into a kind of tax or tribute, whereby those who accepted Islam gave formal expression to that acceptance. As a religious obligation, it retains the meaning of almsgiving.

The five pillars of the faith are positive obligations – duties that a Muslim is required to perform. There is also a wide range of negative commandments – of actions the commission of which is a sin. Many of these – such as the prohibition of murder and robbery – are no more than the basic rules of social coexistence. Others have a more specifically religious connotation, notably the ban on pork, alcohol, fornication, and the taking of interest. The concern with sexual and financial crimes is shared with Judaism and Christianity, though differently defined. The ban on pork is shared with Judaism, though not with Christianity. The ban on alcoholic drinks is uniquely Muslim. The effects of all four prohibitions on social and economic life were – and still are – profound and far-reaching.

Another positive obligation prescribed by the jurists and theologians is that of *jihād*. This is an obligation of the community as a whole in offence, of every individual Muslim in defence. The term '*jihād*', conventionally translated 'holy war', has the literal meaning of striving, more specifically, in the Qur'ānic phrase 'striving in the path of God' (*fī sabīl Allāh*). Some Muslim theologians, particularly in more modern times, have interpreted the duty of 'striving in the path of God' in a spiritual and moral sense. The overwhelming majority of early authorities, however, citing relevant passages in the Qur'ān and in the tradition, discuss *jihād* in military terms. Virtually every manual of *sharī'a* law has a chapter on *jihād*, which regulates in minute detail such matters as the opening, conduct, interruption and cessation of hostilities, and the allocation and division of booty. Fighters in the holy war are enjoined not to kill women and children unless they attack first, not to torture or mutilate prisoners, to give fair warning of a resumption of hostilities, and to honour agreements. The Holy Laws required good treatment of non-combatants, but also accorded the victors extensive rights over the property and also the persons and families of the vanquished. These could be reduced to slavery and, for females, concubinage.

The idea of holy war – a war for God and the faith – was not new in the Middle East. It suffuses the books of Deuteronomy and Judges, and inspired the Christian Byzantines in their wars against Persia and in their struggles to repel the Arab and later Turkish invaders. But these were wars with limited objectives – the conquest of the promised land, the defence of Christendom against non-Christian attack. Even the Christian crusade, often compared with the Muslim *jihād*, was itself a delayed and limited response to the *jihād* and in part also an imitation. But unlike the *jihād* it was concerned primarily with the defence or reconquest of threatened or lost Christian territory. It was, with few exceptions, limited to the successful wars for the recovery of southwest Europe, and the unsuccessful wars to recover the Holy Land and to halt the Ottoman advance in the Balkans. The Muslim *jihād*, in contrast, was perceived as unlimited, as a religious obligation that would continue until all the world had either adopted the Muslim faith or submitted to Muslim rule. In the latter case, those who professed what Muslims recognized as a revealed religion were allowed to continue the practice of that religion, subject to the acceptance of certain fiscal and other disabilities. Those who did not, that is to say idolaters and polytheists, were given the choice of conversion, death or slavery.

According to Muslim law, it is lawful to wage war against four types of enemy: infidels, apostates, rebels, and bandits. While all four are legitimate, only the first two count as *jihād*, regulated by different rules, and conferring different rights on the victors. This is particularly important in relation to enslavement, to which non-Muslims are liable but from which Muslims, even when vanquished as rebels or bandits, are exempt. The object of *jihād* is to bring the whole world under Islamic law. It is not to convert by force, but to remove obstacles to conversion. St Thomas and St Bernard expressed similar views in relation to the Christian crusade.

To those who fight in the *jihād* the Qur'ān promises rewards in both worlds – booty in this one, and the delights of Paradise in the next. Those who are killed 'in the path of God' are called martyrs. The Arabic word '*shahīd*', with the literal meaning of witness, is thus the etymological equivalent of 'martyr' from the Greek *martys*, a witness, but with a different connotation. Muslim jurists and theologians from an early date were aware of the dangers of the misuse of the *jihād*, for example by slave-raiders and looters, and therefore insist on the importance of pious motivation, without which there can be no true *jihād*. Some early *ḥadīths* from the chapters on *jihād* in the major collections give some idea of how this duty was perceived in early times:[5]

> Paradise is in the shadow of swords.
>
> *Jihād* is your duty under any ruler, be he devout or tyrannical.
>
> The nip of an ant hurts a martyr more than the cut and thrust of weapons, for these are more welcome to him than sweet, cold water on a hot summer day.

A frequently cited *ḥadīth* refers to the vast and growing numbers of infidels who were converted to Islam after their defeat and enslavement: 'God marvels at people who are dragged to paradise in chains.'

The holy war for the faith is a recurring and at times dominant theme in Islamic history. It retained its potency on the frontiers of the Islamic world, where the frontier peoples, often themselves recent converts to Islam, tried to carry their new faith, by war and by preaching, to their unconverted kinsfolk in the lands beyond

the frontier. Such localized *jihāds* by the rulers of frontier principalities continued into modern times, notably in Central Asia
and Africa.

In the central lands of Islam, among peoples of more advanced
culture and greater political sophistication, the notion of *jihād* underwent a number of changes. In the heyday of Arab expansion, under
the patriarchal and Umayyad caliphs, the armies of Islam were indeed
sustained by the idea that they were doing God's work, and encouraged
by the belief – plausible enough at the time – that this work would
be completed within a foreseeable future, and the whole world brought
under the rule of Islam. The Byzantines, the first Christians to bear
the brunt of a *jihād*, often speak disparagingly of those engaged in it,
and ascribe their warlike ardour principally to the desire for booty.
But not all. The Emperor Leo VI, in his *Taktika*, speaks with some
respect of the doctrine of the holy war and of its military value, and
even suggests that Christians might be well advised to adopt something
of the same kind.

He was not alone in this. In 846 CE an Arab fleet from Sicily
appeared at the mouth of the Tiber, and Arab forces sacked Ostia and
Rome. A synod held in France decided to send an appeal to all
Christian sovereigns for a combined army to fight against 'the enemies
of Christ', and the pope, Leo IV, offered a heavenly reward to all those
who died fighting the Muslims. A similar promise was made by Pope
John VIII (872–82), offering forgiveness for sins to those who fought
in defence of the holy Church of God and the Christian religion and
polity, and eternal life for those who died fighting the infidel. These
ideas, provoked by the appearance of Arab raiders in the city of the
popes, clearly reflect the Muslim notion of *jihād*, and are precursors of
the Western Christian Crusade that was to follow.

But in the countries of its origin, the *jihād* was, for the time being,
a spent force. Repeated Arab attempts to conquer Anatolia and to
capture Constantinople by assault had failed, and by the ninth century
the rulers of Islam were becoming reconciled to the fact of a more or
less permanent frontier subject to only minor variations, and a more
or less permanent non-Muslim state beyond that frontier, with which
it was possible to have commercial, diplomatic, and at times even
cultural relations. The interruption of hostilities, which according to
strict *sharī'a* doctrine could only be a truce, a brief interlude in the
otherwise perpetual struggle to Islamize the world, became in effect a
peace agreement, no less stable and no less permanent than the treaties

of eternal peace that European states were wont to sign with one another. So far had the idea of *jihād* faded from Muslim consciousness that when, at the end of the eleventh century, the Western crusaders occupied Palestine and captured Jerusalem, their presence and their actions aroused hardly a flicker of interest in the surrounding Muslim countries. Some Muslim rulers were even willing to enter into friendly relations with them. Some went so far as to seek the alliance of Christian princes in the intricate pattern of rivalries between Muslim states.

It was not until almost a century later that a new *jihād*, in the form of a counter-crusade, began to gather force under the leadership of Saladin. It was precipitated by the deliberately provocative actions of the crusader chieftain Reynald of Châtillon, who in 1182, in violation of a treaty existing between the King of Jerusalem and Saladin, attacked and looted Muslim merchant caravans, including a party of pilgrims on their way to Mecca and, most outrageous of all, launched a naval expedition in the Red Sea to raid both the African and Arabian shores. In the course of this expedition, Reynald's buccaneers burned Muslim shipping at Al-Hawra and Yanbu', the ports of Medina, and by 1183 even penetrated as far as Al-Rābigh, one of the ports of Mecca. Like the Saracens at the gates of Rome three centuries earlier, the crusaders at the gates of Mecca offered a challenge which no self-respecting Muslim ruler could ignore. A Muslim fleet promptly dispatched from Egypt accomplished the almost complete destruction of the Christian raiders. The counter-crusade was under way. Saladin was able to defeat both the Latin Kingdom and a new crusade sent from Europe to save it.

Saladin's *jihād* was limited both in purpose and in duration. His successors resumed peaceful relations with the Franks, even those remaining in the Levant, and in 1229 one of them, Al-Malik Al-Kāmil, the ruler of Egypt, was even willing to cede Jerusalem to the Emperor Frederick II as part of a general deal.

A major reason for the relative unconcern of Muslim rulers and peoples with the coming and presence of the crusaders was their pre-occupation with what was, in their eyes, a far greater threat to the integrity of Islam and the unity of the Islamic community. During the two centuries of the crusader presence in the Levant, the Arab historians of the time devote remarkably little attention to them, while other writers – literary, political, theological – hardly mention them at all. Writers of the time, however, show intense concern with the problems of religious disunity within the Muslim fold. The main threat was seen as coming from the Ismāʿīlī Shīʿa. In the tenth century, followers of the Ismāʿīlī imams had created a powerful and active revolutionary movement, and had succeeded in establishing the Fatimid caliphate, a sort of dissident anti-caliphate challenging the ʿAbbasids for the headship of the Islamic world, and doing so on the basis of a doctrine that differed significantly from that of Sunni Islam. In the Sunni Muslim perception, Saladin's major achievement was not halting the crusaders and reducing the area under their control. It was his success in liquidating the Fatimid caliphate in Egypt and restoring the unity of Islam, symbolized by the return of the name of the ʿAbbasid caliph to the bidding prayer in all the mosques in the Egyptian domains.

The classical *jihād* against Christendom was resumed by the Ottomans – of all major Muslim dynasties, the most fervently and consistently committed to the Muslim faith and to the upholding and enforcement of the Holy Law. In the early centuries of Ottoman history, *jihād* forms a major theme in their political, military, and intellectual life alike, and it is clear that the Ottoman sultans, at least until the time of Süleyman the Magnificent, were sustained by a high sense of moral and religious purpose.

The Ottoman *jihād* against Christendom finally foundered under the walls of Vienna in 1683, and since then, despite some occasional attempts, no Muslim state has posed a comparable challenge to Christendom. The old-style expansionist *jihād* continued intermittently on the frontiers. In 1896, the rulers of Afghanistan launched a *jihād* for the conquest of the mountainous region in the northeast, until then politically independent and inhabited by non-Muslims, and for that reason known as Kāfiristān, the land of the unbelievers. After the Afghan conquest and the Islamization of the inhabitants, the country was known as Nūristān, the land of light. At the other end of the Islamic world, militant Muslim leaders in West Africa proclaimed and fought a *jihād* against pagans, against backsliding Muslims, and, towards the end of the nineteenth century, against European imperialist invaders. This last became increasingly the pattern of *jihād* in the late nineteenth and early twentieth centuries, as one Muslim country after another was threatened and then conquered by Christian European powers.

The classical perception and presentation of the *jihād* was as warfare in the field against a foreign enemy. The idea, however, of an internal *jihād*, directed against an infidel, renegade, or otherwise illegitimate regime, was not unknown. It was of course familiar to the different schools of the Shī'a, for whom the Sunni rulers of Islam were all usurpers and mostly tyrants. It gained support among Sunnis living under the rule of heathen Mongols, or of nominally Muslim Mongol princes and protégés, whose commitment to Islam was suspect. It acquired a new relevance in modern times, in the opposition movements to modernizing rulers, seen as having betrayed Islam from within.

Even the classical *jihād* against the infidel did not at all times enjoy universal support. The early nineteenth-century Ottoman historian Esad Efendi tells of a Bektashi dervish who, during the war against Austria in 1690,

> ... went among the Muslim troops when they were encamped from the night, and went from soldier to soldier saying: 'Hey, you fools, why do you squander your lives for nothing? Fie on you! All the talk you hear about the virtues of holy war and martyrdom in battle is so much nonsense. While the Ottoman emperor enjoys himself in his palace, and the Frankish king disports himself in his country, I can't think why you should give your lives fighting on the mountaintops!'[6]

This story, committed to writing at the time when the Bektashi order of dervishes was dissolved by imperial decree, may well be apocryphal, but it reflects a widespread suspicion of the dervish orders, and in particular of their commitment to basic Islamic doctrines and duties.

Most of our information about the dervish brotherhoods dates from the Ottoman period, when they occupied a prominent and recognized place in society, but their origins go back to early Islamic times, and many of their beliefs and practices to a more remote antiquity. Just as the Christianized heathens of southern and northern Europe preserved much of the Roman Saturnalia and the Viking Yule under the disguise of Christian Christmas celebrations, so too did the peoples of more ancient culture that were converted to Islam preserve many of their ancient rites and customs. In the beliefs and practices of the various dervish orders, one may recognize something of the dance cults of the ancient Aegean lands, the seasonal rituals of Egypt, Babylon, and Persia, the shamanistic ecstasies of the Central Asian Turks; and the mystical philosophy of the Neoplatonists.

In the early days after the advent of Islam, converts still found spiritual satisfaction in the new faith, and welcomed the guidance of its authorized exponents. But as these became at once more learned and more remote, they ceased to satisfy the spiritual and social needs of increasing numbers of Muslims, who began to look elsewhere for sustenance and guidance. For some centuries many of them turned to dissident Islamic groups and especially to the different schools of the Shīʿa, who all agreed that the Islamic community under the rule of the caliphs and sultans and the guidance of the Sunni ulema had taken a wrong turning and must be brought back to the true path. But the Shīʿa attempts to revolutionize Islam all failed – some because they were suppressed in the attempt, others because they succeeded, gained power, and changed nothing. As Shīʿism waned, another movement, that of the Sufis, grew steadily in influence.

Sufism began as a purely individual mystical experience, and became a social movement with an extensive following among the general population. In time, Sufis came to be organized in brotherhoods, known in Arabic as *ṭarīqa*, in Turkish as *tarikat*. The Sufis did not formally reject Sunni positions as the Shīʿa had done, and unlike the Shīʿa they were, for the most part, politically quietist. Some of them, indeed, became involved with the government, and maintained links with its various branches. The Bektashis, for example, had a close relationship with the Ottoman janissaries from the beginning to the end of the history of that corps. The Sufi brotherhoods supplemented, in many ways, the austerity of Sunni worship, and the sometimes cold legalism of the ulema. Sufi saints and leaders, in this sense, tried to bridge the gap which Sunni doctrine left open between man and God. Sufi leaders, unlike Sunni ulema, served as pastors and guides. Their faith was mystical and intuitive, their worship passionate and ecstatic. Unlike the Sunnis, they were willing to use music, song and dance to help in the search for God, to help the worshipper achieve mystical union with God. While the ulema became involved with the apparatus of government, the Sufis remained part of the people, and thus retained the influence and respect which the ulema often lost.

Despite its popular, mystical character, Sufism exercised a growing influence on Muslim – and to some extent even non-Muslim – intellectuals. Sufi teachings were brought into the Islamic mainstream by the genius of one of the greatest theologians and philosophers of medieval Islam, Muḥammad al-Ghazālī (1059–1111). His ideas, propounded in a series of major works, some in Persian, most in Arabic, had a profound impact on the subsequent development of the Muslim religious sciences. A native of Ṭūs, in the eastern Iranian province of Khurāsān, he pursued his studies in the colleges of Nīshāpūr and Baghdad, where in 1091 he was appointed a professor in the college (madrasa) established by Niẓām al-Mulk, the Persian chief minister of the Seljuk sultan, and known after him as the Niẓāmiyya. Four years after his appointment, Muḥammad al-Ghazālī suddenly resigned his post, renounced all public functions, and withdrew from the world to ponder in solitude on the basic problems of religion. His soul-searching lasted for ten years, during which he conducted profound studies in theology, philosophy, and law, and travelled extensively, to Mecca, Jerusalem, Damascus, and Alexandria. Visitors to the great mosque of Damascus are still shown the place where al-Ghazālī sat alone with his thoughts. In a remarkable autobiographical work, he explains how he sought but failed to find an answer to his needs in scholastic theology, in rational philosophy, even in Shī'ite doctrines; and how at last he found the truth in Sufism. In 1106 he returned to his birthplace and founded a Sufi lodge.

Al-Ghazālī was no radical. In a series of tracts, he defended mainstream Sunni positions against both the esoterism of the Shī'a and the rationalism of the philosophers. In the same time, he levelled sharp criticism against some of the intellectual trends of the time, denouncing their intellectualism, their scholasticism, their obsession with 'systems and classifications, words and arguments about words', and seeking to give greater importance to subjective religious experience and thus bring at least some Sufi teaching and practice into the Islamic mainstream. His success in this may be measured by the sobriquet given to him by later generations – Muḥyi'l-Dīn, the reviver of the faith.

Some Sufi doctrines and practices remained suspect, notably the unconcern shown by a few Sufi teachers with maintenance of the creed and the law, and even with the barriers between the true faith and others. Such relativism, as it would be called now, is exemplified in the poems of one of the greatest of Sufi poets, Jalāl al-Dīn Rūmī (1207–1273). Born in Balkh in Central Asia, he and his family settled in the Turkish city of Konya, where he spent the rest of his life. Jalāl al-Dīn wrote some of his poems in Turkish, and a few even in Greek, which was still widely used in Anatolia at that time. But his major work is in Persian. Some of his verses illustrate what the scholastics most disliked about Sufism:

If the image of our Beloved is in the heathen temple
Then it is flagrant error to walk round the Ka'ba.

If in the Kaʿba His fragrance is not present
Then it is but a synagogue.
And if in the synagogue we sense the fragrance of union with Him
Then that synagogue is our Kaʿba.[7]

Another poem is even more explicit:

What is to be done, Muslims? I, myself, do not know.
I am neither Christian nor Jew, neither Magian nor Muslim
I am not from east or west, not from land or sea
I am not from the quarries of nature nor from the spheres of heaven
I am not of earth, not of water, not of air, not of fire
. . .
I am not from India, not from China, not from Bulgar, not from Saqsin.
I am not from the kingdom of the two Iraqs. I am not from the land of Khurasan
. . .
My place is placeless, my trace is traceless
No body no soul, I am from the soul of souls. . . .[8]

In the face of such teachings, it was inevitable that the Sunni ulema, and particularly those more directly involved with the administration of justice, should regard the Sufis with suspicion. At various times they accused them of holding pantheistic doctrines and thus denying the transcendental unity of God, of worshipping saints and holy places, in violation of the Islamic ban on idolatry, of thaumaturgic practices, and suspect methods of inducing ecstasy. The common accusation was that while pursuing the impossible aim of union with God, they were negligent in the observance of God's law, and encouraged others in such negligence.

There were other, more political, fears of the dangerous pent-up energies that the dervish leaders could control or release at will. Under the Seljuk and Ottoman sultans, there were even dervish rebellions, which at times offered a serious threat to the established order. It was no doubt to counter such dangers that governments sometimes adopted a dervish order, giving its leaders a privileged place. Such, for example, was the position of the Mevlevi brotherhood, founded by Jalāl al-Dīn Rūmī and known in the West as the 'dancing dervishes'. Mevlevis were the most conformist among the orders. Their followers were mostly urban and middle or upper class; their doctrines were sophisticated and, as put forward, showed only minimal divergence from officially approved doctrines. By the end of the sixteenth century, they had won the favour of the Ottoman sultans, and in 1648 the head of the order officiated for the first time at the ceremony of the girding of the sword of Osman, which marked the accession of a new sultan. Some later heads of the order also participated in the same ceremony.

Dervish orders often differed considerably and even carried on feuds against one another. Sometimes they appeared as defenders of innovation; thus in the seventeenth century the dervishes in the Ottoman Empire defended the lawfulness of coffee and tobacco, which the Sunni ulema condemned along with music and dancing as a blameworthy innovation. In the late eighteenth and early nineteenth centuries, when Russian, British and French rule was extended in Transcaucasia, India and Algeria, it was dervish orders that led the popular resistance to imperialism, rather than the ulema, who in the course of the centuries had developed a practice and even a doctrine of submission to whatever authority was able to seize, hold, and wield effective power.

An old Turkish anecdote illustrated in caricature the complaints of the dervishes about Muslim society, and the suspicions of Muslim society about the dervishes. The story tells that a dervish went one day to the house of a rich man to ask for alms. The rich man, doubtful of the dervish's piety, asked him to enumerate the five pillars of Islam. The dervish responded by reciting the declaration of faith: 'I testify that there is no God but God; I testify that Muḥammad is the Apostle of God,' and was silent. 'And what about the rest?' asked the rich man; 'what about the other four?' To this the dervish replied, 'You rich men have abandoned pilgrimage and charity, and we poor dervishes have abandoned prayer and fasting, so what remains but the unity of God and the apostolate of Muḥammad?'

For Muslims, and therefore also for those others, principally Jews and Christians, who lived under Muslim government and as part of predominantly Islamic societies, religion was not only a system of belief, worship, and communal organization. It was the ultimate basis of identity, the primary focus of loyalty, the sole legitimate source of authority. There were ethnic nations in the Islamic world, such as the Arabs, the Persians, and the Turks. There were territorial states, such as the realms of the Egyptian and Ottoman sultans and of the Persian Shahs. But at no time in traditional Islamic states did these notions acquire the importance which they had in the political and cultural life of Europe, nor did territorial sovereigns or national leaders ever seek to limit, still less to extrude, the authority of religion and of its properly accredited exponents.

CHAPTER 13

CULTURE

The Middle East is an area of ancient civilization, among the most ancient in the world. But if we compare it with other civilizations of millennial antiquity, such as India and China, we shall at once be struck by two distinctive features of the Middle Eastern scene, in sharp contrast with the others.

One of these is diversity, the other discontinuity. Through the millennia of Chinese history there is an element of continuity, from the earliest to most recent times. Though many changes have occurred, modern China and ancient China use recognizable variants of the same language, written in variants of the same script, following variants of the same religion and philosophy. There is a continuity of self-awareness from the most ancient records of Chinese civilization to the present-day People's Republic, which is shared, despite many local differences, by the whole area of Chinese civilization. The same, to a lesser extent, is true of India. Though Indian civilization is neither as exclusive nor as homogeneous as that of China, it remains a cohesive and unifying force. The Hindu religion, the Nagari script, the Sanskrit classics and scriptures, have always been a powerful, indeed a dominant element in Indian civilization and in India's awareness of itself as a continuing entity from antiquity to the present day.

In the ancient Middle East there was no such unity; from the ancient to the modern there is no such continuity. Even in antiquity, the civilizations of the Middle East were highly diverse, with no common binding elements like the Chinese or Nagari script, Confucian philosophy, or Hindu beliefs. Middle Eastern civilization began in a number of different places and evolved along different lines. And although these ultimately moved towards one another, they retained significant differences of culture, belief, and way of life.

But more important than these earlier differences is the dramatic discontinuity in the cultural history of the region. While India and China still cherish and study the records of their ancient past in an unbroken tradition of learning, the ancient Middle East was lost, forgotten, and literally buried. Its languages were dead, its writings locked in scripts that no one could read. Its gods and their worship belong to a remote antiquity known only to a small number of specialists and scholars. The Middle East lacks even a collective name, such as India or China. That indeed is why in our century it has come to be known, first in the Western world, then in other parts of the world, and finally among the peoples of the region itself, by shapeless, formless, colourless, and entirely relative designations, such as 'Middle East' and 'Near East' – designations that obviously lack the dignity, the stature, the evocative power of names like India and China.

The difference once stated, its causes are obvious. The submergence of the ancient Middle Eastern cultures and traditions was the result of a series of cataclysmic changes, the most important of which were the successive processes of Hellenization, Romanization, Christianization, and Islamization, which between them wiped out the greater part of the written culture of the ancient Middle East. All four processes have left their traces to the present day; the fourth, the Islamization of the Middle East, has shaped the region since the seventh century. The most ancient languages – Egyptian, Assyrian, Babylonian, Hittite, old Persian, and the rest – were abandoned and remained unknown until they were exhumed, deciphered, interpreted, and restored by orientalist scholars to history, or rather to historiography, and ultimately to the peoples who live in the region. For a long time the effort was exclusively the work of non-Middle Easterners, and it remains predominantly so. The perceived link with pre-Islamic antiquity, in the corporate self-consciousness of the Middle Eastern peoples, is still tenuous; of late it has indeed been actively challenged by an Islamic revival.

Another comparison, this time with Europe, may be instructive. The barbarian peoples who overran the western Roman Empire made great efforts to preserve at least the forms and structure of the Roman state. They adopted its religion, Christianity, tried to use its language, Latin, and made great efforts to fit their own barbarian rule into the forms of Roman imperial government and law, seeking through these to confer some legitimacy upon themselves. The Muslim Arabs who conquered a large part of the Christian Roman Empire in the Middle East and North Africa in the seventh and eighth centuries, did no such thing. On the contrary, they brought their own religion, Islam, their own language, Arabic, and their own scripture, the Qur'ān, and they established their own imperial state. Though this state, inevitably, was

affected by influences from its non-Islamic predecessors and neighbours, the advent of Islamic domination nevertheless clearly marked
the beginning of a new society and more particularly of a new polity,
in which Islam was not only the basis of identity, but also the source
of legitimacy and authority. In this newly established Islamic world,
the Arabic language assumed the role played by Greek in the Hellenistic
world, Latin in Europe, Sanskrit and Chinese in the civilizations of
south and east Asia. For some time, Arabic was virtually the sole
language of government, law, and administration, as well as of commerce and culture and everyday life. And even when, in time, other
literary languages, notably Persian and Turkish, appeared or reappeared
in the Islamic world, they were written in the Arabic script and had
adopted an Arabic vocabulary as extensive and as important as the
Latin and Greek elements in the languages of the West.

Surely, in the Islamic lands as in Christendom, much of the old
order − of the pre-Arab and pre-Islamic past − survived. But in the
Islamic lands, unlike Christendom, such survivals were not avowed
and conferred no legitimacy. Lexical remnants of a pre-Islamic, pre-
Arab past may be traced in Islamic Arabic usage. Not surprisingly,
these occur principally in the various vernaculars, which preserve
elements of the spoken languages that they replaced. But some occur
also in standard classical Arabic, and a few have been identified even
in the Qur'ān. Identifiable survivals from the more ancient languages
of the region are few and questionable, and most of the survivals date
from the more recent pre-Islamic past. Theological terms from Syriac
and Hebrew, scientific and philosophical terms from Greek, legal and
administrative terms from Latin, and a wide range of social and cultural
terms from Middle Persian, provide the bulk of these lexical survivals.

While such lexical survivals are of relatively minor importance in
the development of classical Arabic and of the other Islamic languages
which were shaped by Arabic usage, they can provide useful evidence
of the process of cultural adapatation. Some are readily recognizable,
such as *kīmiyā* (chemistry), and *falsafa* (philosophy). Some are lightly
disguised, such as *shurṭa* (the police force), from the auxiliary cohort
entrusted with police duties in Roman times, and possibly also *'askar*
(army), from the Latin *exercitus*. A notable example is the 'straight
path', *al-Ṣirāṭ al-Mustaqīm*, which Muslims are enjoined in the very
first chapter of the Qur'ān to follow. *Ṣirāṭ* is of course none other than
the Roman road, or *strata*, and is thus akin to the English word street.
Some borrowings are indirect. Thus *kharāj*, the Islamic legal term for

the land tax, appears in pre-Islamic Aramaic as *keraga*, and derives from the Greek *khorēgia*, a levy which citizens paid to defray the cost of the public choruses on solemn official occasions.

Some of these borrowings were not loan words but loan translations. A modern example is the use of the classical Arabic word *kahrabā'*, itself of Persian origin, in the sense of electricity. The original meaning of *kahrabā'* is amber, and its use in this sense clearly reflects the Western semantic development of the Greek word for amber, *ēlektron*. A more classical example is the epithet applied to Mecca and the Qur'ān, *Umm al-Qurā*, 'the mother of towns', which may well be a calque after the Greek '*mētropolis*'.

By the end of the Middle Ages, the religious and linguistic map of the Middle East and North Africa was fixed in what has remained, with certain exceptions, its modern form. Three languages predominated – Arabic, Persian, and Turkish – each of them used in several forms and in several countries. Arabic, with a common, standard written form and a wide variety of spoken dialects, had become the dominant language not only in the Arabian peninsula, where it was first used, but also in the Fertile Crescent, comprising the present-day states of Iraq, Syria, Lebanon, Jordan, and Israel, and in all the countries of the North African littoral, from Egypt to Morocco, with some extensions southward into sub-Saharan Africa.

Persian – *zabān-i Fārsī*, the language of the province of Fārs, or Pārs, from which the Greek and hence the Western names of the country are derived – was spoken and written in Iran (the ancient name of the country), and in a zone extending eastwards into Central Asia, in regions now included in Afghanistan and in the republic of Tajikistan. Tajik and also Dari, one of the two official languages of Afghanistan (the other is Pashto, also of the Iranic family), are variants of Persian.

The Turkish or Turkic languages, a closely related group of which Ottoman Turkish is the westernmost representative, are spoken in a vast region extending from the northern and southern shores of the Black Sea, across Asia, to the Pacific.

Apart from these three major languages, a number of other languages remained in local use. Some, like Aramaic and Coptic, survivals of more ancient cultures, were used to a diminishing extent by non-Muslims, mostly Christian minorities; others, like Berber and Kurdish, are still widely used by great numbers, but without a standard written form, and therefore without the stability and continuity that a written tradition can provide. Hebrew, which survived as a language of religion and culture among the Jewish minorities, has in modern times reappeared as a spoken and eventually a national language.

In the classical perception, only literature could be ranked among the civilized arts, whose practitioners were worthy of attention and respect. Musicians – both performers and composers – were slaves or other social inferiors, and music was important only as a vehicle, as an accompaniment for poetry. Few musicians are known to us by name, and these because of some mention in a literary context. The visual arts – especially at times and in places where the disapproval of figurative representation prevailed – were the work of craftsmen and artisans. In the earliest period these were mostly non-Muslims, drawn from the native population of the conquered countries. Later, with the progress of Islamization, there were more and more Muslim artists and architects, but in most of the Middle Ages little is known about them. Not until centuries later, in Ottoman Turkey and Safavid Iran, did painters acquire a respected status in court societies. Many of them are known by name with some biographical detail, and with identifiable works. Some of them even formed schools and trained disciples. Architects – by Ottoman times mostly military officers – were in a special category. In addition to their artistic skills, they were organizers and administrators, exercising authority in enterprises with significant payrolls and providing for some of the basic needs of government, religion, and the city: palaces and fortresses for the first; mosques, convents, and colleges for the second; bridges and bathhouses, markets and inns, and dwellings of various kinds for the third. The great architects are not only known by name; they also received the respectful attention of historians and even biographers.

There was little by way of furniture in these domestic interiors, whether palatial or private. Tables and chairs, common in the ancient Middle East, were no longer used in the Middle Ages. Instead, people used wool and leather, readily available from nomads, and interior furniture consisted basically of carpets and mattresses, hassocks and cushions. To complete the interior arrangement they created and used a wide range of metal, glass, and earthenware objects – trays, lamps, bowls, dishes, and a variety of utensils. Engraved and incised metalwork and painted ceramic and glass form an important part of the industrial arts of medieval Islam. They have their place in an interior dominated by the various creations of the textile arts, often with the addition of elaborately worked wooden screens and shutters – the woodcarvers treating their wood with the respect and care due to a rare and precious material.

The earliest known painting of the period of Arab domination also serves a decorative purpose. The frescos that adorn some of the surviving Umayyad palaces illustrate vividly a certain continuity of culture, and in many ways resemble – in their technique, their decorative themes, their iconographic conventions – the still vigorous artistic traditions of Byzantium and pre-Islamic Persia. But in this as in so much else, the older traditions were gradually assimilated and recreated into something new – into an art which, like the civilization that it expressed, is enriched but not dominated by earlier traditions and evolved to meet the needs of Arab taste and Islamic values in a political society created and ruled by Arabs and dedicated to the faith of Islam.

The early frescos, with their nude female figures, can hardly be called Islamic, but already they begin to adapt older themes to newer purposes, for example in the portrayal of a Muslim caliph in the posture used by Byzantine artists to portray the Christian *kosmokratōr*. Before long these nude figures, and indeed any human figures, vanished from Muslim murals and interior decoration, and were replaced by decorative and especially calligraphic designs. Mural paintings do not reappear until centuries later, in some of the palaces and audience chambers of Safavid Persia, and still later of Ottoman Turkey. The next, and in many ways the most important, phase in the development of Islamic painting is in the form of book illustration, an art which flourished among the Arabs, and more especially among the Persians and Turks. Whatever compunction there may have been against the representation of the human face and figure seems to have been overcome, and Muslim painting consists very largely of such portrayals. From late medieval times onwards we find separate pictures, drawings and paintings, mostly on paper but not part of the books. These too are found principally in Turkey and Iran, and in countries under Turkish or Persian rule or influence. Sculpture continued to be effectively forbidden, and even two-dimensional portraiture from living originals was suspect, though not unknown.

Several of the Ottoman sultans were painted by Turkish artists; a few, and notably Mehmed the Conqueror, by European painters. A famous portrait of Mehmed the Conqueror by Bellini hangs in the National Gallery in London. It was sold, along with other paintings, after Sultan Mehmed's death by his pious son and successor Sultan

Bayezid. Royal portraiture, though sometimes patronized in private by late Ottoman and other rulers, remained officially forbidden. With a very few, wholly atypical, exceptions, Muslim sovereigns did not put their faces on coinage nor later on their postage stamps. Yirmisekiz Çelebi Mehmed Efendi, who went to Paris as Ottoman ambassador in 1721, notes in his report, 'The custom of these people is that the king gives ambassadors his own portrait adorned with diamonds. But I explained that pictures are not permitted among Muslims; I was therefore given instead a diamond-studded belt.' Mehmed Efendi goes on to describe his gifts in loving detail. He reports in two lines on the picture gallery which he was shown by the king himself. Pictures hanging on walls were not part of his culture. On the other hand, he speaks eloquently of tapestry, an art form to which he was better attuned. He was enormously impressed by the degree of realistic representation that even a European tapestry could achieve:[1]

> One appears laughing, to show his joy; another sad, to show his sadness. One is shown trembling with fear, another weeping, another stricken by some disease. Thus, at first glance, the condition of each person is known. The beauty of these works is beyond description and beyond imagination.

Since Muslim worship, with the limited exception of some dervish orders, makes no use of music, musicians in the Islamic lands lacked the immense advantage enjoyed by Christian musicians through the patronage of the Church and of its high dignitaries. The patronage of the court and of the great houses, though no doubt useful, was intermittent and episodic, and dangerously subject to the whims of the mighty. Muslim musicians devised no standard system of notation, and their compositions are therefore known only by the fallible and variable medium of memory. There is no preserved corpus of classical Islamic music comparable with that of the European musical tradition. All that remains is a quite extensive theoretical literature on music, some descriptions and portrayals of musicians and musical occasions by writers and artists, a number of old instruments in various stages of preservation, and of course the living memory of long-past performances.

According to traditional accounts, the history of classical Arabic poetry begins in the sixth century CE, when the tribes of the Arabian peninsula created a common formal, literary language and perfected both the pattern and the major variations of the *qaṣīda*, the desert encampment ode which was for long the dominant medium of Arabic poetry.

Many scholars, both Arab and Western, have in modern times cast doubt on the authenticity of much of the extant corpus of ancient Arabian poetry. According to these, the surviving texts contain at most a substratum of authentic material, and in their present form are the work of either poets or philologists – the criterion of choice is presumably poetic quality – of what has been variously described as a neoclassical or as a romantic revival in the eighth century CE. The same criticism has been brought against the poetry attributed to the early Islamic period, and it is not until the time of the Umayyad caliphs in Syria that we have a body of contemporary poetry of unquestioned authenticity.

Much of it consists of *qaṣīdas* produced by the court poets and poet-caliphs in Syria. According to some, the Umayyad *qaṣīda* is a continuation of the pre-Islamic *qaṣīda*, according to others the model which later neoclassicists projected back into an unknown past. Clearly the surviving *qaṣīdas* of the Umayyad period are composed in a tradition that was already old, to a formula that was already stereotyped. The earliest *qaṣīda* was originally a boast, in which the poet, as spokesman of his tribe, vaunted the virtues, prowess and achievements of his tribe, his beasts, and himself. It was composed, by tradition, for public recitation at the poetic contests held during the festivals that preceded the break-up of camp at the time of the seasonal migration of the nomads. The *qaṣīda* begins with an erotic prelude in which the poet, contemplating the ruins of an abandoned camping ground, recalls the happy times when his tribe and that of his beloved occupied adjoining sites there. After this prelude the poet goes on to the later phases of the vaunt proper. In the court *qaṣīda* of the Umayyad century and after, the boast has become a panegyric, and the poet praises his sovereign or patron instead of his tribe.

The prelude reveals a small number of constantly recurring themes. The poet arrives at the abandoned camping ground and enjoys the dubious pleasures of recollection. He apostrophizes the site to all his companions, and weeps for the happy days that are no more. Sometimes his companions try to console him, and chide him for his unavailing sorrows. Often the poet laments the long, dreary night of separation and reproaches the laggard dawn. The phantom of his beloved may visit him in a dream, and even speak to him, leaving him to a still more bitter awakening. Usually the prelude contains the poet's account of his own nocturnal visit to his beloved, when their tribes were camped side by side. This is in part a self-torturing recollection, in part a simple boast. Since his beloved is of another tribe, perhaps a hostile one, he goes to see her at risk of his life, creeping amid the tents of her people to her dwelling-place or to a rendezvous behind a sand dune. Both are constantly aware of the dangers that threaten them, from the guardian – husband, father, or brother – who seeks to protect the lady's honour, and from the slanderer (*wāshī*), who spreads malicious rumours and seeks to sow discord between the lovers. Later these two opponents are joined by a third, the censor (*raqīb*), who also seems to be actuated by ill will against the lovers, but who is ostensibly the guardian of public morals.

The theme of separation is connected with the breaking of camp. The spring grazing season ends, and the tribes move on. The crier bids the tribesmen prepare, the camels are loaded, the tents are struck, and the tribes depart in different directions, leaving the disconsolate lover with nothing but memories. The approach of the dreaded day is foreshadowed by omens and premonitions, especially by the flight of the raven, the bird of parting, whose harsh voice announces the coming departure of the beloved.

Love poetry may best serve to exemplify classical Islamic poetry. Because of the universal human theme with which it deals, it is the easiest of access for the outsider from another culture. Because of the changing social context in which lovers meet and part, it serves to reflect the changing scene in social as well as cultural history.

In addition to the traditional *qaṣīda*, the Umayyad period saw the emergence of a new kind of love poetry – the erotic poetry of the Ḥijāz. The vast conquests of the Arabs had brought immense wealth to their Arabian homeland, and in the towns of the Hijaz, especially in Medina, a new kind of society arose – wealthy, cultivated, pleasure-loving and unrestrained. To the consternation of the pious, the holy city became the pleasure ground of a glittering aristocracy, with great households where slave girls, singers, and dancers vied with free Arab ladies for the attentions of the dissolute heirs of the warriors of the faith.

Of the mass of erotic poetry composed in the Ḥijāz, only a small part has survived, and its study presents special difficulties. Only a few of the poets known by name have left complete *dīwāns* – that is, collections of verse. The majority are known only from fragments and quotations preserved in anthologies and literary histories, many of them of much later date. The romantic haze cast by later tradition around the personalities and adventures of the time makes the authentication of these fragments a special problem. Of many it is impossible even to say whether they are complete poems in themselves, or excerpts from longer poems, and it is not unlikely that some of them are fragments of *qasīdas* the remainder of which has perished. The main themes of these poems are much the same as those of the prelude in the formal *qasīda*, but there are changes. The desert setting is usually omitted, and the adventure takes place with a lady of another household in the town. As in the *qasīda*, the poet is discreet when speaking of a free Arab lady. Usually he conceals her name, and sometimes even praises her virtue. With slaves and tavern girls, the poet is more outspoken.

Islamic law makes generous provision for male sexual needs, and is therefore strong in its condemnation of illicit love. This in time restricted the freer life of the pre-Islamic tribesmen, and modified some of the exuberances of their love poetry. The caliph 'Umar is even said to have forbidden erotic verse-making. And so we find an increased respect for chastity among poets, and a consequent spread of the pangs of unrequited love. Alongside the boastful and insensitive prowler, we find the chaste and submissive adorer from afar, professing a more ethereal passion to which scholars of the following century gave the name 'Udhrī, pertaining to the tribe of 'Udhra, whose sons were said to die of undemanding and unrequited love. Even the 'Udhrī poet adheres to the tradition, paying secret nocturnal visits to the tent of his beloved, but he asks no more than a smile, a handclasp, or a few words of conversation, and he mingles praise and blame for the inclement virtue of his adored one. How far the so-called 'Platonic' love of the 'Udhris corresponds to reality is another matter. A French scholar, Regis Blachère, sees little difference between outspoken libertines like the classical *qasīda* composers and the 'Udhrīs. An Arab scholar, Kinānī, is probably right in describing the 'Udhrī theme as a compromise between sensual love and the new religious morality.

The replacement of the Umayyads by the 'Abbasid caliphs and the transfer of the capital from Syria to Iraq began a new era in Arabic poetry, as in Islamic history. In place of the tribal aristocracy of Arab conquerors, a new cosmopolitan ruling elite of officials and landowners came to dominate the empire. In place of a super-chief of the tribes, an oriental sovereign of a more ancient pattern ruled in the increasingly hierarchic court of Baghdad. Though an Arab dynasty ruled, and

Arabic remained for a while the sole language of government, society and culture, the tastes and traditions of Arabia no longer held undisputed sway. In a great city and a great court, the Arab lady lost her former rank and freedom, and disappeared into the recesses of the harem. Guards and eunuchs made the clandestine visit a perilous if not impossible undertaking. Slave girls and hetairae made it a work of supererogation. For a while, the old literary fashions lingered on, and city poets who had never seen Arabia continued to lament over imaginary camping grounds and to praise the beauties of the fictitious heroines of their literary amours. Some tried to adapt the old themes to real situations. A chronicler tells of a poet in Baghdad who wrote an ode to a lady of the city, begging her in well-worn phrases to send her image in a dream to comfort him in his lonely nights of yearning. The lady replied that if he would send her three gold dinars, she would come and comfort him in person.

But new winds were blowing in Arabic poetry. Among the numberless converts to Islam were many Persians who, though adopting the faith and language of the conquerors, were openly contemptuous of their customs and traditions. Persian and other poets introduced new themes and fashions into Arabic poetry, including love poetry. The person addressed is usually a slave girl, often one of the cultivated hetairae who provided the feminine element in city society. Clandestinity was hardly necessary, and it is in another context that we find the secret meeting and parting. If the Muslim ban on adultery had ceased to be a living issue, that on drinking remained a thorn in the side of the reveller, and it is with the bottle, rather than with the lady, that the poet makes his secret assignation and his secret farewell at dawn.

Despite the Islamic ban on alcohol, wine figures very prominently in Arabic poetry and still more in Persian and Turkish poetic traditions that developed within Islam. Making, selling, and drinking wine were all forbidden to Muslims, but were permitted to the tolerated non-Muslim subjects of the Muslim state. Muslims in need of a drink were therefore obliged to go to the infidels in order to get it. The Christian convent in Arabic poetry, the Zoroastrian lodge in Persian poetry, acquire almost the connotation of tavern. The themes of love and wine are often combined, and sometimes, especially in Persian and Turkish poetry, imbued with a religious significance. Bacchic and erotic imagery is commonly used by Sufi poets to symbolize the mystic union of the devotee with God. The use of erotic means to religious ends is by no means unprecedented, and is familiar to the Judeo–Christian tradition from the Song of Songs in the Hebrew Bible.

Another genre, rich in cultural information, is the poetry – sometimes, especially among the Persians and Turks, embellished by the iconography – of the hunt. Long after hunting ceased to be a significant source of food supply, it retained an important social, cultural, and even military function. Under Islamic rule, the games and athletic contests of the Hellenistic world had for the most part disappeared. Racing with horse and camel, fighting by cocks, camels, and wrestlers, provided some public entertainment, while such martial arts as archery and equitation maintained the professional skills of the military. But until the massive modern development of sports and pastimes the hunt was by far the most popular means of combining exercise, recreation and useful training. The great royal hunts – vast in scale, duration, and numbers – had a special value; they were the closest pre-modern approach to the war-games and military exercises that prepare modern armies for battle, and offered practice in organization and administration, equipment and supply, movement, command and control and, in a manner of speaking, combat.

All this is reflected in an extensive literature. Poets speak eloquently and in sometimes intricate detail of their mounts (horse, camel, sometimes even elephant), their weapons (sword, bow, spear), their adjuncts (hawk, hound, leopard) and their prey. They celebrate the comradeship, the rivalries, and sometimes the romance of the hunters, the thrill of the chase, the fierce joy of the kill, and of course the festivities that follow.

Poetry also served an important social, public, and even political function. Panegyric and satire were the stock in trade of many poets, the former especially their best means of livelihood. In the days before journalism and publicity, propaganda and public relations, poets could fulfil all these functions. This was not a new role for the poet. The Roman emperor Augustus had had court poets in Rome, some of whose compositions represent public-relations work for the Roman Empire in general, and the Roman emperor in particular, and so too no doubt did other ancient rulers. The art of the eulogist reached its peak in the Islamic Middle Ages, when poets praised their rulers in easily memorized and widely repeated verses – one might even say jingles – and thus improved their image throughout the land.

Poetic propaganda could be negative as well as positive. It is surely significant that the Arabic term for satire, *hijā'*, is akin to the biblical Hebrew word *hegeh*, which means witchcraft, or casting a spell. Satire is not just insult and abuse; it is insult and abuse to practical purposes. Stories about the hostile propaganda of tribal satirists date back to very early, probably to pre-Islamic times. According to the traditional biography, the Prophet himself was keenly aware of both the value and the dangers of poetic propaganda. Despite a general disapproval of poetry – one of the greatest of ancient Arabian poets, Imr al-Qays, is described as 'their leader on the road to Hell' – the Prophet himself employed a panegyrist, and took steps to deal with those who composed and disseminated poetry attacking or lampooning him. In one case, not only was the composer of a satire executed, but a singing girl who had sung and recited the poem was also put to death.

Already in the first century of the Islamic era, the Umayyad caliphs employed court poets, and after them virtually all Muslim rulers did so. Nor was this practice limited to rulers. There were many lesser figures who employed poets for publicity and public relations. In this way, composing poetry became a recognized profession, and the chronicles and literary histories provide quite detailed information about the manner and level of remuneration. This obviously depended, in large measure, on the standing of the patron and the skill of the poet. As in other similar professions, the same material could be re-utilized. A poem composed in praise of one ruler could, after a change of employer, be adjusted and re-sold to another. Some rulers were famous for their patronage of poets, i.e. for their extensive propaganda operations. The Hamdanid prince Sayf al-Dawla, who flourished in north Syria in the tenth century, had a considerable staff of poets, who in a sense are still working for him at the present day, and who have misled many unwary historians. The Fatimid caliphs, as one might expect, had ideological poets, presenting a Fatimid world view and a Fatimid case against their 'Abbasid rivals. Sometimes chroniclers give us lists of official poets. An Egyptian encyclopaedist of the later Middle Ages tells us that the Fatimids kept a staff of poets attached to the chancery, and that these were divided into two groups – Sunni poets, who composed respectable Sunni praise, and Ismāʿīlī poets, who produced the more extreme adulation appropriate to an Ismāʿīlī imam.

Poetic propaganda was also used by rebels and sectarians of various kinds, by political and other factions, and sometimes even for personal ends. Poetry could even serve an economic purpose, as is shown by two examples, both from the ninth-century Arabic book of songs – the *Kitab al-Aghānī*. According to one story, a governor of Iraq in the eighth century forcibly expropriated a piece of land which he required for the extension of the public irrigation system. The famous poet Farazdaq, acting on behalf of the expropriated landowner, composed a poem attacking the governor and accusing him of oppression. The result is not recorded, nor is the amount of the fee paid. A second story from the same source bears repeating in its entirety:[2]

> A merchant from Kūfa came to Medina with veils. He sold all but the black ones, which were left on his hands. He was a friend of al-Dārimī and complained to him about this. At that time al-Dārimī had become an ascetic and had given up music and poetry. He said to the merchant, 'Don't worry. I shall get rid of them for you; you will sell the whole lot.' Then he composed these verses:
>> Go ask the one in the black veil
>>> What have you done to a devout monk?
>> He had already girded up his garments for prayer
>>> Until you appeared to him by the door of the mosque.
>
> He set it to music, and Sinān the scribe also set it to music, and it became popular. People said, 'Al-Dārimī is at it again and has given up his ascetisicm', and there was not a lady of refinement in Medina who did not buy a black veil, and the Iraqi merchant sold all he had. When al-Dārimī heard this, he returned to his asceticism and again spent his time in the mosque.

This may well be the earliest known occurrence of the singing commercial.

Narrative poetry was not widely practised by the Arabs in medieval times. Apart from some long popular romances in mixed prose and verse, which are not regarded as formal literature, and from a few short battle pieces, there is little to compare with either the epics or the ballads of classical antiquity and of medieval Europe. The rebirth of the epic in the Islamic Middle East occurred in Persia, where surviving fragments of pre-Islamic Persian poetry attest the existence of an ancient Persian epic tradition. The revival of this tradition was part of the reawakening of Persian national culture, and the emergence of a new Muslim Persian language. The *Shāhnāma*, a long narrative poem telling of the adventures of the gods and heroes of ancient Iran, by the tenth-century poet Firdawsī, has a place in Perso–Turkish culture comparable with that of the *Iliad*, the *Odyssey*, and the *Aeneid* in the West. Like them it found many imitators, and a great number of other epics of varying quality were composed in Persian and in Turkish. Notable among the latter are the heroic poems of the Turkish peoples of Central Asia. Another narrative genre much practised among the Persians and the Turks is the versified romance, often at book length, dealing with the adventures (usually unhappy) of a pair of lovers. These epics and romances provided the occasion for a large part of the Muslim art of book illustration.

A distinctively Arab literary genre is the *maqāma*, an Arabic word with the approximate meaning of a session or occasion. As a literary form, it denoted a fairly short piece written in a medium called *saj‘*, rhymed and often rhythmic prose with the occasional insertion of verses. The *maqāma* is usually one of a collection of *maqāmāt* featuring two imaginary persons, the narrator and the hero. They combine prose and poetry, travelogue and dialogue, sermon and argument, and include a great deal of social comment, often humorously expressed. Some of the collections of *maqāmāt* must be counted among the masterpieces of Arabic literature. *Maqāmāt* were imitated in Persian and Hebrew, but the form remained distinctively and characteristically Arab.

Persian and Turkish poetry are entirely Muslim. Arabic poetry is predominantly but not exclusively Muslim, with a significant Christian component, especially in the very early and very recent periods. There are some Jewish poets in Arabic, but very few. Jewish poets, composing mainly lyrical and religious poetry, used Hebrew, no longer a vernacular but still a language of religion, scholarship and literature, including even secular poetry. Hebrew poetry in the Islamic lands conforms closely to Arabic patterns in prosody, structures, themes, and literary conventions.

The *maqāma* was not the only form of literature for entertainment in classical Arabic. The art of the essay was cultivated to a very high level of sophistication. Somewhat lighter entertainment was provided in the form of fiction – apologue rather than novel – ranging from the anecdote to the book-length story. Many of these sketches and stories are tales of fantasy and wonder, but some present a remarkably vivid portrayal of life under the caliphs in different regions and at different social levels.

Humour is an important element in this literature. The medieval

Arab authors delighted in the pungent anecdote and the witty riposte. They also seem to have had a special liking for parody, using it to poke gentle fun at every genre of Arabic writing, including even the most sacred. Two examples may suffice. Civil servants under the caliphs, as under other regimes in other places, were known for the use of a ponderous and inflated style full of repetition. An eleventh-century collection of 'droll blunders' includes a story about a prince of Aleppo, whose governor in Antioch had a stupid secretary. Two Muslim galleys were lost at sea with all hands, and the secretary reported this, on behalf of his master, to the prince. He wrote: 'In the name of Allah the Merciful and the Compassionate. Be it known to the Prince – God strengthen him – that two galleys, I mean two ships, foundered, that is sank, because of the turbulence of the seas, that is, the force of the waves, and all within them expired, that is, perished.' The prince of Aleppo replied to his lieutenant: 'Your letter has come, that is, arrived, and we understood it, that is to say, we read it. Chastise your clerk, that is, hit him, and replace him, that is, get rid of him, since he is dim-witted, that is, stupid. Farewell, that is to say, the letter is finished.'[3]

According to another story, a certain Ash'ab, a well known narrator of comic tales in the first century of the Hijra, was once reproached for indulging in such frivolities. 'Why', he was asked, 'do you not tell *ḥadīths*, traditions of the Prophet, as a good Muslim should?' 'I also know *ḥadīths*,' replied Ash'ab. 'Then tell me one,' said his interlocutor. Ash'ab began, in traditional manner, with the chain of narrators on whose authority the tradition is told. 'I was told by Nafi', who heard it from Ibn 'Umar, that the Apostle of God said, "There are two qualities such that a man who has them both is one of God's chosen friends."' The interlocutor observed that this was indeed a good tradition, and he asked what the two qualities were. To this Ash'ab replied: 'Nafi' forgot one, and I have forgotten the other.'[4]

Entertainment literature, like other classical Arabic genre, also passed to Persian and Turkish, where they assumed somewhat different forms. The tale and the apologue flourished greatly, but the essay and the conversation-piece changed, becoming less playful and entertaining, more didactic and moralistic. These were the expressions of a sterner and more earnest society.

The theatre, perhaps because of its association with pagan rites in antiquity, disappeared from the Middle East in the Islamic Middle Ages, and did not reappear until many centuries later. Some elements of dramatic performance were familiar and widespread – the arts of the storyteller with theatrical effects, of the mime, the clown, and the dance. There are indications that there may even have been short comic episodes with texts improvised by the actors. These were in the main popular entertainments for the common people, though occasionally court patronage encouraged a somewhat more refined version. Sometimes this refinement gave way to a cruder purpose. The Byzantine princess Anna Comnena, in the mid-twelfth century, describes how her father Alexios Comnenos, who suffered from gout, was ridiculed by actors at the Seljuk court:[5]

> The barbarians, gifted improvisers, burlesqued his pains. The gout became a subject for comedy. They acted the parts of doctor and attendants, introduced the 'emperor' himself and putting him on a bed made fun of him. At these childish exhibitions they roared with laughter.

Another Byzantine emperor, Manuel II Palaeologos, describing a visit to the court of the Ottoman sultan Bayezid at the beginning of the fifteenth century, speaks of companies of musicians, singers, dancers and actors.

The notion of a play – of a connected performance with a narrative thread and a more or less prepared text – is first attested in the fourteenth century, notably in Egypt and Turkey. The characters were played by puppets or by shadows projected on a screen. The words were spoken by a puppet master. The content was usually comic, sometimes farcical, but often contained an element of sharp social and even political comment. The texts of a number of these plays have survived, and some of their authors are known by name.

Puppets were known from antiquity. The shadow-play, far more popular in the central Islamic lands, appears to have been introduced from east Asia, possibly in the time of the Turks or Mongols, who opened new lines of communication between eastern and western Asia.

The introduction of the theatre in the strict sense, with human actors playing roles in a developing story with a prepared text, dates from the Ottoman period and was almost certainly the work of Jewish refugees from Europe, chiefly from Spain, who came in the late fifteenth and sixteenth centuries. We hear of Jewish and later also Christian – Armenian and Greek – troupes performing, presumably in Turkish, at court and other celebrations.

All this, however, was very limited in scope and effect, and the real introduction of the theatre as an art form dates only from the period of European influence in the nineteenth century.

Another kind of dramatic performance of far greater impact is the celebrated *ta'ziya*, the Shī'ite passion play commemorating the martyrdom of Ḥusayn and his family at Karbalā', and performed every year on the anniversary of that event, the tenth day of the month of Muḥarram. Despite its centrality in modern Shī'a religious ceremonies, the *ta'ziya* is comparatively modern, the earliest descriptions of these performances dating from the late eighteenth century.

The greater part of classical prose literature was composed not to amuse but to inform and instruct. A major part of this literature was intended to preserve and transmit knowledge concerning the past – history, biography, and literary history. Islam as a religion and a civilization has been imbued almost from the beginning with a strong sense of history. God himself, says a fifteenth-century Egyptian scholar in a defence of 'history', tells stories about the people of the past, and indeed the Qur'ān itself is full of lessons from history. 'We tell you stories of the apostles, which will strengthen your heart, and thus bring you the Truth, an exhortation and a memorial for the believers' (Qur'ān 11:120). The earliest traditions portrayed a group of people profoundly conscious of the Prophet's place in the historic sequence of revelations and of the predicament of man in the vast design from creation to judgement. The mission of Muḥammad was an event in history; its purpose and meaning are preserved and transmitted through memory and record. The doctrine of *ijmā'*, consensus, according to which the divine guidance was transferred after the death of the Prophet to the Muslim community as a whole, gave a continuing significance to the acts and experiences of that community.

The authority and prestige of the companions and immediate successors of the Prophet gave a strong and recurring incentive to the descendants of these companions and successors in the course of the later struggles to ascertain, sometimes to adjust, and on occasion to rediscover, the truth concerning the personalities and events of the advent of Islam and the rise of the caliphate.

Muslim rulers since early times have been conscious of their place in history, and concerned about the record of their actions left for later times. They have been interested in the deeds of their predecessors, and anxious to record their own for their successors. Historiography begins with the biographies of the Prophet and his companions, and with the heroic sagas of the Arabian tribes. Thereafter, most fortunately for the historian, almost every dynasty that ruled among Muslims, even in the most primitive regions, left annals or chronicles of some kind. In many countries historical writing, in effect, begins with the coming of Islam. For Sunni Muslims – the Shī'a take a different view – God's community was the embodiment of God's design for mankind, and its history, providentially guided, revealed the working out of God's purpose. An accurate knowledge of history was therefore supremely important, since it could provide authoritative guidance in both the profoundest problems of religion and the most practical matters of law.

History was important – that is to say, Muslim history. The history of non-Muslim states and communities, which did not accept God's final revelation nor obey God's law, offered no such guidance and possessed no such value. Muslim historians therefore paid little attention to non-Muslim history, whether of their neighbours in Christian Europe or elsewhere, or of their own Christian, Zoroastrian, and other non-Muslim ancestors. What mattered in ancient history was preserved in the Qur'ān and the tradition. The rest was forgotten and, often literally, buried.

Historiography in the Islamic Middle East is of extraordinary range, richness, and variety, including local, regional, imperial and universal history, old and current history, biography and – very rarely – autobiography, histories of poets and scholars, of soldiers and statesmen, of ministers and secretaries, of judges, theologians and mystics. There are also many different types of historical writing. The tradition of heroic narrative has its roots in pre-Islamic Arabia, in the tales told of the wars and raids of the pagan Arabs. It achieved a new form in accounts of the campaigns of the Prophet against the pagans and of the vast conquests achieved by the early Muslims. Later this type of historiography tends to degenerate into panegyric or propaganda, but still sometimes reaches almost epic form, as for example in the Arabic biography of Saladin, and in the Turkish account of the wars and conquests of Süleyman the Magnificent.

Another kind of historiography is legal, even in a sense theological. Its purpose is to preserve, or, where necessary, recover the record of the actions and utterances of the Prophet, and the decisions of the early 'rightly guided' caliphs, to serve as precedents in the elaboration of the Holy Law of Islam, especially in matters of public policy. By 'Abbasid times, a more sophisticated, more literary form of historical writing seems to be aimed at a vast and growing community of civil servants, and acquaints them with a somewhat different set of governmental precedents – less pious, more practical, often even bureaucratic, and including non-Muslim, especially Persian, examples.

For a while, all Islamic historiography, irrespective of region or authorship, was written in Arabic. Then, as new literary languages developed within the common Islamic civilization, new forms of distinctive cultural self-awareness found expression in literature and particularly in poetry and historiography. There were also other changes. Between the tenth and thirteenth centuries, Sunni Islam fought, and for the most part won, a mighty struggle against three enemies – the Shīʿite dissidents, who were either tamed or overcome, the Christian crusaders, who were repulsed, and the heathen Mongols, who were converted and assimilated. In the course of these struggles, and the great Sunni revival that accompanied them, Islamic state, society, and civilization were transformed, and cultural life began to flow in new channels. These changes are vividly reflected in the literature, and especially in the historical literature of the time. History was no doubt still an essential part of the education of a civil servant, and was, clearly, to some extent written with that in view. But the pious *madrasa*-trained functionary of post-Seljuk times was a very different person from the elegant and worldly-wise scribe of ʿAbbasid days. It is significant that many of the great Arabic historians of the later Middle Ages were men whose main interest and reputation among their own contemporaries lay in fields other than history, and usually in the religious sciences. History never became part of the curriculum of the *madrasa*, but the historian, increasingly, was a graduate of the *madrasa*.

It was a change of no small significance. In the more stable and durable monarchies of the postwar period, and especially in the Ottoman Empire and Iran, the writing of history became a more direct concern of the state, and the historian worked under state sponsorship, patronage, or even employment. This led to some diminution of the traditional concern of the historians, dating back to the early days when the historian was primarily a collector and authenticator of traditions, with the accuracy of his facts and the honesty of his interpretation of those facts. But the older tradition survived, albeit in a somewhat modified form, especially in the Ottoman Empire, where a long series of distinguished historians, although holding the rank and status of imperial historiographer, nevertheless depict the failings and failures of their rulers as well as their virtues and successes.

The treatment by Ottoman historians of Ottoman defeats from the seventeenth century onwards is a model of scholarly integrity.

The Islamic Middle Ages saw the development of many other branches of scholarship. Unlike Christianity, Islam did not encourage the production of translations of Holy Scripture for the benefit of those who could not read it in the original. On the contrary, some Muslim authorities even condemned the attempt to make such translations as impious or even blasphemous. There are therefore no authorized translations of the Qur'ān into Persian, Turkish, or other Islamic languages equivalent to the Syriac Peshitta, the Latin Vulgate, or the Luther or King James versions of the Bible. Some informal translations were provided in the guise of commentaries, but Muslims, whatever their native language, were required to study and recite the Qur'ān in Arabic and only in Arabic. This led to a considerable development of grammatical and lexicographic studies. Their primary purpose was to make Holy Scripture accessible to all believers. Their effect was a development of the linguistic sciences that was without precedent. As well as Arabic, other Islamic languages were in time affected, as was at least one non-Islamic language. Jews in Islamic lands, following the Muslim example, developed textual and linguistic studies of biblical Hebrew to make the Bible accessible to those for whom Hebrew was an acquired language.

The great Arabic dictionaries of the Middle Ages, listing the different meanings of words and illustrating them with examples of their occurrence in classical texts, were a remarkable achievement, and the basis of all subsequent philology in this area. They also served as the model for other alphabetically arranged works of reference. These include geographical dictionaries or gazetteers, often with lengthy essays on the towns, countries, or geographical features named, and a wide range of biographical dictionaries, variously arranged by country, by century, or by profession or vocation.

An important factor in the development of scholarship and more generally of science and learning was the work of the translators who, in the ninth century and after, produced a series of epoch-making Arabic versions of major Greek writings on mathematics and astronomy, physics and chemistry, medicine and pharmacology, geography and agronomy, and a wide range of other subjects including, notably, philosophy. Some of these works were preserved by the local non-Muslims; others were specially imported from Byzantium. Significantly, they did not translate the Greek historians, since the meaningless gyrations of ancient pagans were without sense or value. They did not translate the poets, since the Muslims had their own rich poetic literature, and poetry was in any case untranslatable.

The translators and of course their royal and other patrons were principally interested in what was useful, and that – fortunately for later generations – included philosophy, at that time seen as a useful science which helped mankind to confront the problems of this world and prepare for the judgement in the next. Many important Greek works which were temporarily – or sometimes permanently – lost in the barbarous and for the most part uninterested West, became known through Arabic translations, from which at a later date Latin versions were made. Most of the translators were non-Muslims – Christians, Jews, and above all members of the mysterious sect of the Sabians, since only they were likely to have the necessary knowledge of languages. Some of the texts were translated directly from Greek, others from Syriac versions based on Greek originals. While most of the translated works came directly or indirectly from Greek, there were a few from other sources – translated or adapted from pre-Islamic Persian or even from Indian writings. As far as is known, only one work was translated from Latin – the late chronicle of Orosius, which provided useful background to the Muslim history of Spain.

Thereafter there is little sign of interest in the West until many centuries later when, for good practical reasons, the attention of scholars and scientists was for the first time directed westwards. Two examples may illustrate the different aspects of this new interest. One is a translation into Turkish of a history of France from its origins to the year 1560, made by order of the chief secretary in the office of the Ottoman grand vizier, and completed in 1570. This translation survives in a single manuscript. No comparable exploration into Western history was undertaken until centuries later. The other, more pressing concern with the West is illustrated by a Persian physician called Bahā' al-Dawla (d. *c.*1510), in a work entitled, *Khulāṣat al-Tajārib*, 'The Quintessence of Experiences'. In it he speaks of a new disease, clearly syphilis, which he called 'the Armenian sore' or 'the Frankish pox'. This disease, he says, originated in Europe, and was carried from there to Istanbul and beyond. It appeared in Azerbaijan in 1498, and spread thence to Iraq and Iran. By the seventeenth century, syphilis — known in Turkish and most other Islamic languages as *firengi*, 'the Frankish disease' – is discussed in some detail, largely on the basis of published European writings.

The achievement of medieval Islamic science is not limited to the preservation of Greek learning, nor to the incorporation in the corpus of elements from the more ancient and the more distant East. The heritage which medieval Islamic scientists handed on to the modern world was immensely enriched by their own efforts and contributions. Greek science, on the whole, tended to be rather theoretical. Medieval Middle Eastern science was much more practical, and in such fields as medicine, chemistry, astronomy and agronomy, the classical heritage was clarified and supplemented by the experiments and observations of the medieval Middle East. A good example of these processes may be seen in mathematics. The so-called 'Arabic numerals' – positional numbering with a sign for zero – came from India, but it was Middle Easterners who, in the ninth century if not earlier, made it the starting point of a new arithmetic. Islamic geometry was founded on Greek and influenced by Indian teachings, but its practitioners added much that was new and original, both practical – in surveying, construction and weaponry – and theoretical. Trigonometry was largely, algebra entirely, a medieval Middle Eastern innovation. Among the more famous innovators was the algebrist 'Umar (or Omar) Khayyam (d. 1131), famous in the East for his mathematical writings, and in the West for his quatrains, improvised in his leisure moments. A significant proportion of these scientists, especially of the physicians, were Christians and Jews, mostly of local origin, sometimes refugees from persecution in Europe. But they formed part of a single scholarly community with their Muslim colleagues, and their work is part of the common medieval Islamic civilization of the region. Some of the great Islamic writers whose works were translated into Latin and studied in Europe made a major contribution to the development of modern science. Such, for example, was Muḥammad ibn Zakariyā al-Rāzī (d. 920) from Rayy, near the present site of Teheran, known in Europe as Rhazes, perhaps the greatest of all medieval physicians, and the author of a celebrated work on smallpox. The illustrious Ibn Sīnā (980–1037) of Bukhara, known in Europe as Avicenna, compiled the *Canon*, a vast medical encyclopaedia which, translated into Latin by Gerard of Cremona in the thirteenth century, dominated European medical studies for centuries after that.

There were practical as well as scientific contributions from Middle Eastern to Western medical science. Lady Mary Wortley Montagu, writing from Edirne in 1717, describes the method of smallpox vaccination in use among the Turks:[6]

A propos of Distempers, I am going to tell you a thing that I am sure will make you wish your selfe here. The Small Pox so fatal and so general amongst us is here entirely harmless by the invention of engrafting (which is the term they give it). There is a set of old Women who make it their business to perform the Operation. Every Autumn in the month of September, when the great heat is abated, people send to one another to know if any of their family has a mind to have the small pox. They make partys for this purpose, and when they are met (commonly 15 or 16 together) the old Woman comes with a nutshell full of the matter of the best sort of small-pox and asks what veins you please to have open'd. She immediately rips open that you offer to her with a large needle (which gives you no more pain than a common scratch) and puts into the vein as much venom as can lye upon the head of her needle, and after binds up the little wound with a hollow bit of shell, and in this manner opens 4 or 5 veins. ... Then the fever begins to seize 'em and they keep their beds 2 days, very seldom 3 ... and in 8 days time they are as well as before their illness. ... Every year thousands undergo this Operation, and the French Ambassador says pleasantly that they take the Small pox here by way of diversion as they take the Waters in other Countrys.

Lady Mary was sufficiently impressed by the procedure that she had her own young son vaccinated the very next year. This method of inoculation was subsequently introduced to England and later to the rest of the Western world.

The advancement of literature and learning, and more generally of education, was immensely helped by two innovations, both of them of Far Eastern origin. The introduction of paper, a Chinese invention, is traditionally dated from the year 751 CE, when the Arabs, in a skirmish with Chinese forces in Central Asia, captured some Chinese paper makers. These introduced their craft to the Islamic world, and within a very short time first the use and then the manufacture of paper spread westwards across the Middle East and North Africa, reaching Spain by the beginning of the tenth century. The replacement by paper of such earlier and inefficient writing materials as papyrus, parchment, and the like affected Middle Eastern society in a number of ways. On the one hand, it allowed the cheap and rapid production of books, with beneficial effects on both scholarship and education; on the other it encouraged and facilitated the proliferation of paperwork in both government and commerce. The caliph Hārūn al-Rashīd, according to an Arabic chronicle, gave instructions that paper should be used in government offices, because when something was written on paper it could be neither erased nor altered without leaving traces.

Middle Eastern Islamic society proved much more resistant to another Far Eastern invention, printing. The invention or re-invention of printing from movable type in fifteenth-century Europe did not pass unnoticed in the Ottoman lands, where printing was forbidden by a decree of Sultan Bayezid II issued in 1485. A few years later, this new technology of book production was introduced by Jewish refugees from Spain. By the early sixteenth century, they had established presses in Istanbul and Salonika, and in the following years in a number of other Turkish cities. They were granted permission to set up printing presses on condition that they did not print in Turkish or in the Arabic characters, presumably on the grounds that it would be sacrilegious to use the press for Muslim texts or even for Muslim languages. The powerful vested interest of the scribes and calligraphers may also have had something to do with the ban. The Jewish presses, therefore, confined their work to the printing of Hebrew books, as well as a few in European languages. An Armenian press was established in Istanbul in 1567 by one Abgar Tibir of Tokat, who had studied typography in Venice, and in 1627 a Greek press was established by Nicodemus Metaxas, a native of Cephalonia and a graduate of Balliol College, Oxford, with machinery and types imported from England. Both Armenian and Greek printers were subject to the same restriction as the Jews.

Arabic founts were devised, and Arabic printing presses established, in Italy at the beginning of the sixteenth century. Their production consisted mainly of bibles, prayer books, and other religious texts in Arabic for the use of the Arabic-speaking Christians of the East. The earliest surviving Arabic printed text is a book of Christian prayers, a *horologium breve*, printed at Fano in the states of the Church in 1514. Some non-religious and even non-Christian texts were also printed, notably the medical canon of Avicenna, some geographical works, and – in Paris, in about 1538 – an Arabic grammar. With the rise of Orientalist scholarship, classical Arabic texts, in increasing numbers, were also printed. Some of these found their way into private libraries in Middle Eastern countries.

It was not, however, until the early eighteenth century that printing in Arabic characters was officially authorized in the Middle East. The initiative came from a young man named Said Efendi, who had accompanied his father as Ottoman ambassador to Paris in 1721. There he seems to have acquired both an interest in the art of printing and a conviction of its usefulness. On his return to Turkey, he tried to secure the support of the grand vizier for the setting up of a Turkish printing press in the capital. In this, despite some opposition, both conservative and professional, he was successful. His chief collaborator was one Ibrahim Müteferrika, the founder and director of the first Turkish printing press. Born in Hungary, probably a Unitarian, Ibrahim embraced Islam and made a career in the Ottoman service. In collaboration with Said Efendi, he drafted a memorandum on the usefulness of printing, which he submitted to the grand vizier. Support came from an unexpected quarter, when the chief mufti of the capital, head of the Muslim religious hierarchy of the empire, was persuaded to issue a *fatwā* authorizing the printing of books in Turkish in Arabic characters on subjects other than religion. The printing of the Qur'ān, and of books on Qur'ānic exegesis, tradition, theology, and Holy Law was still excluded. Finally, on 5 July 1727, an imperial *ferman* authorized the establishment of a Turkish press and the printing of Turkish books 'in the high God-guarded city of Constantinople'. Presses and types were at first obtained from the local Jewish and Christian printers already working in the city, and use was also made of Jewish typefounders and typesetters. Later, presses and types were imported from Europe, and especially from Leiden in the Netherlands and from Paris, both of which had established Arabic presses. The first book, a two-volume dictionary, was printed in 1729. The first volume opens with an introduction by the editor, followed by the full texts of the imperial decree authorizing the establishment of the press, the *fatwā* of the chief mufti declaring printing to be licit, and certificates of approval from the two chief judges of the empire and other dignitaries. These are followed by a treatise on the usefulness of printing.

By the time of Ibrahim Müteferrika's death in 1745, the press had printed seventeen books in all, including works on grammar, military affairs, geography, mathematics, and above all history. The number was small, and so too were the print runs – a thousand each for the first two, twelve hundred for the third, and five hundred each for the remainder. Nevertheless they marked the beginning of a new era in the intellectual life of the Islamic world.

The Islamic civilization of the Middle East, at its peak, presented a proud spectacle – in many ways the apex of human civilization achievement to that date. There were other civilizations at the time – in India, in China, and, to a lesser extent, in Europe – that were advanced and sophisticated, and perhaps in some individual respects or areas they may have been ahead of Islam. But all of them remained essentially local, at best regional, civilizations. Islam was not the first religion whose spokesmen claimed that the truths entrusted to them were not only universal but also exclusive – that they were the sole custodians of God's final revelation which it was their duty to bring to all the peoples of the world. But the Muslims were the first to make significant progress in achieving this aim, by creating a religious civilization beyond the limits of a single race or region or culture. The Islamic world in the high Middle Ages was international, multi-racial, poly-ethnic, one might even say intercontinental.

In the late S.D. Goitein's felicitous phrase, the Islamic world was 'the intermediate civilization' – intermediate in both time and space. Its outer limits were in southern Europe, in Central Africa, in southern and southeastern and eastern Asia, and it embraced elements of all of these. It was also intermediate in time, between antiquity and modernity, sharing the Hellenistic and Judaeo-Christian heritage with Europe and enriching it with elements from remoter lands and cultures. Of the alternative routes from Hellenistic antiquity to modern times, it might well have seemed that it was the Islamic civilization of the Arabs, rather than those of Greek or Latin Christendom, that offered the greater promise of advancing towards a modern and universal civilization.

Yet it was the poor, parochial, monochrome culture of Christian Europe that advanced from strength to strength, while the Islamic civilization of the Middle East suffered a loss of creativity, of energy, and of power. Its subsequent development has been overshadowed by a growing awareness of this loss, the search for its causes, and a passionate desire to restore its bygone glories.

PART V

The Challenge of Modernity

CHAPTER 14

CHALLENGE

It has for some time been the custom to define the beginning of modern history in the Middle East, as in other parts of the world, with the impact of the West, or more specifically of European imperialism – its first arrival, its spread, and the processes of transformation which it initiated. The date of this impact has been variously put. For some it begins with the arrival of the French expedition in Egypt in 1798; for others with the disastrous treaty of Küçük Kaynarca imposed by a victorious Russia on a defeated Turkey; for others again with the final Turkish defeat under the walls of Vienna in 1683.

Muslim civilization was, in its own perception, defined by religion. The civilized world was the *Dār al-Islām*, the House of Islam, all the lands in which the law of Islam prevailed and a Muslim government ruled. On all sides it was surrounded by the *Dār al-Ḥarb*, the House of War, inhabited by infidels who had not yet accepted the Muslim faith or submitted to Muslim rule. In the Muslim view, however, as reflected in historical and geographical writings, there is a clear difference between these various regions beyond the Islamic frontier. To the east and to the south of the Islamic world, there was a wide variety of peoples, some civilized, from whom much that was useful could be learnt; some barbarous. There was, however, no serious competitor to Islam as a faith, no serious rival to the Islamic caliphate as a world power. These various infidels, the civilized as well as the barbarous, were seen as teachable, as potential recruits to the Islamic world, and this was indeed the fate of great numbers of them.

From the East there was no threat. The great civilizations of China and of India never seriously challenged, still less threatened, the Islamic world. The one great pagan invasion from the East, that of the Mongols, despite its immense impact, was eventually absorbed with the conversion and assimilation of the conquerors themselves, who became a part, and indeed an important part, of the Islamic world.

A vastly different situation prevailed on the western, more specifically the northwestern frontier of Islam, in the lands of European

Christendom, both Greek and Latin. Here the Muslims rightly recognized a rival – a world faith, with a sense of mission much like their own, whose adherents also believed that they were the possessors of God's final revelation, with the duty to bring it to all mankind. And in Christendom, as in the Islamic world, this belief found political and military support by the creation of strong kingdoms and later great empires, which used warfare as well as other methods to advance their cause. In time the Christian came to be the infidel *par excellence*, and Christian Europe the archetype of the House of War. The Muslims had some respect for the Byzantines, in whom they saw the heirs of ancient Greece and of Christian Rome. They respected them but did not fear them, for the long interrelation between Islam and Byzantium was in the main a story of Byzantine retreat, completed by the Turkish capture of Constantinople in 1453. In the early centuries they neither feared nor respected the barbarous infidels of northern and western Europe, whom they saw as uncouth primitives offering neither threat nor attraction, and of no use except for enslavement. This perception began to change with the western Christian counter-attack – the reconquest of southern Italy and the Iberian peninsula, and the return of Christian arms to the Levant with the Crusades, in the ultimately unsuccessful attempt to retake the holy places of Christendom.

For the first thousand years or so of the long struggle between the two world systems, the Muslims on the whole had the upper hand. True, they suffered reverses; a temporary reverse through the arrival of the Crusaders in the Levant, a more permanent one through the loss of Spain, Portugal, and Sicily. But these were more than compensated by the Turkish advance into southeastern Europe and the creation of a new Muslim power on Christian soil, which for a while threatened the very heart of Europe.

Social and also cultural relations between the European and Islamic worlds can be traced before the Crusades, and became massive and extensive from the Crusades onwards. The Islamic contribution to Europe is enormous, both of its own creations and of its borrowings – reworked and adapted – from the ancient civilizations of the eastern Mediterranean and from the remoter cultures of Asia. Greek science and philosophy, preserved and improved by the Muslims but forgotten in Europe; Indian numbers and Chinese paper; oranges and lemons, cotton and sugar, and a whole series of other plants along with the methods of cultivating them – all these are but a few of the many things that medieval Europe learned or acquired from the vastly more

Thirteenth-century slave market in the Yemen, from an illustrated manuscript of the *Māqāmat,* a classical Arabic masteriece by al-Ḥarīrī.

Arab slave caravan in the desert, nineteenth century.

Two eunuchs on horseback, 1573. The black eunuchs were more numerous and more powerful in the Ottoman household than their white colleagues. Their chief, the Aga of the Girls, was a major figure.

The Aga of the Girls. Eighteenth-century drawing.

The sultan's mother (the *valide sultan*) attended by her suite in one of the palace kiosks, taking a cup of coffee from a servant.

Turkish lady on her way to the bath,
escorted by her servant. Seventeenth century.

Ladies at a wedding procession.

Wie sie im Feren Zimer sizen

Turkish ladies sitting in a drawing room.

AUDIENCE. QUE LE GRAND VISIR DONNE AUX AMBASSADEURS .

(above) The grand vizier grants an audience to a European ambassador, early eighteenth century. (below) The Nuruosmaniye mosque, Istanbul, completed in 1755, with italianate exterior decoration.

Costumes of the Ottomans, c.1825: the aga of the girls, a dwarf jester and a white eunuch. (By Giovanni Brindesi.)

Ottoman military uniforms of the early nineteenth century. (By Giovanni Brindesi.)

From the left: the translator of the Sublime Porte, a European ambassador, the chief secretary, the Bokharan ambassador and the aga of the interior. (By Arif Pasha.)

(above) Bonaparte haranguing his troops before the Battle of the Pyramids, 1798.
Painting by Antoine-Jean Gros. (below) Selim III (1789–1807) by Hippolite Berteaux.

Sultan Mahmud II before and after the destruction of the Janissaries in 1826. The
Sultan's headgear, beard, attire and escort as well as the harness of his horse, illustrate the
change to a Western model. The posture of the horses and riders remains the same.

Muhammad ʿAlı Pasha, Ottoman governor of Egypt from 1805 until his death in
1848, confers with British and French experts.

Persians resisting the advance of Russian troops, early nineteenth century.

The Russians destroy the Ottoman fleet at Sinope on the north coast of Anatolia, 1853.

advanced and more sophisticated civilization of the Mediterranean Islamic world.

There were also a few European contributions to the Islamic world. For a long time, these were mainly material and technical. In arts and letters, science and philosophy, medieval Europe had little that could interest the Muslims, who were in any case predisposed to reject ideas coming from what they regarded as a superseded religion and a primitive society. But Europeans were clever with their hands, and produced a number of things which Muslims found useful and adopted. Clocks and watches to measure time, eyeglasses and telescopes to improve vision, are attested in the Middle East in the fifteenth century, and may well have reached there earlier. Even some food plants were taken over from Europe. Thus, for example, peas are still known in both Arabic and Turkish by their Italian name. The number of food and other plants imported and then transplanted from the West – though few compared with those that travelled the opposite way – increased rapidly after the discovery of America and the arrival in the Islamic lands of maize, the potato, the tomato, and – in many ways most portentous of all – tobacco. But by far the most important contribution of the West to life – and death – in the Islamic world was in weaponry. Already during the Crusades Frankish prisoners of war were employed in building fortifications, and passed something of their skills to their masters. No less a person than Saladin, in a letter to the caliph, justifies his action in allowing the continued presence of European merchants in the seaports which he had reconquered from the Crusaders, by explaining that they were useful since 'there is not one of them that does not bring and sell us weapons of war, to their detriment and to our advantage'.[1] That tradition continued without interruption during the Crusades, the Ottoman advance and retreat, and into modern times.

From time to time there were some, in both church and state, who condemned and tried to stop this traffic in weapons of war. Governments denounced other governments for condoning and even encouraging it. The church was unequivocal. Papal bulls of the sixteenth and seventeenth centuries, for example, 'excommunicate and anathematize ... all those who take to the Saracens, Turks, and other enemies of the Christian name, horses, weapons, iron, iron wire, tin, copper, bandaraspata, brass, sulphur, saltpetre, and all else suitable for the making of artillery, and instruments, arms, and machines for offence, with which they fight against the Christians, as also ropes and timber and other nautical supplies and other prohibited wares.'² This trade, and the attempts to stop it, continued.

By far the most important Western importation in weaponry was of course firearms: siege guns, field guns, and handguns of many kinds. At first there was some resistance to the use of these infidel and unchivalrous weapons. But the Ottomans adopted them on a vast scale, and by so doing gained an enormous advantage over the other Muslim powers who vied with them for the mastery of the Middle East.

The turning-point in the power relationship between Islam and Christendom, like other turning-points in history, is difficult to place with any precision. As always happens in such changes, the beginnings of the new order are discernible long before the dramatic events which first made it apparent. Similarly, much of the old order continued to function long after its apparent abrogation. All such 'turning points' are in varying measure arbitrary and artificial – a device of the historian, not a fact of history. But they are a useful, indeed a necessary adjunct to historical discussion. Of the many major events that punctuate the changing relationship between Europe and the Islamic world, those which took place in the last years of the seventeenth century probably provide the best basis for exposition.

On 12 September 1683, after a siege of sixty days, the Turkish armies encamped outside Vienna began to withdraw. It was their second attempt and their second failure to take Vienna, but between the two there was a vast difference. In 1529, when the armies of Süleyman the Magnificent first reached the walls of Vienna, they marked the crest of a wave of conquest which in the course of the preceding centuries had engulfed the whole of southeastern Europe and now threatened the very heart of Christendom. Süleyman failed to capture the Imperial city, but the failure was far from final or decisive. The Turkish retreat was orderly, their defeat inconclusive; the siege initiated a century and a half of stalemate during which the two empires – those of the Habsburgs and those of the Ottomans – battled for the control of Hungary and ultimately of Central Europe. The second siege and the second withdrawal were quite a different matter. This time, the failure of the Turks was clear and unequivocal. The withdrawal of the Turkish armies from Vienna was followed by crushing defeats in the field, the loss of many cities and provinces, and finally the destruction of the Ottoman armies.

The peace treaty of Carlowitz, signed 26 January 1699, marked a new stage not only in the relations between Ottoman and Habsburg empires, but more profoundly, between Christendom and Islam. The transformation can be seen both in the content of the Treaty and in the procedures by which it was negotiated. For the Ottomans, this was diplomacy of an entirely new kind. During the early stages of their advance into Europe there had been no treaties in the proper sense, and very little negotiation – just terms dictated by the victors to the vanquished. At Sitvatorok in 1606, for the first time, they negotiated with the enemy as equals. At Carlowitz, in an even more dramatic change, the Ottomans were compelled to sign a peace in a war which they had unmistakably lost in the field, and on terms which were basically determined by their victorious enemies. In seeking to mitigate the consequences of this defeat, they adopted the new tactic of seeking the help of Western European countries, notably England and Holland, to mediate on their behalf and to counterbalance the power of their nearer neighbours. This new diplomacy, based on the new military relationship, set the patterns for the centuries to follow. The defeat that was suffered at Vienna and sealed at Carlowitz inaugurated a long period of almost unrelieved Muslim retreat before Christian power.

The Ottomans were under no illusion as to what had happened. In the words of the contemporary Turkish chronicler: 'This was a calamitous defeat, of such magnitude that there has never been its like since the first appearance of the Ottoman state.'³ Significantly, the debate about its causes began almost immediately after. Discussion of what was going wrong with the state and the world had been a commonplace of Muslim religious and even political literature since the early days of Islamic glory. Now for the first time the debate was conducted in terms of 'us' and 'them' – why were the miserable infidels, previously always vanquished by the victorious armies of Islam, now winning the day, and why were the armies of Islam suffering defeat at their hands? The debate was opened in Ottoman official memoranda at the beginning of the eighteenth century, and for a long time was confined to an inner circle of Ottoman officials, officers, and intellectuals, while the great mass of the population, more particularly in the inner provinces of the empire, remained blissfully unaware of the changed world situation. But gradually the debate spread from the upper classes to the generality of the population, from the Turks – for long the sword and buckler of Islam in the confrontation with Christendom – to the rest of the Muslim world. Awareness of the change was strengthened on the one hand by the steady advance of European arms – first Russian and then West European – and the establishment of European domination over many Muslim lands, and then also by a dramatic change in the terms of trade, to the immense disadvantage of the Muslim lands. Efficient manufacture in the West and low-cost production in the Western colonial dependencies flooded Middle Eastern markets with cheap textiles and other commodities. In time even such products as coffee, sugar and cotton, once prominent among Middle Eastern exports to the Western world, were produced in the colonies and exported by Western merchants to the Middle East.

In Iran, the Safavid dynasty, despite its defeat at the hands of the Ottomans at the beginning of the sixteenth century, continued to rule for more than two centuries. This period saw a number of significant changes – the imposition and general acceptance of Shīʿism as the dominant and ultimately the majority religion of the Iranians; the extension of European trade and, with it, European commercial and political rivalries to Iran; the continuation of the political, military, and religious struggle with the Ottomans; and the simultaneous development of a new system of relations with Muslim states further to the East in Central Asia and in India. The Safavid period was one of notable achievement in the arts and especially in architecture, painting and the industrial arts. But behind this imposing façade, the Safavid state and society were in rapid decay. This became evident in the early eighteenth century when Iran was invaded by Afghans from the east, Ottomans from the west and Russians from the north.

To an increasing extent, the rivalries of the Middle Eastern Muslim powers were being overshadowed by a new threat from the two great Christian powers in the north – Austria and Russia. In a series of wars these gained considerable territorial and other advantages at Ottoman and Iranian expense. The Austrians were first concerned to recover the former Austrian and Hungarian lands lost to the Turks in earlier times, and then to add to them at Turkish expense. While their penetration into the Balkan peninsula was modest, they secured the important right to navigate the Danube as far as its mouth and first entered the valley of the Morava, the lane to Istanbul.

Of far greater significance was the southward advance of the power of Muscovy. A new phase in Russian imperial expansion to the south began during the eighteenth century. At first this did not go too well. In 1710, Russian forces crossed the River Prut and attached the Ottoman Empire, but were compelled to withdraw and relinquish their conquests. In 1723, the Russians, profiting from the chaos in

Iran, tried again, advancing into the Caucasian region, where they occupied the cities of Derbent and Baku. This time the Russians acted more or less in concert with the Ottomans, who were concerned to forestall a Russian presence on their eastern as well as their northern borders, and to ensure an Ottoman share if the Iranian state was indeed collapsing. Their successes and acquisitions were, however, short-lived. Under a brilliant military commander, Nāder Khan, the Iranian state began to recover. In a series of major victories in both east and west, Nāder, who became shah on the death of the ruler in 1736, was able to expel the Afghans, the Ottomans and the Russians from Iranian soil and even to invade and conquer new areas.

Despite these successes by both Ottoman and Iranian arms, the balance of power between the Islamic states and their European rivals was inexorably changing. By the latter part of the eighteenth century, this was becoming clearer to both parties. In 1768, the Russians began a new offensive against the Ottoman Empire, this time with overwhelming superiority. The Russian armies carried all before them; Russian naval squadrons sailed around Europe into the Mediterranean and threatened even the coasts of Anatolia and Syria.

The resulting treaty of Küçük Kaynarca (1774) recorded the utter humiliation of the Ottomans and, in a larger sense, marks a turning point in the relations between Europe and the Middle East. The Empress Catherine II of Russia rightly described it as a success 'the like of which Russia has never had before'.

The advantages obtained by Russia from this treaty may be grouped under three main headings: territory, trade, and influence. The territory ceded to Russia, though of small extent, was of major strategic importance. By the annexation of Azov at the head of the Gulf of Taganrog at the beginning of the eighteenth century, Russia had already secured a foothold on the northern shore of the Black Sea, until then entirely under Turco-Muslim control. The treaty of Küçük Kaynarca gave Russia two important additions: the ports of Kertch and Yenikale on the eastern tip of the Crimean peninsula, at the junction of the Gulf of Taganrog and the Black Sea; and the fortress of Kinburn, at the mouth of the River Dniester. At the same time the Crimean peninsula itself, for centuries the seat of a Tatar Khanate under the suzerainty of the Ottoman sultan, was now declared independent, and the Tatar khan and his various dependencies along the northern shore of the Black Sea east and west of the Crimea were removed from Ottoman control or influence. This opened the way for further Russian expansion, notably the annexation of the Crimea in 1783.

This brought a very significant change. In previous wars against the Austrians, the Turks had been obliged to withdraw from several of their European provinces. Most of these were, however, recent conquests, inhabited by mainly Christian populations. The Crimea was another matter. Its people were Turkish-speaking Muslims, commonly if inaccurately known as Tatars, who had lived in the Crimea since the Mongol conquests of the thirteenth century and perhaps earlier. This was the first loss, to Christian conquerors, of an old Muslim land and people. It was a bitter blow to Muslim pride. The humiliation was to some extent assuaged by a face-saving formula according to which the Crimean Tatars did not pass to Russian control but became independent, and the sultan, though no longer suzerain of the Tatars, retained religious authority over them in his capacity as caliph or Head of Islam. Both Tatar independence and Ottoman religious jurisdiction were of brief duration.

The second Russian advantage from the Treaty of Küçük Kaynarca was in trade. Russia gained freedom of navigation and commerce in the Black Sea and through the Straits into the Mediterranean, as well as access to the ports and to overland trade in the European and Asiatic provinces of the Ottoman Empire. This too was a major step towards the commercial penetration of the Ottoman Empire by all the European powers during the nineteenth century.

The third major Russian advantage lay in the acquisition of positions of power and influence within the Ottoman realms. The most immediately important was the recognition of a special status for Russia in the Danubian principalities of Moldavia and Wallachia, the modern Romania. Though these remained in principle under Ottoman suzerainty, they were now granted an increased measure of internal autonomy – and of Russian influence. Russia also gained the right to open consulates at will in Ottoman cities – a privilege long sought in vain by the Western powers – and, in another seemingly minor concession, to erect a Russian church in Istanbul and to 'make, upon all occasions, representations in favour of the new church' (article VII).

If the religious authority of the Ottoman sovereign as caliph over the Tatars was ineffective, quite the contrary is true of the concession made to the Russian empress in return. Though limited in the text of the treaty to a single Russian church in the capital, this right of representation was, by careful misinterpretation, expanded into a right of intervention on behalf of all the orthodox Christian subjects of the Ottoman sultan.

A new phase of Russian territorial expansion began with the annexation of the Crimea in 1783. From there the Russians advanced rapidly in both directions along the northern shores of the Black Sea, subjugating and settling lands previously ruled and inhabited by Turks, Tatars, and other Muslim peoples. To the east they formed an imperial province in Caucasia in 1785 and strengthened their rule over the native peoples and chieftains of the area. This led to a war with Turkey, at the end of which, in 1792, the Turks had to recognize the Russian annexation of the Tatar Khanates and accept the Kuban river in Circassia as the border between the two empires. In 1795 the Russians established the port city of Odessa in former Tatar territory and in 1812, after another war with Turkey, they annexed the Ottoman province of Bessarabia, now called Moldava. The Russians had ended the centuries-long Muslim domination of the Black Sea, and were threatening the frontiers of the Ottoman Empire at both its eastern and western ends.

They were also threatening Iran, where in 1794 a new dynasty, the Qājārs, had acceded to power. After restoring some measure of unity and authority at home, the Qājārs tried to recover the Caucasian lands which had been lost to Russia, but without success. A Persian invasion led some of the inhabitants of the ancient Christian kingdom of Georgia to appeal for Russian protection against Muslim conquest, and the Tsar responded by proclaiming, in January 1801, the annexation of Georgia to the Russian Empire. This was followed in 1802 by the reorganization of Daghistan (the lands between Georgia and the Caspian Sea) as a Russian-protected federation of native chiefs, and rounded off by the annexation of Imeretia, another small Georgian kingdom, in 1804.

The way was now clear for Russia to attack Iran itself. Two Russo-Iranian wars, in 1804–13 and 1826–8, resulted in the Russian acquisition, partly from local rulers and partly from Iran, of the regions which later formed the Soviet republics of Armenia and Azerbaijan.

A month after the signing of peace with Iran in 1828, Russia declared war on Turkey, in support of the Greeks, who had begun their war of independence in 1821. By September 1829, the Russians were at Edirne, two or three days' march from the Turkish capital, and were able to impose a peace treaty giving them considerable advantages. Apart from territorial gains on both the Balkan and Caucasian frontiers between the two empires, Russia extended her influence in the internal affairs of the Danubian principalities, and reaffirmed the rights of her merchants and merchant shipping.

While the Russians continued their advance southwards into the Middle East, another threat was developing from the West. Since the latter part of the fifteenth century, Europe had been expanding at both ends, from Russia overland, from Western Europe across the sea. In both East and West the advance against Islam had begun as a process of recovery and reconquest – of Russia from the Tatars, of Spain and Portugal from the Moors. Reconquest was followed by counterattack, carrying the war into enemy territory. While the Russians advanced south and east into Asia, the Spaniards and the Portuguese, having recovered their peninsula from the rule of the Muslim Arabs and Moors, pursued their former rulers into Africa and then far beyond.

For many, the great voyages of discovery were a religious struggle, a continuation of the Crusades and of the reconquest against the same Muslim enemy. When the Portuguese arrived in Asian waters it was the Muslim rulers of Turkey, Egypt, Iran and India who were their main opponents and who tried without success to stop them. After the Portuguese came the other maritime peoples of Western Europe – the Spaniards, the French, the Dutch, and the English. These between them established a West European hegemony in Africa and in southern Asia which endured until the twentieth century.

After the initial Portuguese impetus, West European activities in southern Asia were mainly commercial and maritime, and only gradually led to the establishment of political domination. Even then it was confined in the main to India, Southeast Asia and East Africa, affecting the Middle East indirectly. There, the interests of the Western powers continued to be predominantly commercial. Significantly, until the beginning of the nineteenth century the British Embassy in Istanbul was maintained and paid by the Levant Company, the chartered company which was the main instrument of British trade in the area.

The consolidation of Dutch and British power in Asia confronted the Middle East with West Europeans on both sides, and it is this development, rather than the earlier circumnavigation of Africa by the Portuguese, that greatly reduced the spice trade through the Red Sea and Persian Gulf. While European imperial rule in Asia and Africa did not as yet directly encroach on the Middle East, it did lead to a growing Western interest in the strategic routes through the region. The global character of the revolutionary and Napoleonic wars gave a new acuteness to these considerations. The concern of the British and the French with each other and of both of them with the Russians brought about a Western intervention in the heart of the Middle East. The Turks no longer had to deal only with Austria and Russia, but with four powers, now including Britain and France.

It was from France that, for the first time since the Crusades, a military expedition was launched against the heartlands of the Middle East. In 1798, a French army commanded by General Bonaparte landed in Egypt, then an Ottoman province, and occupied it with little difficulty. An attempt to extend the French occupation from Egypt into Palestine failed, however, and in 1801 the French withdrew from Egypt. Neither the Egyptians nor their Turkish suzerains accomplished this result. The struggle was mainly between the French and British forces, with local elements playing a comparatively minor role. The French occupation proved of brief duration, and Egypt was subsequently restored to Muslim rule. The arrival of the French revealed that even a small expeditionary force from a Western power could conquer and occupy one of the heartlands of the Middle East with ease. Their departure demonstrated that only another Western power could get them out. It was a portentous double lesson.

For most of the first half of the nineteenth century the countries of Western Europe continued to be concerned mainly with commerce and diplomacy in the Middle East, and more particularly with their rivalries among themselves. While their activities in the Middle East often involved a high degree of interference in internal affairs, they stopped short of attacking the central lands, preferring to nibble at the edges. In 1830 – a year after the Russo-Turkish Treaty of Adrianople – the French invaded and annexed Algeria, then ruled by an autonomous dynasty under Ottoman suzerainty. During the same period the British were establishing themselves around Arabia. Aden, useful as a coaling station on the route to India, was occupied in 1839. Similar commercial and strategic considerations led to the gradual establishment of British naval paramountcy in the Persian Gulf, completed by the Treaty of 1853 with the local rulers.

Towards the mid-century the Russians were again pressing very heavily on the Ottoman Empire. In the course of a complicated diplomatic crisis, the Russians invaded the Danubian principalities in July 1853. Britain and France gave support to Turkey, and in March 1854 became her allies against Russia. The war – commonly known as the Crimean War – ended two years later with the Treaty of Paris, by which Russia made some territorial and other concessions and the powers agreed to admit Turkey to the Concert of Europe and undertook to respect her independence and territorial integrity. This was the first war in which the Turkish empire was involved with West European allies whose troops were present in considerable numbers on Turkish soil. These direct contacts with the West brought immense changes.

Thwarted in the Middle East, the Russians turned their attention to Central Asia where they made important advances. The area east of the Caspian Sea, extending towards the Chinese border, had for centuries been divided among three Islamic Turkish states: the Amirate of Bukhara, and the Khanates of Khoqand and Khiva. In a series of swift military campaigns these were now brought under Russian control. Part of the territory was annexed; the remainder was left under 'native princes', subject to Russian occupation and protection.

The peace treaty of 1856 had restricted Russian activity in the Black Sea. In 1870, while Western Europe was preoccupied with the Franco-Prussian War, the Russians seized the opportunity to repudiate these restrictions. This inaugurated a new phase of Russian pressure on Turkey, culminating in a declaration of war on 25 April 1877. The Turks, distracted by rebellion in the provinces and a constitutional crisis at the centre, were unable to withstand the advance of the Russian armies, who reached San Stefano (nowadays called Yeşilköy), only a few miles from the capital, and dictated a draconian treaty to the Sultan. Only the intervention of Western, chiefly British, diplomacy was able to save Turkey from total disaster, and the treaty of Berlin of 1878 again set limits to Russian expansion at Ottoman expense.

The Russians once more turned eastwards, and in 1881 began a new advance, which concluded with the formal annexation of the trans-Caspian regions. In the course of same decade, Russian armies also pacified the region between the Caspian Sea and the Oxus River. With the capture of Marv in 1884, Russian imperial power was established as far as the Central Asian borders of Iran and Afghanistan.

Once again an advance from Eastern Europe was paralleled by a wave of expansion from the West. The French occupied Tunisia in 1881, followed by the British in Egypt in 1882. In both of these places, as in Russian Central Asia, the indigenous monarchies and political systems were preserved more or less intact, but subject to military occupation and overall political and economic control.

British diplomacy in the Middle East was based on the principle of preserving 'the integrity and independence of the Ottoman Empire' as a shield against foreign threats to the road to India. But attacks continued. Both the French and to a lesser extent the Russians were able to make considerable inroads into the Ottoman Empire, and from 1880 onwards Germany, already Britain's main imperial rival, began to display mounting interest in the Middle Eastern area. Successive Ottoman regimes showed what seemed to British eyes a disquieting acquiescence in German purposes. German financiers and industrialists won concessions; German officers trained and reorganized the Ottoman army; German scientists and archaeologists explored the Asian territories of the Empire. In 1889 work began on the famous Baghdad Railway, intended ultimately to link Berlin with the Persian Gulf via Istanbul, Aleppo, Baghdad and Basra.

The perception of this German threat from the north was one of the main considerations which determined Britain to maintain the occupation of Egypt, at first meant to be temporary. Similar concerns led to the conclusion of an agreement with Russia in 1907 dividing Iran into Russian and British spheres of influence. This was designed to prevent the further expansion of Germany eastwards and southwards from Ottoman Iraq.

A new phase of advance began in 1911, with a Russian military invasion of the northern provinces of Iran. From this time until the outbreak of the First World War, despite some resistance, Iran was effectively under Russian domination. In the meantime the French extended their influence in Morocco and in 1912 established a pro-tectorate. The Italians, frustrated by the French occupation of Tunisia and alarmed by the French advance in Morocco, declared war on the Ottoman Empire in September 1911 and announced the annexation of the Ottoman provinces of Tripolitania and Cyrenaica, both of which became Italian colonies.

The Islamic Middle East was now caught in a pincer movement formed by the expansion of Europe at both ends since the sixteenth century. The Russian arm of the pincers had come down from the north and was squeezing both Turkey and Persia. The West Europeans came first round Africa and then across the Mediterranean, reaching into the Arab world.

CHAPTER 15

CHANGE

The same period saw a tremendous growth in European economic and political influence in the Middle East. As in the political and military spheres, this was due, in the first instance, to a growing disparity of strength. In comparison with Europe, both Eastern and Western, by the nineteenth century the Middle East had become far weaker than it had been in the great days of the sixteenth century. There is some evidence, though this is less certain, that the decline in the economic power of the Middle East was absolute as well as relative.

Several factors combined to bring about this change. In its dealings with Europe, the Middle East was affected by the increasing complexity and resulting higher cost of armament and war. Its internal economy was adversely affected by the great inflation of the sixteenth and seventeenth centuries and the rise in prices which continued after that. Its external trade suffered from the development of transoceanic trade routes across the Atlantic, around southern Africa, and into South Asian waters, resulting in the deflection of much of the transit trade and a fall in the relative importance of the Middle Eastern area. Another element in the situation was the continuing unfavourable balance of trade of the Ottoman Empire with the countries to the east of it and the steady flow of gold and silver eastwards to Iran and India. These processes were accelerated by a lack of technological progress in agriculture, industry and transportation within the Middle East.

There were other changes. One was the transformation of the landholding system. Because of the growing need for cash to meet the higher costs of administration and warfare, the government abandoned the traditional military grant system and replaced it with tax-farming, with adverse effects both in the countryside and at the centre. Another change was a rapid decline in population, particularly in the villages and especially during the eighteenth century. From such evidence as is available it would seem that the populations of Turkey, Syria, and Egypt were all lower in 1800 than they had been in 1600.

A major shift in prices seems to have begun in the latter part of the sixteenth century. This was a Middle Eastern reflection of the wider process resulting in part from the disruptive effects of the inflow of American gold and silver. The purchasing power of these precious metals was greater in the Ottoman Empire than in the West, but less than in Iran and India. Persian goods, especially Persian silk, were in great demand both in the Ottoman lands and in Europe, where however there was no demand of comparable magnitude and persistence for any Ottoman product. Grain and textiles were the two most important exports to Europe. The latter had at one time consisted largely of manufactured goods, but this trade was gradually reduced, only cotton cloth remaining for a little longer as a significant item among the exports from the Middle East to Europe. The balance had shifted overwhelmingly the other way, with Europe sending manufactured textiles, including Indian cloths, to the Middle East, and importing raw materials, cotton and mohair, and especially silk, much of it from Iran. Not surprisingly, despite the inflow of gold and silver from the West, Ottoman records reveal a chronic lack of precious metals even to meet the needs of minting coins.

While agriculture derived some benefit from the introduction of new crops from the West, the general situation was one of technological and economic stagnation. The European agricultural revolution found no parallel in the countries of the Middle East; still less the European industrial revolution. Middle Eastern industry continued to be in the form of handicrafts which flourished until the latter part of the eighteenth century but showed few if any signs of technological development.

Two of the most important areas of technological backwardness were shipbuilding and weapons. Already in the eighteenth century, the Ottoman Empire employed European naval engineers and bought vessels for both civil and military use from Sweden and from the United States. Within the Empire, there was little attempt to improve the network of roads and canals. In the greater part of the Middle East at the beginning of the nineteenth century wheeled transport was almost unknown. Apart from a few dignitaries' carriages in the cities and a few farmers' carts in the villages, mainly in the Turkish lands, transport was still almost entirely by pack animals or by river and canal boats.

The terms of trade were also changing, to the disadvantage of the Ottoman Empire and other Middle Eastern states. The opening and development of the oceanic routes bypassed the Middle East; even the

Persian silk trade, which had been important as a source of raw materials and also of tax revenue to Turkey, was now diverted, and to a large extent, controlled by west European merchants. Parallel changes in the Black Sea also weakened the Turkish position. The expansion of Russian power on the northern shore led to a great increase in East European commerce in the region. The commercial rights obtained by Russia under the Treaty of Küçük Kaynarca enabled Russian merchants and skippers to deal directly with Ottoman subjects and to send ships through the Straits to the Mediterranean, thus bypassing the Turkish capital. The rights obtained by Russia were soon claimed and gained by other European powers, and the Black Sea trade was to a large extent lost by Turkey to Europeans, and especially, to Greeks.

In general, the Turkish share in European trade dropped considerably. With France it fell from one half in the late sixteenth century to one-twentieth in the late eighteenth, and with Britain from one-tenth in the mid-seventeenth century to one-hundredth at the end of the eighteenth. At the same time there was a large increase in imports, especially from France and Austria, and European goods – cheaper and sometimes better – drove many local products from the market.

At the same time new markets were opening in Europe for Ottoman agricultural products, especially from the predominantly Christian Balkan provinces. This had important social consequences for the Ottoman population. The decline of the traditional crafts impoverished the artisans and craftsmen, most of them Muslims, and reduced them to the level of unskilled labourers. Members of the Christian minorities, however, found new opportunities as farmers, merchants, and shippers. Their new position, together with the favour and encouragement shown to them by the European powers with whom they traded, brought them wealth, and with it, access to education and to the power and influence which wealth and education give. In time most of the trade between the Ottoman Empire and Europe passed into hands of Europeans or members of the minorities, mostly Christian and occasionally Jewish.

In the Arab provinces the economic decline seems to have gone further than in Turkey proper. In Iraq, Syria and even Egypt, the area of cultivation and the numbers of population both decreased considerably. In Egypt, for example, the population is said to have dropped from an estimated 8 million in Roman times to about 4 million in the fourteenth century and 3.5 million in 1800. While the main decrease in population seems to have taken place in the countryside, there was some decline also in the cities, and there is evidence that industry not only did not advance but actually fell back. The number of craftsmen and the quality of their work had declined in most of the cities, while some of the major seaports dwindled into insignificance.

To some extent these changes in the Middle East resulted from political factors – notably the breakdown of authority, the emergence of more or less independent local rulers, and the growing damage inflicted in the provinces by indigenous nomads and imported soldiery. In general, the ruling military and bureaucratic groups showed little concern with promoting local economic development, and what few efforts they made were easily thwarted by European economic interests. In part the decline was due also to permanent economic factors, notably the long continuing shortages of timber, minerals and water. The shortage of fuel and energy inhibited the development of transport and industry, and any kind of worthwhile technology. Even such early technological innovations as the water mill, the windmill, and improved harness for the better use of animal traction had little or no impact in the Middle East, which remained far behind Europe in this respect. All this, added to the greater richness of Europe in timber, minerals, water power and transport, helped to weaken the Middle East in relation to Europe and to facilitate the establishment and maintenance of European economic domination in the area.

The decline of the Ottomans was due not so much to internal changes as to their inability to keep pace with the rapid advance of the West in science and technology, in the arts of both war and peace, and in government and commerce. The Turkish leaders were well aware of this problem, and had some good ideas for its solution, but they could not overcome the immense institutional and ideological barriers to the acceptance of new ways and new ideas. As a distinguished Turkish historian put it: 'The scientific wave broke against the dikes of literature and jurisprudence.'[1] Unable to adapt to the new conditions, the Ottoman Empire was destroyed by them, much as was the Soviet empire in our own day.

In comparing the fate of the Ottomans with that of the Soviets, attention has focused mainly on the political and ideological elements – the explosive forces of nationalism and liberalism, the bankruptcy of old ideologies, the collapse of old political structures. In all these, the Russians have indeed been following the path once trodden by the

Turks. If they are fortunate, they will find a Kemal Atatürk to open a new chapter in their national history.

But there is another aspect of the Ottoman decline that suggests a different present-day parallel. The economic weakness of the Middle East, unlike that of the Soviet Union, was not due to an excess of central control. Such control, on the contrary, was almost entirely lacking. There was some economic regulation, mainly at the level of the craft guild and the country market, but in the mobilization and deployment of economic power the Ottoman world had fallen far behind Western Europe. It had also become a predominantly consumer-oriented society.

In contrast, the rise of mercantilism in the producer-oriented West helped European trading companies, and the states that protected and encouraged them to achieve a level of commercial organization and a concentration of economic energies unknown and unparalleled in the East, where – as a matter of fact more than of theory – 'market forces' operated without serious restrictions. The Western trading corporation, with the help of its business-minded government, represented an entirely new force. Thanks to this growing disparity of economic strength and will, Western merchants, later manufacturers, and eventually governments, were able to establish an almost total control of Middle Eastern markets, and ultimately even of major Middle Eastern manufactures.

In the same period, even the trade in manufactured textiles was affected by the expansion of the West, and English merchants brought Indian cotton and other cloths in increasing quantities to the ports of the Ottoman and Persian Empires. Middle Eastern textiles, once highly regarded in the West, were driven first from external, and then even from domestic markets by more cheaply produced and aggressively marketed Western goods. The changing commercial relationship is graphically illustrated in that familiar Middle Eastern indulgence, a cup of coffee. Both coffee and the sugar used to sweeten it were first introduced to Europe from the Middle East. In the last quarter of the seventeenth century coffee was an important item among imports to Europe from the Middle East. By the second decade of the eighteenth century, the Dutch were growing coffee in Java for the European market, and the French were even exporting coffee grown in their West Indian colonies to Turkey. By 1739 West Indian coffee is mentioned as far east as Erzurum. Colonial coffee from the West was cheaper than that coming from the Red Sea area and the supply from there dwindled into insignificance.

Sugar too was originally an Eastern innovation. First refined in India and Iran, it was imported by Europe from Egypt, Syria and North Africa, and was transplanted by the Arabs to Sicily and Spain. Here again the West Indian colonies provided an opportunity which was not missed. In 1671, by order of Colbert, the French built a refinery in Marseilles from which they exported colonial sugar to Turkey. Consumption there increased enormously when the Turks took to sweetening their coffee, perhaps as a consequence of the more bitter flavour of the West Indian bean. Hitherto they had relied largely on Egyptian sugar, but West Indian sugar was much cheaper and soon dominated the Middle Eastern market. By the end of the eighteenth century, when a Turk or Arab drank a cup of coffee, both the coffee and the sugar had been grown in the European colonies and imported by Europeans. Only the hot water was of local provenance. During the nineteenth century, even that became doubtful, as European companies developed the new utilities in Middle Eastern cities.

Western economic domination in the Middle East was buttressed and maintained in a number of ways. While the import of Middle Eastern products to the West was restricted and in some cases excluded by protective tariffs, Western trade in the Middle East was sheltered by the capitulations system, which amounted to a right of free and unrestricted entry. The term 'capitulations' (Latin *capitula*, 'chapters' – i.e. an itemized document) was used in Ottoman times for the privileges granted by the Ottoman and other Muslim rulers to Christian states, allowing their citizens to reside and trade in the Muslim dominations without becoming liable to the fiscal and other disabilities imposed by these Muslim rulers on their own non-Muslim subjects. Privileges of this kind were accorded to the Italian maritime states during the fourteenth and fifteenth centuries. In the sixteenth century the practice was extended to France (1569), England (1580) and other countries. A contemporary translation of the English capitulation of 1580 includes the following provisions:[2]

> We most sacred Musulmanlike Emperor ... most mightie prince Murad Can, in token of our Imperiall friendship, doe signifie and declare, that now of late Elizabeth Queene of England ... that the people and subjects of the same Queene, may safely and securely come to our princely dominions, with their goods and marchandise, and ladings, and other commodities by sea, in great and smal vessels, and by land with their

carriages and cattels, and that no man shall hurt them, but they may buy and sell without any hinderance, and observe the customes and orders of their owne countrey. . . .

Item, if any Englishman shall come hither either to dwel or trafique, whether hee be married or unmarried, he shall pay no polle or head money. . . .

Item, if any variance or controversie shall arise among the Englishmen, and thereupon they shall appeale to their Consuls or governours, let no man molest them, but let them freely doe so, that the controversie begunne may be finished according to their owne customes. . . .

Item, if the ships of warre of our Imperiall highnesse shal at any time goe forth to sea, and shall finde any English ships laden with marchandise, no man shall hinder them, but rather shall use them friendly, and doe them no wrong, even as wee have given and granted articles, and privileges to the French, Venetians, and other Kings and princes our confederats, so also wee have given the like to the English: and contrary to this our divine law and privilege, let no man presume to doe anything.

. . . and, as long as the Queene of England on her part shall duely keepe and observe this league and holy peace, expressed in this privilage, we also for our Imperiall part, do charge and commaund the same so long to be straightly kept and observed.

The relationship was concerned with other things besides commerce. A letter of June 1590 from Sultan Murad III to Queen Elizabeth I – one of many preserved in the Public Record Office – concludes:[3]

When you turn and proceed against the Spanish infidels with whom you are ever in conflict and strife, with the help of God you will be victorious. Do not refrain from making those who come to hand food for the sword and targets for the arrow. Do not omit to inform us of those of your affairs which it is necessary to communicate. For please God – may He be exalted – we on our side will not be idle; we will at the right time take the necessary measures and harass the Spanish infidels, and we will in any case give you help and assistance. Let it be noted.

With the progressive decline in power of the Muslim states and the change in the effective relationship between them and their Christian neighbours, the capitulations came to confer privileges greatly in excess of those originally intended. By the late eighteenth and early nineteen centuries the protection of a European power carried important commercial and fiscal advantages, and the practice grew up whereby European diplomatic missions distributed *berats*, documents or certificates of protection, in abusive extension of their capitulatory rights. Originally these certificates were intended only to protect locally recruited officers and agents of the European consulates. They were by abuse sold or granted to increasing numbers of local merchants who thus acquired a privileged and protected status. The Ottoman authorities tried in vain to curb this abuse. At the turn of the eighteenth and nineteenth centuries the sultan Selim III, unable to beat the consuls of the European powers, decided to join them, and himself issued such *berats* – not to Muslim but to Ottoman Christian and Jewish merchants. These conferred the right to trade with Europe, together with certain legal, fiscal and commercial exemptions and privileges, and were intended to enable Ottoman subjects to compete on more or less equal terms with foreign subjects. Their effect was to create a new privileged class in which Ottoman Greeks, thanks to their maritime skills and opportunities, soon won a position of pre-eminence. Early in the nineteenth century the system was extended to Muslim merchants, but very few availed themselves of it.

There are other examples in history of a relatively simple economy that is stimulated by the commercial impact of a more active and more complex society. In the Middle East, exceptionally, the agents and also the immediate beneficiaries of change, both inside and outside, were themselves outsiders. The foreigners were of course Europeans, but even inside the Muslim countries the main actors, if not actually foreigners, were members of religious minorities, regarded as marginal by the dominant majority society. A common Turkish phrase distinguished between 'Franks', i.e. foreigners from Europe, and 'sweet-water Franks', i.e. the superficially Europeanized local Levantine population.

The predominance of foreigners and members of minorities in financial matters was, in the early years of the twentieth century, overwhelming. In a list of forty private bankers in Istanbul prepared in 1912, those who can be identified by their names include twelve Greeks, twelve Armenians, eight Jews, and five Levantines or Europeans. A similar list of thirty-four stockbrokers in Istanbul includes eighteen Greeks, six Jews, five Armenians and no Turks.

Greeks, Armenians, and Turkish Jews were separated from their neighbours not only by religion but even by language. In the Arabic-speaking countries this division at least was lacking, since both Christians and Jews shared a common Arabic language with their Muslim neighbours. This enabled the new Christian commercial bourgeoisie which arose in and around the port of Beirut from the 1830s onward to develop, by the mid-century, into something previously lacking – a prosperous, educated Arabic-speaking middle class. Though they were still inhibited by their Christian identity from playing any great social or political role, nevertheless their mastery and use of the Arabic language enabled them to make a major contribution to the Arab cultural revival.

The religious minorities were also involved in a second form of Western infiltration – acquisition of positions of power and influence within the countries of the Middle East. After the Treaty of Küçük Kaynarca, the Russians had established a virtual protectorate over the Orthodox Christian communities of the Ottoman Empire. Orthodox Christians formed the overwhelming majority of the inhabitants of the Greek and Balkan provinces, and substantial minorities in Anatolia and in the Syrian lands. The status of protector of Orthodoxy assumed by the tsars thus gave them considerable influence among an important element of the Ottoman population. The French developed a similar protectorate of the Roman Catholic subjects of the sultan. These, though less numerous than the Orthodox Christians, were not insignificant, and in particular included the vitally important uniate Maronite church of Lebanon. In this quest for religious minorities to protect, Britain was at something of a disadvantage compared with her French and Russian rivals. The Protestant communities were insignificantly few, despite efforts by British, German, and American missionaries to add to them. British foreign secretaries from time to time experimented with the idea of extending British protection to other groups, such as the Jews or the Druze, whose claim to such protection – or need for it – might be in doubt, but whose services to the protector could possibly be useful. Germany, as a predominantly Protestant power, was similarly disadvantaged, but eventually solved this problem by extending her protection to the Ottoman Empire as a whole.

Such religious protection took many forms. An obvious concern was for the interests and welfare of Ottoman subjects of the protected religion. In the conditions of the nineteenth century, of Ottoman weakness and European strength manifested in the capitulations system, this amounted to an almost unlimited right of interference in almost every aspect of Ottoman internal affairs. In addition, the religious and educational needs of the Ottoman Christians and Jews were met by an increasingly ramified network of missions, schools, and other educational, cultural, and social institutions. These were mostly Christian, a few Jewish, and some designated as secular, and they attracted a growing number of Muslim as well as minority pupils. Products of Western schools in the Middle East went to universities in the West for their higher education, and from the second half of the nineteenth century Western colleges were established in a number of Middle Eastern cities. Education became an important means of extending the cultural and therefore also ultimately the economic and political influence of the sponsoring power. In this area the French were at first the most successful, followed by the Italians and later by the British, the Germans and the Americans. The Russian effort, though important among the Orthodox Christians, was comparatively small. Western missionaries were able to register few converts among the Muslims, who were their ostensible targets – apostasy is a crime punishable by death in Islamic law – but they had some impact among the Christian populations, and a small number of Orthodox, Armenian, and other Eastern Christians were converted to one form or another of Protestantism or to Roman Catholicism.

Another religious concern of the Powers was the protection of the Christian holy places in Jerusalem and elsewhere in Palestine. For centuries these had been hotly disputed by the local churches, with the Turkish authorities acting as contemptuous but on the whole effective mediators. The involvement of the Great Powers as protectors of their respective churches raised minor local disputes to the status of international conflicts, and played some part in the events leading to the Crimean War.

Protection was exercised through the embassies and consulates which, thanks to the capitulatory system, acquired extensive jurisdiction and powers within the Ottoman Empire. They administered their own laws, and had their own courts, prisons and even post offices.

In the educational effort of Europe in the Middle East one element was particularly important – military instruction. The test of battle had shown that in the current era the military arts of Europe were superior to those of Islam, and perforce the Muslim states had to turn to Europe as pupils. For quite a long time individual Europeans had gone to Turkey to seek their fortunes as military experts or advisers, some of them achieving remarkable careers. But by the latter part of the eighteenth century such private arrangements no longer sufficed. In the autumn of 1793 the sultan sent a message to Paris with a list of the officers and technicians whom he wished to recruit from France. A couple of years later a second and longer list went from Istanbul to the Committee of Public Safety. In 1796 the new French ambassador to Turkey brought a whole group of French military experts with him. Franco-Turkish military co-operation was interrupted by the war of 1798–1802, in which France and Turkey were on opposite sides, but was resumed when they became allies and reached a high level during the Anglo-Russian attack on Turkey in 1806–7.

A new start was made in the 1830s, when the reforming sultan Mahmud II sought the aid of Western governments in modernizing his armed forces. A Prussian military mission arrived in 1835, and a British naval mission in 1838, initiating relationship – which continued through the nineteenth and into the twentieth century.

A parallel development began even earlier in Egypt, where the Ottoman governor Muḥammad ʿAlī Pasha was trying to create an independent principality. He too began by recruiting individual foreign and especially French military and technical experts, and then in 1824 invited a whole military mission from France, where, after the final defeat of Napoleon, many military men were available for employment. This mission was the first of a long series.

In Iran, further from the European centres of power, change was slower. Iran first became involved in European politics during the Napoleonic period, and both France and Britain sent military missions, the first in 1807–8, the second in 1810, to train the Iranian armies. Thereafter a number of Russian, French and Italian officers served as instructors, but with limited effect. The modernization of the Iranian army did not really begin until the twentieth century.

Military instruction came in the main from Western Europe and chiefly from Britain, France and Prussia, later Germany. Some Italians also appear as instructors, and after the end of the American Civil War, a number of American officers whose services were no longer required at home were able to find a career in Egypt. Except in Iran, Russians do not appear as teachers or advisers until the twentieth century.

The ramifications of military instruction were considerable. They included the sending of Middle Eastern pupils to Western military and naval academies, the invitation of Western officers to teach in Middle Eastern staff colleges, the employment of Westerners as advisers, sometimes as executive officers, in the armed forces, and of course the supply from the West of arms, equipment and technological skills. Though this process never approached the scale and significance which it acquired during the 1950s and after, it was nevertheless a factor of some significance in nineteenth- and early twentieth-century power politics.

In the course of the nineteenth century the European powers became more directly active also in the internal economic affairs of the Middle East, which in turn was increasingly involved in the international network of trade and finance. The resulting changes involved almost every aspect of Middle Eastern life.

One immediate consequence was a vast extension of the area of cultivation, by the use of cultivable land which had been neglected for centuries. This was facilitated by the improvement of security conditions, by reclamation, and in many parts, by the construction of extensive irrigation systems. Cash crops were introduced or greatly expanded for export purposes, notably cotton, silk, tobacco, dates, opium, coffee, wheat and barley. The change from subsistence to cash crops, occurring at the same time as the Westernization of the legal system, brought important changes in land tenure, the general effect of which was the decline of village or communal or tribal ownership and the extension of European-style freehold. This agricultural expansion was largely indigenous in origin, initiated partly by governments, partly by a newly emerging class of freehold landowners. Much of the necessary capital, however, came from abroad in the form of loans or investment, and European companies, protected from government control by the extraterritorial privileges of the capitulations, predominated in the exploitation of the resources of Middle Eastern countries.

Foreign enterprise and foreign skills also played a decisive part in the development of services – the telegraph, the main ports of the eastern Mediterranean, the railways of Egypt, Turkey, Syria, and Iraq, as well as such public amenities as water, gas, municipal transport, and later electricity and telephones in the major cities.

Local steamship passenger lines linked Istanbul with the Black Sea and the Aegean, but it was foreign lines that provided the first links with Europe. An Austrian company began operations in 1825, and was soon followed by French, British, Russian and Italian lines sailing between Ottoman and European ports and also between different parts of the Empire. An important new development began in 1837, when regular British steamship services were started linking Europe with Alexandria and India with Suez, with an overland transfer between the two ports for mails, then goods and passengers. At first these were carried in steamboats on the inland waterways and in wheelcarts on the newly built roads. The building of the Egyptian railways from 1851, and still more the opening of the Suez Canal in 1869, made

Egypt once again the main route between Europe and southern Asia, and a nodal point in world traffic. During these years the development of steam navigation in the Caspian Sea and the Persian Gulf linked Iran more closely with both Russia and Western Europe.

A new phase in European financial penetration began during the Crimean War. The Ottoman government had made attempts to raise money by internal loans as far back as the late eighteenth and early nineteenth centuries. The needs and opportunities of the Crimean War encouraged them to seek a new kind of loan, floated on the money markets of Europe. The first such loan, for £3 million at 6% interest, was raised in London in 1854; the second, for £5 million at 4%, was arranged in the following year. Between 1854 and 1874 foreign loans were raised almost every year, reaching a nominal total of about £200 million. During the same period there was a rapid extension of banking activities in the area. During the preceding twenty or thirty years, British and other private bankers had already established themselves in various Mediterranean seaports. From the mid-1850s there was a series of major developments, including the founding of such incorporated banks as the Bank of Egypt (1855), the Ottoman Bank (1856), the Anglo-Egyptian Bank (1864), and others, as well as branches of the major British, French, German, and Italian banks, in the Middle East. These banks were entirely European, and between them dominated the finances of the Middle East. It was not until after the First World War that genuinely Turkish, Iranian, Egyptian or Arab banks were established, and not until after the Second World War that these controlled any significant proportion of total financial business.

Since Turkey was seen as a poor risk, loans were usually granted on very unfavourable terms. The money was for the most part used to cover regular budgetary expenditure, or else was spent on uneconomic development projects. The result was the Crash of 6 October 1875, when the Ottoman government defaulted on its payments of interest and amortization. After some negotiation, agreement was reached with representatives of the European bondholders, and incorporated into a decree of 20 December 1881 setting up a 'Council of the Administration of the Public Debt', directly controlled by and answerable to the foreign creditors. Its duty was to ensure the service of the consolidated Ottoman public debt, for which purpose certain revenues were ceded to the Council by the Ottoman government 'absolutely and irrevocably ... until the complete liquidation of the debt'. By 1911 the total staff of the Council of the Administration of the Debt stood at 8,931 persons, more than that of the Ottoman Ministry of Finance itself. A parallel process of indebtedness, bankruptcy and receivership in Egypt ended with the Law of Liquidation of 1880, assigning half of the total revenues of Egypt to the Egyptian government for administrative purposes, and the rest, apart from a sinking fund, to the service of the debt. In both countries further loans were contracted in the early years of this century, but by this time the various bodies set up by the bondholders to protect their investment ensured that the capital or at least a large part of it was used productively.

Yet amid all these changes, and despite the rapidly expanding activity of European enterprise and its foreign and minority beneficiaries, the position of the mass of the population altered very little. In one respect significant change can be measured – in population where, after centuries of stagnation or decline, the nineteenth century saw the beginnings of a major increase. A few examples must suffice from the figures available to us. The population of Istanbul, Anatolia and the Islands rose from about 6,500,000 in 1831 to 11,300,000 in 1884 and 14,700,000 in 1913. The estimated population of Egypt rose from about 3,500,000 in 1800 to 4,580,000 in 1846; 6,800,000 in 1882; 9,710,000 in 1897; and 11,290,000 in 1907. But there were few signs of improvement in the living standard of the rural and urban working populations, and perhaps even some deterioration. At the same time the social Westernization of the upper classes, without any corresponding change among the lower classes, weakened the complex network of loyalties, obligations, and shared values that had bound them together in the old order, and opened the way to new conflicts and new leaderships.

The military, political and economic weakness of the Ottoman world as compared with Christian Europe has been variously explained. On the one hand, there was the tremendous leap forward of the Western world in the period following the great discoveries, involving a series of technological, economic, social and political changes which had no counterpart in the world of Islam. But European progress is not a sufficient explanation. Within the Ottoman lands themselves many signs of weakness can be discerned. At a time when the governments of Europe were just acquiring wealth and strength to sustain their new role, the sultan was losing all power: in the capital to ministers and courtiers; in the provinces, to autonomous and hereditary rulers under what was becoming a largely nominal suzerainty.

This devolution of power was accompanied by extensive changes in the system of land tenure and taxation. In the traditional Ottoman order, the kingpin of both the military and fiscal agrarian systems was the *sipahi* cavalryman, holding a grant known as a *timar.*

The *sipahi* system was at its height in the early and middle sixteenth century. Thereafter it began to decline, though it did not disappear until the early nineteenth century. As the *sipahis* lost their importance, they were replaced in the field by regular troops and in the countryside by tax-farmers. When *timars* were vacated by the death or dismissal of the *sipahis*, they were with increasing frequency not reassigned to new *sipahis*, but instead re-incorporated into the imperial domain so as to ensure greater tax revenue for the exchequer. These revenues were, however, for the most part not collected directly by state officials. Instead, they were sold as tax-farms, at first on a fixed annual basis, the tax-farmer paying in advance for the right to collect taxes for one year. By abuse, the period for which such a tax-farm was granted became longer and longer, until it finally developed into a system known as *malikâne*, a form of tenure which, though in theory a tax-farm for a limited period, in fact became a form of freehold granted for life and even became heritable and alienable. By the end of the seventeenth century, this system had been introduced to many provinces of the empire, and in the course of the eighteenth, despite attempts to abolish it, it became general.

The *malikâne* system provided an economic basis for the *a'yān*, who became the real rulers of the countryside. The weakness of the central government and its loss of effective control in the provinces helped the *a'yān* to acquire political power and even sometimes to become autonomous local rulers. Tax-farms were converted into freehold in various ways: by purchase or by grant from the government, by prescription, or by simple usurpation in defiance of the authorities.

These *a'yān* were of diverse origins. They included rich landowners, traders, a certain number of *sipahis* who found this a more profitable and less dangerous form of tenure than the military grant and, in time, a whole series of functionaries of the court and the harem, engaged in business on their own account and through agents. The *a'yān* now begin to resemble a freeholding, landed gentry, choosing their own leaders and representatives who were recognized rather than appointed by the government.

As their economic power grew, so the functions of the *a'yān* expanded to include the maintenance of law and order. For this in turn they raised and maintained their own armed forces, some of them even becoming hereditary rulers of definite territories. As they became more powerful, the government in Istanbul found it convenient to delegate to the a'yān, to a very large extent, the conduct of most provincial affairs and the running of some provincial cities. In 1786, the sultan and his government, fearing their growing power, tried to oust them from town government and to appoint city provosts, but they were soon compelled to abolish the provosts and restore the rule of the a'yān.

By this time, the a'yān had become more than a provincial gentry and magistracy. From the beginning of the eighteenth century, local rulers in Anatolia began to assume control of very large areas. These, known as the derebeys, valley lords, were of various origin. Some first appear as provincial functionaries of the central government; others arose from local leading families. Tolerated and at times recognized by the central government, they established autonomous, hereditary principalities in a relationship of vassalage rather than subordination to the sultan. In times of war they served with the other contingents in the sultan's armies, which came to consist, to a large extent, of such quasi-feudal levies. They were given formal titles as governors and intendants by the Porte, but were effectively independent in their own territories. By the beginning of the nineteenth century almost the whole of Anatolia was in the hands of the various derebey families, with only two provinces, Karaman and Anadolu, remaining under the direct administration of Istanbul.

A parallel development took place in the Balkan peninsula. Effective control was exercised by such local rulers as the famous Tepedelenli 'Alī Pasha, the governor of Yannina, and Pasvanoglu Osman Pasha, the governor of Vidin, who raised their own armies, levied their own taxes, coined their own money, and even maintained diplomatic relations with foreign powers. Many of 'Alī Pasha's military as well as civilian retainers were recruited among the Greek population, who thus acquired a taste for independence and the skills needed to exercise it. In the Arabic-speaking regions of the Empire, Egypt had become virtually autonomous, while in Iraq and in central and southern Syria, the governors nominally appointed by the central government in fact acted like independent dynasts, and even contended for power with local tribal and feudal chiefs. In the Arabian peninsula, Ottoman authority had never been firmly established, and it was now openly flouted by the rise of a new dynasty, the House of Saʿūd, inspired by a religious revivalist movement, the Wahhābīs.

By the eighteenth century, Caucasian slaves provided the bulk of the intake of the palace School of Pages, from which a large proportion of the governors and administrators of the Empire still emerged. This does not mean that the Caucasians had entirely replaced men of Balkan origin in the positions they had once held in the governing elite. Significant numbers remained, and in the palace as in the other sections of what had once been the slave establishment, recruitment was opened to freeborn Muslim subjects, at first by abuse, then by accepted custom. The reduction and eventual cessation of the intake of new blood through the *devshirme* was only partially made good by the acquisition of slaves of Caucasian origin. The resulting shortage of suitable recruits for the state service led to a weakening of the barriers which had previously separated the different branches, and to the appearance of men of civilian background in offices such as provincial governor or even grand vizier, previously the perquisite of the military and administrative slave elite.

By the eighteenth century, there were two main civilian career structures in the Ottoman system – one the bureaucracy, often staffed by the descendants of *devshirme* recruits; the other, the religious hierarchy, collectively known as the ulema. In all branches of the service, there was a tendency for professions and careers to become hereditary. This was particularly noticeable among the ulema, who managed to use the Muslim law of pious foundations to preserve and transmit their family property in a period of general insecurity. The point was noted as far back as 1717 by that keen English observer, Lady Mary Wortley Montagu, who remarked of the ulema:[4]

> This sect of men are equally capable of preferments in the Law or the Church, these 2 Sciences being cast into one, a Lawyer and a preist [sic] being the same word. They are the only men realy considerable in the Empire; all the profitable Employments and church revenues are in their hands. The Grand Signor, thô general Heir to his people, never presumes to touch their lands or money, which goes in an uninterrupted succession to their Children. 'Tis true they lose this privelege by accepting a place at Court or the Title of Bassa, but there are few examples of such fools amongst 'em. You may easily judge the power of these men who have engross'd all the Learning and allmost all the Wealth of the Empire. 'Tis they that are the real Authors, thô the Souldiers are the Actors of Revolutions.

Thus, at the same time that the sultan was losing control of the provinces to a newly formed gentry and magistracy, he was also forced to share the central power itself with a new group, or rather groups, of hereditary holders of authority. The long and at first successful struggle of the Ottoman sultans to prevent the formation of a hereditary class of proprietors and even rulers had finally failed; in this time of weakness, new elements appeared that owned the land, collected taxes, dispensed justice and fought with one another for the mastery of the provinces and, ultimately, of the capital and of the sovereign himself.

In the present state of Ottoman historical studies, these groups cannot be identified and defined with any precision. We can, however, detect in the general obscurity certain shifting outlines that suggest, albeit vaguely, the shapes of the warring groups and interests whose clashes and embraces determined the course of events in Istanbul in the late seventeenth and eighteenth centuries.

One of them is the office of the grand vizier, later known as the Sublime Porte, which, as the real power of the sultan and the Imperial Council decreased, became the effective centre both of authority and of government. Under the grand vizier were a hierarchy of senior officials and a large bureaucratic staff with a strong sense of corporate professional loyalty. These offices were the home of many of the great administrative families of the capital whose origins went back to the Balkans. They also provided a career for the free-born, educated Muslim population of the capital and of provincial towns.

The great rival of the vizierate was the Imperial palace – in part also becoming a hereditary social group, but still strongly influenced by new intakes of Caucasian and also of African slaves. The latter were mainly menial, but as eunuchs could reach positions of great power. The Chief Black Eunuch, known as the Aga of the Girls (*Kızlar Agası*), was one of the most influential personages at the Ottoman court. The palace faction enjoyed the immense advantage of controlling access to the person of the sovereign and was often able to exercise vast power in the Empire and even to appoint its own nominees to the Grand vizierate. Historians sympathetic to the vizierate stigmatize such periods of palace domination as 'the rule of odalisques and eunuchs' and condemn the courtiers and their agents as selfish, greedy and irresponsible.

It would be an oversimplification to describe the struggle for power simply as a clash between the Porte and the palace – the bureaucrats and the courtiers. Each was subdivided into many cliques and factions, at times joining in transitory coalitions which crossed the dividing line. There were other interests too that affected the struggle – the janissaries and the religious hierarchy, independent corporations with their own policies and interests; the central and provincial bureaucracy; the provincial notables and princes, many of whom had their agents in Istanbul well endowed with ready cash; the merchants and financiers, chiefly Greek, who though formally excluded from political life had their partnerships and understandings at both the court and the Porte; even the survivors of the feudal cavalry who, though dwindling in numbers and importance, still managed to play a role at certain critical periods.

While courtiers and bureaucrats, slaves and free-born, Caucasians and Rumelians wrangled for the control of the apparatus of government and extortion, the Empire itself, so it seemed to many at the time, lay dying. Yet it did not die. Even in the darkest days of the eighteenth century, the Empire could muster sufficient strength to safeguard almost all its Muslim provinces from permanent loss to foreign or local rivals. What is still more remarkable, it could still find enough men of loyalty and integrity to serve it in the capital and the provinces and to save it from the worst consequences of its own disunity and disorder.

But by the end of the eighteenth century, the sultan and his advisers were well aware that they had reached a crisis. Though the Empire was still resilient enough to recover a brief sovereignty over the rebellious rulers of the provinces, they could not halt the disintegration of territory and the contraction of authority. They knew, too, that their moderate successes in the wars against Russia and Austria were due less to their own merits than to the disagreements and suspicions amongst their enemies, the fear of Prussian expansion and the unknown menace of the new upheaval in France.

CHAPTER 16

RESPONSE AND REACTION

For many centuries, Muslims had been accustomed to a view of history in which they were the bearers of God's truth with the sacred duty of bringing it to the rest of mankind. The Islamic community to which they belonged was the embodiment of God's purpose on earth. The Islamic sovereigns who ruled over them were the heirs of the Prophet and the custodians of the message which he had brought from God, with the God-given duty of maintaining and applying the Holy Law and extending the area in which it prevailed. To this process there were in principle no limits. In the sixteenth century, the Turkish author of the first and for long the only Muslim work on America describes the European discovery and conquest of what he calls 'the New World', and piously hopes that it would, in due course, be illuminated by Islam and added to the Ottoman realm.

Between the Muslim state and its infidel neighbours there was a perpetual and obligatory state of war which would only end with the inevitable triumph of the true faith over unbelief and the entry of the whole world into the house of Islam. In the meantime, the Islamic state and community were the sole repositories of enlightenment and truth, surrounded by an outer darkness of barbarism and unbelief. God's favour to his own community was manifested by victory and power in this world as it had been since the days of the Prophet himself.

These beliefs, inherited from the Middle Ages, had been amply reinforced by the great Ottoman successes of the fifteenth and sixteenth centuries, when the armies of Islam had reached the very heart of Christendom, and were revived again by the transient but sometimes impressive successes won by Muslim arms in the eighteenth century. It was a slow and painful readjustment for Muslims to accept and adapt themselves to a new situation, in which the course of events was determined not by the Muslim state but by the Christian adversary, and in which the very survival of that state might at times depend on the help or even the goodwill of some of the Christian powers.

Defeat in the field is the most cogent and perspicuous of arguments, and it was after the signature of the Treaty of Carlowitz, enshrining the first major Ottoman defeat, that the first attempts were made in Ottoman ruling circles to explore the ways of the West and seek out those deserving of imitation.

At first, the Turks saw the problem primarily in military terms and propounded military remedies. Christian armies had proved superior to them in the field; there might therefore be some advantage to adopting the weapons, the techniques and the methods of training of the victors. Several times in the course of the eighteenth century, the Ottoman government established training schools for European methods of warfare, employing European instructors to teach Turkish officers and cadets. From this small beginning, vast changes in time followed. Whereas previously young Muslims had been accustomed to despise the barbarous and unbelieving Westerners, they now received them as teachers and were compelled to learn their languages and read their books. By the end of the eighteenth century, the young Turkish cadets in the artillery and engineering schools who had learned French in order to read their manuals also found access to other reading matter. Some of the ideas they found proved more explosive than anything that their artillery instructors could offer them.

The military reforms were followed by other breaches in the barrier that had separated the two worlds. In 1729, the long-sustained Turkish resistance to the printing press was at last overcome, and at last a Turkish printing press was authorized. By 1742, when it was closed, the printers had produced seventeen books. They included a treatise on the military arts of the armies of Europe and a lengthy description of France, written by a Turkish ambassador who was there in 1721.

The cultural influence of the West remained very small. The number of books translated was minimal, and most of these dealt with practical, largely political and military matters. European exports, however, were beginning to condition Turkish taste, and European influences can be seen in even so essential a matter as religious architecture, even in an Ottoman imperial mosque. The architecture of a society reveals a great deal about its nature, its condition and its perception of itself. Like the skyscrapers of modern New York or the pyramids and temples of ancient Egypt, the great imperial mosques of Istanbul express the strength and self-confidence of a thriving and expanding society. The Ottoman Empire, like its predecessors in the Middle East, was above all an Islamic state, and its most characteristic and magnificent buildings are without exception places of worship. By comparison, the Topkapı Palace, where the sultans lived for centuries, seems almost insignificant. True, it covered a vast area and housed great luxury, but it consists in the main of a series of small buildings, none of them particularly imposing. It was no doubt in the same spirit that on the accession of a new sultan the celebrating crowds greeted him with cries of 'Sultan, do not be proud, God is greater than you'.

The beginning of a profound change of mood can be seen in the Nuruosmaniye Mosque, built in 1755 at the entrance to the Great Bazaar. In general structure it is an Ottoman imperial mosque in the grand style, but its ornamentation suggests Italian baroque. This alien decoration, in something as central to Ottoman state and society as an imperial mosque, is as startling as would be arabesque decorations in a Gothic cathedral. It is the first sign of faltering self-confidence.

We see many more such signs in the nineteenth century, none perhaps more striking than the Dolmabahçe Palace, built in 1853. Two changes are notable. The first is that it is now the palace, and not the mosque, on which the sultans and their architects lavish their resources and with which they seek to impress the outside world. The other change is the almost complete collapse of the traditional values, standards, and one might even say good taste, that had marked Ottoman buildings in the past. The Dolmabahçe Palace, with its wedding-cake architecture, its vast and lavish decoration and its extraordinary mixture of styles and themes imported from Europe, graphically illustrates the ambitious aims and confused directions of the nineteenth-century reforms.

All in all Western influence remained small and the exposure to European ideas was confined to very small groups of the population; and even this limited intrusion was contained and sometimes reversed by reactionary movements such as that which led to the destruction of the first Turkish printing press in 1742. If military defeat was the main stimulus, its impact was somewhat weakened in the course of the eighteenth century, during which the Ottomans were able to hold their own and, at times, even score some successes. But the stimulus was renewed, with unmistakable force, by the Treaty of Küçük Kaynarca, the loss of the Crimea, and the French conquest of Egypt.

From the early years of the nineteenth century, the Ottoman Empire faced yet another threat to its territorial integrity. In addition to the foreign powers advancing on its borders, there were now local leaders and movements in many parts, seeking autonomy or even independence. Some of these continued a trend already clear in the eighteenth century – the regional autonomies achieved by the *a'yān*, the *derebeys* and a number of insubordinate pashas who managed to carve out principalities for themselves in the provinces which they had been sent to govern. The attempts of the imperial Ottoman government to restore the authority of the capital aroused resistance. At first the resisters achieved considerable successes, and in 1808 a coalition of *a'yān* and *derebeys* convened in Istanbul where they, together with some dignitaries of the central government, signed an agreement of mutual support setting forth their claims. This was ratified, much against his will, by the newly enthroned Sultan Mahmud II. Thus, at the beginning of the nineteenth century the Ottoman sultan was obliged to sign a charter recognizing feudal privileges and regional autonomies in the Ottoman Empire.

In the central provinces of the Empire the sultan was gradually able to restore and strengthen his authority. In the remoter provinces this proved more difficult. In the Arabic-speaking countries in particular – in Arabia, Iraq, Lebanon and above all in Egypt – independent rulers of various kinds contended for real control, and gave only nominal allegiance to their Ottoman suzerain. The famous Muḥammad 'Alī Pasha, governor of Egypt from 1805 to 1848, conducted a diplomatic and even military struggle against the Ottoman sultan, and was prevented only by the intervention of the European powers from utterly defeating him. He was, however, able to make Egypt an autonomous and hereditary principality, and to launch it on the way to modernization. His successors reigned until the mid-twentieth century. They changed their title several times – first from pasha to khedive, to symbolize their quasi-monarchical status within the Ottoman Empire, and then, consecutively, to sultan and, later, king, to proclaim their independence and assert their equality with the Ottoman and, later, the British monarchs.

The century and a half of Western influence and domination in the Middle East, from the end of the eighteenth century to the middle of the twentieth, brought immense changes on every level of existence. To some extent these changes were due to the action or intervention of Western rulers and advisers. These, however, on the whole tended to be cautious and conservative in their policies, and the most crucial changes were due less to Westerners than to Middle Eastern westernizers.

In the economic field, the direct contribution made by Middle

Eastern rulers was comparatively small. In some countries, notably Turkey and Egypt, governments tried from time to time to devise and implement programmes of state-controlled economic development, especially through forced and rapid industrialization, in which they saw the key to Western wealth and power. Such programmes were introduced on a fairly extensive scale during the first half of the nineteenth century but had little permanent effect. During the second half of the nineteenth century, governments turned their attention instead to what has been called the 'social overhead capital', consisting of irrigation works, transport, communications and the like, leaving more directly productive economic activities to private enterprise. With the exception of agriculture, this normally meant leaving it to foreigners and members of minorities.

The main effort of Middle Eastern governments was directed towards two aims: military modernization and administrative centralization. The purpose of these interlinked designs was to restore and maintain the authority of the government, both at home, against separatists and other dissidents, and abroad against increasingly powerful enemies. To achieve these results governments began what developed into an elaborate programme of reform.

Its beginning was purely military – the need to survive in a world dominated by the armed might of Europe. But creating modern armies was more than just a question of training and equipment to be solved by hiring instructors and buying arms. Modern armies needed educated officers to command them – and a reform of education; departments to maintain them – and a reform of administration; factories to supply them – and a reform of the economy; money to pay for them – and a series of far-reaching financial innovations and adventures.

The military reformers had intended no more than to open a sluice in the barrier that had for long separated Islam from Christendom – a sluice with a limited and regulated flow. Instead they started a flood which they could not control. With European weapons and technology and the men who brought them came European ideas, no less disruptive of the old order. The growth of personal communications through education, diplomacy, trade, and other forms of travel helped greatly in the dissemination of these new ideas. They were carried still further by the increasing study of foreign languages among Middle Easterners, the preparation of a growing body of translations and the distribution of these by means of the printing press, and from the 1820s, by periodical and later daily newspapers.

The shattering of the age-old conviction of superiority by the impact of Western arms engendered a deep malaise in Islamic society. This found its first expression in the reform movements, aiming at the modernization of the Muslim army and hence of the Muslim state, and the adoption of certain products of Western civilization, in what was intended to be the limited area of technology. But before long the penetration of alien ideas and still more the intrusion of alien powers evoked a powerful reaction.

At first this took a religious form. Already in the eighteenth century two important new movements expressed, in different ways, the Islamic reaction against the growing power of the West. In their beginnings, both were protests against what was seen as a process of internal decay in Islam – as a falling away from the pristine purity of the faith; both, inevitably, became concerned with foreign encroachment.

One of these movements, the reformed order of Naqshbandi dervishes, was of Sufi origin. Introduced from India to the Middle East, it spread first to the Arab countries, then to Turkey, and finally into the Caucasian lands. In Egypt, an Indian Naqshbandi scholar gave a vital impulse to the revival of Arabic learning and to the beginnings of an Egyptian renaissance, which was aborted by the French invasion. In Arabia, another Indian Naqshbandi wrote of the greatness of the ancient Arabs and the purity of their original Islam, distorted by later accretions. This idea may have contributed to the rise, in central Arabia, of the second major movement of the time, that of the Wahhābīs. These were, however, bitterly opposed to the mysticism of the Sufis, which they regarded as a part of the decay and corruption of the faith of their day. Puritanical in precept, militant in practice, the Wahhābīs conquered much of the Arabian peninsula and by the end of the eighteenth century they were able to challenge the Ottoman Empire on the borders of the Fertile Crescent. Their power was destroyed in 1818, but the Wahhābī faith survived. It enjoyed more than one revival in Arabia and exercised considerable though indirect influence in other Muslim lands. Though the full Wahhābī doctrine found few disciples in the Middle East, the religious revivalism which it represented influenced Muslims in many countries and imbued them with a new militancy in the coming struggle against European invaders.

When the invaders came, the resistance was led and inspired not by sultans or viziers or soldiers or scholars, but by popular religious leaders who represented one or other of these revivalist movements, and were able to evoke strong passions and direct great energies.

It was in the colonial empires – in Russian Central Asia, British India, and French North Africa – that the next phase in the Islamic response to the impact of the West, that of adaptation and collaboration, is most immediately apparent. In all three areas, leaders arose who urged their peoples to learn the languages of their masters and thus gain access to the modern knowledge necessary for their advancement. In the heartlands of the Middle East there were still no foreign masters, but the same lesson was taught and driven home by reforming rulers and modernizing intellectuals.

In the reform movements and activities of the nineteenth century two distinct trends can be discerned, between which there was continuous struggle. One derived from the Central European enlightenment, and brought ideas which were welcome and familiar to authoritarian reformers. They too, like their Central European models, knew what was best for the people and did not wish to be distracted by so-called popular government from the business of applying it. The inert masses, accustomed by ancient tradition to follow and to obey, could not yet, according to this view, be entrusted with their own fate but had to be taught and commanded by those whose historic function it is to teach and to command – that is, the intellectuals and the soldiers.

The other view drew its inspiration from Western rather than Central Europe, and was inspired by doctrines of political and, to a lesser extent, economic liberalism. For the disciples of this trend, first in Turkey and then in other countries, the people had rights which were to be secured, along with the general advancement of the country, by means of representative and constitutional government. Freedom was seen as the true basis of Western power, wealth and greatness.

The word freedom has many meanings. In the early nineteenth century, after the introduction of European political ideas but before the establishment of direct European rule in their countries, Middle Easterners did not yet use it, as later, primarily to denote a group attribute – the absence of alien domination, in other words what might more accurately be termed independence. They used it rather in the Western sense, in relation to the position of an individual within the group – the immunity of the citizen from illegal or arbitrary government action and, by further development of the notion, his right to participate in the formation and conduct of government. The importation, adaptation, and in some measure application of these ideas constitute one of the major political developments of the nine-teenth and early twentieth centuries.

The first tentative experiments with consultative councils and assemblies, all appointed, date back to the early nineteenth century, when both in Turkey and in Egypt councils of this kind were convened to discuss such matters as agriculture, education and taxes. In 1845 the Ottoman sultan even convened an assembly of provincial rep-resentatives, two to be chosen from each province, 'from among those who are respected and trusted, are people of intelligence and knowledge, who know the requisites of prosperity and the charac-teristics of the population'.[1] Despite these fine qualifications the exper-iment led nowhere and was abandoned. Much the same happened in Iran shortly after.

But while the sultan and the shah and the pashas experimented with such nominated advisory bodies, some of their subjects began to play with more radical ideas. Visitors to Europe extolled the merits of parliamentary government which they saw functioning there, and before long the students and official emissaries who had hitherto been the main travellers from the Middle East to Europe were joined by political exiles. By the 1860s and 1870s constitutionalism seemed to be gaining ground. In 1861 the ruler of Tunis, then an autonomous dynastic state under loose Ottoman suzerainty, proclaimed a con-stitution, the first in any Islamic country. It was suspended in 1864, but the trend continued. In 1866 the ruler of Egypt convened a consultative assembly of seventy-five delegates elected on a restricted franchise by indirect collegiate elections for a term of three years. Meanwhile the constitutional movement was growing in Turkey, and its more active supporters, who in 1867 had been compelled to seek refuge in England and France, appeared to triumph when in 1876, amid great fanfare, an Ottoman constitution was promulgated by the new sultan Abdülhamid II.

The first Ottoman constitutional interlude did not last long. Two elections were held, and when Parliament began to show signs of vigour it was summarily dismissed by the sultan. The first Ottoman parliament sat for two sessions of about five months in all; it did not meet again for thirty years.

After the prorogation of the Ottoman parliament by Abdülhamid it was only in Egypt that parliamentary elections of any kind survived. Several assemblies were elected and functioned, and the process con-tinued after the British occupation of 1882. An 'Organic Law' published in 1883 provided for two quasi-parliamentary bodies with restricted electorates, limited powers, and brief and rare meetings. They were merged and given somewhat greater powers in 1913, but the whole business of elections and assemblies ended with the outbreak of war in 1914.

Meanwhile more radical developments had been taking place elsewhere. The victory of constitutional Japan over autocratic Russia in 1905, the first victory in centuries won by an Asian over a European power, brought a message too clear to be denied. It was heard even in defeated Russia, where under popular pressure a form of parliamentary regime was installed. Constitutionalism was the elixir of life, and an immediate dose was required. The first was taken in Iran where in the summer of 1906 a constitutional revolution obliged the shah to convene a national assembly and accept a liberal constitution. Two years later a group of Ottoman officers, commonly known as the Young Turks, compelled the unwilling sultan to restore the constitution of 1876 and thus inaugurated a second, somewhat longer, and much more important interlude of constitutional and parliamentary government in the Ottoman Empire.

These early constitutional reforms were obviously the result of European influence and example, and of a desire to face Europe on equal terms. They also were gestures of propitiation – to qualify for loans and other benefits and at the same time ward off intervention and occupation. They had little success in securing these aims. Neither the Tunisian nor the slightly longer Egyptian parliamentary experiments halted the plunge to bankruptcy, disorder, control and occupation. Some indeed would argue that they accelerated the process.

In the meantime the advance of Europe from both ends continued, and once again the reaction of the Middle Eastern Muslims against these new encroachments was expressed in religious terms. The idea of pan-Islamism, of a common front of the Muslim peoples against the common threat of the Christian empires, seems to have originated in the 1860s and 1870s. It was probably at least in part inspired by the successes of the Germans and Italians in unifying their peoples and countries. There were some in Turkey who thought that the Ottoman Empire, as the most important surviving independent Muslim power, could do what Prussia had done for the Germans and Piedmont for the Italians. Significantly this was seen as achieving a solidarity and unity of all the Muslims, that is to say of a group defined by religion or rather by community, and not of the Turks or of any other ethnic, linguistic, or territorial nation, concepts which would have had little appeal for most Muslims at that time.

A limited and controlled pan-Islamism became official Ottoman policy. It was useful both at home, where it helped the sultan in his appeals to his Muslim subjects for loyalty against subversives of various kinds, and abroad, where it served to win support among non-Ottoman Muslims and especially among Muslim subjects of the European empires. The second task called for a more radical and militant form of pan-Islamism than the officially sponsored Ottoman variety. This was provided by a succession of leaders, some of whom came to exercise considerable influence. For the time being, however, pan-Islamism was not a major factor in the political programmes of the radical elites of the time, being overshadowed by the liberal ideologies which they had learned from Europe and also by a new idea – that of the country or nation.

CHAPTER 17

NEW IDEAS

In September 1862, Âli Pasha, at that time foreign minister of the Ottoman Empire, wrote a letter to his ambassador in Paris in which he gave what diplomats call a '*tour d'horizon*'. He surveyed the diplomatic situation in Europe generally, going from country to country, and ended with Italy, at that time in the throes of the national unification struggle. Âli Pasha observed in his letter:[1]

> Italy, which is inhabited only by a single race speaking the same language and professing the same religion, experiences so many difficulties in its unification. For the moment all it has achieved is anarchy and disorder. Judge what would happen in Turkey if free scope were given to all the different national aspirations. ... It would need a century and torrents of blood to establish even a fairly stable state of affairs.

Âli Pasha was an accurate prophet, though his estimate of 'a century' fell short of the reality. He was, in fact, rather better as a prophet than as an observer of the contemporary scene, since the virus of nationalism which he feared so greatly, one might even say so justly, had already entered the body politic and begun the processes by which it inflamed, enfeebled and finally destroyed the Ottoman Empire.

The source, manner, and time of infection can be determined with a precision that is rare in historical study. It began with the ideas of the French Revolution, promoted energetically by the French and accepted eagerly by a minority – at first minute, but always increasing and at times dominant – of the Ottoman population. Interchange between the worlds of Middle Eastern Islam and Christian Europe was nothing new. Exchanges of commodities and even of technologies had been going on for centuries, sometimes on a very considerable scale. In earlier times, the Middle East had been the supplier and the teacher of new tastes and techniques to Europe. More recently, with the rise of the military and economic power of Europe, the major movement was no longer westwards but eastwards. It had remained, however, almost entirely material, with little or no intellectual aspect. In medieval times, the movement of ideas had been overwhelmingly from East to West, and the poor and backward societies of Western Europe were the pupils of the Islamic world in medicine and mathematics, chemistry and astronomy, philosophy and even theology. But by the end of what Western historians call the Middle Ages, the Islamic East no longer had much to teach to Europe, nor did Europe have any more need for such teaching. Some influences remained, in painting and literature and the arts, but they were comparatively unimportant. The theme of Defoe's *Robinson Crusoe* was probably taken from a medieval Arabic philosophic novel, an English translation of which had been published some years earlier. A French translation of the great Arabic collection of tales known as the *Thousand and One Nights*, published between 1704 and 1717, provoked a whole literature of adaptations and imitations in virtually all the languages of Europe. The music of the Moors in Spain and the Turks in the Balkans had a recognizable impact on both the folk music and later the art music of the European borderlands, while from time to time the visit of an Ottoman ambassador and his suite to one or other European capital launched a new fashion of *turquerie* in architecture, interior decoration, and sometimes dress.

In the opposite direction, intellectual communication was virtually zero. In the Middle Ages Europe had little to offer to the far more advanced and sophisticated societies of Islam. By the time that the intellectual as well as the material balance of power had changed, the Islamic world had lost its earlier receptivity. It was, in particular, immunized against anything coming from Christendom – that is to say, from a society which, according to the Muslim perception, represented an earlier and outdated stage of the religious civilization of which Islam represented the final perfection. There were some cultural imports, principally related to military matters, in which European proficiency was recognized at an early date. These included some geographical and cartographic information, and even an early description and map of the New World. But this information seems to have had little or no impact on intellectual life. The same is true of the very limited amount of historical information required to assist the Ottoman government in its dealings with European powers. The literature available on European history was minimal, and its impact infinitesimal. Such major movements as the Renaissance, the Reformation, the Enlightenment, and the Scientific Revolution passed unnoticed and without effect. Islam had had its own Renaissance some centuries earlier, with significant effects even in Europe. There was no response to the European Renaissance, and no Reformation. All these ideas and others that followed them were seen as Christian and discounted accordingly. They were simply irrelevant – of no interest and of no concern to Muslims.

The French Revolution was the first movement of ideas in Europe which had a significant impact on the Middle East, and which began to change the processes of thought and action of its peoples. One reason for this is obvious. This was the first major upheaval in Europe that did not express its ideas in Christian terms, and that was even presented by some of its exponents as anti-Christian. Secularism as such had no appeal to Muslims; if anything, the reverse. But a movement free from the taint of a rival and superseded religion, and opposed by all the traditional enemies of the Ottomans in Europe, was another matter. It could at least be looked at on its merits, and might even yield the elusive secret of Western power and wealth, about which Muslims were becoming increasingly concerned.

Another contrast between the French Revolution and earlier movements in Europe was that the French took active steps to promote their ideas among the peoples of the Middle East. At first, the response to French revolutionary propaganda was minimal, and confined in the main to the Christian subject peoples. But among these they spread rapidly, and before very long affected the masters as well as the subjects of the Empire. To adopt a simile used by several contemporary Ottoman writers, these new Frankish ideas spread like the new Frankish disease.

Liberty, equality, and fraternity were not entirely new and strange ideas to the peoples of Islam. Fraternity – the brotherhood of the believers – was a basic principle, as was equality between them, untrammelled by ethnic or aristocratic privilege. In the course of human affairs, such privileges inevitably arose in the Islamic lands as elsewhere, but they arose in despite of Islam, not as a part of it, and such privileges never acquired the stability and recognition which they had in Europe.

Equality between believers and unbelievers was another matter. But even that self-imposed disability could at any time be removed by the simple act of conversion. The unequal status of the slave and the woman was not that easily shed, but seems to have aroused no strong feelings at the time nor for long after. Liberated slaves could rise to high office, and the slaves of the sultan were in many ways the real rulers of the empire. As for women, their inferior status – established by divine revelation and enshrined in Holy Law – was for the time being not open to question. The impact of the Holy Law was not entirely negative, since it allowed Muslim women some rights, for example in matters of property, which their Western sisters still lacked. This point was noted by several women visitors from the West.

The abolition of legal chattel slavery was accomplished, in the main, by Western rule, interference, or influence, and did not evoke much concern or debate. The emancipation of women, in contrast, though clearly inspired by Western ideas, owed nothing to Western pressure or interference, and whatever progress was made was due to internal initiatives accompanied by passionate internal debates. And even that limited measure of progress has constituted one of the main grievances of Islamic militants, both traditional and radical. One of the most noticeable consequences of Islamic revival has been the return, by women though not by men, to full traditional attire. In Iran since the Islamic revolution, men have signalled their rejection of the West by wearing Western-style clothes without a necktie. From women considerably more has been required.

In contrast to equality and fraternity, liberty, at least in a political sense, was a new idea. The words 'free' and 'freedom', in Islamic usage, had a primarily legal, secondarily social connotation. A free man or woman was one who was not an owned slave. The term was also used in some contexts to denote certain privileges and immunities, for example from forced labour and other exactions and impositions. The term 'freedom' was not, however, used in the very extensive Muslim discussions of the nature of government and the contrasts between good and bad government. In Muslim tradition, the converse of tyranny was not freedom but justice, and this was seen primarily as a duty of the ruler rather than a right of the subject. The Western concept of citizenship, with the accompanying notions of participation and representation, first became known through the influence, and still more the impact, of revolutionary France.

From quite an early stage, the French Embassy in Istanbul became a centre of propaganda. Revolutionary literature was translated into the various languages of the Empire – Turkish, Arabic, Greek, Armenian – and imported from France or printed in a press set up in the embassy grounds. In 1793, the hoisting of the new tricolour flag of the Republic on two French ships moored opposite Seraglio Point provided the occasion for a solemn celebration. In the words of the

French ambassador: 'The Ottoman and American flags, and those of some other powers that have not soiled their arms in the impious league of tyrants, flew on these two ships.'[2] The prolonged festivities ended when the French and their friends danced 'a republican carmagnole' around the tree of liberty which they had planted in the soil of Turkey, in the courtyard of the French Embassy.

These activities caused some alarm, but principally among the embassies of the European powers rather than among the Turks themselves. An Ottoman historian reports a joint Austrian, Prussian and Russian demand for a ban on the flaunting of tricolour cockades and other revolutionary emblems by the French in Turkey. To this request, the chief secretary of the Sublime Porte replied:[3]

> My friends, we have told you several times that the Ottoman Empire is a Muslim state. No one among us pays any attention to those badges of theirs. We recognize the merchants of friendly states as guests. They wear what headgear they wish on their heads, and it is not the business of the Sublime Porte to ask them why they do so. You are troubling yourselves for nothing.

According to another version, the Ottoman official replied that the Porte did not concern itself with either the headgear or the footwear of its foreign guests. From this and other early documents it would appear that the Turks initially believed that as in the past they were still immunized by their religion against Western contagion.

They were speedily disillusioned. In October 1797, the Habsburg emperor was forced to make peace with the revolutionary France in the treaty of Campo Formio. Among other provisions, the treaty sealed the end of the long history of the Republic of Venice, and divided its possessions between the Habsburg empire and the French Republic. The Ionian Islands, together with the port of Preveza and the adjoining coasts of Greece and Albania, became French. French rule in this area was of brief duration – from 1797 to 1799, and again from 1807 to 1814 – but it had a considerable impact. For centuries past, these territories had been under Venetian, not Turkish rule, but the inhabitants were Greek, and the radical and revolutionary changes introduced during the interlude of French rule could not fail to affect and influence their Greek neighbours in the Ottoman imperial provinces of the Morea.

The French had long presented themselves as the traditional friend of the Ottoman Empire. The old friend now became a new neighbour, and friendship did not survive the shock. Soon, alarming reports began to arrive in the capital from Ottoman Greece about events in the areas under French rule – decrees depriving the nobility of their privileges and freeing the peasants from forced labour, the holding of elections, and, in general, talk of liberty and equality. Most ominous of all, in the words of an Ottoman historian, 'By recalling and evoking the days of the states of ancient Greece, they incited the Orthodox in that region to republicanism, and they set to work to corrupt the minds of the neighbouring subjects of the Ottoman state.'[4]

The lesson was driven home in a more acute form when the French, having conquered Egypt, an overwhelmingly Muslim Ottoman province, with alarming ease and speed, started the same dangerous and subversive talk there about ancient glory and modern freedom.

The combination of these two ideas, mixed in varying proportions for different tastes, proved irresistible. Freedom in the sense of citizenship was an unfamiliar and acquired taste, with at first limited appeal. Its potency was enormously increased when it was mixed with two other new ideas imported from Europe – patriotism and nationalism, the acceptance of country and nation instead of religion as the determinants of identity and loyalty and therefore of legitimacy and allegiance.

The danger – especially its secularist implications – did not pass unnoticed or unopposed. A contemporary refutation distributed in both Turkish and Arabic by the sultan's government warns its readers that:[5]

The French ... do not believe in the unity of the Lord of Heaven and Earth ... but have abandoned all religion ... They ... pretend that ... there is no resurrection and no reckoning, no examination and no retribution, no question and no answer ... They assert ... that all men are equal in humanity and alike in being men; none has any superiority or merit over any other, and every one himself disposes of his soul and arranges his ... life. And in this vain belief and preposterous opinion, they have erected new principles and set new laws, and established what Satan whispered to them, and destroyed the bases of religions, and made lawful to themselves forbidden things, and permitted to themselves whatever their passions desire, and they have enticed into their iniquity the common people, who are as raving madmen, and sown sedition among religions, and thrown mischief among kings and states. With lying books and meretricious falsehoods, they address themselves to every party and say: 'We belong to you, to your religion and to your community' ... They are wholly given up to villainy and debauchery, and ride the steed of perfidy and presumption, and dive into the sea of error and impiety, and are united under the banner of Satan.

The recurring reference to Satan to designate such a challenge is revealing. In the words of the final chapter of the Qur'ān (114:5), Satan is 'the insidious whisperer who whispers in the hearts of men'. The same theme reappears in late twentieth-century attempts to counteract the attraction of European and later American ideas and lifestyles.

The traditional political and social order which flourished in the Ottoman Empire and, with some modifications, in the realms of the shahs of Iran, had its roots in classical Islamic law and custom, and beyond that in the remoter civilizations of the ancient Middle East. As in other religious cultures, it was based frankly on inequality, since it would be inappropriate and indeed absurd to accord equal treatment to those who accept God's final revelation and those who wilfully reject it. Some modern apologists, in justly praising the religious tolerance of traditional Islamic regimes, have described it as a system of equal rights. It was not, and such equality would indeed have been seen at the time not as a merit but as a dereliction of duty. In refusing equality to the unbeliever, the Islamic state was following the common practice of religions in power. Where it differed from most others was in according to these unbelievers a recognized status in society, defined and maintained by Holy Law, and accepted by the mass of the Muslim populations. This was not equal status, but it did provide a level of toleration which in states guided by other dispensations was not achieved until religion was disestablished or, at the very least, deprived of much of its influence in public affairs. Muslim religious tolerance was of course limited to monotheists who accepted what Islam recognized as earlier revelations. In practice, in the Middle East this meant Christians of various denominations, and Jews. In Iran there was also a small surviving community of Zoroastrians. In the Ottoman Empire, these minorities were constituted into what were known by the name of *millet*.

A *millet* was a religio-political community defined by its adherence to a religion. Its members were subject to the rules and even to the laws of that religion, administered by its own chiefs, naturally in so far as these did not conflict with the laws and interests of the state. In return for this measure of religious freedom and communal autonomy, non-Muslim *millets* owed allegiance to the state and accepted the limitations and disabilities of *dhimmi* status.

In the Ottoman Empire, there were four major *millets*; in order of ranking, the Muslims, the Greeks, the Armenians, and the Jews. All four were defined exclusively in religious terms. The Muslim *millet*, also known as '*millet-i hakime*', the dominant *millet*, included speakers of Turkish, Arabic, Kurdish, Albanian, Greek, and several Balkan and Caucasian languages.

The second *millet*, that of the Greeks, was equally diverse. As well as ethnic Greeks, it included the followers of the Orthodox Church of many other origins – Serbs, Bulgars, Romanians, and Albanians in Europe; Arabic and Turkish speakers in Asia, who by Western classification might be called Christian Arabs and Turks.

The third *millet*, that of the Armenians, was much more homogeneous, and consisted, in the main, of members of the Armenian nation who were adherents of the Armenian Church. It included, however, a considerable number of Turkish-speakers, who wrote Turkish in Armenian characters. It also included, at certain periods, followers of the Coptic Church of Egypt and the Jacobite Church of Syria, linked with the Armenian Church by their monophysite Christology. It is noteworthy that neither the Greek nor the Armenian *millet* included Uniate or other Catholic Greeks or Armenians, or later, converts to Protestantism from either group.

The Jewish *millet* included Spanish-speaking immigrants who fled from Spain before and after the edict of expulsion of 1492, the native Arabic-speaking Jewish communities of Syria and Iraq, and the Greek-speaking Jews of the Morea, as well as smaller communities speaking several other languages.

Thus each of these religiously defined *millets* included a variety of ethnic and sometimes also tribal groups. These internal divisions were not without importance. They formed the basis of solidarity groups in political, bureaucratic, commercial and social rivalries. They gave rise to a variety of ethnic stereotypes and prejudices of a familiar kind, attested in literary sources for centuries, and still familiar at the present day. But when the classical *millet* system was still functioning in accordance with its own inner logic, such ethnic solidarities did not define basic identity, nor did they determine ultimate allegiance. The people whom we call, and who now call themselves, Turks and Arabs, did not describe themselves by these names until fairly modern times. The language was known as Turkish, but the civilized citizens of Istanbul and other cities did not call themselves 'Turk', reserving that epithet for the primitive peasants and nomads of Anatolia. Similarly, the Arabic-speaking inhabitants of Egypt and the Fertile Crescent called their language Arabic, but reserved the substantive 'Arab' for the Bedouin inhabitants of the desert fringes. It was only in modern times, under the impact of European ideas of nationality, that literate city-dwellers began to describe themselves by these ethnic terms.

The impact of these European ideas was naturally stronger and more immediate among the Christian peoples of the Ottoman Empire. First, the Greeks and Serbs, later the other Balkan peoples, and eventually the Armenians, encountered and responded to the new and potent ideologies of nationalism. Even the Jews, the smallest, weakest and least disaffected of the non-Muslim minorities, in time developed their own nationalism. In 1843, a rabbi called Yehuda Alkalai wrote a little book in which he advanced the novel idea that the Jews should return to the Holy Land and rebuild it by their own efforts without waiting for divine redemption. Rabbi Alkalai was born and lived in the Ottoman city of Sarajevo.

During the nineteenth century, the Christian minorities in the Ottoman Empire pursued three different and ultimately irreconcilable objectives. The first of these was equal citizenship in the Ottoman state, that is to say equal rights with the Muslim majority. This idea of equal citizenship regardless of religion was urged on the Turks by the European powers, sometimes in striking contrast with their own procedures at home; it was embraced by the Ottoman liberals and reformers. Anything less was seen as demeaning and unacceptable by the standards of enlightened opinion at the time.

It was not only new ideas that made the old inequalities unacceptable; it was also a new prosperity. During the Revolutionary and Napoleonic wars, and in the early years of the nineteenth century, the non-Muslim communities on the whole did pretty well. They had a higher level of education than was usual among the Muslims; they had the advantage of easier communication with the outside world. As a result, they were growing more and more prosperous. All this made the social and political inferiority imposed on them by the old order increasingly irksome. The equalization of rights was formally enacted in a series of major reform edicts promulgated by the Ottoman government in the course of the nineteenth century. The results fell somewhat short of the enactments, but were by no means inconsiderable.

The second objective pursued with increasing energy by more and more of the Ottoman Christians was that of independence, or at least autonomy within a national territory of their own. In the course of the nineteenth and early twentieth centuries, first the Serbs and Greeks and then the other peoples of the Balkan peninsula were able to establish sovereign independent states in what they regarded as a part of the national territory – all of them with irredentist claims on their neighbours and on the remaining Ottoman territories. The position of the Armenians, scattered through almost all the Ottoman dominions in Asia but forming a majority in none of them, was far more difficult. Much of the special bitterness of the Armenian struggle derived from the fact that, unlike the Balkan peoples and later the Arabs and the Jews, they had never achieved a sovereign state in modern times – never, that is, until the collapse of the Soviet Union and the attainment of genuine independence by the former Soviet Republic of Armenia.

The third aim, rarely avowed but nevertheless tenaciously pursued, was the retention of the privileges and autonomies which the *millets* had had under the old order – the right to the maintenance and enforcement of their own religious laws, to the control of their own educational systems in their own languages, and generally to the maintenance of their own distinctive cultures. The introduction in the nineteenth century, among other European innovations, of conscription, added an important item to the list, since now what had previously been the demeaning disability of exclusion from bearing arms became the valued privilege of exemption from compulsory military service. The retention of the old polltax, renamed the military service exemption tax, seemed a small price to pay for this privilege.

In the long run, these three objectives were incompatible. Even in the short run, there were some immediate disadvantages. Equal citizenship meant levelling down as well as up. A contemporary Ottoman observer, Cevdet Pasha, in an account of the promulgation of the great reform edict of February 1856, notes:[6]

The patriarchs ... were displeased. ... Whereas in former times in the Ottoman state, the communities were ranked, with the Muslims first, then the Greeks, then the Armenians, then the Jews, now all of them were put on the same level. Some Greeks objected to this, saying, 'The government has put us together with the Jews. We were content with the supremacy of Islam.'

This response on the part of 'some Greeks' was understandable.

During the seventeenth and eighteenth centuries, the Greek aristocracy of the capital had established an almost symbiotic relationship with the Ottoman state. In particular, the group of patrician families known as the Phanariots, from their residence in the Phanar district of Istanbul, in the neighbourhood of the Greek patriarchate, virtually monopolized a number of important positions in the Ottoman service. These included the office of Grand Dragoman of the Sublime Porte – nominally a mere interpreter, but in fact for most day-to-day affairs in charge of the foreign relations of the Empire. Every Ottoman ambassador sent to Europe was accompanied by his Greek interpreter from the office of the Grand Dragoman, who similarly conducted much of the business of the embassy. Other positions held by the Phanariots included the governorships of the two Danubian principalities which later formed the Kingdom of Romania.

The demand for independence, and still more the attainment of independence, inevitably raised doubts about the loyalty and reliability of the non-Muslim subjects, and in particular of the non-Muslim servants of the state. The change came slowly. At the beginning of the Greek insurrection which became the Greek War of Independence, the Grand Dragoman of the Porte was summarily hanged on a charge, probably unfounded, of intelligence with the rebels. As late as 1840, when the Ottomans opened their first diplomatic mission in Athens, their first envoy was a Phanariot Greek, Kostaki Musurus, who later became Ottoman ambassador in London. But the Ottoman Greeks as a whole lost and never regained the positions of trust and power which they had previously enjoyed in the Ottoman state.

Meanwhile there were other changes in the relative positions of the minorities. In the sixteenth century, when Jews were the only community possessing European knowledge and skills but not suspected of sympathy with the European enemies of the state, successive Ottoman rulers had found them useful in both economic and political matters. But Jews, more than any other minority community, were caught up in the decline of Ottoman power. Unlike Ottoman Christians, they could not count on the favour of European merchants and the protection of European governments. Unlike them again, they did not, until the second half of the nineteenth century, experience any educational or intellectual revival such as those which had revitalized the Christian communities. In business and in government they were gradually replaced, both in the capital and in the provinces, by Christians, that is to say, Greeks, Armenians, and an important new element, the Arabic-speaking Christian minorities of the Levant.

Of these, the Greeks were becoming increasingly suspect, while the Arabic-speaking Christians were still confined to one rather remote region of the Empire, and had not yet attained their subsequent prominence and influence. The main beneficiaries of these changes were the Armenians. Long known as *millet-i Sadika*, the faithful *millet*, they were regarded, not only by the Ottomans but also by Western observers, as the minority group most loyal to the Ottoman state. Like the Greeks before them, they profited from their Western educational and commercial opportunities, and prospered accordingly. As late as the early years of the twentieth century, an Armenian leadership co-operated with the Young Turk committees in overthrowing the despotic rule of Sultan Abdülhamid II, and in accomplishing the Young Turk revolution of 1908. In the post-revolutionary government there was even, for a while, an Armenian minister of foreign affairs.

But for Armenians, as for Greeks, the old symbiotic relationship ceased to be possible. As with the Greeks, the new prosperity brought better education and a cultural revival, making them more receptive to new ideas from the outside world. These came from both West and East, often with conflicting and contradictory messages; from the West, national independence and liberal democracy and, through the rapidly expanding mission schools, a feeling of Christian reassertion; from the East, both the proffered protection of the Russian state and the message – and method – of subversion of the Russian revolutionaries. All these ideas found disciples, for whom the status of *dhimmī*, even if well-appointed, was no longer tolerable.

The visible decline of Ottoman power raised new hopes. The Bulgarian crisis of 1876, followed by the defeat of the Ottoman Empire and the involvement of the powers in its internal affairs, seemed to show the way to their fulfilment. Article 61 of the Treaty of Berlin (1878), retaining the provision of article 16 of the superseded Treaty of San Stefano, is at once vague and specific. In it, the Ottoman government 'undertakes to carry out, without further delay, the improvements and reforms demanded by local requirements in the provinces inhabited by the Armenians, and to guarantee their security against the Circassians and Kurds. It will periodically make known the steps taken to this effect to the [European] Powers, who will super-intend their application.'

The clear message of the concluding sentence was reinforced by events. The Bulgars, like the Greeks before them, had won their

independence through the painful but effective sequence of insurrection, repression, and intervention. By this same road, so it seemed
at the time, an independent Armenia might also be achieved. Agitation
led to armed action, and rekindled long dormant religious and ethnic
hostilities. From 1890, and especially in 1895–6, the grim cycle of
rebellion and repression, terror and massacre raged in eastern Turkey
and even, briefly, affected the capital. Great numbers of Armenians
were killed, many of them by the Hamidiye, a locally raised irregular
force authorized by the Sultan Abdülhamid II to deal with Armenian
insurgents and with any suspected of helping, hiding, or sympathizing
with them. The effect was to encourage, not discourage, the revolutionary movements. Raiding and warfare between Christian, i.e.
Armenian, and Muslim, i.e. Turkish, Circassian and Kurdish villagers
and nomads became endemic.

The Armenians were in significant respects worse off than the Balkan
Christians who preceded them in the struggle for independence. The
Ottoman towns and regions in which they formed majorities were
scattered, and no longer cohered into a national homeland like Greece
or Bulgaria. In all the provinces where they lived they had become
minorities, among Muslim majorities increasingly disquieted by
Armenian aspirations and activities. The Armenian heartlands, with
their ancient capital, had been incorporated in the empire of the tsars,
who might variously offer patronage or incitement but who had no
interest in a free Armenia.

In time, even the Muslim peoples of the Empire – Turks, Arabs and
others – lost their previous immunity and succumbed to the infection
of European ideas – liberal, patriotic and nationalist.

These ideas, which did so much to undermine the traditional
structure of legitimacy and allegiance and thus to destroy the old
political order, came in two stages, first in the form of patriotism, from
Western Europe, later, in the form of nationalism, from Central and
Eastern Europe.

In the traditional Islamic world, as in Christendom, nations and
countries often had a strong sense of national and regional identity.
The three major peoples of Middle Eastern Islam, the Arabs, the
Persians and the Turks, were proudly conscious of their national
heritage – their languages and literatures, their history and culture,
their presumed common origins, their distinctive manners and
customs. There was also a natural attachment to the land of one's
birth – love of country, local pride, homesickness, are all familiar in

327

Islamic as in Western literature. But these carried no political message, and at no time before the intrusion of Western ideas was the idea accepted or even known that the nation or the national homeland was the unit of political identity and sovereignty. For Muslims, their identity was the Faith, and their allegiance belonged to the ruler or dynasty that ruled over them in the name of that Faith.

Both patriotism and nationalism were alien to the world of Islam. Alike in the titulature of monarchs and in the writings of historians, nation and country neither delimited sovereignty nor defined identity. The introduction of these ideas, as Âli Pasha observed, was devastating in its impact.

Patriotism – not just the natural love of one's place of birth, but a political and, if necessary, military duty owed to one's country and payable on demand to its government – is deep-rooted in Western civilization, with its origins in ancient Greece and Rome. In Britain, France, and later the United States, it became associated with two other ideas: the unification of the diverse elements of the population of the country in a single national allegiance, and the growing conviction that the people, rather than Church or State, is the true and only source of sovereignty.

Patriotism welded the numerous peoples that inhabited Britain and France – sometimes speaking different languages, sometimes professing divergent religions – into united and powerful nations. Some Ottoman observers of the European scene felt that such an idea could also serve to bind together the different ethnic and religious communities of the Ottoman Empire in a common loyalty to their homeland and, as a matter of course, to the Ottoman state which governed that land.

The patriotic idea was taken up at a slightly later stage in Egypt, which had many advantages for this purpose. Egypt, more than any other country in the region, is sharply defined by both geography and history. Consisting of the valley and delta of a single river, it possessed, despite its Arabization and Islamization, a continuing identity through the millennia and a degree of homogeneity and centralization that were unique in the region. The progress of this new idea of patriotism defined by country was also helped by the ambitions of the Khedivial dynasty, which had established a virtually autonomous state in Egypt under the nominal suzerainty of the Ottoman sultanate. The khedives had an obvious interest in an ideology which would promote the idea of a distinctive Egyptian entity, to be expressed in separate nationhood and statehood. It was much easier to see Egypt as a country, as a nation in the Western sense of the word, than the polyglot and pluralistic Ottoman Empire of the nineteenth century. But even in Egypt, the acceptance of this new identity was slow, gradual, and contested, and has by no means been fully accepted by all Egyptians even at the present day.

From the mid-century onwards, patriotism was followed and in large measure superseded by a very different idea – nationalism. Patriotism had served well in Western Europe, where country and state on the one hand, and nation on the other, became virtually identified. It did not fit the very different conditions in Central and Eastern Europe – the fragmentation of Germany, the ethnic diversity of Austria-Hungary, the 'prison-house of nations' of the empire of the tsars. Patriotism in such a situation could mean support for the status quo – and for increasing numbers, that was becoming unacceptable. The idea of the nation, defined not by country and status but by language, culture, and presumed common descent, corresponded much more closely to the realities of their everyday life. It also corresponded much more closely to the realities of the Middle East, where nationalism of the Middle European kind was at once more intelligible and more acceptable than the liberal patriotism of the West.

Both patriotic and nationalist ideas, when introduced to the Middle East, were associated with libertarian and opposition movements. In general, patriotism tended to reinforce, nationalism to subvert, the existing political order. For the patriot, the independence of his country is axiomatic, and freedom is concerned with the status of the individual in the country. For the nationalist, the state may be alien and oppressive, and both country and nation subject to foreign, sometimes also divided rule. Freedom means the ending of these aberrations and the achievement of national independence and unity.

The first to feel the influence of these new ideas were the non-Muslim subjects of the Empire – more open to ideas emanating from Christian Europe, more easily persuaded that the government that ruled them was an alien tyranny. And not only the government. The same process can be seen within the Greek *millet*, which, under the old dispensation, had united all Orthodox Christians of the Empire. In the nineteenth century, non-Hellenic adherents of the Greek Orthodox Church began to chafe under an ecclesiastical authority whose higher ranks of which were occupied almost entirely by ethnic Greeks. First the Balkan peoples, then later – with rather less success –

Arabic-speaking Orthodox Christians in Syria, demanded a greater say in their own communal affairs, and in their ecclesiastical organization. The new nationalist ferment was disrupting the Greek *millet*. It later destroyed the Ottoman Empire.

In Iran, more distant from Europe and cushioned by the Russian and Ottoman empires against the immediate impact of the West, the influence of Western ideas was slower, later, and weaker. The terrain, too, was in some respects less favourable. The shahs, like the sultans, ruled over a diverse population, professing several religions and speaking a number of languages. But the role of these linguistic and religious minorities was far less important in Iran than in the Ottoman Empire, and at no time did they constitute a comparable threat to the established political and social order. By comparison with the Ottoman situation, the non-Muslim minorities were less numerous, less prosperous, more subdued. The Jews and Zoroastrians were culturally integrated, speaking only Persian, and with historical roots going back to pre-Islamic times. But legally and socially they were isolated, and politically powerless. The only Christian community of any size was that of the Armenians. In most respects they were far better placed than their Jewish and Zoroastrian fellow subjects. But unlike them, they were separated from the Persians not only by religion but also by the proud possession of a separate ethnic, linguistic, and cultural identity. The non-Muslim communities in Iran were also organized in their separate communities with a certain degree of autonomy, but these communities were insignificant compared with the *millets* of the Ottoman Empire.

At first sight it might have seemed that the ethnic and religious minorities among the Muslims would be of greater importance. There was a small Sunni minority, and a more active minority of adherents of the new Bahā'ī faith. But the former were quiescent, and the latter subject to severe constraints. Persian speakers comprised not much more than half of the population of Iran, the remainder being made up of a variety of ethnic minorities – Azeris and Kurds in the northwest, Kashgai and Arabs in the southwest, Turkmen in the northeast, Baluchi in the southeast. Many of these spoke Turkic languages related to those spoken beyond the frontiers in the Ottoman Empire and in the Transcaucasian and Central Asian dominions of the tsars. But in fact, ethnic differences were far less important than among the Ottomans. All these peoples were Muslims, most of them Shī'ites, and they were bound by ties of religious loyalty and cultural affinity far stronger than the new notions of nationality that were drifting in from Europe.

Yet in many ways, Iran was a country well suited to the reception and acceptance of the new ideas – if not of nationalism, then assuredly of patriotism. The Iranians, unlike the peoples of the Fertile Crescent, of Egypt, and of North Africa, which became the Arab world, had retained an awareness of their pre-Islamic past, and a certain pride in its achievements. Their memories of that past were more mythic than historic, owing more to legend and to epic than to serious historical evidence, but they were no less vivid for that, and these memories retained an important place in the literature, the art, the self-perception of Persians everywhere. Again unlike the countries of the Arab world, they had retained their own language – written in the Arabic script, with a large vocabulary of Arabic loan-words, but still basically and unmistakably Persian and not Arabic. Since the rise of the Safavid dynasty at the beginning of the sixteenth century, they had formed a separate realm, united under a single royal government and clearly marked off from their neighbours by their Persian language and culture, and still more by their Shī'ite faith, which since the rise of the Safavids had been first the official and then the dominant religion of the country. All their neighbours – the Ottomans, the Muslim states of Central Asia, of Afghanistan, of India – were Sunni, and their Shī'a faith brought sharp contrast and permanent conflict with these neighbours. Patriotism came late to Iran, and when it came it exercised an irresistible appeal even for the anti-Western, anti-modern, anti-secular leaders of the Shī'ite radical movements.

On 9 January 1853, the Tsar of All the Russias entered into a conversation with the British ambassador, Sir George Hamilton Seymour, at a reception in St Petersburg. Speaking of the Ottoman Empire, according to Seymour's report, the tsar remarked: 'We have a sick man on our hands, a man gravely ill. It will be a great misfortune if one of these days he slips through our hands, especially before the necessary arrangements are made.'[7] Seymour suggested that the sick man should be treated with gentleness and helped to recover. What was needed, he said, was a physician, not a surgeon.

There were many physicians, both at home and abroad, and despite their sometimes acrimonious disagreements, they seemed to be making some progress in restoring the sick man to health. With time and tranquillity, they might even have succeeded. But neither time nor tranquillity was allowed to them.

CHAPTER 18

FROM WAR TO WAR

For more than a century until its final dissolution, the Ottoman Empire was engaged in almost continuous warfare against both internal and external enemies. One of these wars, fought in 1821–3, was against Iran – the last of the long series waged between the two countries since the beginning of the sixteenth century, to decide which of them was to be the dominant power in the Muslim Middle East and, in the second place, where precisely the frontier between them was to lie. The frontier was finally stabilized and eventually demarcated by a joint commission. It later formed the eastern frontier of the republics of Turkey and Iraq, though with the latter some border disputes remained to be settled. The Ottoman–Iranian contest for regional hegemony was resolved by the eclipse of both contenders and their replacement by external powers, whose rivalries and struggles, sometimes inside, sometimes outside the region, dominated its political history for almost two centuries. It was against these competing outside powers and their local protégés that the Ottoman Empire fought a long, bitter and finally unsuccessful rearguard action.

Many wars were fought against enemies within the Empire. Some were against nationalist movements seeking independence. All these movements were Christian; almost all of them were ultimately successful, with external help. Another kind of rebellion was led by ambitious Ottoman pashas seeking to profit from the disarray of the Empire and to carve out autonomous principalities in the provinces that they governed. The most successful was Muḥammad 'Alī Pasha, who, while remaining nominally under Ottoman suzerainty, founded a new dynasty ruling a quasi-independent state in Egypt. Other pashas achieved similar autonomies in Iraq and Syria, though of smaller extent and briefer duration.

Most of these pashas, though operating in Arab territories, were not Arabs but Turkish-speaking Ottomans of Balkan or Caucasian origin. Only in two areas did Arabic-speaking leaders manage to gain some regional autonomy. One was Lebanon, where local rulers, some

Christian, some Druze, managed to create a virtually autonomous principality in the mountain, which formed the nucleus of the later Republic of Greater Lebanon. This principality, and the adjoining areas still under Ottoman rule, saw from the mid-century the beginnings of an Arab cultural and economic renaissance.

The other centre of Arab activity was the Arabian peninsula, especially in the Gulf area, disputed between Ottoman, Iranian, and, increasingly, British power. From the late eighteenth century onwards, tribal and regional chiefs were able to turn these rivalries to their advantage and secure a large measure of autonomy. Notable among them was the principality of Kuwait – an Arabic diminutive of an Indian word meaning fortress – where the ruling Ṣabāḥ family gained power around 1756.

Only one Arabian movement challenged the legitimacy of the Ottoman state, and that was Wahhābism. Its founder, a theologian in Najd called Muḥammad ibn ʿAbd al-Wahhāb (1703–1787), called for a return to the pure, authentic Islam of the Prophet, and the rejection of the accretions that had corrupted and distorted it – superstitions, false beliefs, evil practices, and the regimes that upheld and encouraged them. Among his converts was Muḥammad ibn Saʿūd (correctly ibn al-Suʿūd), the emir of Darʿiyya in Najd. According to some narratives, Muḥammad ibn ʿAbd al-Wahhāb instructed his converts both in his doctrines and in the use of firearms. From about the middle of the eighteenth century, these new warriors of the faith, led by the military skill of Ibn Saʿūd and inspired by the religious teachings of Ibn ʿAbd al-Wahhāb, conquered much of Arabia and in time even threatened the borderlands of Syria and Iraq. Their struggle to purify the faith resembled, or was presented as, a renewal of the original rise and expansion of Islam in the days of the Prophet and his immediate successors. But even the weakened Ottoman Empire, despite all its many problems, was able to repel the Wahhābī Saudi attack without undue difficulty, succeeding where the great empires of Byzantium and Persia had failed. In the seventh century, attackers and defenders used much the same weaponry. In the eighteenth and nineteenth centuries, the Ottomans had artillery.

The Ottoman armies were strong enough to crush rebellious Bedouin, but not to repel the European powers. Some foreign wars developed from the involvement of outside powers in domestic rebellions; others arose from the rivalries among the powers themselves. Between 1806 and 1878, Russia went to war with the Ottomans four times, and all four wars ended with significant loss of territory. The Ottoman defeats would have been far worse, had the Russians not been obliged by Western intervention or involvement to relinquish a part of their gains.

These interventions illustrate an important change – the transformation of the Ottoman retreat into what diplomatists began to call 'the Eastern question'. In this phase, the survival of the Empire was due not only to the stubborn but ultimately unavailing defence offered by the Ottoman forces, but to this new factor – the involvement of other European powers concerned about Russian aggrandizement, and the increasing skill of the Ottoman government in recognizing these rivalries and taking advantage of the opportunities that they offered.

As far back as 1699, after the second and final retreat from Vienna, when the Ottomans were negotiating the first treaty which they had to sign after a defeat, they benefited from the advice and help of the British and Dutch ambassadors in Istanbul, both representing governments concerned about the advancing power of Austria. In the course of the nineteenth century, not only diplomatic but also military involvement became normal. During the Revolutionary and Napoleonic Wars, the Turks were helped by Britain against France and later by France against Russia. In 1829, it was a Prussian mediator who persuaded the victorious Russians to moderate their terms. In the Crimean War, Britain and France fought side by side as allies of the Ottomans against Russia. In 1878 British diplomatic intervention was able to alleviate the political consequences of the Ottoman military defeat, postponing the dissolution of the Empire until the following century. In the meantime, the Western allies also secured a preliminary share of the sick man's heritage – not indeed directly administered Ottoman provinces, but more distant lands under some local administration and a vague Ottoman suzerainty.

In the nineteenth and early twentieth centuries, the Iranians faced many of the same challenges as the Ottomans. Their task was on the whole simpler, though no less dangerous. In 1806–7 Iran was briefly involved in the European struggle when Napoleon sent a mission to Tehran offering to help the shah, both to recover the lands lost to the Russians in the north and to attack the British in India to the south. But after the Franco-Russian peace signed at Tilsit in 1807, the French lost interest. The Russians and the British remained, and for more than a century, the history of Iran was dominated by the rivalry of the two greatest European empires in Asia. Russian conquests, at the expense of local rulers and of the shah, made Russia the immediate northern neighbour of Iran first on the western then on the eastern side of the Caspian Sea. The consolidation of British rule in India brought British power to the southeastern border of Iran, and British influence far beyond it. As Russian forces advanced southwards, and Russian influence grew in Tehran, the British saw this advance as a threat to their imperial interests, and made great efforts to counter Russian encroachments by extending their own.

The French had, in effect, withdrawn; the Germans did not appear in force until the First World War, when they moved in from the territory of their Ottoman allies. Until then, the Iranians, unlike the Ottomans, had faced only two imperial powers, Russia in the north and Britain in the south.

In some respects, the Iranians were better situated than the Ottomans. Their religious minorities were too small to matter, especially after the loss of their Armenian provinces to Russia; their ethnic minorities, though by no means always submissive to the Iranian state, did not seek to join or create any other state. These were no small advantages.

The policies the shahs adopted were similar to and in some degree modelled on those of the Ottoman sultans – to modernize and centralize their armed forces and, as a necessary concomitant, their administration and education; to build, or allow others to build, a modern infrastructure, especially in communications; to adopt and then adapt the necessary minimum of Western techniques and methods; and, while doing this, to preserve their independence by playing the rival imperial powers off against one another.

But in all these policies, both domestic and external, the Iranians had less scope and achieved fewer successes than the Ottomans. Their military and civilian reforms were less thorough; their measures of centralization were impeded and sometimes nullified by regional and tribal particularism. This in turn frustrated their attempt to prevent the advance of the rival empires.

Russian pressure was mostly military, and a succession of treaties ratified the stages of Russian conquest and annexation. British infiltration was mostly economic and diplomatic, and was marked by a series of accords and concessions. But neither power neglected the methods of the other. At times, British forces were brought from India to impose Britain's will in Iran; increasingly, Russian businessmen and diplomats worked to extend the range and depth of Russian activity and influence. In 1864, British interests opened the first telegraph in Iran as part of the line of communication to India. This was followed by the so-called Reuter Concession of 1872, which granted a British firm the exclusive right to develop the mineral resources of Iran, to establish a bank, to install a network of telegraph lines and to build railways. The Iranian customs were pledged by way of payment. In the face of both practical difficulties and fierce Russian opposition, this concession was cancelled by the Iranian government. The year 1879 saw an important Russian success with the establishment of the Cossack Brigade, ostensibly the imperial guard of the shah, but a force trained, armed, equipped and in part officered by Russia. The Russian advances in Central Asia solidified Russian power in northern Iran and provided a base for its extension southwards. The British oil concession of 1901 was the only important exception to a series of Russian successes and advances.

The year 1905 brought a major change not only for Iran but for the whole region. Russia had just suffered a humiliating defeat in the Russo-Japanese War – the first in which a European imperial power was defeated by an Asian nation. This defeat brought grave troubles in Russia, leading in October 1905 to the promulgation, for the first time, of a constitution providing for representative and parliamentary government. In Iran, the lesson was clear. The despotism of the tsars had been defeated. The victors were the Japanese, who had themselves promulgated a constitution in 1889. The Russians themselves were following their example, thus demonstrating the potency and effectiveness of liberal democracy.

The Persian constitutional revolution began in December 1905, and, after some struggle, the first Majlis, national assembly, met in Tehran in October 1906 and drew up a constitution which was signed by the shah.

But in the meantime, the international situation had changed greatly to Iran's disadvantage. A common fear of the rising power of Germany drove Russia and Britain into each other's arms, and in August 1907 they concluded an *entente* which, in effect, divided Iran into a Russian sphere in the north, a British sphere in the south around the Persian Gulf, and a central belt open to both powers. A period of struggle followed – between the shah and the Majlis, between reactionary and liberal forces among the Iranians, and before very long, once again, between Russian and British interests. When war broke out in 1914, the Russian invasion and occupation of northern Iran was already well under way.

The Ottoman constitutional revolution of 1908 began under more auspicious circumstances and seemed at the time to herald the dawn of a new age. The despotism of Sultan Abdülhamid was overthrown; the constitution, in abeyance for thirty years, was again proclaimed. Free elections were announced and, in the meantime, Turks and Armenians, Muslims, Christians and Jews embraced in the streets and promised a new era of freedom and brotherhood. Of that revolution, a Turkish historian, in a book published in 1940, remarked: 'There are few movements in the world that have given rise to such great hopes ... there are likewise very few movements whose hopes have been so swiftly and finally disappointed.'[1]

While both the Ottoman Christians and the European powers welcomed the Young Turk Revolution as a major step forward, they did not allow it to interfere with their other plans. On the contrary, they seem to have seen it as an opportunity not to be missed. Without delay, Austria-Hungary annexed Bosnia and Herzegovina, Bulgaria declared independence, and Crete, which after the Greco-Turkish War of 1896 had been accorded autonomous status within the Empire, announced its union with Greece. In 1909 a counter-revolutionary mutiny was suppressed after bloody fighting.

In September, 1911, the first of a new series of wars began with an Italian attack on Tripoli. By this time, almost the whole of the North African littoral from Egypt to Morocco was under British or French control. Only the two Ottoman sanjaks of Cyrenaica and Tripolitania remained. Italy, a latecomer to the imperial game, was determined to stake at least a toehold on the sick man's estate and, with the prior consent of the European powers, launched a military and naval attack. The Italian advance in North Africa encountered unexpectedly strong Ottoman and local resistance, but in October of the same year that resistance was abandoned, as the Ottomans faced a new, closer and more dangerous threat.

The first Balkan war began on 18 October 1912 and ended on 30 May 1913. The Balkan allies, Bulgaria, Serbia and Greece, made substantial territorial gains at Ottoman expense and Albania was added to the roster of independent states. A second Balkan war in June and July 1913 between the victorious allies gave the Ottomans the opportunity to recover a small part of their lost territories and notably the region of Edirne up to the line of the Maritza river. This remains the Turkish frontier in Europe.

Amid all these troubles, the fragile democracy of the Young Turks, established with such high hopes, foundered, and a *coup d'état* in January 1913 installed what was in effect a military dictatorship. The following year the Young Turks blundered into a world war on the side of the Central powers and found themselves involved in a death struggle, in which their traditional friends and their traditional enemies were united against them.

The First World War was the last which the Ottoman Empire fought as a great power among other great powers. At the end of October 1914, Turkish warships, accompanied by two German cruisers, bombarded the Russian Black Sea ports of Odessa, Sevastopol and Theodosia. The sultan-caliph proclaimed a *jihād* against all who bore arms against him and his allies. Britain, France and Russia, the three principal Allied powers, all ruled over vast Muslim populations in Central Asia, North Africa, and India, and the Turks and their German allies hoped that these Muslim subjects would respond to the call to *jihād* and rise in revolt against their imperial masters. In fact, they did not, and the Ottomans found themselves obliged to confront the might of both imperial Russia and imperial Britain, on their eastern and southern borders.

At first, things went fairly well for the Turks. In December 1914 they began an offensive in eastern Anatolia, recaptured Kars, ceded to Russia in 1878, and briefly captured the city of Tabriz, in Iran, from the Russians, who had been operating freely in that country despite the neutrality which the shah's government had proclaimed but was too weak to enforce. In the south, at the beginning of 1915, Ottoman forces from Palestine crossed the Sinai desert and attacked the Suez Canal in British-occupied Egypt.

But these successes were of brief duration. In the east, the Russians counterattacked in strength and, with local help, entered and for a while held Van. In the south, the Turkish assault on the Suez Canal was repulsed by the British who, in the meantime, had sent an expedition from India to the Persian Gulf. On 22 November 1914, a British force occupied what was then the Ottoman port of Basra. The immediate British purpose was to protect the oil pipeline from Iran, but this initial success encouraged more ambitious plans. During 1915 British forces occupied a number of places on both the Tigris and Euphrates rivers, and began to advance northwards towards Baghdad.

In the meantime, the Ottomans faced a far more dangerous attack within striking distance of the capital. In February 1915, the British

The opening of the
Suez Canal in 1869.

The British in Egypt. Satirical comment on the British presence
in Egypt as a 'protector', from the French magazine *Petit Journal*, 1893.

The Dolmabahçe Palace, a
new residence for the sultan
in a new style, 1853.

Silk mercers' bazaar, Cairo,
1840s, by the Scottish artist
David Roberts. An example of
a new genre of 'Orientalism' –
picturesque portrayals of Middle
Eastern scenes and personalities
by Western artists.

European and Turkish ladies in Sultan Ahmed Square, Istanbul, 1907.

Atatürk, the founder and first president
of the Turkish republic.

Atatürk in an Istanbul park, 1928.
The leader as teacher, teaching the
new Latin alphabet.

The Arabian revolt against Ottoman rule:
Arab forces advance towards the port of Akaba in July 1917.

Austrian soldiers march out of Jerusalem, 1917.

Jerusalem, 1947: the last days of the British Mandate.

The nomadic life: Bedouin tribesmen in Saudi Arabia.

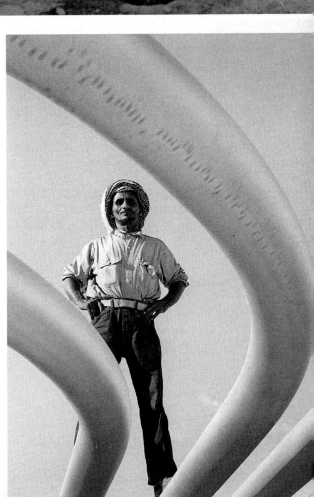

Oil pipelines in the desert. The discovery and exploitation of oil has brought huge changes to the Middle East in the twentieth century.

Demonstration in support of
Ayatollah Khomeini, Tehran,
January 1979.

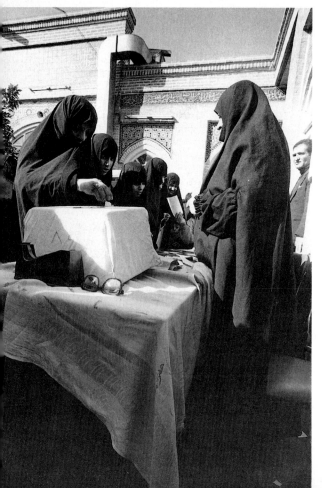

Iranian women vote on a new Islamic
constitution, December 1979.

The Great Mosque and the Kaʿba at the centre of the holy city of Mecca.

The faithful at prayer, Congress of the Islamic Research Academy, Cairo.

Istanbul, 1988.

began a naval action in the area of the Dardanelles and occupied the island of Lemnos, where they established a base. During the spring and summer, British and Australian troops were landed at a number of places in the Gallipoli peninsula, in a major attempt to break through the Ottoman defences in the Straits and link up with the Russians in the Black Sea.

In late 1915 and early 1916, things again went rather better for the Ottomans. The Russians were driven out of Van, the British were defeated and forced to surrender in Iraq, and the sultan's forces launched a second attack against the Suez Canal. By the beginning of 1916, after bitter fighting and heavy losses, the British and Australians withdrew from Gallipoli and abandoned the attempt to force the Straits.

But in the long run, the superior power of the Allies prevailed. After the Russian Revolution in 1917, the pressure from the East was relaxed, but the British advance from the south could no longer be halted.

During all these struggles and upheavals, the vast majority of the subjects of the Ottoman Empire, irrespective of their ethnic and religious identities, remained loyal. There were, however, two exceptions, among the Armenians in Anatolia and the Arabs in the Ḥijāz, in Arabia. Even among the Armenians and the Arabs, most were peaceful and law-abiding, and their menfolk served in the sultan's armies. But among nationalist leaders in both groups, there were some who saw the war as an opportunity to throw off Ottoman rule and achieve national independence. Clearly, this could only be accomplished with the help of the European powers which were now the sultan's enemies. In 1914 the Russians formed four large Armenian volunteer units, and three more in 1915. These, though primarily raised in Russian Armenia, all included Ottoman Armenians, some of them deserters, some of them well-known public figures. One of these units was commanded by an Armenian former member of the Ottoman Parliament. Armenian guerrilla bands were active in various parts of the country and, in several places, Armenian populations rose in armed rebellion, notably in the eastern Anatolian city of Van and the Cilician town of Zeytun.

In the spring of 1915, when Armenian rebels had gained control of Van, the British were at the Dardanelles, the Russians attacking in the east, and another British force apparently advancing on Baghdad, the Ottoman government decided on the deportation and relocation of the Armenian population of Anatolia – a practice sadly familiar in the region since biblical times. Some categories of Armenians, along with their families, were declared exempt from the deportation order: Catholics, Protestants, railway workers, and members of the armed forces. But the great mass of Armenians in Anatolia, extending far beyond the endangered areas and the suspect groups, was included in both the deportation and its deadly consequences.

The deportees suffered appalling hardships. In an embattled empire desperately short of manpower, neither soldiers nor gendarmes were available, and the task of escorting the deportees was entrusted to hastily recruited local posses. Estimates vary considerably as to the numbers, but there can be no doubt that at least hundreds of thousands of Armenians perished, perhaps more than a million. Many succumbed to hunger, disease and exposure; great numbers were brutally murdered, either by local tribesmen and villagers, through the negligence or with the complicity of their unpaid, unfed, and undisciplined escorts, or by the escorts themselves.

The Ottoman central government seems to have made some effort to curb these excesses. The archives contain telegrams from high Ottoman authorities, concerned with the prevention or punishment of acts of violence against the Armenians. They include records of almost fourteen hundred courts martial at which Ottoman civil and military personnel were tried and sentenced, some of them to death, for offences against the deportees. But these efforts had limited effect, and the situation was certainly worsened by the bitterness accumulated in decades of ethnic and religious strife between the Armenians and their once-peaceful neighbours. Istanbul and Izmir were exempted from the deportation orders, as were Ottoman Syria and Mesopotamia, to which the surviving deportees were consigned.

The Arab revolt against Ottoman rule was better placed, better planned, better timed, and better supported than that of the Armenians. While the Armenians were situated in the heart of Turkey in Asia among a predominantly Muslim population, the Arab revolt was launched in the Ḥijāz in Arabia, in a quasi-autonomous province, governed by a hereditary Arab ruler, the sharīf Ḥusayn, in a territory that was purely Arab and Muslim, and included Mecca and Medina, the two holiest places of Islam. It had the further advantages of being remote from Ottoman centres of power and easy of access for the British in Egypt. The Arab rebels also had something useful to offer to the British, and it was after long and careful secret negotiations that in 1917 the sharīf first proclaimed the independence of Ḥijāz, and later proclaimed himself as 'King of the Arabs'. The British government, which in letters to Ḥusayn had made certain promises concerning an ill-defined Arab independence, endorsed both proclamations.

The military significance of a few thousand Bedouin irregulars, in battles involving vast regular armies, may have been minor, but the moral significance of an Arab army fighting the Turks and, still more, of the ruler of the holy places denouncing the Ottoman Sultan and his so-called *jihād,* was immense, and was of particular value to the British and incidentally also to the French empires in maintaining their authority over their Muslim subjects. The Arab revolt was also more auspiciously timed, and coincided with the major retreat of the Ottoman forces in all the Arab provinces. Perhaps most important of all, the Arabs were more fortunate in their patrons. The British, unlike the Russians, were not incapacitated by a revolution at home, and were able to follow through in their military support. The subsequent fulfilment of their political promises was another matter, but at least they saved the Arab rebels from Ottoman retribution.

At the end of 1916, British forces began to advance from Egypt into Ottoman Palestine, while another British force landed in Iraq and resumed the interrupted advance northwards. By the spring of 1917, British forces had occupied Baghdad in Iraq and Gaza in Palestine. In December 1917 they captured Jerusalem and in October 1918 Damascus. On 29 October 1918, after three days of preliminary negotiation, an Ottoman delegation went on board the British warship HMS *Agamemnon,* at anchor off Mudros in the island of Lemnos. They signed an armistice next day.

The First World War marked the culmination of the retreat of Islam before the advancing West. Iran, though officially neutral, was overrun by foreign soldiers and their local auxiliaries. In the Ottoman lands this final war, like the Crimean War, brought a far more intense involvement with Europe and an acceleration of all the processes of change. Unlike the Crimean War, it ended in defeat, and the Turks were compelled to relinquish their Arab territories to Britain and France. Only in the Anatolian Turkish homeland did they manage to defy the victors and, after a struggle, establish an independent Turkish republic.

The years from 1918 to 1939 are commonly known in the context of European history as the inter-war period, though some have seen them rather as a long armistice between two phases of the same war. In the context of the Middle East, however, neither of these formulations is particularly helpful. These years may be better understood as an interlude in the history of the region, even as an intervention, if only in the sense in which surgeons use that word. In the Middle Eastern context, the period may be deemed to include both world wars as well as the years of fitful peace between them.

This period begins with the collapse or, more precisely, the destruction of the old order which, for better or for worse, had prevailed for four centuries or more in much of the Middle East. The Ottomans, building on the work of their predecessors, had erected a political structure which endured and a political system which worked. They had also created a political culture which was well understood and in which each group and indeed each individual knew his position, his powers and limits and, most important, what was due from him and to him, to whom and from whom. The Ottoman system had fallen on bad times, but despite many difficulties, it was still functioning. It had lost the loyalty and acceptance of most of its Christian subjects, but it was still accepted as legitimate by most of the Muslim population. During its last decades, the Ottoman order was beginning to show signs of recovery and even of improvement. Any such development was, however, diverted and terminated by the Ottoman entry into the First World War and the resulting end of the Empire – the collapse of the state and the fragmentation of its territories.

Since the arrival of General Bonaparte's expedition in Egypt at the end of the eighteenth century, the course of events in the Middle East had been profoundly influenced, and in times of crisis dominated, by the interests, ambitions, and actions of the European Great Powers. When the Ottomans finally departed and the Western powers were unequivocally present as rulers of the region, imperial rivalries took a new and more direct form.

In these rivalries there were three main phases. In the first, the British and French had the region much to themselves, and the major theme of international relations was the competition between the two. In the second phase, the 1930s and 1940s, the Anglo-French domination faced new challenges, first from Fascist Italy, then from Nazi Germany. In the third phase, during the Second World War, the Italians and then the Germans were eliminated. Thereafter the French, then the British were weakened to the point when they could no longer play a dominant role. And, in the distance, a new contest was developing between remoter outside powers, the Soviet Union and the United States, a portent of the shape of things to come.

As the smoke of battle and the mists of diplomacy cleared from the Middle Eastern scene after the First World War, it became apparent that major changes had taken place. Some of these brought new hope to the peoples dominated by both the Eastern and Western European empires. In Russia, the revolution and the consequent relaxation of authority from the centre permitted the establishment of liberal nationalist Muslim regimes both in Central Asia and in the Transcaucasian lands, while further south Britain and France promised self-determination and ultimate independence to the Arab peoples who now came under their rule. Even in North Africa, nationalist leaders proclaimed a Tripolitanian republic in November 1918, to which the Italians were for a while willing to grant recognition.

But these hopes were swiftly disappointed. In Central Asia and Transcaucasia, the action of the Red Army and the restoration of Moscow's control soon ended the experiments in independence in these countries, which were firmly reincorporated into the Russian orbit. In Tripolitania and Cyrenaica the Italians likewise conquered the local rulers and imposed their own authority. The two became Italian colonies, and were combined and renamed Libya in January 1934.

In southwest Asia, the peace settlements did not satisfy the hopes that had been aroused among the Arabs, but nevertheless gave them a great deal. Britain and France divided the Fertile Crescent not, as in the old days, into colonies and dependencies, but into new states, with new frontiers and nomenclature, which they held and administered under mandate from the League of Nations to prepare them for independence. In these new states they established regimes modelled on their own. The eastern arm, first called Mesopotamia and then Iraq, became a monarchy under British Mandate, ruled by King Faysal, a son of the Sharīf Ḥusayn. The western arm, previously loosely known as Syria or the Levant, was divided, the central and northern parts being assigned to France, and the south, under the name of Palestine, to Britain. Both mandatary powers then further subdivided their territories. The French, after some experiments, set up two republics, of which one was called Lebanon while the other retained the name of Syria. Similarly, the British split their area in two: they formed an Arab emirate ruled by 'Abdallah, another son of the sharīf, in the eastern part, renamed Transjordan, and set up direct administration in the Western part, to which the name Palestine was now restricted.

In Arabia, the course of events was very different. Apart from the British colony and protectorate of Aden in the southwest and the sheikhdoms of the Persian Gulf, most of which had for some time been under varying degrees of British control, the greater part of the peninsula enjoyed effective independence. The most notable development was the second and more successful expansion of the Wahhābī doctrine and the House of Saud which carried it. By the outbreak of war in 1914, the current head of the house, 'Abd al-'Azīz ibn Saud, had extended his rule to much of eastern Arabia and had entered into relations with the British whose help he needed against the Turks. After the war he resumed his career of conquest, capturing and annexing further territories in both northern and southern Arabia and deposing or expelling their previous rulers.

Well aware of the British imperial interest in eastern and southeastern Arabia, he took no action against the sheikhdoms and principalities of the east, but instead concentrated his efforts on western and southwestern Arabia, where only two serious rival states remained. One was the Kingdom of the Ḥijāz, ruled by Ḥusayn, the hero of the Arab revolt against the Turks; the other was the Imamate of the Yemen in the southwestern corner of the peninsula.

In 1924 Ibn Saud began operations against the Ḥijāz. By the end of 1925, Mecca, Medina and Jedda were in his possession, and King Ḥusayn had abdicated in favour of his son 'Alī who, in turn, was obliged to leave the country. On 8 January 1926 Ibn Saud was proclaimed King of the Ḥijāz and Sultan of Najd, retaining this title until September 1932, when the kingdom was renamed Saudi Arabia. A period of peaceful consolidation followed, during which Ibn Saud signed treaties of friendship with Turkey, Iran, Iraq, and, finally, after long and bitter disputes, with Transjordan.

A new war began in the spring of 1934, this time against Yemen. The Saudis were able to win a military victory, but Ibn Saud had to be content with a peace agreement, with British mediation, giving him some frontier rectifications but preserving Yemeni independence.

By the end of 1918, Turkey and Iran, which had for centuries disputed or shared the hegemony of the region, were themselves in acute danger of losing their independence. The Ottoman Empire lay supine in defeat, its capital occupied, its victorious enemies apportioning its territories among themselves and their satellites. Iran, despite its nominal neutrality, had served as a battleground for the belligerent powers, with foreign forces – Turks, Russians, Germans, British – operating on Iranian soil as if the sovereign Iranian state did not exist. Nothing, it seemed, could save them from sharing the fate of other Asian and African countries overwhelmed by the rising power of the West.

In fact, both of them, by different routes, escaped this fate. The change began in 1919, when a Turkish officer called Mustafa Kemal, later surnamed Atatürk, organized and led a movement of resistance in the heart of Anatolia against foreign invaders and occupiers. In a series of remarkable victories, he was able to rid the country of foreign forces, annul the draconian peace treaty which the victors had imposed on the sultan's government and, since the sultan's government had refused to align itself with these new forces, abolished the sultanate and proclaimed a republic. Under Atatürk's leadership, the republic carried through an extensive and comprehensive programme of modernization and – uniquely in the Muslim world – of secularization.

In Iran, the same year, 1919, saw the conclusion of an Anglo-Persian agreement which recognized the independence and integrity of Iran but at the same time provided for effective British ascendancy. The Iranian Parliament, summoned to ratify this agreement, refused, and the situation was further complicated by a reappearance of Russian power, this time in Bolshevik guise, in northern Iran. After a period of anarchy, an officer in an Iranian Cossack brigade, called Reza Khan, seized power in February 1921 and established a virtual dictatorship, which he consolidated in 1925 by declaring the shah deposed and proclaiming himself as shah. The dynasty founded by Reza Shah, later surnamed Pahlavi, lasted until 1979, when it was overthrown by the Iranian Islamic revolution. Like Atatürk, Reza Shah pursued a policy of centralization and modernization; unlike him, he made no attempt to disestablish Islam.

Only in three areas of the Middle East did independent Muslim states survive. For a time the Anglo-French domination seemed secure and was threatened only by the quarrels between the two powers themselves. But between the two world wars their will to dominate began to fail. Suffering from both economic weakness and moral discouragement, they no longer had the assurance or strength of will of their empire-building predecessors.

Their growing hesitancy was matched by a new mood of revolt among their subject peoples. At the beginning of the century the

Japanese, by defeating Russia, had shown the invigorating qualities of constitutional democracy and industrial modernization; now the Turks, by freeing themselves from the settlement imposed by the victors, demonstrated the efficacy of nationalism. The Turkish forces led by Mustafa Kemal achieved the first successful nationalist revolution in Asia or Africa; their victory and their successful defiance of the victorious Allies gave new hope to Muslim and indeed other peoples who saw for the first time a way to meet and defeat the West with its own weapons. For a while, the modernizing Turkish republic, like the Islamic Ottoman Empire before it, seemed to be showing the way for the whole Islamic world. But Kemal Atatürk had no such desire. His disestablishment of Islam, his secularization of the state and the law, and his oft-declared intention of making Turkey part of Europe, antagonized many Muslims who had at first acclaimed his victories.

Outbreaks of violence against the new masters occurred in almost all the Arab countries and demonstrated that a simple policy of direct rule was unworkable. Instead, the mandatary powers sought to achieve their purposes by indirect rule through Arab governments. To these they proposed to concede some degree of independence, and at the same time to sign treaties with them safeguarding their own privileged position, including the right to maintain armed forces on the national territory.

This policy was a failure. The concessions made by the mandatary powers to nationalist demands were always too small and too late to satisfy. Where treaties were obtained, they were signed either with unrepresentative governments lacking the support of the politically active elements, or under the shadow of some common external threat. Such was the Anglo-Egyptian Treaty of 1936, signed when the Italian invasion of Ethiopia was seen as posing a threat to both Britain and Egypt.

Arab disappointment found expression in a series of vigorous nationalist movements. The struggle they waged was bitter, sustained and in the main successful, at least in attaining its political objectives. Egypt and Iraq were soon accorded formal independence, the protectorate in the one, the mandate in the other, being officially terminated. But the British presence remained – the Royal Air Force establishments in Iraq, the army bases in the canal zone and elsewhere in Egypt – and the nationalist effort continued, to transform formal into real independence by the final withdrawal of foreign forces and the abrogation of unequal treaties.

In the Levant states the mandatary system survived much longer. The French remained in Syria–Lebanon, and the British continued to rule directly in Palestine, though allowing an increasing degree of autonomy to the amir of Transjordan.

In both the areas there were complicating factors. Lebanon was a special case among the new Middle Eastern states fashioned from the debris of the Ottoman Empire in Asia. Unlike the others it was not a new creation, but an existing and indeed deeply rooted historic entity, with a well-established tradition of separate autonomy maintained, often in conditions of great difficulty, during the centuries of Ottoman rule. The French created a 'greater Lebanon' by adding a number of adjoining districts to the original Lebanese heartland – that is, the mountain and its immediate neighbourhood. This heartland, inhabited mainly by Christians and by non-Sunni Muslims, had for long been a refuge of social, intellectual and in some measure even political independence within the Ottoman world. In the regions north of Beirut, Christian farmers had established what was then virtually the only community of independent smallholders in the whole of the Middle East, while in the nineteenth century a flourishing Christian bourgeoisie had developed in and around the port of Beirut. Their energy and their skills enabled them to make an enormous contribution to the Arab revival, politically and intellectually as well as economically. While the rise of Muslim nationalism greatly diminished the Christian role, Lebanon for some time continued to fulfil a unique function as the only surviving centre of cultural and religious pluralism and of economic and political freedom within the Arab world.

If the Christian redoubt in the Lebanon was one exception in the Arab-Islamic world, immediately to the south an even more dramatic exception was coming into existence. There had been Jews in Palestine since remote antiquity, but in late Roman times they ceased to constitute a majority of the population. From time to time the Jewish population of the country was reinforced by immigration, most of it religiously inspired. In the last quarter of the nineteenth century, an entirely new factor entered the situation, when a number of young Jews arrived in Palestine from Eastern Europe. Their inspiration was Zionism – a movement drawn partly from Jewish religious tradition, partly from a Jewish version of the new nationalist ideologies current at the time and, increasingly, driven by the need to find an answer to rejection and persecution in Europe and later the Middle East. The settlements which they and their successors founded formed the nucleus of what eventually became the state of Israel.

By the end of the First World War the Jewish community, old and new, had reached sizeable proportions, and the British government gave the Zionist enterprise formal recognition in the Balfour Declaration of November 1917, declaring British government support for the project of establishing an undefined 'National Home for the Jews'. The terms of this promise were incorporated into the League of Nations Mandate under which Britain administered Palestine. The promise and its implementation gave a special acuteness to the Arab struggle against the British mandate and the Jewish presence.

From the 1930s Western domination in the Middle East faced another kind of threat – not from rebellious subjects, but from two new contenders for imperial power: Fascist Italy and Nazi Germany.

In the course of the 1930s, liberal and constitutional institutions began to lose the attraction which they had once held in the region. Not surprisingly, they were not working very well. Limited to a small Westernized elite, they had no real basis of support in the society as a whole. Alien in both conception and appearance, they were in every way ineffective – unable alike to evoke people's memories of the past, to respond to their needs in the present, or to illuminate their hopes for the future. Worst of all, they were associated in the minds of most Arabs with the by now hated imperial powers of Western Europe.

Germany and Italy offered a seductive alternative. Both were countries which had only recently achieved unity by forcibly freeing and uniting a number of small states. Their example was an inspiration to the leaders of peoples who saw their own predicament, and its solution, in similar terms.

Best of all, they were the opponents, at once politically, strategically and ideologically, of Britain, France and of the growing Jewish presence in Palestine.

As far back as 1933, immediately after Hitler's accession to power, the British-appointed Mufti of Jerusalem, Ḥāj Amīn al-Ḥusaynī, made contact with the German consul to declare his support and offer his help. After years of uncompromising struggle against the British and the Jews, the Mufti left Palestine, and with stops in Beirut, Baghdad and Tehran en route, reached Berlin in 1941. The most important of these stops was Baghdad, where in April 1941, an Iraqi politician called Rashīd 'Alī al-Gaylānī, with military support, seized power and established a pro-Axis regime. Despite some help from Syria, at that time still controlled by the Vichy authorities, the Axis powers were too far away to save him, and his regime was overthrown by British and British-led forces. In Syria a committee was formed to mobilize support for the Rashīd 'Alī regime. This was the nucleus of what later became the Ba'th party, rival branches of which came to govern both Syria and Iraq.

Rashīd 'Alī fled and later joined the Mufti in Berlin. Among the many who supported or sympathized with the Axis during the war years were some who later became famous. Nasser (Nāṣir) recorded his sympathy and his disappointment at Germany's defeat; Sādāt, according to his own memoirs, was a willing co-operator in German espionage. Even Rashīd 'Alī has been resuscitated as a hero in Ṣaddām Ḥusayn's Iraq.

At first sight, this enthusiasm for the Nazi cause seems very strange. Nazi racism cannot have had much appeal for a people who, according to Nazi pseudo-science, were themselves racial inferiors. Nazi propaganda, in so far as it was specifically anti-Jewish rather than generally anti-Semitic, had considerable support. But it was, after all, the persecution of Jews by the Nazis in Germany and their imitators elsewhere that was the driving force of Jewish migration to Palestine and the consequent strengthening of the Jewish community in that country. The Nazis not only caused this migration; they even encouraged and facilitated it until the outbreak of war, while the British, in the forlorn hope of winning Arab good will, imposed increasing restrictions. Nevertheless, significant numbers of Arabs favoured the Germans, who sent the Jews to Palestine, rather than the British, who tried to keep them out.

The Axis powers tried in different ways to profit from this mood. First Fascist Italy and later Nazi Germany launched massive programmes of propaganda and penetration in the Arab world, with considerable impact on the new generation of political thinkers and activists. The Nazis in particular, by preaching hatred of Jews, were able to exploit a problem which they themselves had in large measure created.

In part, this turn towards the Axis was precautionary. In the early years of the war and especially in 1940–1, between the fall of France and the invasion of Russia, when Britain stood alone, it seemed to many that an Axis victory was inevitable and that elementary prudence dictated the opening of lines of communication to the victors – the more so since few in the Middle East felt that they owed any allegiance or loyalty to their imperial rulers. Thus even political figures acclaimed – or denounced – as friends of the West, such as Naḥās Pasha of Egypt, Nūrī al-Saʿīd of Iraq, and Ibn Saud of Arabia tried to establish contact with Berlin. They were not successful, since the Nazis had already received more offers of help than they found it convenient or expedient to accept. Support for the Axis was in part based on ideology, but owed much more to the old and still valid principle that 'the enemy of my enemy is my friend'. The main attraction of the Axis was that it was the implacable enemy of the West. At a later date, the same attraction worked in favour of a very different power, the Soviet Union, which was also able to win considerable support, some-times even the same supporters.

In the event, both sides in the Second World War disappointed their supporters in the Middle East, and were disappointed by them. Both sides managed to mobilize some military help. The Transjordanian Arab Legion played an important part in the overthrow of Rashīd ʿAlī and the maintenance of the Allied order in the Middle East. The Germans raised some volunteer forces in the so-called 'Orient Legions'. These were recruited in part from Allied prisoners of war – French North Africans, British Indians, Red Army conscripts from the Central Asian and Transcaucasian republics, supplemented by volunteers from among the diasporas of these peoples in German-occupied Europe. But none of these had any great significance. A Jewish brigade, raised in Palestine despite considerable official mis-givings in London, played a part in the North African and Italian campaigns, but this too was of relatively minor military importance.

The main contribution to the Allied cause by Middle Eastern countries was the use of their territories, resources and facilities. In most of these countries, this was made possible by the military garrisons established under the mandates and protectorates. In neutral Iran it was achieved by the simultaneous invasion of Iranian territory by Russian and British forces in 1941. Only Turkey was able to maintain neutrality almost until the last weeks, when the Turkish government declared war in order to qualify for a seat at the victors' table. As one Turkish statesman later put it: 'We wanted to be on the guest list, not on the menu.'

The results were no less disappointing for the Middle Eastern peoples and governments. The Germans disappointed their Arab followers and suitors. They were fairly generous with declarations, though even these were sometimes couched in equivocal language and fell con-siderably short of a ringing endorsement of Arab aims. The Nazis, with their eyes focused on Europe, were not really interested in the Middle East, and time and again showed their readiness to sacrifice their Middle Eastern protégés to satisfy their European friends – Fascist Italy, Vichy France and, from August 1939 to June 1941, the Soviet Union.

Despite promises of independence and withdrawal, the war ended with Allied troops still massively present in most Arab countries. Some of these countries, as in North Africa, were still under colonial rule; others were governed by regimes which, though mistrusted by the Allies, were detested by their own people as Allied puppets. And even the Jews in Palestine, though obviously no sympathizers of the Third Reich, were alienated from their rulers by the determined effort the British authorities had made both before and after the end of hostilities to prevent the remnants of European Jewry from reaching the shores of Palestine.

During the war, two requests were repeatedly made to the warring parties – by Jewish organizations in London and Washington, urging their governments to bomb the death camps in Auschwitz; by the Mufti's office in Berlin, urging the German government to bomb Tel Aviv. Neither request was accepted – not because of any ill will on the one side or good will on the other, but for the same basic reason – that such a bombardment would serve no military purpose and make no direct contribution towards winning the war. It did not therefore, in purely military terms, justify the risks and costs involved.

The war years of 1939 to 1945 thus brought little satisfaction to either side in the Middle East. Despite the great effort made by the Axis powers and the widespread sympathy for their cause, the effective response was small. The only tangible gains achieved by the Germans were some facilities in Vichy-occupied Syria and a pro-Axis coup in Iraq in 1941. Both were of brief duration. The British attempt to win the friendship of Arab nationalism fared even worse, and the Allies could at best count on a sullen neutrality, assured by their massive military presence. The defence of Egypt against first the Italians and then the Germans was left to British and imperial forces; the liberation of North Africa, to the Americans.

Once again, as on earlier occasions, involvement in a major war brought rapid and far-reaching change. Axis and Allied propagandists competed in encouraging the aspirations of nationalist movements. Axis and Allied armies camped and fought on Arab soil, bringing with them the stresses and dislocations inseparable from modern war. By now several Arab states were enjoying greater or lesser degrees of independence and beginning to pursue foreign policies of their own. The Arab League, founded in 1945, grouped all the Arab sovereign states of the Middle East for the joint pursuit of common political objectives. Originally a British-sponsored project, it rapidly shook off British leading strings and developed according to the sometimes conflicting purposes of its members.

One of the most important changes of this century in the area was the discovery, exploitation, and use of petroleum. The process began in the Russian-ruled parts of the Middle East, where a first drilling for oil took place in the Apsheron peninsula as far back as 1842. The development of the oil industry in Russian Azerbaijan was roughly contemporary with American development in Pennsylvania. The first refinery was built in Baku in 1863, and a pipeline constructed from the Apsheron oil fields to Baku in 1877–8. By the eve of the Russian Revolution, the Baku oil fields were providing 95 per cent of all Russia's oil. Further south, in the still independent Iranian and Ottoman lands, European and American businessmen were making the first attempts to obtain concessions. At the beginning of the twentieth century the first major concession was granted by the shah of Iran to a British businessman – actually a New Zealander – called William Knox D'Arcy. The D'Arcy concession was acquired by the subsequently created Anglo–Persian (later renamed Anglo–Iranian) Oil Company. This was the first of a series of similar arrangements whereby the oil of the Middle East was exploited by concessionary companies, most of them British, French, Dutch and American, under royalty agreements with Middle Eastern governments. First in Iran, then in Iraq, later in Arabia and elsewhere, great new oil fields were opened up, and the Middle East became one of the major oil-producing areas of the world.

This new development affected the countries of the Middle East in several ways. The use of the internal combustion engine transformed overland communications. It was now possible to link major centres and move persons, commodities, printed matter and ideas on a scale and at a speed undreamt of in earlier ages. The replacement, on a massive scale, of the horse, donkey and camel by car, bus and truck, coupled with rapid economic development and the spread of such other Western means of communication as printing, newspapers, cinema, radio and television, began a far-reaching social transformation and made it visible to all.

What, it may be asked, did the British and French want in the Middle East, and what did they get? There is by now general agreement that the prime motive which brought both powers to the region and kept them there for more than twenty-five years was strategic – concern with the military potentialities and dangers of the area. The nature of this strategic purpose has been expressed in a variety of images: the Middle East as a buffer, as a junction, as a nodal point in communications, as a base, as a *place d'armes*. An obvious strategic purpose was to deny the area to others who, it was thought, would inevitably enter if the Western powers were not there to exclude them. A consideration of some significance for both the British and the French was the safeguarding of their other, richer, imperial possessions. The British were much concerned with India, the French with their rule in North Africa. Both felt the need to protect these possessions from destabilizing forces which they believed, with some plausibility, would come out of the Muslim Middle East, unless the countries and peoples of that region were kept safely under imperial control or at least influence.

There were of course other elements. Apologists for the French presence at the time often referred to the cultural and religious mission of France – the protection of the Christian and especially the Catholic minorities and the dissemination of French culture. Parallel considerations counted for rather less with the British.

Economic motives, contrary to a once prevalent interpretation of imperialism, were of minor importance, and there was little expectation of economic gain. On the contrary, a major preoccupation of both the British and the French seems to have been with the financial cost, that is to say, with the high price of achieving the strategic and political purposes that were desired. Both powers were always anxious to keep this cost as low as possible. It was only fairly late in the period that oil emerged as a significant factor and even then it was by no means as important as it subsequently became. In the inter-war period, the interest in oil was at least as much strategic as economic.

In retrospect, it is clear that the position of both the British and French in the Middle East was flawed by several basic weaknesses. They were unwilling to incur costs to maintain power and reluctant to use force to overcome opposition. In both Britain and France there was hesitancy, uncertainty and weakness. Almost from the start, doubts were expressed about whether the whole enterprise was feasible or worthwhile. Winston Churchill is even quoted as suggesting that it might be better to give the whole place back to the Turks – a gift that the Turkish Republic would certainly have refused.

As the Anglo-French position in the Middle East was weakened, it was threatened by other hostile forces – nations and regimes still possessing that special mixture of greed, ruthlessness and smugness which are the essential ingredients of the imperial mood, and which, among the British and French, had given way to weariness, satiety and self-doubt. For a while, both were most keenly aware of the threat which each offered to the other. Both showed weakness and irresolution in dealing with other and ultimately far more important challenges, whether from those in the region who sought to overthrow their rule or those outside who wanted to replace them.

The Anglo-French position was further weakened by constant quarrelling or rather bickering. This took place at many levels and in many ways: the British and French against the rest; the British and French against each other; the British and French amongst themselves – the innumerable and persistent squabbles between home governments and local authorities, and between a multiplicity of bureaucratic factions, departments and services, divided by social origins and by conflicting interests and purposes, all of which helped to delay and deflect what is nowadays known as the decision-making process.

The Ottoman Empire had provided the Middle East with a structure and a protective screen, sheltering it from the many dangers that threatened from outside. Now all that was gone. The Ottoman structure and system were replaced by new ones which failed and ultimately broke down. There was now no lack of protective screens, but the protection, such as it was, was given by the European powers against one another, and this was of small comfort to most of the inhabitants of Middle Eastern countries.

What was the final balance for the British and French on the one hand and the peoples of the Middle East on the other? What did the Anglo-French interlude of power in the Middle East achieve before its sordid and wretched ending, after one of the greatest military victories in modern history? What resulted that was of any value, either for the Western powers themselves or for the Middle East and its peoples?

At this stage, it is possible to offer no more than tentative and preliminary answers to some of these questions. On the whole, the most positive results were probably in relation to those objectives to which, at the time, the least importance was given: the economic and the practical. There can surely be no doubt that for most people in the Middle East, life was better in 1939 than in 1918 or even 1914. The standard of living was higher for most, if not all, sectors of the population. The amenities were greater and more numerous, the prospect of living to a ripe old age far better than they had ever been before. A new infrastructure had been built and all kinds of services provided.

These benefits were less noticeable in the territories of the Middle East than in those directly administered by an imperial power, such as British India or French North Africa. In this respect, Middle Easterners were unfortunate in that they suffered most of the drawbacks of imperialism but missed its main advantages or received them only in an attenuated form. But even this attenuated benefit was not negligible, and by 1939, the peoples of the region were better off in most material respects.

They had also gained another very important benefit, that of language – the English and French languages, previously known to very few people in the region outside Egypt and Lebanon. With these languages came access to the modern world, its culture and its science. The introduction of Western, or more precisely modern, science is generally recognized as a gain for the peoples of the region. Western culture, and especially its social consequences, evoked a more varied response. While some embraced it with enthusiasm, others saw it as at best a mixed blessing, while others again denounced it as an unmixed curse.

The Anglo-French domination also gave the Middle East an interlude of liberal economy and political freedom. That freedom was always limited and sometimes suspended, but in spite of these limitations and suspensions, it was on the whole more extensive than anything they experienced before or after. Most of these Western-style institutions have now gone. They have been abandoned, even condemned. It is only very recently there is a new beginning, a reawakening interest in liberal ideas and practices, for which changing circumstances in some of the countries of the region may at last provide a more favourable setting.

For the Western powers and perhaps ultimately even for the Middle Easterners themselves the most positive result of the period of Anglo-French domination was probably the attainment of the primary strategic goal, as can be seen in the role of the Middle East during the Second World War. The greatest service the Middle East rendered to the West was the provision of base and support facilities for the war against the Axis. And in return, the greatest service of the West to the Middle East was in saving it from the direct experience of Axis rule.

CHAPTER 19

FROM FREEDOM TO FREEDOM

The defeat of the Axis and the victory of the Allied powers in 1945 did not bring immediate peace to the world. The advance of the Soviet Empire in Eastern and Central Europe and the retreat of the Western colonial empires in Asia and Africa posed grave problems in these regions. Both the loss and the gain of sovereign independence revived old hatreds and created new ones, displacing millions of refugees. The Middle East also had its share of post-war, post-imperial upheavals. Peace in this region was fitful, uneasy, and frequently interrupted by struggles against internal and, on occasion, external enemies. On the whole, its troubles were less intense and less traumatic than those which accompanied the clamping down of Soviet rule in Central and Eastern Europe, or the winding down of British rule in South and Southeast Asia. But the problems of the Middle East, though of smaller dimensions, proved to be of greater intensity and far less amenable to diplomatic treatment and political solutions.

In the Middle East, as elsewhere in the ex-colonial world, the first and, for a while, the only, issue of public concern was independence.

In the aftermath of the First World War, three states in the region, Turkey, Iran and Afghanistan, possessed full sovereign independence and had lengthy experience in exercising it. The inter-war period added four Arab states, Saudi Arabia, Yemen, Iraq and Egypt. The first two enjoyed a large measure of practical as well as theoretical independence, but the last two were bound to their former rulers, both diplomatically by unequal treaties and militarily by the presence of British bases and forces. The enforced departure of France from the Levant added Syria and Lebanon to the roster of Arab sovereign states. The 'League of Arab States' was formed in March 1945 by Egypt, Iraq, Syria, Lebanon, Saudi Arabia, Yemen and also Transjordan, though the last named was still in principle part of the British-mandated territory of Palestine. A year later, in March 1946, Transjordan, subsequently renamed Jordan, also gained independence.

The first objective in all these states was to turn nominal into real independence by abrogating treaties and eliminating the foreign presence. As the Western empires withdrew from almost all their possessions, this was completed by the early fifties.

At the same time, the process was extended to the rest of the Arab world. Libya became independent in 1951, the Sudan, Tunisia and Morocco in 1956, Mauritania in 1960, Kuwait in 1961, Algeria in 1962, South Yemen (the former Aden colony and Protectorate) in 1967, and the Gulf States in 1971. All of them joined the Arab League. Some, notably South Yemen and Algeria, acquired their independence only after a long and bitter struggle. In most of the others, independence was achieved more or less peaceably, by sometimes tough negotiations ending in agreement.

With the exception of Israel, established in 1948 after the termination of the Palestine mandate, all the new states that became independent in the post-war period were Arab. This situation changed dramatically in the early nineties. With the break-up of the Soviet Union in 1991, the Transcaucasian and Central Asian territories, acquired by the tsars in the nineteenth century and retained by the Soviets in the twentieth, suddenly had thrust upon them an independence for which they were ill prepared. Historically, all these countries had been part of or dependent on the Middle East. Two of them, Armenia and Georgia, were Christian, but had for many centuries been subject to Muslim empires, either Turkish or Persian. The rest, Azerbaijan and the five republics of Central Asia, were predominantly Muslim, speaking languages closely related to either Turkish or Persian, and tied by a thousand historical, religious, and cultural bonds to their southern neighbours in the Middle East. One of them, Tajikistan, was Persian by speech and culture. The other four – Kazakstan, Uzbekistan, Kyrgyzstan, and Turkmenistan – spoke languages related to Turkish. With the exception of Kazak, the differences between these various languages were no greater than between the vernaculars spoken in the Arab lands from Iraq to Morocco. Unlike the Arabs, the Turks had no common standard written language, but the coming into existence of a world of Turkish states analogous to the Arab world, which had for so long dominated and in large measure shaped the politics of the Middle East, was a new and portentous development. The previous experience of these new states provided them with little preparation for the attainment or exercise of either national or personal freedom. And it soon became apparent that, despite the demise of the Soviet Union, the new Russian state still had concerns and interests in these republics and a consequent desire to maintain some form of Russian presence. In many ways it seemed that the Turkish world was about to re-live some of the experiences of the Arab world a few decades earlier in disengaging from their former imperial masters.

But even the political troubles of the region did not end with the attainment of sovereign independence. Old conflicts remained, and new conflicts emerged at several levels – internal, intra-regional, and international. Of the newly independent nations of the Arab world, a few represented old and continuing historical entities with long experience of separate identity – notably Egypt and Morocco. Others were new creations, both as countries and as regimes. Saudi Arabia, though assembled by conquest from different tribal and regional groups, did at least have the advantage of homogeneity. It was all Arab, all Muslim and, except for the eastern province, overwhelmingly Sunni. Most of the other newly created states lacked this advantage, and were riven by inner rivalries and hatreds. Sometimes these broke out into armed conflict, variously described as rebellion, revolution, or civil war – the differences between these are of perspective as well as of dimension.

The most persistent and destructive were the struggles in Lebanon between rival groups and often between rival factions within the groups themselves – religious and sectarian, ethnic and tribal, regional and local. These struggles were complicated and protracted by the intervention of outside powers. Such were the civil wars in Lebanon in 1958, in 1975–6, and, with interruptions and uneasy truces, between 1983 and 1991.

Another region of persistent conflict was southern Arabia. In 1962, a revolutionary movement with Egyptian support overthrew the traditional rule of the imam, and installed a republic in its place. The resulting struggle, between outside forces – Saudi and Egyptian – and between rival factions espousing either the royalist or the republican cause, endured for many years. The greater United Yemen, formed in 1990 by the union of the territories of the former Imamate and the former British possessions with their centre at Aden, was again convulsed by a deadly civil war between the north and the south in 1994. Yemenis also were involved in the long-running conflict in Dhofar which, between 1965 and 1975, tried to separate itself from the Sultanate of Oman, of which it was a part. The Dhofar rebellion was finally suppressed with the help of an Iranian expeditionary force provided by the shah. This secessionist rebellion acquired a more than local significance because of the involvement of South Yemen, at that time a Marxist state closely aligned with the Soviet Union.

There were many other Middle Eastern countries in which governments used force to suppress dissident minorities or provinces. Both Turkey and Iraq had to confront disaffection and sometimes insurrection among their Kurdish minorities. Iraq also resorted to military action against the Shī'a population – actually a majority in the country as a whole – in the central and southern regions. In the Sudan, the Arabic-speaking, Muslim north was often at war with the non-Arab, non-Muslim Africans in the south. In Jordan, differences between the Palestinian leadership and the Royal Jordanian establishment came to a head in September 1970, when the Palestine Liberation Organization openly challenged the authority of the Jordanian state and suffered a bloody defeat. Perhaps most ominous of all was the civil war in Algeria in the early 1990s, when a powerful Islamic fundamentalist movement and leadership questioned the legitimacy and challenged the authority of the Algerian government.

One of the basic principles of the Arab League is that no Arab state should take up arms against another Arab state to settle a dispute. There had been many disputes between Arab states. Sometimes a state claimed the entire territory of a neighbouring state, seen as a part of the national soil detached and separated by imperialist intervention. Such were, notably, the Moroccan claim to Mauritania, the Egyptian claim to the Sudan, the Syrian claim to Lebanon, and the Iraqi claim to Kuwait. The Egyptians renounced their claim to the Sudan in 1953 and recognized its separate sovereignty. The Moroccans recognized Mauritania in 1970. In November 1994 the government of Iraq was induced to recognize the sovereignty and integrity of Kuwait – a renunciation achieved only after a long and bitter conflict.

The Iraqi claim came in two forms – sometimes for a frontier rectification, sometimes for Kuwait in its entirety. A threatening movement by Iraq in 1961 was countered by the swift dispatch of British troops to Kuwait. This stopped the Iraqi advance for the time being, but did not end the Iraqi claim. The Syrian claim to Lebanon and, more remotely, to all the lands of the former Palestine mandate also remained unresolved. There were some minor border disagreements and skirmishes – between Morocco and Algeria in 1963, between Libya and Chad in 1980 and again in 1986–7 and some others, but these were of purely local importance and had little or no effect on the general pattern of development. The first major violation of the Arab League principle occurred in 1990 with the Iraqi invasion, occupation, and annexation of the sovereign state of Kuwait. Beginning as an inter-Arab conflict, this rapidly developed into a major international crisis.

Sometimes, in pursuit of the ideal of pan-Arabism, attempts were made to combine previously sovereign Arab states in some form of direct but voluntary association. The most notable of these was the United Arab Republic, formed by the merging of Egypt and Syria in 1958. After some years of uneasy cohabitation, Syria seceded from the UAR and resumed its separate existence in 1961. Several other attempts, mostly initiated by the government of Libya, were without effect.

The post-imperial Arab states, with few exceptions, are of extraneous origin and artificial character, but they have proved remarkably persistent – and successful – in preserving their independent statehood and their territorial integrity. Despite many attempts in both directions, no Arab state has yet been pulled apart; no two Arab states – with the questionable exception of Yemen – have successfully been joined together.

Of all the wars that originated and were fought within the region in recent times, two were especially deadly, bitter and protracted: the series of short wars between Israel and the Arab states that began in 1948 and may have ended in 1994, and the long war between Iraq and Iran from 1980 to 1988.

The Arab–Israel wars had their origins in events long before the establishment of the state of Israel, when the Arab leadership in Palestine was striving to halt and reverse the build-up of the Jewish national home in that country. This struggle began when Palestine, not yet known by that name among its inhabitants, was still part of the Ottoman Empire. The struggle became more acute after the establishment of the British mandate, the terms of which embodied a formal recognition of the principle of a national home for the Jews in Palestine. It reached crisis proportions in the 1930s and 1940s, with the rise to power of the Nazis in Germany and the spread of Nazi ideas and practices, by force and otherwise, to many other countries. The enthronement of militant anti-Semitism in the heart of Europe seemed to confirm the Zionist analysis of the Jewish predicament; the closed doors of the former countries of immigration, their economies racked by the depression, left the mounting tide of Jewish refugees from Europe and later from the Middle East with nowhere else to go.

By the end of the war in 1945, the vast majority of the Jews of German-occupied Europe were dead, and only a few hundred thousand remained alive, mostly in the so-called 'displaced persons' camps. Those who had come from Western Europe returned home and were re-integrated without undue difficulty. Those who came from Central and Eastern Europe, from countries suffering from internal upheavals and foreign invasions and occupations, faced far greater problems; all too often, when they tried to return, they were received by their former neighbours with hostility and violence. Many, therefore, rather than endure a new cycle of repression and persecution at the hands of their reluctant compatriots, preferred to risk the hazards of a journey to the Promised Land.

For the British government, struggling to brace the crumbling pillars of empire, and keenly aware of the mounting resentment of the Arabs in Palestine and elsewhere, the sudden flood of Jewish immigrants presented an impossible dilemma. For almost two years, the British government made a sustained effort – by diplomacy in the countries of origin and transit, by naval action on the high seas, by police action in mandatary Palestine – to prevent, divert, or repel the incoming tide. But the naval and police efforts were of limited effectiveness, and at a time when the Western world, still stunned by the revelations of the Nazi Holocaust, was sympathetic to the Jews, and the Soviet bloc, for its own reasons, supported the Jews against Britain, the diplomatic effort was unavailing and even counterproductive.

Meanwhile, with the ending of British rule in India, the primary motive for staying in the Middle East had gone, and there seemed little reason for the weakened and impoverished Britain of the post-war years to pursue a policy that was difficult, unsuccessful and increasingly unpopular both at home and abroad. On 2 April 1947 the British government announced that it would return to the United Nations the mandate which it had received from the defunct League of Nations, and would relinquish the Palestine Mandate. Some months later the date of termination and withdrawal was set on Saturday, 15 May 1948.

For more than a year, the British still remained in Palestine, but now functioned only as a caretaker government, while the responsibility for deciding what happened next in the former mandated territory reverted to the United Nations. After long and complex negotiations, the General Assembly adopted a resolution on 29 November 1947 for the partition of Palestine into three entities – a Jewish state, an Arab state, and a *corpus separatum* under international jurisdiction for the city of Jerusalem. The General Assembly passed this resolution by the necessary two thirds majority, but made no provision for its execution or enforcement.

There were others, however, who made provision for its prevention. On 17 December, the Council of the Arab League declared that it would oppose the proposed partition, if necessary by force. The Palestinian leadership resumed its armed resistance to the mandatary government and to the Jewish national home. The Jewish leadership in Palestine accepted the UN plan. Since the mandate ended on the Sabbath, they anticipated its end by some hours, and on Friday, 14 May 1948 announced the establishment of a state, which they called Israel, in the territories assigned by the UN partition plan. The Palestinian leadership had already been at war for some time to prevent its establishment; they were now reinforced by the armies of the neighbouring states, with some support from remoter Arab countries.

Fighting between Jews and Arabs in Palestine had abated during the war years. It began again in 1947 and continued until the end of the mandate and after. The Palestinian Arabs were assisted by a volunteer force from Syria known as the Arab Liberation Army. With the establishment of the state of Israel – immediately recognized *de facto* by the United States of America and *de jure* by the Soviet Union – and the armed intervention of the neighbouring Arab states, the conflict acquired a formal international dimension. The struggle for Palestine was now an Israel–Arab war.

Against such odds there seemed little chance that the new state would survive. But after a few weeks of desperate struggle, the situation changed dramatically. The Israelis, caught between their enemies and the sea, showed unexpected strength, while the Arab coalition was misled by overconfidence and weakened by dynastic and national rivalries.

This first war continued for several months, punctuated by fragile truces negotiated under the auspices of the United Nations. During these consecutive phases, there was a decisive change in the military situation. The Israeli state withstood the first Arab attack and was able not only to hold but even to extend its ground. The remainder of Palestine was held by the forces of the neighbouring states – the Egyptians in Gaza and in what became known as 'the Gaza Strip'; the Jordanians on the West Bank and in east Jerusalem, and the Syrians in a small enclave on the eastern shore of the Sea of Galilee. In January–April 1949, armistice agreements between Israel and the neighbouring Arab states were negotiated and signed on the island of Rhodes.

For decades these remained the only formal legal instruments recognized by both parties that regulated relations between the signatories. The Arab states made it clear that their acceptance of the armistice agreements in no sense constituted a recognition or acceptance of the state of Israel or of its frontiers. The agreement with Lebanon confirmed the former international boundary between the two sides; the agreements with Egypt, Jordan, and Syria recognized only armistice demarcation lines, leaving the drawing of political and territorial boundaries to 'the ultimate settlement of the Palestine question'.[1]

In the course of the fighting, great numbers of Palestinian Arabs in the Israeli-held areas fled or were driven from their homes and became refugees in the neighbouring Arab countries. The evidence is contradictory, claims conflicting, but it seems likely that both descriptions are true of different places. Their numbers were estimated at the time by United Nations agencies at 726,000.

Amid the confusions and uncertainties of battle and diplomacy, in the agonies of flight and expulsion, the Palestinian refugees shared the fate of millions of other victims of conflict who fled or were driven from their homes in India, in Eastern Europe, and elsewhere, in the bloody reshaping of the world after the Second World War. Their position, however, was unique in that, unlike all these others, they were neither repatriated nor resettled but were left or kept in camps where they and their descendants remained for generations as stateless refugees. The one exception was Jordan, where the Hashimite government formally annexed the Jordanian-held territories west of the river and later offered citizenship to all Arab Palestinians. At about the same time, Israel absorbed some hundreds of thousands of Jews who fled or were driven from Arab countries. In a time of intense Arab-Jewish conflict, their position had become untenable.

The war of 1948–9 was the first of a series fought between Israel and its Arab neighbours, sometimes together, sometimes separately. The responsibility for the immediate outbreak of these wars is about evenly divided. The wars of 1948 and of 1973 were unmistakably launched by the decision of Arab governments; those of 1956 and of 1982, by Israel. Responsibility for the war of 1967 is more difficult to allocate. As more information becomes available about the sequence of events leading to the opening of hostilities, it seems that the participants were like characters in a Greek tragedy, in which at every stage the various actors had no choice but to take the next step on the path to war.

The most dramatic of these wars was certainly that of 1967, when in six days the Israeli armed forces inflicted crushing defeats, in rapid succession, on the armies of Egypt, Jordan, and Syria, and on an Iraqi expeditionary force. By the end of the war, Israel was in possession not only of the whole territory of mandatary Palestine west of the Jordan, but also of the Golan Heights, taken from Syria in the north, and the Sinai peninsula, taken from Egypt in the south. Israel's military frontiers were now on the Suez Canal, the Jordan River and the Golan Heights, some thirty miles from Damascus. The Sinai Peninsula remained in Israeli hands until, in 1979, a peace agreement was signed between Israel and Egypt – the first with any Arab country – under the terms of which peace and normal diplomatic relations were established between the two states and Israeli forces withdrew in agreed stages to the old, international frontier between mandatary Palestine and the Kingdom of Egypt. In October 1994, a second peace treaty with an Arab country was signed between Israel and Jordan. Negotiations, apparently of a similar purport, had already begun between Israel and Syria.

The extension of Israeli rule to the West Bank and the Gaza Strip added a new dimension to the dispute: the active involvement of a Palestinian leadership. Between 1949 and 1967, the Arab League, and in particular the Arab states occupying parts of Palestine, claimed to speak for the Palestinians and discouraged – at times even prevented – any active Palestinian participation in the political process. The total defeat of these states in 1967 ended such claims and gave a new importance to the Palestine Liberation Organization, founded three years previously and until then principally an instrument of inter-Arab politics. It now acquired an entirely new role and, as the advancing guerrilla replaced the retreating soldier as the symbol of Arab opposition to Israel, the Palestine Liberation Organization rapidly became a major international player. For twenty-five years, the PLO leadership carried on a struggle variously designated from different perspectives as resistance, guerrilla warfare and terrorism. Their first base was in Jordan, until, in 1970, a clash with the Royal Jordanian government led to their departure for Lebanon. There, the circumstances of the civil war and the weakening of the authority of the central government enabled them to set up a virtual state-within-a-state under PLO control. This phase ended in 1982, when the Israeli forces entered Lebanon and secured the expulsion of the PLO. The leadership and headquarters were then transferred to Tunis, where they remained until 1994.

During this final phase, the PLO's struggle against Israel changed in character. Until then, its actions had consisted mainly of attacks on Israeli and other targets abroad, with publicity as the prime objective. The late eighties and early nineties saw the transfer of the struggle to the occupied territories, and the emergence of a new phase of resistance and rebellion, known as the Intifāda. The Intifāda was directed, not against neutral targets abroad, but against the personnel and instruments of the occupation at home, and its primary purpose was to weaken and discourage that occupation, rather than to attract attention. Finally, in 1993, the PLO and the government of Israel decided to recognize each other and enter into negotiations. These eventually produced interim agreements for the transfer of authority from the Israeli police and military to the Palestinians in the Gaza Strip and the West Bank.

Inevitably, these developments were affected, and sometimes determined, by the international context of the Arab-Israel conflict. In 1948-9, both the United States and the Soviet Union gave diplomatic support to the new state of Israel. Stalin in those days still regarded Britain, not the USA, as his principal world adversary, and saw in the new state of Israel the best chance of undermining the British position in the Middle East. In pursuit of this objective, he allowed Czechoslovakia, then a Soviet satellite state, to provide the weapons which enabled Israel to survive its first war. Some military help also arrived from private sources in the United States, despite a generally maintained official embargo on weapons to all the contending parties. In 1956, when Britain and France landed forces in Egypt, ostensibly to interpose between the Israelis and the Egyptians but almost certainly in prior agreement with the Israelis, the United States government, followed by that of the Soviet Union, took up a strong position against the three invading powers and by various means compelled their withdrawal from Egyptian territory.

But by this time, the strategic situation had radically changed. In the immediate post-war years, Soviet pressure was directed mainly against the so-called Northern Tier states, Turkey and Iran. Resisting both the pressures and the blandishments of the Soviet government, these countries turned for help to the United States, which became increasingly involved in the affairs of the Middle East, first in the attempt to shore up the crumbling British position, and then, with the realization that this objective was unattainable, in the attempt to create a Middle Eastern defence system against possible Soviet attack. In 1952, both Greece and Turkey were accepted as members of the North Atlantic Treaty Organization. In 1955 the government of Iraq was induced to join with Turkey, Iran, and Britain in a new alliance that came to be known as the Baghdad Pact. The United States at that time preferred informal association to formal membership of the alliance.

In the event, the attempt to include an Arab country in a Western-sponsored alliance proved counterproductive. Turkey and Iran were old sovereign states. Lying on the southern frontier of the Soviet Union, they were keenly aware, from both past experience and current realities, of the threat from the north. The Arab states had no such experience, and their recent political history had consisted largely of attempts to free themselves, first from Western rule, and then from Western entanglements. In Iraq, the inclusion of that country in the Baghdad Pact was seen as a retrograde step restoring Western dominance; in other Arab countries, and especially in Egypt under the new republican regime, it was seen as a Western attempt to change the regional balance of power against Egypt. When in the mid-1950s the Soviets, leap-frogging the Northern Tier states, established close relations with Egypt and other Arab states, they were generally welcomed, and were quickly able to establish positions of strength and influence – even to the extent of persuading Arab governments to sign treaties and accord base facilities.

An important element in Soviet policy from the mid-fifties, and more strongly in the sixties and seventies, was their support for the Arab case against Israel – diplomatically, at the United Nations and other international fora; militarily, by the provision of sophisticated weaponry and technical and logistical support for the Arab armies. This in turn led the United States to enter into a new and closer strategic relationship with Israel, of which it became the principal source of diplomatic, strategic, and in time also financial, support.

These developments made the Arab–Israel conflict a major issue of the Cold War. In Middle Eastern as in some other problems, super-power involvement on the side of their various protégés served to contain crises and limit their effects, but also at the same time to prevent any real movement towards a solution. For the Middle Eastern peace process, as for parallel peace processes in other parts of the world, the ending of the Cold War was an essential prerequisite.

Of all the wars between Middle Eastern states and peoples, the Arab–Israel conflict has attracted most attention in the outside world, in part because of the direct involvement of the rival superpowers, in part, no doubt because of interests and concerns only tenuously related to the issues and merits of the case. These outside concerns have prevented a clear resolution of the conflict by the victory of one side or the other. The struggle thus consisted, in effect, of a series of short, sharp wars, ended by international intervention, with at best tactical and never strategic victories. The unintended result was that, in dealing with this issue, the role of the international agencies was not the resolution but rather the conservation of conflict.

The response to the war fought between Iraq and Iran from 1980 to 1988 was very different. Unlike the Arabs and Israelis, neither side could command any strong international support – if anything, the contrary, since both regimes had aroused powerful antagonisms in the outside world. Neither the powers nor the international bodies seemed disposed to make any great effort or take any great risk to bring the fighting to an end. The result was a conflict which lasted longer than the Second World War and which, in its toll of death and destruction, greatly exceeded all the Arab–Israel wars put together.

The issues were also more complex. Those of the Arab–Israel conflict were basically clear and simple. They were, consecutively, three questions. Should Israel exist; if so, where should its frontiers be, and who should rule on the other side of these frontiers? The Iraq–Iran war had many different aspects. It could be and was portrayed in personal terms, as a confrontation between two charismatic leaders, Khomeini and Saddam Hussein; in ethnic terms, between Persians and Arabs; in ideological terms, between Islamic revivalism and secular modernism (Saddam Hussein later changed his mind on this point); in sectarian terms, between Sunni and Shīʿa; in economic terms as a contest for control of the oil of the region; and even in old-fashioned power political terms as a quarrel over territory and a struggle for regional hegemony. A notable feature of the struggle was the patriotic loyalty of both Iranians and Iraqis to their countries and to the governments that ruled them. The Arab minority in southwestern Iran did not rally to the Iraqis; the Shīʿa population of Iraq, with few exceptions, showed little sympathy with the Iranian revolution or regime.

Impeded by neither domestic nor international pressures, nor yet – since both were oil exporters – by serious financial constraint, the two sides were able to pursue their mutually destructive war for eight years.

At first, the Iranians seemed to be gaining the upper hand. After halting the opening Iraqi offensive, they mounted a powerful counter-attack and advanced into Iraqi territory. The Iraqis, with significant intelligence and logistical support from the United States and financial support from the wealthier Arab states, were in turn able to halt this attack and eventually Iran was compelled to agree to a peace which left Iraq in a slightly better position.

Saddam Hussein's quasi-victory over Iran and the acquiescence of the outside world in his attack emboldened him to start a new war, with the invasion, occupation and annexation of Kuwait in August 1990.

In starting these two wars, Saddam Hussein made both political and military calculations, both correct and incorrect. In attacking Iran, he calculated – rightly – that neither regional nor outside powers would lift a finger in support of a revolutionary regime that had both outraged and alarmed them. He also calculated – wrongly – that the invasion of Iran at a time of revolutionary upheaval would be quick and easy. In his invasion of Kuwait ten years later, the balance of correct and incorrect calculation was the other way round. His military calculation that the invasion and annexation of Kuwait would be quick and easy was correct. His political assumption, that the regional powers would be supportive or at least acquiescent and that outside powers would not go beyond some perfunctory and ineffectual protest was, from his point of view, disastrously mistaken.

This error arose from a failure to take account of the changing configuration of world affairs. By the summer of 1990 processes had begun which, within the following months, led to the unravelling of the Soviet Union and the ending of the Cold War. Saddam Hussein was no longer held back from dangerous adventures, as he might have been in the past, by the caution of a superpower patron, and he took full advantage of this new freedom. But there was a price. As the sequel soon demonstrated, he could no longer summon his superpower patron to protect him from the other superpower invoked by his victims within the region.

A new pattern was emerging in the region. In this new con-figuration, outside powers no longer determined or directed the course of events in the Middle East, but the policies and actions of Middle Eastern governments provoked or invoked the intervention of increas-ingly reluctant outside powers. The war over Kuwait in 1990–1 was not, like so many previous struggles in the region, inspired or prolonged by external rivals. It was a regional and, indeed, an inter-Arab conflict in which external powers, led by the United States, became involved. The war and its aftermath showed that not one but both of the superpowers were in effect withdrawing from the battle for the Middle East – the one lacking the ability, the other the desire, to play an imperial role or even, more modestly, to provide the region with police protection against its more dangerous denizens.

The defeat of Saddam Hussein's army by a coalition of regional and external forces proved quick and easy, in striking contrast with the eight-year war between Iraq and Iran. But having expelled the Iraqi forces from Kuwait, the United States and its allies were content to . leave matters at that; that is to say, to leave Saddam Hussein and his regime in power. Several explanations, of varying plausibility, have been offered for this decision, but one basic reason seems fairly clear. In the situation prevailing in 1991, to destroy the regime would have meant installing another in its place, and that in turn would have required a level of sponsorship and protection perilously reminiscent of the mandates and protectorates, both overt and disguised, of earlier times. The United States, it was said at the time, had no desire to install a proconsul in Baghdad, nor would America's Arab allies have been willing to accept such an action. Instead it was decided to leave to the Iraqi people – as was their right – the choice of retaining, changing or replacing the government of their country. The practical implications of this policy were seen in the period immediately fol- lowing a cease-fire between Iraqi and coalition forces, when Saddam Hussein proceeded to the ruthless repression of opposition movements among the Kurds in the north, the Shī'a in the south, and dissident elements of all persuasions at the centre.

The lesson was clear. The United States might act vigorously to defend its own basic interests and those of the international community, the definition of these interests to be determined by trial and error. Otherwise, the governments and peoples of the Middle East were on their own. The Middle East was a freer, and also a more dangerous place.

The ending of the Cold War, and the collapse of the bi-polar discipline which the two superpowers, sometimes acting in com- petition, sometimes in accord, had managed to impose, confronted the peoples of the Middle East, like those of other regions liberated from superpower control or interference, with an awful choice. They could move, however slowly and reluctantly, to settle their disputes and live peacefully side by side, as happened in some parts of the world; or they could give free rein to their conflicts and hatreds, and fall into a descending spiral of strife, bloodshed and torment, as happened in others. It was surely the prospect of this bloody descent into chaos, and the awareness that there were forces – inside not outside the region – actively working to this end, that impelled the government of Israel, the leadership of the Palestine Liberation Organization, and a number of Arab governments to embark on negotiations which, with external and particularly American help, seemed to be leading to mutual recognition, to a measure of mutual tolerance, and, more practically, to the transfer of the occupied territories from Israeli to Palestinian rule.

With the agreement to end Israeli rule in the occupied areas, the last of the Arab peoples, the Palestinians, seemed about to realize their dream of freedom. But among the Palestinians, as earlier among other Arab peoples, a different and increasingly urgent question was discussed – after the achievement of freedom from foreign rule, what kind of freedom would they in fact enjoy? For peoples under foreign rule, the first objective – and for many, the only objective – was to end that rule. But even under foreign rule, the debate began on the nature of the regime to follow its ending. The debate became urgent and immediate once independence was attained.

Both the British and the French had created new states in their own images. The French set up parliamentary republics, the British constitutional monarchies. After the departure of their patrons, almost all of them collapsed or were abandoned and the peoples of the region looked for other models.

While the political and strategic threat offered to the Middle East by the Axis powers ended with their defeat, the impact of their ideas on the rising nationalist and related movements remained and even grew. This new pattern of thought and of social and political organization had a double appeal – first, because it was opposed to the dominant West and was already attractive for that reason; and second, because the ideologies and social strategies that were being offered corresponded in many ways much more closely to both the realities and the traditions of the region. In countries of still uncertain territorial definition and of shifting national identity, ethnic nationalism was much more understandable than patriotism. Similarly, radical and authoritarian ideologies had greater appeal than liberal and libertarian ideas. Communal and collective identities and rights made better sense than the more individualistic formulations of the West, which at that particular point seemed both irrelevant and inappropriate. These influences were and remain more active in Syria and in Iraq than in Egypt, which had a stronger national identity, an older liberal tradition and a much more extensive and effective parliamentary experience.

The failure of the combined Arab forces to prevent the birth of Israel gave rise to profound heart-searching in the Arab countries and, within a few years, to the violent removal of the rulers and sometimes even of the regimes that were held responsible. The first regime to fall was that of Syria, where in March 1949, Colonel Ḥusnī Zaʿīm, in a bloodless coup, terminated the presidential and parliamentary order and inaugurated a series of military *coups d'état*. The period of army government ended in 1954 with the restoration of the parliamentary regime and the holding of elections. This restoration was of brief duration. Between 1958 and 1961, Syria was part of the United Arab Republic. After its secession, the country moved rapidly towards a dictatorship of the Baʿth party. In Jordan, King ʿAbdullah, held responsible for the Arab defeat in Palestine and, worse, for having tried to make peace with Israel, was assassinated in 1951. But the Hashimite monarchy, which to many at the time seemed the most fragile of Arab regimes, held firm, and King ʿAbdullah, the founder and creator of his kingdom, was succeeded by his son and grandson.

The most dramatic changes were in Egypt where, in 1952–4, in a series of moves, King Fārūq was deposed and exiled, the monarchy abolished and a republic was proclaimed. The first ruler, General Muhammad Neguib, the nominal leader of the revolution, was soon set aside and replaced by Colonel Nasser, the real head of the group of so-called 'Free Officers', who had planned, organized and executed the change of regime. The republican government gradually lost its military character. It remained authoritarian.

In time, other Arab states were affected by the revolutionary wave. In Iraq in 1958, the monarchy, discredited especially by its Western alignment, was overthrown and replaced by the first of a series of military dictators. As in Syria, the army rule eventually gave way to a party dictatorship run by the Baʿth. Though sharing a common origin with the Syrian ruling party, the two branches of the Baʿth were profoundly hostile to one another.

Of the Arab states bordering Israel, only Lebanon, which had taken no significant part in the military action in 1948, and which alone had recognized an international frontier with Israel in the Rhodes armistice agreement, retained its parliamentary and democratic system until in time that, too, was overthrown in a civil war, due in large measure to external intervention.

Among the remoter Arab regimes, the two Yemens in southern Arabia, Libya and Algeria in North Africa, also succumbed to revolutionary takeovers. Elsewhere, in Morocco and in the Arabian peninsula, more remote from the conflict in Palestine, traditional regimes were able to survive.

In the countries more actively involved, revolutions came and went, and revolutionary regimes removed and replaced one another. But the basic problems which had brought each new regime to power remained unresolved – the immediate problem of the presence of Israel at the centre of the region and beyond that, the agonizing dilemmas posed by the survival and even the flourishing of Israel in spite of the hostility of the entire Arab world.

The initial survival of Israel after months of bitter fighting could plausibly be explained as a victory of desperation against overconfidence. This explanation did not, however, suffice for the greater and swifter victories achieved by Israel over vastly bigger and better equipped armies in the wars that followed.

For some, the establishment and development of Israel was a continuation of the aggressive acts of Western imperialism against the Arab and Islamic lands. In this perspective, Israel was created to serve as a bridgehead of Western influence, penetration and domination; Zionism was simply the tool of imperialism and Israel an instrument of Western power. Later, in the desperate search for explanations, there were some who, drawing on the themes and imagery of European anti-Semitism, depicted events in the same dramatic terms but with the roles reversed.

Others, concerned less to detect and condemn the misdeeds of foreigners than to discover and remedy the faults of their own societies, pointed to the disparities between the two sides – to the scientific and technological attainments, the economic and social structures, the political liberties of Israel as contrasted with their own situation. In all this, Israel, despite its predominantly Middle Eastern population, was seen as part of the West – not merely in the crude instrumental sense of being a tool of Western power, but in the profounder sense of being a part of Western civilization. The question of Israeli success was therefore part of the larger problem that had been exercising Muslim minds for centuries – the problem of Western wealth and power contrasted with the relative poverty and powerlessness of the Muslim states and peoples.

There were many answers to this dilemma. For some, the root cause of their difficulties was disunity – the fragmentation of the once great Arab world into a score of petty, squabbling states, incapable of agreeing among themselves and frittering away their energies on sterile rivalries and conflicts. Their answer was pan-Arabism – the ideal of a higher loyalty to a greater nation, purer and nobler than the often squalid parochial politics of the various Arab states. This ideal reached its peak in the days of the struggle against imperial control. It declined in appeal and in strength when the states attained effective independence and their leaders became increasingly reluctant to surrender that independence to some larger body. In any case, the history of Europe and, indeed, of the Western world in general provided ample proof that disunity was not necessarily an obstacle to material and intellectual progress and, in certain circumstances, could even contribute to its attainment.

As the states into which the region was divided became more stable and more permanent, both in the awareness of the political classes and in the realities of the region, governments and peoples began to look more to problems that could be formulated and solutions that could be applied within the structure of national sovereignty. As the struggle for political independence receded into an ever more distant past, attention was increasingly focused on economic problems and, more specifically, on the need for rapid economic development. Only in this way, it was felt, could these countries take their place in the modern world and acquire the strength to confront their modern enemies. The economic situation in most of these countries was deteriorating, not just relatively, as compared with the West and the rising economies of the Far East, but absolutely, as expressed in the falling standard of living of the rapidly increasing population.

For a long time, the solutions to these problems were seen almost exclusively in socialist terms. Developing countries, it was argued and widely accepted, did not have the time to wait for the gradual and erratic progress of the market economy; nor did they have the patience for the upheavals and the uncertainties of political democracy. Only a firm hand and central planning, that is to say, authoritarian socialist government, could achieve the requisite rapid development. This approach was, of course, enormously encouraged by the influence and example of the Soviet Union, the most respected power in much of the Middle East and North Africa at that time.

By the mid-century, socialism was already popular among many intellectuals, but it was not they who brought it to power and put it into effect. Socialism, like liberalism in an earlier generation, was imposed from above, and fared no better. In Egypt, it was applied by a decision of the Nasserist regime nine years after its accession to power; in other countries, by military and nationalist regimes of various complexions which shared the belief that this was the only way to rapid economic development. There were several varieties of socialism – some of them more or less Marxist, more or less Soviet style; others, the so-called 'Arab socialism', seen as more humane, less rigid and better adapted to Arab conditions.

By the early 1990s it was clear that both Arab and Marxist socialism had failed and that the often misguided and inept reforms introduced by reformist governments had impeded rather than advanced the economic development that governments had so plausibly promised and peoples had so eagerly awaited.

Only in one respect were the economic policies successful – in underpinning a series of ruthless and pervasive dictatorships in which both the decencies of the traditional Islamic order and the liberties of the new Western order were undermined and destroyed. In their place, in the so-called socialist countries, the new political order consisted of a range of totalitarian dictatorships copied – sometimes with imported expert guidance – from the worst Central and East European models.

Despite the failure of economic policies, this was a period of very rapid economic change and perhaps even more of social and cultural transformation. Politically Western influence was reduced to a minimum but, in every other respect, Western influence grew apace.

The most visible, the most pervasive and the least recognized aspects of Western influence are in the realm of material things – the infrastructure, amenities and services of the modern state and city, most of them initiated by past European rulers or concession holders. Here there was clearly no desire to reverse or even deflect the processes of modernization. Nor indeed were such things as aeroplanes and cars, telephones and televisions, tanks and artillery, seen as Western or as related to the Western philosophies that preceded and facilitated their invention.

More remarkably, even some avowedly anti-Western states have retained the Western political apparatus of constitutions and legislative assemblies. The Islamic Republic of Iran claims to be restoring true Islamic government but it does so in the form of a written constitution and an elected parliament – neither with any precedent in Islamic doctrine or history.

Perhaps the most powerful and persistent of Western political ideas in the region has been that of revolution. The history of the Islamic Middle East, like that of other societies, offers many examples of the overthrow of governments by rebellion or conspiracy. There is also an old Islamic tradition of challenge to the social and political order by leaders who believed that it was their sacred duty to dethrone tyranny and install justice in its place. Islamic law and tradition lay down the limits of the obedience which is owed to the ruler and discuss – albeit with considerable caution – the circumstances in which a ruler forfeits his claim to the allegiance of his subjects and may or rather must lawfully be deposed and replaced.

But the notion of revolution, as developed in sixteenth-century Holland, seventeenth-century England and eighteenth-century America and France, was alien and new. The first self-styled revolutions in the Middle East were those of the constitutionalists in Iran in 1905 and the Young Turks in the Ottoman Empire in 1908. Since then there have been many others, and by the last decade of the twentieth century, a clear majority of states in the region were governed by regimes installed by means of the violent removal of their predecessors. In early days, this was sometimes accomplished by a nationalist struggle against foreign overlords. Later it was usually achieved by military officers deposing the rulers in whose armies they served. All of these, with equal fervour, laid claim to the title 'revolutionary', which in time became the most widely accepted claim to legitimacy in government in the Middle East.

In a very few cases, the change of regime resulted from profounder movements in society, with deeper causes and greater consequences than a simple replacement of the men at the top. One such was surely the Islamic Revolution of 1979 in Iran, which invites comparison with the French and more especially Russian Revolutions in its origins, its modalities and perhaps also its ultimate fate.

For better or for worse – and from the start there have been different views on this – what happened in Iran can be seen as a revolution in the classical sense: a mass movement with wide popular participation that resulted in a major shift in economic as well as political power and that inaugurated, or perhaps more accurately continued, a process of vast social transformation.

In Iran under the Pahlavis, as in France under the Bourbons and in Russia under the Romanovs, a major process of change was already under way, and had advanced to a point at which it required a shift in political power in order to continue. And in the Iranian, as in the other revolutions, there was also the possibility that something might happen whereby the process of change was deflected, perverted or even annulled. From an early stage, some Iranians, arguing from different and sometimes contrasting premises, claimed that this had already happened. As the revolutionary regime ensconced itself in power, more and more came to agree with them.

The revolution in Iran, unlike those earlier movements designated by that name, was called Islamic. Its leaders and inspirers cared nothing for the models of Paris or Petrograd, and saw European ideologies of the left no less than of the right as all part of the pervasive infidel enemy against whom they were waging their struggle. Theirs was a different society, educated in different scriptures and classics, shaped by different historical memories. The symbols and slogans of the revolution were Islamic because these alone had the power to mobilize the masses for struggle.

Islam provided more than symbols and slogans. As interpreted by the revolutionary leaders and spokesmen, it formulated the objectives to be attained and, no less important, it defined the enemies to be opposed. These were familiar from history, law and tradition: the infidel abroad, the apostate at home. For the revolutionaries, of course, the apostate meant all those Muslims, and especially Muslim rulers, who did not share their interpretation of authentic Islam and who, in their perception, were importing alien and infidel ways and thus subverting the community of Islam and the faith and law by which it lived. In principle, the aim of the Islamic revolution in Iran, and eventually in other countries where such movements established themselves, was to sweep away all the alien and infidel accretions that had been imposed on Muslim lands and peoples in the era of alien dominance and influence and to restore the true and divinely given Islamic order.

An examination of the record of these revolutionaries, however, in Iran and elsewhere, reveals that the rejection of the West and its offerings is by no means as comprehensive and as undiscriminating as

377

propaganda might indicate, and that some at least of the importations from the lands of unbelief are still very welcome.

Some of these are obvious. The Islamic revolution in Iran was the first truly modern revolution of the electronic age. Khomeini was the first charismatic orator who sent his oratory from abroad to millions of his compatriots at home on cassettes; he was the first revolutionary leader in exile who directed his followers at home by telephone, thanks to the direct dialling that the Shah had introduced in Iran and that was available to him in France but not in Iraq, his previous place of exile. Needless to say, in the wars in which they have been engaged, both formal and informal, the Iranian revolutionary leaders have made the fullest use of such weapons as the West and its imitators were willing to sell them. Naturally, such weapons as fax, internet and the satellite dish are also available to those who seek to overthrow them.

There was, tragically, another respect in which the revolutionary regime in Iran borrowed from Europe. While their symbols and allusions were Islamic rather than European, their models of style and method were often more European than Islamic. The summary trial and execution of great numbers of ideologically defined enemies; the driving into exile of hundreds of thousands of men and women; the large-scale confiscation of private property; the mixture of repression and subversion, of violence and indoctrination that accompanied the consolidation of power – all this owes far more to the examples of Robespierre and Stalin than to those of Muḥammad and ʿAlī. These methods can hardly be called Islamic; they are, however, thoroughly revolutionary.

Like the French and the Russians in their time, the Iranian revolutionaries played to international as well as domestic audiences, and their revolution exercised a powerful fascination over other peoples outside Iran, in other countries within the same culture, the same universe of discourse. The appeal was naturally strongest amongst Shīʿite populations, as in south Lebanon and some of the Gulf states, and weakest among their immediate Sunni neighbours. It was for a while very strong in much of the Muslim world where Shīʿism was virtually unknown. In these, the sectarian difference was unimportant. Khomeini could be seen, not as a Shīʿite or an Iranian, but as an Islamic revolutionary leader. Like the young Western radicals who, in their day, responded with almost messianic enthusiasm to events in Paris and Petrograd, so did millions of young and not-so-young men and women all over the world of Islam respond to the call of Islamic revolution – with the same upsurge of emotion, the same uplifting of hearts, the same boundless hopes, the same willingness to excuse and condone all kinds of horrors, and the same anxious questions about the future.

The years that followed were difficult years in Iran. The people suffered greatly from foreign wars, internal strife and repression, and a steadily worsening economic crisis. As in other revolutions, there was recurring conflict between rival factions, sometimes described as extremists and moderates, more accurately as ideologues and pragmatists. Because of these and other changes, the ideal of the Islamic revolution, Iranian-style, lost some of its appeal – but not all. Islamic revolutionary movements derived from, inspired by, or parallel to the revolution in Iran developed in other Muslim countries where they became serious and sometimes successful contenders for power.

All these various revolutionary regimes, as well as the surviving monarchies and traditional regimes, shared the desire to preserve and utilize both the political apparatus and the economic benefits which modernization placed at their disposal. What was resented was foreign control and exploitation of the economic machine, not the foreign origin of the machine itself.

Like the British and the French before them, the Soviets and the United States in their rivalry in the Middle East tried to create societies and polities in their own image. Neither task was easy, one of them especially difficult. The sponsorship of authoritarian government presented no problem, but it was quite another matter to create a Marxist, socialist regime in an Islamic country. The task of creating a liberal democracy was even more difficult. But if democracies are more difficult to create, they are also more difficult to destroy. This in the long term worked to the advantage of the democracies, both inside and outside the region, and to the detriment of their authoritarian enemies.

In the long debate about how the hard-won independence should be used, and the lot of the people bettered, there were two main ideological streams: Islam and democracy. Both came in many variant and competing forms. At a time when all the different imported methods that Muslims had used or copied or imitated had visibly failed, there was considerable force in the argument that these were the ways of foreigners and unbelievers, and that they had brought nothing but harm. The remedy was for Muslims to return to the faith and law of Islam, to be authentically themselves, to purge state and society of foreign and infidel accretions, and create a true Islamic order.

The alternative programme was democracy – not the shoddy imitations of Western democracies practised in the interwar period, and operated only by small cliques of magnates at the top, but authentic, free institutions functioning at every level of public life, from the village to the presidency. Where fundamentalists and democrats are both in opposition, the former have an immense advantage. In the mosques and preachers, they dispose of a network for meeting and communication that no government, however tyrannical, can entirely control and no other group can rival. Sometimes a tyrannical regime has even eased the path of the fundamentalists by eliminating competing oppositions. Only one other group in society has the cohesion, the structure, and the means to take independent action, and that is the army – the other major motor of political change in the region. At different times and in different places, the army has acted for democracy, as in Turkey, or for fundamentalism, as in the Sudan.

The proponents of both Islamic and democratic solutions differed considerably among themselves, and many variants of both have been propounded. For some, the two ideas were mutually exclusive. The so-called Islamic fundamentalists – a minority, but an active and important one among Muslims – had no use for democracy, except as a one-way ticket to power; the militant secularists among the democrats made little effort to conceal their intention of ending, or at least reducing, the role traditionally played by Islam in the public life of a state. The interaction between the Islamic tradition of a state based on faith and Western notions of separation between religion and government seems likely to continue.

For men and for women alike, the interlude of freedom was too long, and its effects too profound, for it to be forgotten. Despite many reverses, European-style democracy is not dead in the Islamic lands, and there are some signs of a revival. In some countries, parliamentary and constitutional systems are becoming increasingly effective. In several others there have been steps, still rather tentative, towards political as well as economic liberalization.

In cultural and social life, the introduction and acceptance of European ways went very far and persisted in forms which even the most militant and radical either did not perceive or were willing to tolerate. The first to change were the traditional arts. Already by the end of the eighteenth century, the old traditions of miniature painting in books and of interior decoration in buildings, were dying. In the course of the nineteenth century they were replaced in the more Westernized countries by a new art and architecture that were at first influenced and then dominated by European patterns. The old arts of miniature and calligraphy lingered on for a while but those who practised them, with few exceptions, lacked originality and prestige. Their place in the artistic self-expression of society was taken by European-style painters, working in oils on canvas. Architecture too, even mosque architecture, conformed in the main to Western artistic notions as well as to the inevitable Western techniques. At times there were attempts to return to traditional Islamic patterns, but these often took the form of a conscious neo-classicism. Only in one respect were Islamic artistic norms retained and that was in the slow and reluctant acceptance of sculpture, seen as a violation of the Islamic ban on graven images. One of the main grievances against such secular modernizers as Kemal Atatürk in Turkey and the Shah in Iran was their practice of installing statues of themselves in public places. This was seen as no better than pagan idolatry.

The Westernization of art was paralleled in literature, though at a slower pace and at a later date. From the mid-nineteenth century onwards, traditional literary forms were neglected, except among some die-hard circles with limited impact. In their place came new forms and ideas from the West – the novel and the short story, replacing the traditional tale and apologue; the essay and the newspaper article, and new forms and themes that have transformed modern poetry among all the peoples of the region. Even the language in which modern literature is written has, in all the countries of the region, been extensively and irreversibly changed under the influence of Western discourse.

The change is least noticeable in music, where the impact of European art music is still relatively small. In Turkey, where European influence has lasted longest and gone deepest, there are talented performers, some of them with international reputations, and composers working in the Western manner. Istanbul and Ankara are now on the international concert circuit, as are of course the chief cities of Israel, itself in effect a cultural component of the West. In these places, there are audiences large enough and faithful enough to make such visits worthwhile. Elsewhere in the Middle East, those who compose, perform or even listen to Western music are still relatively few. Music in the various traditional modes is still being composed and performed at high level and is accepted and appreciated by the vast majority of the population. Of late there has been some interest in the more popular types of Western music but even this is, in the main, limited to comparatively small groups in the larger cities. Music is perhaps the profoundest and most intimate expression of a culture, and it is natural that it should be the last to yield to alien influence.

Another highly visible sign of European influence is in clothing. That Muslim armies use modern equipment and weaponry may be ascribed to necessity, and there are ancient traditions declaring it lawful to imitate the infidel enemy in order to defeat him. But the adoption of infidel dress is another matter, and has a significance at once cultural, symbolic, even religious.

In the nineteenth century, the Ottomans, followed by other Muslim states, adopted European style uniforms for both officers and men, and European harness for their horses. Only the headgear remained un-Westernized, and for good reason. After the Kemalist Revolution in Turkey, even this last bastion of Islamic conservatism fell. The Turkish army, along with the general population, adopted European hats and caps, and before long they were followed by the armies, and eventually even many civilians in almost all other Muslim states.

The position was different for women. During the nineteenth and early twentieth centuries, the Europeanization of female attire was slower, later, and more limited. It was strongly resisted, and affected a much smaller portion of the population. At many levels of society, where the wearing of Western clothes by men became normal, women still kept – or were kept – to traditional dress. By the mid-twentieth century, however, more and more women were adopting a Western style of clothing – at first among the modernizing leisured classes, and then, increasingly, among working women and students. One of the most noticeable consequences of the Islamic revival has been a reversal of this trend and a return, by women far more than by men, to traditional attire.

Of all the changes attributable to Western example or influence, the profoundest and most far-reaching is surely the change in the position of women. The abolition of chattel slavery made concubinage illegal, and though it lingered on for some time in the remoter areas, it ceased to be either common or accepted. In a few countries, notably Turkey, Tunisia, and Iran until the fall of the shah but not after, even polygamous marriage was outlawed, and in many of the Muslim states, while still lawful, it was subject to legal and other restrictions. Among the urban middle and upper classes, it became socially unacceptable;

for the urban lower classes, it had always been economically impractical.

A major factor in the emancipation of women was economic need. Peasant women had from time immemorial been part of the work-force and had, in consequence, enjoyed certain social freedoms denied to their sisters in the cities. Economic modernization brought a need for female labour, which was augmented by mobilization for modern war. This became a significant factor in the Ottoman Empire during the First World War, when much of the male population was in the armed forces. The economic involvement of women and the social changes resulting from it continued in the inter-war period and after, and even brought a few legislative changes in favour of women. These had some effect in social and family life. Education for women also made substantial progress, and by the 1970s and 1980s, considerable numbers of women were enrolled as students in the universities. They began in so-called 'women's professions', such as nursing and teaching, traditional in Europe and gradually becoming so in the lands of Islam. Later, women began to appear in other faculties and professions. Even in Iran there are women physicians for women patients and, more remarkably, women members of parliament.

The enrolment of women even in the traditional professions was too much for some of the militants. Khomeini spoke with great anger of the immorality which he believed would inevitably result from the employment of women to teach boys.

The political emancipation of women has made significant progress in those countries where parliamentary regimes function. It matters little in the dictatorships, controlled by either the army or the party. Both are overwhelmingly male. Westerners tend to assume that the emancipation of women is part of liberalization, and that women will consequently fare better under liberal than under autocratic regimes. Such an assumption is dubious and often untrue. Among Arab coun-tries, the legal emancipation of women went furthest in Iraq and South Yemen, both ruled by notoriously repressive regimes. It lagged behind in Egypt, in many ways the most tolerant and open of Arab societies. It is in such societies that public opinion, still mainly male and mainly conservative, resists change. Women's rights have suffered the most serious reverses in countries where fundamentalists have influence or where, as in Iran, they rule. The emancipation of women is one of the main grievances of the fundamentalists and its reversal is in the forefront of their programme.

Nevertheless, it is clear that irreversible changes have taken place.

Even those claiming to restore the Holy Law in its entirety are unlikely to reintroduce legal concubinage, nor is there much probability of a return to polygamy among the educated classes in Middle Eastern cities. Fundamentalist influences and rulers have in many ways changed the content and manner of education for women, but they have not returned them – nor are they likely to return them – to their previous condition of ignorance. And while, in Islamic lands as in Europe and America, there are women who speak and work against their own emancipation, the long-term trend is clearly for greater freedom. There are now significant numbers of educated, often Western-educated, women in Islamic lands. They are already having a significant impact, and Islamic public life will be enriched by the contributions of the previously excluded half of the population.

These changes, and the legal, social, and cultural transformations which preceded, accompanied and followed them, have evoked sharply differing reactions among the population. For many women, they brought release and opportunity; for many men, they opened a way to a previously hidden world. In some places, the impact of the West brought wealth, often beyond any that could be imagined. Western technology and Western-style business introduced new ways of acquiring money; Western consumer culture offered a wide range of new ways of spending it. But for many, and not only those directly and adversely affected, the new ways were both an affront and a threat – an affront to their sense of decency and propriety, and a mortal threat to the most cherished of all their values, the religious basis of their society.

Modernization – or as many saw it, Westernization – widened the gap between rich and poor. It also made that gap more visible and more palpable. In most cities outside the Arabian peninsula, the rich now wore different clothes, ate different food, and lived by different social rules from the unmodernized mass of the population. And all the time, thanks to Western means of communication, especially the cinema and television, the deprived masses were more aware than ever before of the difference between them and the wealthy, and of what, specifically, they were missing.

In some countries, the pain and discomfort inevitable in a period of rapid change were palliated by wise and moderate governments. But in most they were aggravated by the economic mismanagement of autocratic regimes. There were real problems, notably the rapid growth of population unaccompanied by any corresponding increase in domestic food resources. But often even the considerable assets enjoyed by some countries were squandered. Part of the problem was the heavy cost of the security and military apparatus required to maintain order at home and to confront or deter potential enemies abroad. But these costs are not the whole explanation. The sad comment of an Algerian interviewed in a French news magazine is typical: 'Algeria was once the granary of Rome, and now it has to import cereals to make bread. It is a land of flocks and gardens, and it imports meat and fruit. It is rich in oil and gas, and it has a foreign debt of twenty-five billion dollars and two million unemployed.' He goes on to say that this is the result of thirty years of mismanagement.

Algeria has a small oil income and a large population. Some other countries have large incomes and small populations, but have nevertheless managed to devastate their economies and impoverish their peoples. In the longer perspective, oil may prove to be a very mixed blessing for the countries endowed with it. Politically, oil revenues strengthened autocratic governments by freeing them from the financial pressures and constraints which, in other countries, induced governments to accept measures of democratization. Economically, oil wealth often produced a lopsided development, and left these countries dangerously exposed to such outside factors as the fluctuations in the world price of oil, and even, in the long run, to the position of oil itself. There are other sources of oil besides the Middle East; there are other sources of energy besides oil, and both are being actively pursued by a world that has grown weary of Middle Eastern pressures and uncertainties.

In the last decade of the twentieth century, the Middle East faces two major crises. One of them is economic and social: the difficulties arising from economic deprivation and, still more, economic dislocation, and their social consequences. The other is political and social – the breakdown of consensus, of that generally accepted set of rules and principles by which a polity works and without which a society cannot function, even under autocratic government. The break-up of the Soviet Union exemplifies the consequences of such a loss of consensus, and the difficulties and dangers of creating a new one.

In the last decade of the twentieth century, it became increasingly clear that in facing these problems, the governments and peoples of the Middle East were substantially on their own. Outside powers were no longer interested in directing, still less dominating, the affairs of the region. On the contrary, they displayed an extreme reluctance to become involved. The countries of the outside world – that is to say, of Europe, the Americas, and increasingly, of the Far East – were basically concerned with three things in the Middle East: a rich and growing market for their goods and services, a major source of their energy needs, and, as a necessary means to safeguarding the first two, the maintenance of at least some semblance of international law and order.

The circumstances which would provoke outside military intervention were epitomized by Saddam Hussein's invasion and annexation of Kuwait, and the consequent immediate threat to Saudi Arabia and the Gulf states. This confronted the outside world with a double threat. The first was that the oil resources of the region, that is to say, a significant part of the oil resources of the world, would fall under the monopolistic control of an aggressive dictator. The second threat was to the whole international order established in the aftermath of the Second World War. Despite all the many conflicts in many continents, this was the first time that a member state of the United Nations in good standing was simply invaded and annexed by another member state.

Had Saddam Hussein been allowed to succeed in his venture, the United Nations, already devalued, would have followed the defunct League of Nations into well-deserved ignominy, and the world would have belonged to the violent and the ruthless.

He was not allowed to succeed, and an impressive range of forces, both from inside and from outside the region, was mobilized to evict him from Kuwait. But – this is the most telling indication of the new era – he was evicted from Kuwait, not from Iraq, and was allowed to resume his distinctive style of government and many of his policies in that country. The message was clear. If the Iraqis want a new and different form of government, they must do it for themselves; no one else will do it for them.

This broadly has been the message of the outside powers in the last decade of the twentieth century. These powers will, at most, act to defend their own interests, that is to say, markets and oil, and the interests of the international community, that is to say, a decent respect for the basic rules of the United Nations. Otherwise, the peoples and governments of the Middle East, for the first time in two centuries, will determine their own fate. They may produce new regional powers, perhaps acting in concert, perhaps contending for regional hegemony.

They may go the way of Yugoslavia and Somalia, to fragmentation and internecine chaos – and there are movements and individuals in the region who have made it clear that they would choose this rather than compromise on what they believe to be their religious duties or national rights. Events in Lebanon during the civil war could easily become a paradigm for the entire region. They may unite – perhaps, as some are urging, for a holy war, a new *jihād* which, again as in the past, might well evoke the response of a new Crusade. Or they may unite for peace – with themselves, their neighbours, and the outside world, using and sharing their spiritual as well as their material resources in the search for a fuller, richer, freer life. For the moment, the outside world seems disposed to leave them in peace, and perhaps even to help them achieve it. They alone – the peoples and governments of the Middle East – can decide whether and how to use this window of opportunity while, in an interval of their troubled modern history, it remains open.

NOTES

INTRODUCTION

1. Kâtib Çelebi, *Mīzān al-Haqq* (Istanbul, AH 1290), pp. 42–3. English translation by G. L. Lewis, *The Balance of Truth* (London, 1957), p. 56.
2. Abū 'Abdallah Muḥammad b. 'Abd al-Wahhāb, *Riḥlat al-wazīr fī iftikāk al-asīr*, ed. A. Bustani (Tangier, 1940), p. 67.
3. *Takvim-i Veka'i'*, 1 Jumada I 1247/14 May 1832.
4. Mehmed Efendi, *Paris Sefaretnamesi*, ed. Ebüzziya (Istanbul, AH 1306), pp. 139–46.

CHAPTER 1   *Before Christianity*

1. Sabbath 33b; for another translation, see *The Babylonian Talmud: Seder Mo'ed*, trans. I. Epstein (London, 1930), vol. 1, p. 156.

CHAPTER 2   *Before Islam*

1. Ammianus Marcellinus, trans. John C. Rolfe (Cambridge, Mass.: Loeb Classical Library, 1963).
2. Menander, *Excerpta de legationibus*, ed. C. de Boor (Berlin, 1903), vol. I, pp. 205–6; translation as in *Cambridge Medieval History*, vol. IVa, p. 479.

CHAPTER 3   *Origins*

1. Al-Mas'ūdī, *Murūj al-Dhahab*, ed. Barbier de Meynard and Pavet de Courteille, rev. Charles Pellat (Beirut, 1970), vol. 3, pp. 76–7.
2. Ibn Qutayba, *'Uyūn al-Akhbār*, ed. Aḥmad Zakī al-'Adawī (Cairo, 1343–8/1925–30), vol. 2, p. 210; English translation in Bernard Lewis, ed. and trans., *Islam from the Prophet Muhammad to the Capture of Constantinople*, 2 (1974), p. 273.
3. Al-Muqaddasī, *Descriptio Imperii Moslemici*, ed. M. J. Goeje, 2nd edn (Leiden, 1906), p. 159.

CHAPTER 6   *The Mongol Aftermath*

1. Al-Suyūṭī, *Ḥusn al-Muḥāḍara* (Cairo, AH 1321), p. 39.

2. As cited in Colin Imber, *The Ottoman Empire 1300–1481* (Istanbul, 1990), p. 24.

3. *The Reign of the Sultan Orchan, Second King of the Turks, translated out of Hojah Effendi, an Eminent Turkish Historian, by William Seaman* (London, 1652), pp. 30–1.

CHAPTER 7   *The Gunpowder Empires*

1. Ibn Kemal, *Tevârih-i Âl-i Osman* VII *Defter*, ed. Şerafettin Turan (Ankara, 1957), p. 365.

2. Kemalpashazade, *Mohaczname*, ed. M. Pavet de Courteille (Paris, 1859), pp. 97–109.

3. Rudolf Tschudi, *Das Asafname des Lutfi Pasha* (Berlin, 1910), pp. 32–3.

4. Peçevi, *Tarih* (Istanbul, AH 1283), vol. i, pp. 498–9.

5. *The Turkish Letters of Ogier Ghiselin de Busbecq*, trans. Edward Seymour Forster (Oxford, 1922), p. 112.

6. Guglielmo Berchet, ed., *La Repubblica di Venezia e la Persia* (Turin, 1865), p. 181; English version in *A Narrative of Italian Travels in Persia in the 15th and 16th Centuries* (London, 1873), p. 227.

7. As cited in Ismail Hakkı Uzunçarşılı, *Osmanlı Devleti Teşkilâtından Kapıkulu Ocakları*, vol. 1 (Ankara, 1943), p. 306, note 1.

8. Selaniki Mustafa, *Tarih-i Selâniki*, ed. Mehmet Ipşirli (Istanbul, 1989), p. 471.

9. Koçu Bey, *Risale*, ed. Ali Kemali Aksüt (Istanbul, 1939), p. 32; following quotation, p. 45.

CHAPTER 8   *The State*

1. Ernest Barker, ed. and tr., *Social and Political Thought in Byzantium from Justinian I to the Last Palaeologos: Passages from Byzantine Writers and Documents* (Oxford, 1957), pp. 54–5.

2. Barker, op. cit., pp. 75–6.

3. Text and translation in M. Back, *Die Sassanidischen Staatsinschriften, Acta Iranica* 18 (1978), p. 284–5.

4. *The Diwans of 'Abīd b. al-Abraṣ, etc.*, ed. and tr. Sir Charles Lyall (Leiden, 1913), pp. 81 (Arabic text), 64 (trans.).

5. *Répertoire chronologique d'épigraphie arabe*, vol. 1 (Cairo, 1931), no. 1.

6. Al-Jāḥiz, *Rasā'il*, ed. A. M. Hārūn (Cairo, 1964–5), vol. 2, pp. 10–11.

7. Ibn Qutayba, op. cit., vol. 2, p. 115.

8. Mustafa Nuri Pasha, *Netaic ül-vukuat* (Istanbul, AH 1327), vol. 1, p. 59.

9. Lûtfi Pasha, *Tevarih-i Āl-i 'Osman* (Istanbul, AH 1341), p. 21; Yazıcıoglu Ali, *Selcukname*, as cited in Agah Sırrı Levend, *Türk Dilinde Gelişme ve Sadeleşme Safhaları* (Ankara, 1949), p. 34.

10. 'Abbās Iqbāl, *Vezārat dar 'ahd-i Salātīn-i Buzurg-i Saljūqī* (Tehran, 1959), pp. 302ff.

11. Ibn al-Rāwandī, *Rāhat-us-Sudūr*, ed. Muhammad Iqbāl (Leiden, 1921), p. 334.

12. Al-Jahshiyārī, *Kitāb al-Wuzarā' wa'l-Kuttāb*, ed. Mustafā al-Saqqā, Ibrāhīm al-Abyārī, 'Abd al-Hāfiz Shalabī (Cairo, 1938), p. 53.

13. Lûtfi Pasha, *Asafname*, pp. 14–15.

14. Hilāl al-Sābi', *Kitāb al-Wuzarā'*, ed. H. F. Amedroz (Leiden-Beirut, 1904), p. 64.

15. Al-Balādhurī, *Futūh al-Buldān*, ed. M. J. de Goeje (Leiden, 1866), vol. 1, p. 263.

16. Ibn Qutayba, op. cit., vol. 1, pp. 2, 6, 9, 10.

CHAPTER 9   *The Economy*

1. Ibn al-Faqīh, *Mukhtasar Kitāb al-Buldān*, ed. M. J. de Goeje (Leiden, 1885), pp. 187–8.

2. Peçevi, op. cit., vol. 1, p. 363.

3. *Akhbār al-Sīn wa'l-Hind*, ed. J. Sauvaget (Paris, 1948), p. 18.

4. Cited from Ralph S. Hattox, *Coffee and Coffeehouses: the Origins of a Social Beverage in the Medieval Near East* (Seattle, Wash., 1985), pp. 14–15.

5. Ibn Khaldun, *Al-Muqaddima*, ed. E. Quatremère (Paris, 1858), vol. i, p. 272.

6. Jean de Thevenot, *Relation d'un voyage fait au Levant* (Paris, 1665), as trans. in A. Lovell, *The Travels of Monsieur de Thevenot into the Levant* (London, 1687), pt. 1, p. 144.

7. Volney, *Voyage en Égypte* (Paris, 1825), vol. II, p. 254.

8. Karl Jahn, *Die Frankengeschichte des Rašīd al-Dīn* (facsimile edition with German translation) (Vienna, 1977) fol. 415 v. (Persian text), p. 54 (German translation).

9. Pierre Dan, *Histoire de Barbarie et de ses Corsaires* (Paris, 1637), p. 277. The captives are listed in the *Calendar of the State Papers relating to Ireland of the reign of Charles I, 1625–1632, preserved in the Public Record Office*, ed. R. P. Mahaffy (London, 1900), pp. 621–2.

CHAPTER 10   *The Elites*

1. Mālik ibn Anas, *Al-Mudawwana al-Kubrā* (Cairo, AH 1323), vol. 4, pp. 13–14; idem, *Al-Muwaṭṭaʾ* (Cairo, AH 1310), 3, pp. 57, 262.
2. ʿAbd al-Ḥamīd, *Risāla ilaʾl-kuttāb*, in Aḥmad Zakī Ṣafwat, *Jamharat Rasāʾil al-ʿArab* (Cairo, 1356/1937), ii, p. 534; English translation in B. Lewis, ed. and trans., *Islam from the Prophet Muhammad to the Capture of Constantinople* (New York, 1974), vol. I, p. 186.
3. Paul Rycaut, *The History of the Present State of the Ottoman Empire*, 4th ed. (London, 1675), p. 45.
4. Abū ʿAmr Muḥammad al-Kashshī, *Maʿrifat Akhbār al-Rijāl* (Bombay, AH 1317), p. 249.
5. Ibn Samāʿa, *Al-Iktisāb fiʾl-rizq al-mustaṭāb* (Cairo, 1938), pp. 16ff.

CHAPTER 11   *The Commonality*

1. Text in al-Maqrīzī, *Al-Khiṭaṭ* (Būlāq, 1270/1854), pp. 199–200; English translation in Yūsuf Faḍl Ḥasan, *The Arabs and the Sudan, from the Seventh to the Early Sixteenth Century* (Edinburgh, 1967), p. 23.
2. Aḥmad Shihāb al-Dīn ibn Salāma al-Qalyūbī, *Nawādir al-Shaykh*, (Cairo, 1955), p. 154.
3. Abū Dulaf, *Qaṣīda Sāsāniyya*, lines 17–23; trans. C. E. Bosworth in *The Mediaeval Islamic Underworld: The Banū Sāsān in Arabic Society and Literature* (Leiden, 1976), pt. 2, pp. 191–2.

CHAPTER 12   *Religion and Law*

1. Mīrzā Abū Ṭālib Khān, *Masīr -i Ṭālibī*, ed. H. Khadīv-Jam (Tehran, 1974), p. 251.
2. Al-Jāḥiẓ, *Kitāb al-Ḥayawān* (Cairo, 1938), vol. i, p. 174.
3. Al-Ghazālī, *Fayṣal al-Tafriqa bayn al-Islam waʾl-zandaqa* (Cairo, n.d.), p. 68.
4. As cited in Ignaz Goldziher, *Vorlesungen über den Islam* (Heidelberg, 1925), pp. 185–6.
5. ʿAlī al-Muttaqī al-Hindī, *Kanz al-ʿUmmāl*, part 1 (Hyderabad AH 1312), nn. 5350, 5445, 5451, 5987.
6. Mehmed Esad, *Uss-i Zafer* (Istanbul, AH 1293). As translated and cited in B. Lewis, *Istanbul and the Civilization of the Ottoman Empire* (Norman, Okla., 1963), p. 156.
7. Jalāl al-Dīn Rūmī, *Rubāʿiyyāt*.

8. Jalāl al-Dīn Rūmī, *Dīvān-i Shams-i Tabrīz*, no. 31.

CHAPTER 13 *Culture*

1. Mehmed Efendi, *Paris Sefaretnamesi*, ed. Ebüzziya (Istanbul, AH 1306), p. 109; French translation, *Le Paradis des infidèles*, ed. Gilles Veinstein (Paris, 1981), p. 163.
2. Abu'l-Faraj al-Isfahānī, *Kitab al-Aghānī* (Cairo, 1372/1953), vii, pp. 13–14.
3. Ghars al-Ni'ma al-Ṣābi', *Al-Hafawāt al-Nādira*, ed. Ṣāliḥ al-Ashtar (Damascus, 1967), pp. 305–6.
4. Ibn Qutayba, op. cit., vol. 2, p. 55.
5. Anna Comnena, *Alexiad*, 15.1; trans. E. R. A. Sewter (London, 1969), p. 472.
6. *The Complete Letters of Lady Mary Wortley Montagu*, ed. Robert Halsband (Oxford, 1965), vol. 1, pp. 338–9.

CHAPTER 14 *Challenge*

1. Abū Shāma, *Al-Rawḍatayn fī Akhbār al-Dawlatayn*, ed. M. Ḥilmi Aḥmad and M. Muṣṭafā Ziyāda (Cairo, 1926), 1/ii, pp. 621–2.
2. Cited in B. Lewis, *The Muslim Discovery of Europe*, p. 193.
3. *Sılıhdar Tarihi* (Istanbul, 1928), vol. II, p. 87.

CHAPTER 15 *Change*

1. Abdülhak Adnan (Adıvar), *La Science chez les Turcs Ottomans* (Paris, 1939), p. 57.
2. Richard Hakluyt, *The Principall Navigations of the English Nation*, vol. 5, pp. 178–83.
3. State Papers 102/61/23.
4. *Letters*, op. cit., vol. 1, pp. 316–17.

CHAPTER 16 *Response and Reaction*

1. Ahmed Lûtfi, *Tarih* (Istanbul, AH 1290–1328), vol. 8, pp. 15–17.

CHAPTER 17   *New Ideas*

1. Published by Cavid Baysun in *Tarih Dergisi* 5 (1953), pp. 137–45.
2. E. de Marcère, *Une ambassade à Constantinople: la politique orientale de la Révolution française* (Paris, 1927) vol. II, pp. 12–14.
3. Cevdet, *Vekâyi-i Devlet-i Aliye* (Istanbul, 1294/1877), vol. 5, p. 130.
4. Cevdet, op. cit., vol. 6, pp. 280–1.
5. The Turkish text, from a document in the Istanbul archives, was published by E. Z. Karal, *Fransa-Mısır ve Osmanlı Imparatorlugu (1797–1802)* (Istanbul, 1940), pp. 108ff. The Arabic text as brought to Acre by Sir Sidney Smith was included in an Arabic biography of Jazzār Pasha: *Taʾrīkh Aḥmad Bāshā al-Jazzār* (Beirut, 1955), pp. 125ff. There are variations between the two versions.
6. Cevdet, *Tezakir 1–12*, ed. Cavid Baysun (Ankara, 1953), pp. 67–8.
7. As cited in Harold Temperley, *England and the Near East: the Crimea* (London, 1936), p. 272.

CHAPTER 18   *From War to War*

1. Hikmet Bayur, *Türk Inkılâbı Tarihi* (Istanbul, 1940), vol. 1, p. 225.

CHAPTER 19   *From Freedom to Freedom*

1. Israel–Egypt agreement of February 1949, article V, subsection 2, with similar clauses in the Syrian and Jordanian agreements.

BIBLIOGRAPHICAL NOTE

The literature on the history of the Middle East during the past two thousand years is of vast extent and of varied content and quality. Fortunately, works of reference and critical bibliographies are available for much, though not all, of the region and period. The following lists are in no sense a comprehensive bibliography, but rather a small selection of useful reference works on the major topics treated in this book. I have laid the main emphasis on works that are recent, authoritative, and comprehensive.

(1) Bibliographies and Handbooks

J. D. Pearson, *et al.*, *Index Islamicus, 1906–1955. A Catalogue of Articles on Islamic Subjects in Periodicals and Other Collective Publications.* Cambridge, 1958. Supplements: i, 1956–1960 (Cambridge, 1962); ii, 1961–1965 (Cambridge, 1967); iii, 1966–1970 (London, 1972); iv, 1971–1975 (London, 1977); v, 1976–1980 (London, 1982). *Quarterly Index Islamicus* (London, 1977–).

Denis Sinor, *Introduction à l'étude de l'Eurasie centrale.* Wiesbaden, 1963.

Jean Sauvaget, *Introduction to the History of the Muslim East: A Bibliographical Guide.* Berkeley and Los Angeles, 1965. (Based on the second French edition of Sauvaget as recast by Claude Cahen.)

J. D. Pearson, *A Bibliography of pre-Islamic Persia.* London, 1975.

Diana Grimwood-Jones, Derek Hopwood, and J. D. Pearson, eds, *Arab Islamic Bibliography: The Middle East Library Committee's Guide.* Hassocks, Sussex, 1977.

Margaret Anderson, *Arabic Materials in English Translation: A Bibliography of Works from the Pre-Islamic Period to 1977.* Boston, 1980.

Claude Cahen, *Introduction à l'histoire du monde musulman médiéval VII–XV siècle: méthodologie et éléments de bibliographie.* Paris, 1982.

Wolfgang Behn, *Islamic Book Review Index.* Berlin/Millersport, PA, 1982– .

L. P. Elwell-Sutton, ed., *A Bibliographical Guide to Iran.* Totowa, NY, 1983.

Jere L. Bacharach, *A Middle East Studies Handbook*, rev. edn. Seattle and London, 1984.

R. Stephen Humphreys, *Islamic History: A Framework for Enquiry*, rev. edn. Princeton, NJ, 1991.

(2) Genealogy and Chronology

Eduard von Zambaur, *Manuel de généaologie et de chronologie pour l'histoire de l'Islam*. Hanover, 1927; 2nd edn, 1955.

C. E. Bosworth, *The Islamic Dynasties: A Chronological and Genealogical Handbook*. Edinburgh, 1967.

H. U. Rahman, *A Chronology of Islamic History 570–1000 C.E.* London, 1989.

Robert Mantran, ed., *Les grandes dates de l'Islam*. Paris, 1990.

(3) Atlases

Donald Edgar Pitcher, *An Historical Geography of the Ottoman Empire from the Earliest Times to the End of the Sixteenth Century*. Leiden, 1972.

Tübinger Atlas des Vorderen Orients. Wiesbaden, 1977– .

William C. Brice, *An Historical Atlas of Islam*. Leiden, 1981.

Jean Sellier and Andre Sellier, *Atlas des peuples d'Orient, Moyen Orient, Caucase, Asie Centrale*. Paris, 1993.

(4) Documents

Sylvia G. Haim, *Arab Nationalism: An Anthology*. Berkeley and Los Angeles, 1962.

Charles Issawi, ed. and trans., *The Economic History of the Middle East, 1800–1914* (Chicago, 1966); *The Economic History of Iran, 1800–1914* (Chicago, 1970); *The Economic History of Turkey, 1800–1914* (Chicago, 1980); *The Fertile Crescent, 1800–1914* (New York, 1988).

Kemal H. Karpat, ed., *Political and Social Thought in the Contemporary Middle East*. London, 1968.

Lewis, Bernard, ed. and trans., *Islam, from the Prophet Muhammad to the Capture of Constantinople*, 2 vols. New York, 1974.

J. C. Hurewitz, *The Middle East and North Africa in World Politics: A Documentary Record*, 2nd rev. edn. New Haven and London, 1975.

Andrew Rippin and Jan Knappert, ed. and trans., *Textual Sources for the Study of Islam*. Chicago, 1986.

Norman Stillman, *The Jews of Arab Lands* (Philadelphia, 1979); *The Jews of Arab Lands in Modern Times* (Philadelphia, 1991).

(5) Encyclopedias

The Encyclopedia of Islam, new edn. Leiden, 1954– .

Encyclopedia Iranica, ed. Ehsan Yarshater. London and Boston, 1982– .

The Cambridge Encyclopedia of the Middle East and North Africa. Cambridge and New York, 1988.

The Oxford Dictionary of Byzantium. New York, 1991.

NOTE ON CALENDARS

All dates in the Chronology and in the body of the book are given in the calendar traditionally starting from the birth of Christ (AD), now universally adopted, and known to scholars as the Common Era (CE). Reformed in 1582 by Pope Gregory XIII, the so-called Gregorian, or 'New Style' calendar was introduced at different times in various parts of the world. Christians of the Orthodox and most other Eastern churches retained the earlier, Julian, era, also known as 'Old Style' (O.S.), until modern times, and still use it for religious purposes. At the present time, the Orthodox Christmas falls on a date corresponding to 7 January of the Gregorian calendar.

Since the advent of Islam, the Muslim calendar has been the most widely used in the Middle East. The Muslim era (AH) dates from 16 July 622 CE, that is, the beginning of the Arab year in which the Hijra (sometimes misspelt Hegira), the migration of Muḥammad from Mecca to Medina, took place. The Muslim year consists of twelve lunar months, 354 days in all, without adjustment to the solar year. The months thus do not correspond to seasons, and major religious occasions, such as the fast of Ramaḍān and the Pilgrimage, traverse the entire solar year. There are rough-ly 103 Hijri years to 100 Gregorian years. Conversion tables are readily available.

The Hijri calendar, being purely lunar, was inconvenient for fiscal and administrative purposes, and Muslim governments from early times worked out a series of solar adaptations of the Hijri year with Iranian, Christian, and other months. The most important of these are:

(1) The Turkish financial year, *Maliye*. This was an adaptation of earlier 'fiscal' calendars combining the Hijri date with a solar year, and was intro-duced into the Ottoman revenue administration in 1789 CE. The *Maliye* was a Julian year, with most of the old Syrian month names combined with a Hijri era and a system of 'sliding' at intervals to bring the *Maliye* and Hijri eras into line.

(2) The Persian solar year. Introduced in 1925, it is based on the Hijra, but is calculated in solar years, using an adaptation of the old Iranian month names. To convert Iranian solar years to Gregorian, add 622 to dates 1 January–21 March; 621, to dates 21 March–31 December. The New Year, 1 *Farvardin*, falls in the third week of March. This era is now used in Iran for all but purely religious purposes.

The Jewish calendar, traditionally dated from the creation of the world, is used for religious, and, in the State of Israel, some other purposes. It consists of twelve lunar months, adjusted to the solar year by the intercalation of an extra month at seven points in a nineteen-year cycle. The new year of 5756 coincides with 25 September 1995.

CHRONOLOGY

25 BCE	Roman expedition to Arabia
c.30 CE	Crucifixion of Jesus Christ
47–49	First mission of the Apostle Paul
54–59	Roman conquest of Armenia
63	Peace between Rome and the Parthians
65	Pompey visits Petra: first Roman contact with the Nabatean kingdom
66–70	First Jewish revolt
70	Roman capture of Jerusalem; end of Jewish revolt, destruction of the Temple
106	Annexation of the Nabataean region of Arabia
114–17	Trajan's war against the Parthians
115–17	Second Jewish revolt, in eastern provinces
117	Death of Trajan; Hadrian abandons eastern conquests
132–5	Third Jewish revolt
161	Parthian invasion of Syria and Armenia
197–202	Eastern campaigns of Septimus Severus
224	Accession of the Sasanid dynasty in Persia
226–40	Establishment of the Sasanid dynasty
229–32	Perso-Roman war
231–2	Campaign of Severus Alexander against the Sasanids
240	Persians capture Nisibis
241–4	Perso-Roman war
241–72	Reign of Sasanid Emperor Shapur I
242	Beginning of the preaching of Mani
258–60	Perso-Roman war
260–3	Reign of Odenathus in Palmyra
267	Wahballat, the son of Odenathus, and his mother, Zenobia, become independent rulers
272	Capture of Palmyra by Aurelian
296–7	Perso-Roman war; peace treaty of 297 recognizes Roman victory
303	Diocletian begins persecution of Christians
306	Constantine proclaimed emperor
310–79	Reign of Shapur II
312	Edict of Milan; legalization of Christianity
325	Council of Nicaea

330	Foundation of Constantinople
337–50	Perso-Roman war
359–61	Perso-Roman war
363	War against Shapur II
371–6	Perso-Roman war
381	Edicts of Constantinople, establishing Christianity and prohibiting pagan cults
384	Perso-Roman peace
395	Death of Theodosius; split between eastern and western Roman empires
503–5	Perso-Roman war
524–31	Perso-Roman war
527–65	Reign of Justinian; reconquest of Africa and Italy
527–32	Perso-Byzantine war
531–79	Reign of Chosroes I
533	'Endless peace' between Rome and Persia
537	Dedication of Hagia Sophia in Constantinople
540–62	Perso-Byzantine war
572–91	Perso-Byzantine war
606–28	Perso-Byzantine war; 614, Persian capture of Jerusalem
622	Hijra of Muḥammad from Mecca to Medina: beginning of the Islamic era
628	Truce of Ḥudaybiyya. Byzantium under Heraclius concludes victorious peace; Persian conquests returned to Byzantine control
630	Muḥammad conquers Mecca
632	Death of Muḥammad. Abū Bakr becomes the first Caliph
633–7	Arabs conquer Syria and Mesopotamia
634	'Umar becomes Caliph
635–6	Capture of Damascus
637	Battle of Qādisiyya. Fall of Ctesiphon
639–42	Conquest of Egypt
642–6	Capture of Alexandria
644	Murder of 'Umar. 'Uthmān becomes Caliph
656	Murder of 'Uthmān: beginning of first civil war in Islam
661	Murder of 'Alī: beginning of Umayyad dynasty
674–8	First Arab siege of Constantinople
680	Battle of Karbalāʾ
691	Construction of the Dome of the Rock in Jerusalem
696	'Abd al-Malik introduces Arabic coinage, as part of

	reorganization of imperial administration
705–15	Construction of the Umayyad Mosque in Damascus
710	Muslims land in Spain
717–18	Siege of Constantinople
750	Fall of Umayyads, accession of 'Abbāsids
751	Arabs defeat Chinese near Tālās. Chinese prisoners of war introduce paper-making.
762–3	Foundation of Baghdad by al-Manṣūr
767	Death of Abū Ḥanīfa
809–13	Civil war of al-Amīn and al-Ma'mūn
813–33	Reign of al-Ma'mūn; development of Arabic science and letters
820	Death of al-Shāfi'ī
833–42	Reign of al-Muʿtaṣim: beginning of Turkish domination
869–83	Revolt of black slaves in southern Iraq
910	Establishment of Fātimid Caliphate in North Africa
945	Buwayhids occupy Baghdad
950	Death of al-Fārābī
969	Fāṭimids conquer Egypt, found Cairo
c. 970	Seljuk Turks enter territories of Caliphate from the east
1037	Death of Ibn Sīnā (Avicenna)
1055	Seljuks take Baghdad
1070–80	Seljuks occupy Syria and Palestine
1071	Defeat of Byzantine armies at Manzikert, Seljuk expansion into Anatolia
1094	Death of Fātimid Caliph al-Mustanṣir; split in Ismāʿīlī movement: Ḥasan-i Ṣabbāḥ leads extremist (Assassin) wing
1096	Crusaders arrive in Near East
1099	Crusaders take Jerusalem
1111	Death of al-Ghazālī
1171	Saladin declares Fātimid Caliphate at an end; foundation of Ayyūbid dynasty in Syria and Egypt
1187	Battle of Ḥattīn: Saladin defeats Crusaders and captures Jerusalem
1220	Mongols conquer eastern territories of the Caliphate
1229	Frederick II obtains Jerusalem from Al-Malik al-Kāmil by negotiation
1244	Muslims retake Jerusalem
1250–60	Emergence of Mamlūk Sultānate in Egypt and Syria from the decay of the Ayyūbid kingdoms

1252	Khan of Golden Horde becomes a Muslim
1258	Mongols capture Baghdād
1273	Death of Jalāl al-Dīn Rūmī
c. 1290–1320	Rise of Ottoman principalities in western Anatolia
1295	Il-Khan of Persia becomes a Muslim
1326	Ottomans take Bursa
1331	Ottomans take Nicaea
1354	Ottomans take Gallipoli
1366	Ottomans in Adrianople (Edirne)
1371–5	Ottomans invade Serbia
1389	Battle of Kosovo; Ottoman rule in Serbia
1400–1	Tīmur ravages Syria
1402	Tīmur defeats Ottomans at Ankara
1406	Death of Ibn Khaldūn
1444	Battle of Varna; Ottoman rule in Bulgaria
1453	Capture of Constantinople by Mehmed II
1462	Annexation of Bosnia
1475	Ottomans in Crimea
1492	Christians take Granada
	Jews expelled from Spain
	Columbus sails west
1498	Vasco de Gama sails to India via Cape of Good Hope. Arab pilot Ibn Mājid guides Vasco de Gama from Africa to India
1501	Shah Ismāʿīl founds Safavid dynasty in Iran
	Shah Ismāʿīl imposes Shīʿism as the official religion of Persia
1514	Ottoman-Persian war
1516–17	Ottomans conquer Syria and Egypt, destroy Mamlūk Sultānate. Sharīf of Mecca accepts Ottoman suzerainty
1520–66	Reign of Süleyman the Magnificent
1521	Ottomans take Belgrade
1522	Ottomans conquer Rhodes
1526	Battle of Mohacs
1529	First Ottoman siege of Vienna
1534	Ottoman capture of Baghdad. First Ottoman conquest of Iraq
1539	Ottoman capture of Aden
1552	Russians take Kazan
1555	Ottoman-Persian war
	Peace of Amasya between Ottoman Empire and Iran

1556	Russians take Astrakhan
1557	Construction of Süleymaniye mosque in Istanbul
1565	Ottoman siege of Malta
1571	Battle of Lepanto
1573	Ottomans conquer Cyprus
1587–1629	Reign of Shah 'Abbās in Iran
1589	Ottoman-Persian treaty records Ottoman victory
1598	Isfahān becomes capital of Persia
1602–27	Ottoman-Persian wars
1606	Treaty of Sitvatorok
1607	Ottomans driven from Persian territory
1612	Construction of Masjid-i Shah in Isfahan
1630–8	Ottoman-Persian wars
1631	Insurrections in Egypt, Yemen, Lebanon
1639	Final Ottoman conquest of Iraq
1683	Second Ottoman siege of Vienna
1699	Treaty of Carlowitz
1726	First Turkish printing press in Istanbul
1733	Ottoman-Persian war
1736–47	Nader Shah in Persia
1743–7	Ottoman-Persian war
1768–74	Ottoman-Russian war
1774	Treaty of Küçük Kaynarca
1783	Russian annexation of Crimea
1789	Accession of reforming Sultan Selim III
1794	The Qājār dynasty established
1795	The Qājār shah takes Teheran as capital
1798–1801	French occupation of Egypt
1800	Russians annex Georgia
1803	Wahhābīs occupy Mecca and Medina
	Treaty of Gulistan: Persia cedes Caucasian provinces to Russia
1803–12	Insurrection in Serbia
1805	Muḥammad 'Alī becomes effective ruler of Egypt
1809	Beginning of regular shipping service from India to Suez
1821–9	Greek War of Independence
1826–8	New Russo-Persian war; Persia cedes Armenia to Russia
1827	Ottoman naval defeat at Navarino
1828	First official newspaper published in Egypt
1830	French invade Algeria

1831–2	First official newspaper published in Istanbul
1839	British take Aden; reform edict of the Rose Chamber
1844	Ottoman currency reform on European model
1853–5	Crimean War
1855	Introduction of telegraph
1856	Congress of Paris
1861	Creation of autonomous Lebanon
1863	Foundation of the Ottoman Bank
1869	Opening of the Suez Canal
	Foundation of University of Istanbul
1876–8	Ottoman war with Serbia and then Russia
1876	Ottoman constitution proclaimed
	Al-Ahrām, first Arabic daily paper in Egypt
1878	Ottoman constitution suspended
1878	Treaty of San Stefano
1878	Congress of Berlin: independence of Serbia, Romania, Bulgaria; occupation of Bosnia and Herzegovina by Austria-Hungary; occupation of eastern provinces by Russia
1881	French occupy Tunisia
1882	British occupy Egypt
1894–6	Armenian revolts and their suppression
1897	Ottoman-Greek war
1906	Persian constitutional revolution
1908	Young Turk revolution. Opening of Ḥijāz railway
1911	Italians conquer Tripoli
1912	First Balkan war
1913	Second Balkan war
1914	Ottoman alliance with Germany
1916	Arab revolt in Ḥijāz; Sharīf Ḥusayn assumes title of king
1917	British occupy Baghdad and Jerusalem
	Adoption of Gregorian calendar in the Ottoman Empire
1918	End of Ottoman rule in Arab lands
1919	Greek landing in Izmir
1920	Grand National Assembly in Ankara: beginning of Turkish War of Independence
	Mandates established for Syria (French), Palestine and Iraq (British)
	Ibn Saud becomes Sultan of Najd
1922	Armistice of Mudanya
	Anglo-Egyptian treaty

1923	Treaty of Lausanne
1924–6	Ibn Saud's forces occupy Ḥijāz
1925	Accession of Reza Shah, first ruler of Pahlavi dynasty
1926	Ibn Saud adopts title of king
1932	Iraq becomes independent
	Ibn Saud proclaims Saudi Arabian Kingdom
1936	Anglo-Egyptian treaty, recognizing independence of Egypt
1945	League of Arab States formed
1945	Jordan becomes independent
1948	End of Palestine Mandate: establishment of Israel; first Arab-Israel war
1951	Libya becomes independent
1952	Military coup in Cairo; King Fārūq abdicates
1953	Egypt becomes a republic
1956	Sudan, Tunisia, and Morocco become independent
	Egypt nationalizes Suez Canal; Israel-Egypt war; Anglo-French expedition to Suez
1957	Tunisia becomes a republic
1958	Formation of United Arab Republic
	Civil war in Lebanon
	Revolution in Iraq, which becomes a republic
1961	Kuwait becomes independent
	Syria secedes from the United Arab Republic
1962	Slavery abolished in Yemen and Saudi Arabia
1967	Israel-Arab war
	South Yemen becomes independent
1969	Libya becomes a republic
1970	Death of Nasser: Sadat succeeds
1971	Gulf states become independent
	Formation of Union of Arab Emirates
1973	Arab-Israel war
1975–7	Civil war in Lebanon
1979	Egypt and Israel sign peace treaty
	Revolution in Iran
1980–8	Iran-Iraq war
1981	Murder of Anwar Sadat
1982	Israeli invasion of Lebanon
1990–1	Iraq invades Kuwait: Gulf War
1994	Jordan-Israel peace treaty

MAPS

Note. Shaded areas on the maps indicate only the approximate areas of empire or conquest.

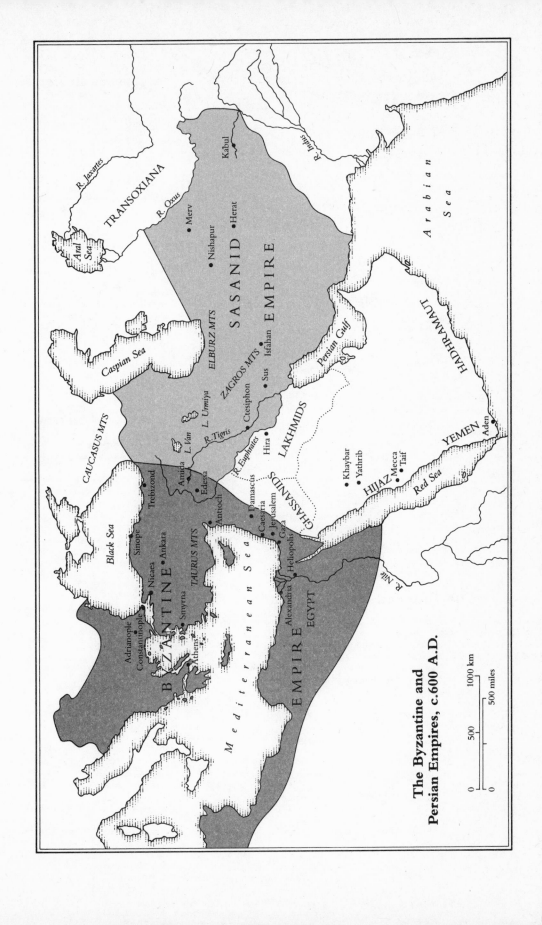

The Byzantine and Persian Empires, c.600 A.D.

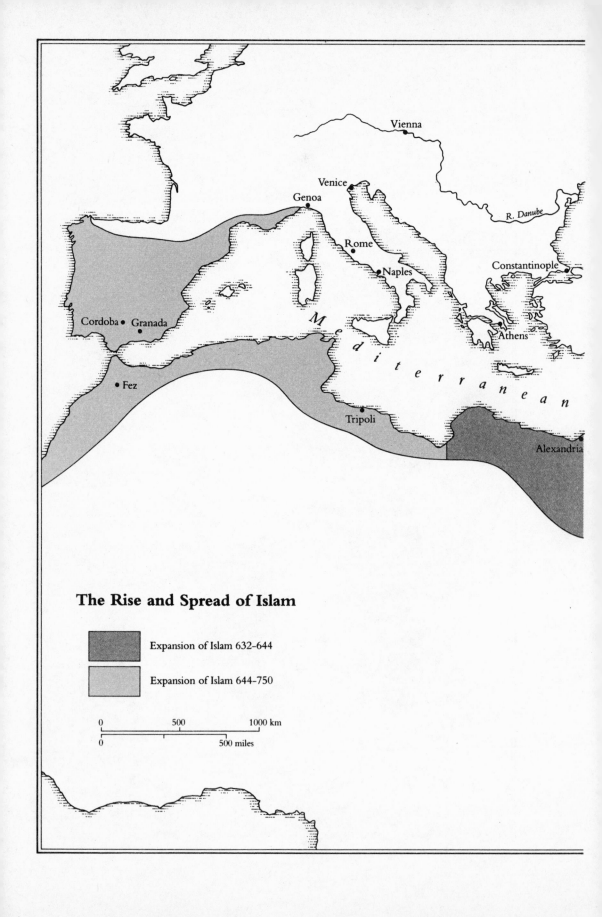

Vienna

Venice

Genoa

Rome

Naples

Constantinople

M e d i t e r r a n e a n

Athens

Cordoba ● ● Granada

● Fez

Tripoli

Alexandria

R. Danube

The Rise and Spread of Islam

Expansion of Islam 632–644

Expansion of Islam 644–750

0		500		1000 km

| 0 | | 500 miles | |

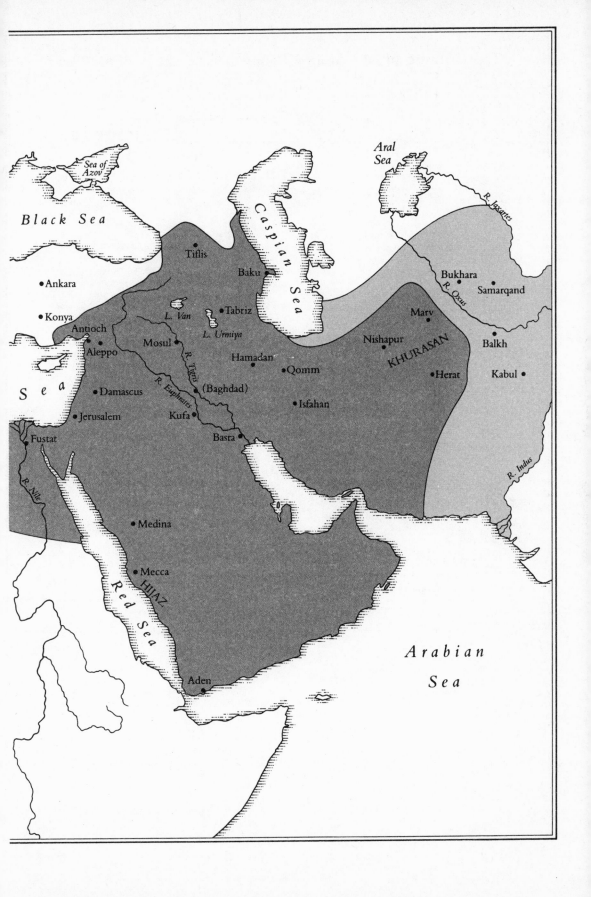

Black Sea

Sea of
Azov

Aral
Sea

Caspian Sea

• Ankara

• Konya

Antioch •
• Aleppo

S e a

• Damascus

• Jerusalem

Fustat •

R. Nile

• Tiflis

Baku •

L. Van
• Tabriz
L. Urmiya

Mosul •

R. Tigris

Hamadan •

R. Euphrates

(Baghdad) •

Kufa •

Basra •

• Qomm

• Isfahan

R. Jaxartes

Bukhara •
Samarqand •

R. Oxus

Marv •

Nishapur •

KHURASAN

Herat •

Balkh •

Kabul •

R. Indus

• Medina

• Mecca

HIJAZ

Red Sea

• Aden

Arabian

Sea

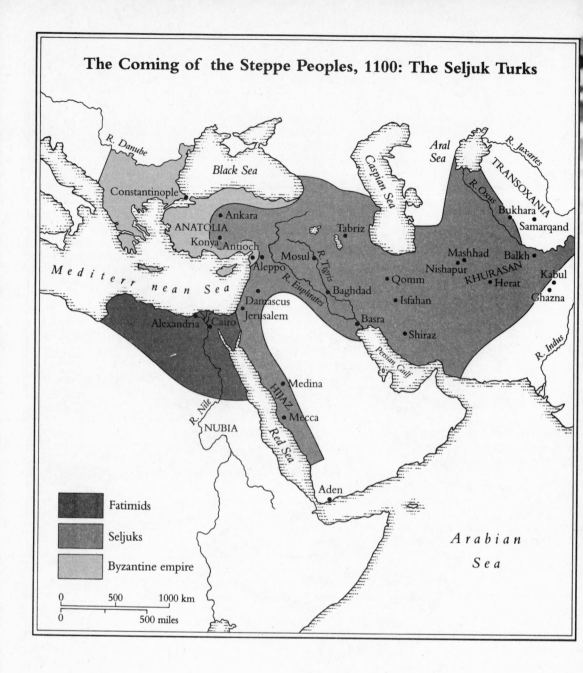

The Coming of the Steppe Peoples, 1100: The Seljuk Turks

R. Danube

Black Sea

Constantinople

• Ankara

ANATOLIA

Konya • Antioch

Aleppo

Mosul

Tabriz

Caspian Sea

Aral Sea

R. Jaxartes

TRANSOXANIA

R. Oxus

Bukhara

Samarqand

Mashhad

Balkh

Nishapur

KHURASAN

Kabul

Herat

Ghazna

Mediterranean Sea

R. Tigris

Qomm

Baghdad

R. Euphrates

Isfahan

Damascus

Jerusalem

Basra

Alexandria • Cairo

Shiraz

Persian Gulf

R. Indus

Medina

HIJAZ

R. Nile

NUBIA

Mecca

Red Sea

Aden

Arabian Sea

Fatimids

Seljuks

Byzantine empire

| 0 | 500 | 1000 km |
| 0 | 500 miles | |

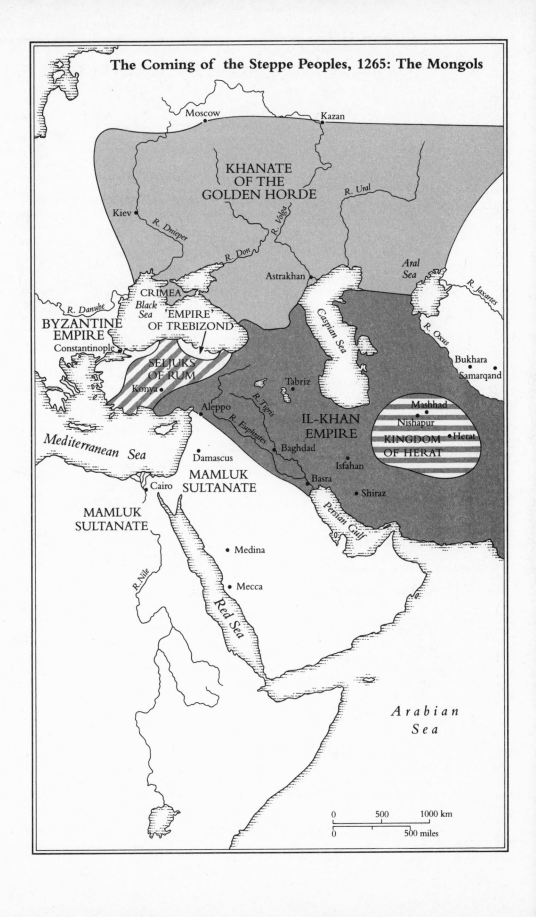

The Coming of the Steppe Peoples, 1265: The Mongols

Moscow

Kazan

KHANATE OF THE GOLDEN HORDE

R. Ural

Kiev

R. Dnieper

R. Don

R. Volga

Astrakhan

Aral Sea

R. Jaxartes

CRIMEA

Black Sea

'EMPIRE' OF TREBIZOND

Caspian Sea

R. Oxus

BYZANTINE EMPIRE

Constantinople

R. Danube

Bukhara

Samarqand

SELJUKS OF RUM

Konya

Tabriz

MASHHAD

Nishapur

Herat

KINGDOM OF HERAT

Aleppo

R. Tigris

R. Euphrates

IL-KHAN EMPIRE

Baghdad

Isfahan

Mediterranean Sea

Damascus

Basra

Shiraz

MAMLUK SULTANATE

Cairo

Persian Gulf

MAMLUK SULTANATE

R. Nile

Medina

Mecca

Red Sea

Arabian Sea

| 0 | 500 | 1000 km |
| 0 | 500 miles | |

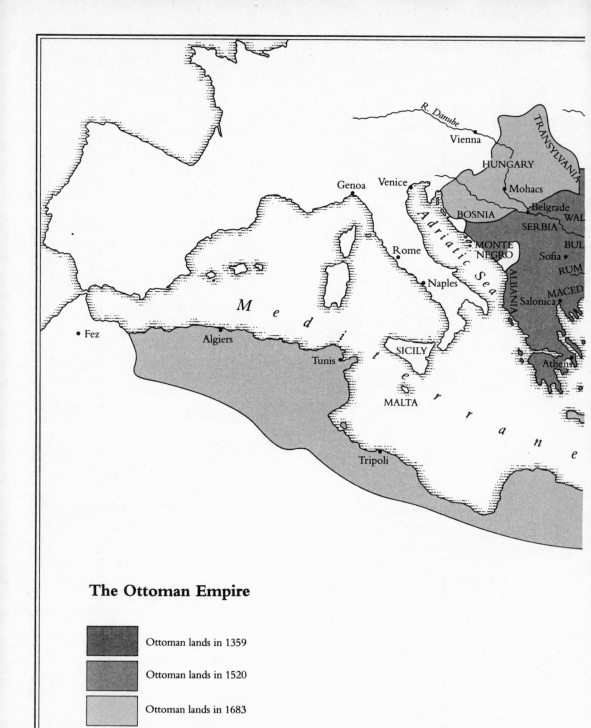

The Ottoman Empire

Ottoman lands in 1359

Ottoman lands in 1520

Ottoman lands in 1683

| 0 | | 500 | | 1000 km |

| 0 | | | 500 miles |

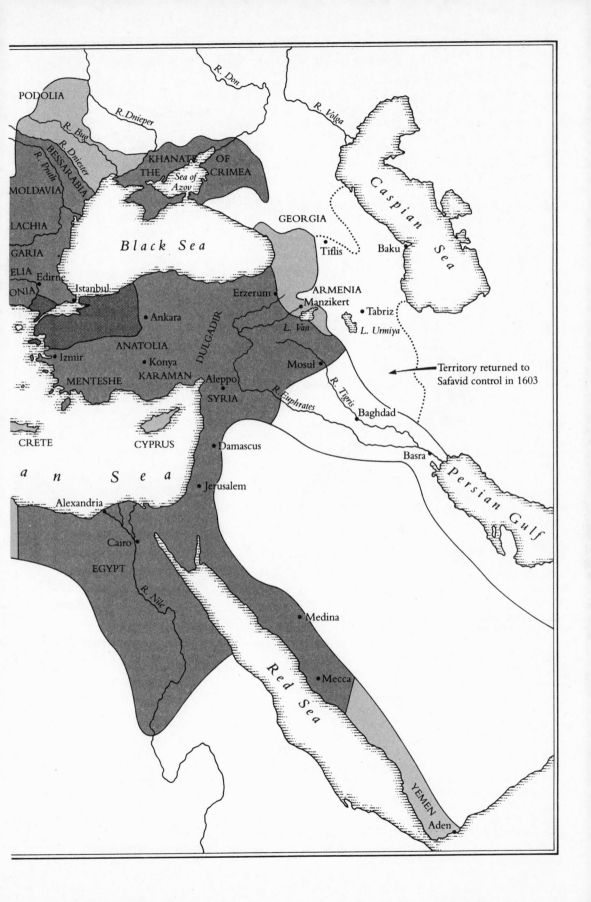

PODOLIA

R. Don

R. Volga

R. Dnieper

R. Bug

R. Dniester

BESSARABIA

R. Prut

MOLDAVIA

LACHIA

KHANATE OF
THE CRIMEA

Sea of
Azov

GARIA

GEORGIA

*Caspian
Sea*

ELIA

Tiflis

Baku

ONIA

Edirne

Black Sea

Istanbul

ARMENIA

Erzerum

Manzikert

Tabriz

Ankara

L. Van

L. Urmiya

Izmir

ANATOLIA

DULGADIR

Territory returned to
Safavid control in 1603

MENTESHE

Konya

KARAMAN

Aleppo

Mosul

R. Tigris

SYRIA

R. Euphrates

CRETE

CYPRUS

Damascus

Baghdad

a   n   S   e   a

Jerusalem

Basra

Persian Gulf

Alexandria

Cairo

EGYPT

R. Nile

Medina

Red Sea

Mecca

YEMEN

Aden

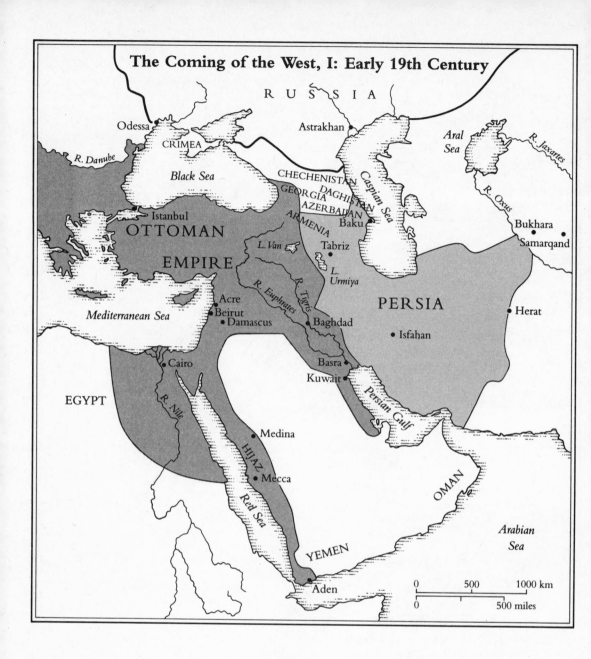

The Coming of the West, I: Early 19th Century

RUSSIA

Odessa

CRIMEA

Astrakhan

Aral
Sea

R. Danube

Black Sea

R. Jaxartes

CHECHENISTAN

DAGHISTAN

Caspian Sea

GEORGIA

AZERBAIJAN

R. Oxus

Istanbul

ARMENIA

Baku

Bukhara

OTTOMAN

L. Van

Tabriz

Samarqand

EMPIRE

L.
Urmiya

R. Euphrates

R. Tigris

PERSIA

Mediterranean Sea

Acre

Herat

Beirut

Baghdad

Damascus

Isfahan

Cairo

Basra

EGYPT

Kuwait

R. Nile

Persian Gulf

Medina

HIJAZ

OMAN

Mecca

Arabian
Sea

Red Sea

YEMEN

500   1000 km

Aden

0   500 miles

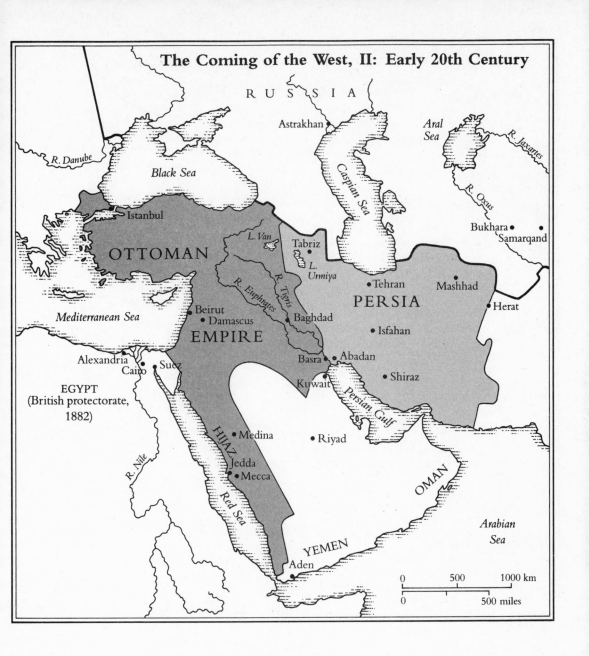

The Coming of the West, II: Early 20th Century

INDEX

Dates given are CE unless otherwise stated.